Mass Shootings in America

Mass Shootings in America

Understanding the Debates, Causes, and Responses

Jaclyn Schildkraut, Editor

Foreword by
Frank DeAngelis, Former Columbine
High School Principal

ABC-CLIO™

An Imprint of ABC-CLIO, LLC
Santa Barbara, California • Denver, Colorado

Library of Congress Cataloging-in-Publication Data

Names: Schildkraut, Jaclyn, editor.
Title: Mass shootings in America : understanding the debates, causes, and responses / Jaclyn Schildkraut, editor ; foreword by Frank DeAngelis, Former Columbine High School Principal.
Description: Santa Barbara, California : ABC-CLIO, LLC, [2018] | Includes bibliographical references and index.
Identifiers: LCCN 2017060019 (print) | LCCN 2018011609 (ebook) | ISBN 9781440856259 (ebook) | ISBN 9781440856242 (print : acid-free paper)
Subjects: LCSH: Mass murder—United States. | Firearms and crime—United States. | Violent crimes—United States. | Gun control—United States.
Classification: LCC HV6529 (ebook) | LCC HV6529 .M378 2018 (print) | DDC 364.152/340973—dc23
LC record available at https://lccn.loc.gov/2017060019

ISBN: 978-1-4408-5624-2 (print)
        978-1-4408-5625-9 (ebook)

22 21 20 19 18   2 3 4 5

This book is also available as an eBook.

ABC-CLIO
An Imprint of ABC-CLIO, LLC

ABC-CLIO, LLC
130 Cremona Drive, P.O. Box 1911
Santa Barbara, California 93116-1911
www.abc-clio.com

This book is printed on acid-free paper ∞

Manufactured in the United States of America

To the victims of the Pulse nightclub shooting, my hometown of Orlando, FL, and other communities devastated by such senseless violence, may this book honor your legacies and may positive changes stem from your losses.
#OrlandoUnited

All editor royalties from the sale of this book are being donated to the onePULSE Foundation in honor of the victims and survivors of June 12, 2016. For more information on the foundation or to make your own contribution, please visit www.onepulsefoundation.org.

Editor's Note

As this book went to press, three additional senseless tragedies struck the United States. On October 1, 2017, a shooter opened fire on a crowd at the Route 91 Harvest Festival in Las Vegas, Nevada. A total of 58 people were killed and 489 others were injured before the shooter committed suicide.

Just five weeks later, on November 5, 2017, an armed attacker entered the First Baptist Church in Sutherland Springs, Texas. As parishioners were participating in their Sunday morning prayer service, he opened fire, killing 26 people and wounding 20 others. The shooter committed suicide after fleeing the scene and being chased by a pair of local residents who heard the attack and responded.

Then, on February 14, 2018, a former student entered the freshman building of Marjory Stoneman Douglas High School in Parkland, Florida, and opened fire. Within minutes, 14 students and 3 of their educators had been killed. The shooter fled the school and was apprehended a short time later nearby.

Though we were unable to incorporate these mass shootings into this encyclopedia's coverage due to the timing of the events (as they fell beyond the scope of the section), we believe it is important to recognize these events and those who were impacted by them. We hold the communities of Las Vegas, Sutherland Springs, and Parkland, as well as all those affected, close to our hearts and hope that these terrible tragedies will further highlight the need for Americans to engage in serious and somber discussion of the phenomenon of mass shootings in the United States.

Contents

Mass Shootings Q&A: The Experts Weigh In

Pivotal Documents in Mass Shootings Research

Foreword

Columbine High School opened its doors in 1973 and its first senior class graduated in 1975 with the motto of "Stretch for Excellence." Although Columbine's mailing address is Littleton, that is misleading. Littleton is the seat of Arapahoe County and Columbine is about five miles west of Littleton's downtown. I am guessing that until 1999, most Denver-area residents thought of the Columbine area as being in the Jefferson County city of Lakewood, not Littleton. The high school is 14 miles southwest of the Colorado State Capitol building in downtown Denver.

I describe the Columbine community and the school to provide context. If you had said to me years ago that something horrific would happen at Columbine, I would have said, no, no way, not in *this* community. Jefferson County had 162 schools. An impressive 92 percent of our kids graduated on time and over 88 percent went on to college, with 25 percent of the student body getting some type of scholarship. It was a community of pride and tradition. There was a lot of parental support; it was and still is a highly respected school. I thought—we all thought—that it could not happen *here*. And the reaction I hear from others when they ask me about the shooting often is: "Frank, your community is just like ours!" I tell them that no one is immune. What happened at Columbine, I tell them, can happen in any community "On Any Given Day!"

I started my career at Columbine High School in the fall of 1979. I was hired to teach social studies, but I also worked as the assistant football coach, head baseball coach, and Senate sponsor. I went on to serve as the dean of students, an assistant principal, and then, in 1996, I was hired as the principal at that wonderful high school. It was a dream job.

I had a difficult time leaving the classroom to start my administrative career. I loved teaching and each day I had the opportunity to interact with the students. When I was encouraged to pursue a career as an administrator, I was hesitant because I was afraid that the opportunities for daily interactions with the students would diminish, and that I would have to change if I accepted the position. As I struggled to make a decision, a dear colleague of mine stated, "Your position is changing but you do not have to change as a person. As a social studies teacher, you interact with 150 students who are in your classes, but as the principal you will have the opportunity to interact with 2,000 students and 150 staff members." I made my choice and I have no regrets.

On April 20, 1999, I was nearing the end of my third year as principal and my twentieth year at Columbine High School. It was a beautiful Colorado spring day—about 70 degrees, the sun was shining, and the sky was blue. It was 11:20 a.m. when my secretary ran into my office and screamed about a report of gunfire in the hallway and bombs exploding. My first response was that this had to be a senior prank, that such violence could not possibly be occurring at this wonderful school. As I ran out of my office and into the hallway, I encountered the gunmen. They fired their weapons at me as I ran down the hallway to protect some female students who were unaware of the danger they were in. I realized that "Any Given Day" had become a reality; it was really happening.

Twelve of my beloved students and my dear friend, Dave, lost their lives on that terrible day. Twenty-six additional students were injured. I was witnessing the unthinkable. The lives of the members of the Columbine High School community changed forever when the first shots were fired. To this day, people ask me, "When did it get back to normal?" I respond that after that day, we had to redefine normal. I told the nation that I became a member of a club that no one wanted to join.

I can remember thinking in the aftermath of our tragedy that I would not allow our beloved 13 "to die in vain." Unfortunately, mass shootings in our schools have not stopped but I am not going to give up hope. There is not a day that goes by that I do not think about the tragedy at Columbine and all the lives affected, and all the lives that have been lost in mass shootings at other schools and locations across America. I made a promise to continue to do what I can to stop these senseless shootings from occurring.

Since the tragedy, I have had many opportunities to be interviewed by people writing books and articles and making documentaries. I have met with FBI profilers and numerous law enforcement officers and psychologists to try to find answers to the unthinkable. I have read many books about the Columbine tragedy and other mass shootings. One book in particular piqued my interest: *Mass Shootings: Media, Myths, and Realities,* written by Drs. Jaclyn Schildkraut and H. Jaymi Elsass.

As I continued my crusade, I had the opportunity to meet Jackie and Jaymi when they were in Denver for a conference. I soon realized that in meeting them, my life changed for the better. Their passion for their work is undeniable. The extensive research in *Mass Shootings: Media, Myths, and Realities* helped me to appreciate the complexities in trying to understand mass shootings.

This new book by Jackie is another important contribution to our understanding of mass shooting events in America. *Mass Shootings in America: Understanding the Debates, Causes, and Responses* presents arguments for the never-ending debates surrounding the topic, as well as research to aid in our efforts to stop mass shootings. It is safe to say that no single step or reform can stop the mass shootings from occurring, but if research shows that there are things that enhance the chances of preventing the senseless violent acts from occurring, then it is our responsibility to continue to study and learn.

Jackie and I continued to have conversations over the subsequent years, and in March 2017, I had the opportunity to be a keynote speaker at the State University of New York at Oswego, where Jackie is a professor. I had the honor to share the stage with Virginia Tech survivor Kristina Anderson. As a result of my interactions with many of Jackie's students and colleagues at the conference, I discovered Jackie's vast knowledge about school shootings and her abiding interest in using her research to try to keep others from losing their lives to school violence.

When Jackie asked me to write the foreword for this book, I was honored to be able to share my thoughts about it. After having many dialogues with Jackie, something that kept resonating with me is our agreement that they are "all of your kids!" I cannot tell you the number of times after the shooting at Columbine that I was asked "What are you going to do?" and my response always was "What are *we* going to do?" I think back to the policies and practices that were in place at Columbine on April 20, 1999. Schools, law enforcement agencies, mental health workers, psychologists, and criminologists were working together as separate entities. I believe it was after Columbine that we began working as one. We checked our egos at the door and started "putting the pieces to the puzzle together"; we started "connecting the dots." We must be a team to protect our most precious commodity, our children. As adults, we are not supposed to bury children.

After coming to know Jackie and her passion on the topic, I did not hesitate in accepting her invitation to write this foreword. The book provides a unique hybrid approach to understanding the broader problem of mass shootings in America. We have learned that there is not a "quick fix." We live in a society where people want answers and they want them now. Jackie was able to solicit research from a variety of experts in writing the book to help provide those answers.

I am amazed as I continue to do presentations throughout the United States, Canada, and Europe that people are in such disbelief about the response protocol that was in place on April 20, 1999. Columbine forced our schools and communities to change what we were doing and learn to do things differently. The chapter "Issues and Challenges for Law Enforcement Responding to Mass Shootings" has that discussion, and lets the reader know what has changed and what we can do to improve. Special attention is given to first responders dealing with post-traumatic stress disorder (PTSD). This is a topic I spend a great deal of time discussing during my presentations, for PTSD has had a profound effect on me and many other members of the Columbine High School community.

As a result of extensive media coverage of the Columbine tragedy and its aftermath, people formed their opinions about mass shootings. The first viable question is "Are mass shootings increasing?" Needless to say, opinions varied because of the basic essence of what constitutes a mass shooting. In the book, this issue is confronted. There is extensive research defining the criteria for qualifying an event as a mass shooting and whether it should be included in the statistical analysis. In addition, there are chapters detailing "Mass Shootings as Hate Crimes" and "Mass Shootings as Acts of Terrorism." This was a major breakthrough. The authors had to develop a relevant definition of a mass shooting, particularly as these events now can overlap with hate crimes and acts of terrorism. There has not been a universally accepted definition. The book does an outstanding job of getting the reader to think by presenting extensive data and research to consider when weighing the causes and consequences of mass shootings. The book helps in developing critical thinking skills.

An eye-opener for many is that fact that Columbine was not the first mass school shooting. A major topic that resonated with me is that no one is immune and as I have stated during my presentations, if someone had told me that a Columbine tragedy could have happened at Columbine, I would have stated unequivocally, "Not in our community." As this book makes clear, schools, churches, hospital, airports, movie theaters, and other locations are potential targets for mass shooting events. Jackie does a wonderful job of giving the grim history of mass and school shootings in America and the different types of school shootings that have taken place over the years. I must confess that in reading Glenn W. Muschert's "School Shootings" chapter, I did have chills and was retraumatized when he stated: "The 1999 Columbine High School shootings in Littleton, Colorado, have become a cultural touchstone for rampage-type or 'Columbine-style' attacks." It seems that each time another mass shooting occurs in our world, it is referenced as another "Columbine-like attack" or shooting.

The role the media plays in the aftermath was a subject that hit close to home. I made a statement that "you do not get in an argument with people who buy ink by the barrel." It is my humble opinion that the reason we are still talking about Columbine after all this time is the role the media played in keeping the story relevant. Once again, the book does a marvelous job of statistically supporting my statement. The unbiased presentation of research by Jackie and the other contributors in this book will encourage people to think, converse, and yes, passionately argue their point of view. It will also get people to realize that when it comes to mass shootings, there are no simple answers and no "one size fits all" solution.

As Americans struggle to understand recent mass shooting events such as the ones that took place at the Pulse nightclub in Orlando, Florida, at an outdoor concert in Las Vegas, Nevada, and at a church in Sutherland Springs, Texas, chapters such as "The Role of Firearms in Mass Shooting" are even more relevant. This chapter does a superb job of giving both sides of a highly emotional topic. I hear the passionate arguments from both sides of the aisle on the floor of Congress, as well as from families directly impacted by mass shootings. What intrigues me about this book is that both anti-gun and pro-gun advocates give testimony. Schildkraut does not give you her own opinions, but rather gives you research and arguments from experts on both sides so you can make the decision. With our country so divided on this topic, I hope that *Mass Shootings in America: Understanding the Debates, Causes, and Responses* can help people understand other perspectives and come together to forge compromises that can help us address the senseless violence that is occurring in our country today.

Another issue covered in this book that resonates with me is the role mental health plays in the shootings that occur in America. The chapter "Mass Shooters and Mental Illness" does an excellent job of looking at the research and determining the role of mental health in mass shooting events. I do not believe that the killers came out of their mothers' wombs hating or planning a mass shooting. I think of the two killers at Columbine. I have seen pictures of them when they were youngsters in their soccer uniforms or smiling for their elementary school pictures. I also remember how they fired their long rifles at me. Did mental illness play a role in their act of terrorism, or in acts carried out by the gunmen at Virginia Tech or Sandy Hook? This chapter looks at the extensive research done on mental health. Are there predictors that can prevent the violent acts from occurring? Once again various sides are presented; of particular interest to me is the copycat or imitator theory.

There is evidence that the killers at Virginia Tech and Sandy Hook mentioned the names of the two killers at Columbine. It frightens me to think that there are students who were not born when the Columbine tragedy occurred who are using the template of the two Columbine killers to develop elaborate plans to carry out a school shooting. It frightens me that we are allowing the two killers from Columbine to remain relevant, and I question whether this give support to potential killers who are struggling mentally. Once again, the "Mass Shooters and Mental Illness" chapter addresses some of my concerns. The conclusion, which stresses the importance of "holistic programs," is a must read.

The various chapters in the book also do an outstanding job of presenting extensive research on whether or not video games, music, and other potential factors are contributing factors in mass shooting events. The book also shares research on gender and mass shootings. Also of great importance is the fact that many scholars believe that killers often broadcast their intentions. The two killers at Columbine had been videotaping their plans of terrorism for almost a year prior to the attack. The chapter "Insight from Averted Mass Shootings" by Eric Madfis shares valuable knowledge about this topic, and hopefully alerts people to keep their eyes and ears open for potential threats. This is especially important in this age of ubiquitous social media. A vital point I share during my presentations is that a student who has an adult that he or she can go to has the potential to avert a tragedy from occurring.

Another vitally important chapter in the book is "School Security Responses after Mass Shootings." History shows that each time a school shooting occurs, safety measures are implemented. This chapter discusses the security measures that have proven to be effective in preventing violent acts. I truly believe that there are people who believe if they do not talk about it or practice drills, it will not happen. This cannot be the attitude. Once again, this chapter talks about the benefits of school security, the monetary issues confronting institutions in implementing the security measures and programs, and the unintended consequences of failing to be proactive in school safety.

"Reponses to Mass Shootings" is a chapter in which Kristina Anderson, founder of the Koshka Foundation and a survivor at Virginia Tech, and Michele Gay, who tragically lost her daughter Josephine at Sandy Hook and started a school safety organization called Safe and Sound: A Sandy Hook Initiative, join Jackie to share their wealth of knowledge and lessons learned from their personal experiences. I have had the opportunity to share the stage with them on several occasions and their stories and knowledge are valuable on the topic. I applaud Jackie for soliciting their knowledge for the book.

This book also includes an "Encyclopedia of Mass Shooting Events, 1966–2016." This section provides a wealth of knowledge about mass shootings that have occurred on American soil from 1966 to 2016. Each event is structured similarly. The Columbine tragedy event was accurately reported and did debunk many of the myths that circulated following the tragedy and continue to circulate 19 years later.

One of the many strengths of the book is that Jackie does not try to tell you what works or does not work in preventing mass shooting events. She accumulates the evidence from professionals in the field who share their knowledge and extensive research and then you can decide. For example, the book shares articles from both sides of the gun control debate, including arguments regarding the meaning and extent of the Second Amendment. Also included in this section is Schildkraut and Elsass's thought-provoking research entitled "Presenting Mass Shootings: Using Theory to Drive Evidence-Based Practice."

As stated earlier, the book does an outstanding job giving details about mass shooting events from 1966 to 2016. The book does focus on three shootings that have had a particularly large and lasting impact: the Columbine High School tragedy in 1999, the Virginia Tech tragedy in 2007, and the Sandy Hook tragedy in 2012. In the "Pivotal Documents in Mass Shootings Research" section, excerpts from government reports will help readers reach a deeper understanding of each of these shootings. "The Report of Governor Bill Owens' Columbine Review Commission" (2001) was reported accurately, and I can make this statement without hesitation because I testified before the committee. The Virginia Tech Review Panel report in 2007 and the Final Report of the Sandy Hook Advisory Commission in 2015 serve as excellent resources as well. Many of the precautions and antiviolence practices being used today are a direct result of the work done by those three committees. Many of the recommendations have led to legislation that provides greater protection to our children and staff members.

Another key document in this section is the New York City Police Department's report on active shooters, including recommendations based on its findings. The section also references gun laws enacted during the administrations of President Johnson and President Clinton—and the loopholes associated with each piece of legislation. Other documents present the perspectives of Presidents Clinton, Bush, and Obama; members of Congress; and the National Rifle Association on school violence and mass shooting events. I do feel that President Obama stated it well when he said that he would "sign a directive that would give law enforcement, schools, mental health professionals, and the public health community the tools that they need to help reduce gun violence." The key point is that we must work as a team. As noted, I always respond, "What are *we* going to do?" when questioned about how to respond to these events. Our children are our most precious commodities.

In conclusion, I would encourage you to read the book with an open mind. Throughout the book, after reading the research presented, I do see the different points of view. I know that we continue to witness school shootings and other acts of violence, but how many potential acts have been thwarted because of new laws and policies that have been enacted? We must continue to look for answers. *Mass Shootings in America: Understanding the Debates, Causes, and Responses* does an outstanding job of looking at all the research on this subject and presenting it in a way that will hopefully encourage Americans of every ideological and political stripe to approach the topic of mass shootings with an open mind and see what is working and what is not working. As stated in the book, although researchers can find evidence that correlates for these events, it will be extremely difficult if not impossible to determine causation for all mass shooters. It is imperative that scholars continue to engage in individual offender case studies as well as examinations of the phenomenon of mass shootings as a whole in order to further the knowledge base about these events and facilitate both proactive and reactive responses to such tragedies. We must continue to fight the good fight because another life lost is one too many.

Frank DeAngelis
Principal (Retired)
Columbine High School

Acknowledgments

This book would not be possible without the support and dedication of so many individuals.

To the contributors, thank you for sharing your ideas and visions as part of this bigger project. Your insight is invaluable and I appreciate having such amazing minds lending their expertise to this volume.

To my research assistants—Hannah Brennan, Courtney Cherry, Sonali Kumar, Rolando Mejia, Michael Rotolo, and Jenna Testa—thank you for putting time and dedication into seeing my vision through, especially as you were finishing up your collegiate careers. This book would not be what it is without your efforts. Thank you also to Collin Carr for serving as my right hand in editing this work.

Finally, to my editors, Steve Catalano and Kevin Hillstrom, thank you for choosing me for this project. It has been both an honor and a privilege to work with you to make this book a reality, and I could not have asked for better editors or sounding boards. Your support and enthusiasm have been irreplaceable.

Introduction

It brought the nation to its knees, but now that we have gotten back up how
have things changed; what have we learned?
An inscription on the Wall of Healing at the Columbine Memorial

On April 20, 1999, two high school seniors opened fire at Columbine High School
in Littleton, Colorado. By the end of their nearly one-hour-long rampage, 12 students and a teacher had been killed before the shooters committed suicide (Columbine Review Commission, 2001). The Columbine shootings were not a new event,
nor would they be the last mass shooting to occur in the United States (Schildkraut
& Elsass, 2016). Something about the event, however, changed the way the phenomenon of mass shootings, both in and out of schools, was viewed. Columbine
came to be viewed as what experts call a "watershed" moment (Muschert, 2002,
p. ii; see also Altheide, 2009; Kalish & Kimmel, 2010; Larkin, 2007, 2009;
Muschert, 2007; Muschert & Larkin, 2007), an archetypal case to which all other
mass shootings would be compared. In its wake and in the aftermath of each similar tragedy that followed, the nation has been left with the question inscribed on the
memorial: "What have we learned?"

The lessons learned in the aftermath of Columbine and other similar tragedies
are important for several reasons. First, by examining how these horrific events
unfolded, we are better able to work toward addressing such issues that may prevent future attacks. Through the years, there have been advances in threat assessment protocols, safety measures and practices, and improvements in security
technology in response to mass shooting events. Second, advancements in response protocols for both law enforcement and other first responders, as well as
civilians, have been informed by previous tragedies. These reforms have, at least
in some cases, shortened the duration of mass shooting events, reduced arrival
times for first responders, and potentially mitigated the loss of life. Many of these
lessons serve as the foundation for this book and are discussed in the following
chapters and sections.

The loss of just one life to these senseless acts of violence is one too many. Yet
the lessons learned in the aftermath of these tragedies also mean that these lives
were not lost in vain. In order for these lessons to evolve, we must be willing to
have difficult conversations about issues such as safety, security, mental health,
violence in society, and more. These discussions should be sustained; yet the

reality is that often such dialogues only take place in the immediate aftermath of the event, at a time where emotions are running high and reactions often are knee-jerk (see, generally, Burns & Crawford, 1999; Schildkraut & Hernandez, 2014; Soraghan, 2000; Springhall, 1999). As a result, no real meaningful action is achieved and when the next event happens, society often finds itself back at square one.

An important part of that discussion needs to be research. Research is critical when informing policy, but it also helps to provide much-needed context to a problem like mass shootings. Sir Francis Bacon once said that knowledge is power. If that is true, then research is the knowledge necessary to make advancements toward the goal of reducing mass shootings in the United States.

WHAT IS A MASS SHOOTING?

This might seem like an easy question, right? Wrong. The reality is that as complex a phenomenon as mass shootings are (Harris & Harris, 2012), defining these episodic violent crimes is equally as challenging. Depending on the way that the description is crafted, mass shootings can look like infrequent events or occurrences that take place with alarming regularity. The broader impact of the definition has to do with the policies offered in the aftermath of mass shootings. If the severity of the problem is exaggerated by stakeholders (e.g., politicians, the media), then responses implemented may be too broad to address the issue at hand due to overprediction. Conversely, if not enough attacks are recognized under the definition proposed, the responses may be too narrow to be impactful.

In their book *Mass Shootings: Media, Myths, and Realities*, Jaclyn Schildkraut and H. Jaymi Elsass (2016) confronted this very issue. The manner in which a mass shooting is defined depends upon the agency providing the description, and often it is contingent upon a particular end goal or position. Everytown for Gun Safety, for example, has a definition of school shootings that is particularly broad in nature. Under its definition (Everytown for Gun Safety, 2014), incidents where a firearm discharges on school grounds but does not injure anyone counts as a school shooting. The end result of this is that the number of incidents is overinflated, thereby contributing to hysteria and panic about the safety of students in America's schools. In reality, however, such events are statistically rare in the context of how many children attend K–12 schools each year. In fact, the statistical likelihood of any one of those children falling victim to a mass shooting in his or her school is less than *one in five ten-thousandths* (Bernard, 1999; Donohue, Schiraldi, & Ziedenberg, 1998), meaning that the same student has a greater statistical likelihood of being struck by lightning. Furthermore, this relative risk has remained stable over time, meaning that one's likelihood of victimization is *not* increasing with each new event. Making these events appear more common, however, leads to a greater demand for action and change, which aligns with the organization's gun control initiative.

Variations in definition have also been found at the federal level. Differences in how these events are characterized can be found among the Centers for Disease

Control (2014), U.S. Department of Homeland Security (2008), Congressional Research Service (Bjelopera, Bagalman, Caldwell, Finklea, & McCallion, 2013), and a joint collaboration between the U.S. Department of Education and U.S. Secret Service (Vossekuil, Fein, Reddy, Borum, & Modzeleski, 2002; see also U.S. Secret Service, 2002), to name a few. The main discrepancies in definition among these and other agencies and organizations concern the location where the shooting takes place or how many victims (with respect to either fatalities or injuries) must be present for the shooting to be considered "mass." Even the federal government has weighed in by offering a definition of "mass killing" as part of the Investigative Assistance for Violent Crimes Act of 2012 (H.R. 2076, 2013). Still, no universally accepted definition by which to categorize these events has been found.

Schildkraut and Elsass (2016) proposed a definition that seeks to overcome such limitations while incorporating a reconceptualization of mass shooting events in four key ways:

1. Rather than considering only those killed, the meaning of the term "victim" needs to be reevaluated to account for everyone who is impacted directly by the event. Aside from those individuals also injured in the attacks, there often are many other individuals present at the scene who are victimized and traumatized by the experience and also could have been killed or wounded in the shooting.

2. The location of the shooting is often public and chosen at random or for symbolic value. It is common for these attacks to happen at places of opportunity (such as schools or workplaces for shooters who already have access to such locations). Further, as more perpetrators are becoming mobile (e.g., the 2014 mass shooting in Isla Vista, California, in which the shooter attacked from a moving car), it must be acknowledged that mass shooting events can be spread across several scenes.

3. There is also a time component with mass shootings, such that these events happen within a 24-hour period, though most often they last only minutes or hours (see, for example, Blair & Schweit, 2014). This distinct time period is what differentiates mass shootings from spree killings or serial murders (Morton & Hilts, 2006).

4. The potential motivation of the shooters (though often unable to be confirmed, particularly in cases where the offender commits suicide or is otherwise killed in the attack) also must be considered, as there is a qualitative difference between mass shooters and perpetrators of gang homicides, terrorism, or other episodes of mass violence.

Through such reconceptualization, and in an attempt at offering a potential universal definition by which such events could be understood, Schildkraut and Elsass (2016) carefully crafted the following definition of a mass shooting:

> A mass shooting is an incident of targeted violence carried out by one or more shooters at one or more public or populated locations. Multiple victims (both injuries and fatalities) are associated with the attack, and both the victims and location(s) are chosen either at random or for their symbolic value. The event occurs within a single

24-hour period, though most attacks typically last only a few minutes. The motivation of the shooting must not correlate with gang violence or targeted militant or terroristic activity. (p. 28)

This definition seeks to overcome the limitations identified in the descriptions mentioned above while simultaneously extracting those facets that make sense in the context of understanding these events. It is for these reasons that this definition serves as the basis for identifying the events included in the encyclopedia of shootings found later in the book.

WHAT DO WE KNOW ABOUT MASS SHOOTINGS?

In addition to the absence of a universally accepted definition about mass shootings, we also are without a similarly comprehensive data source that tracks these events. Those databases linked to organizations such as Everytown for Gun Safety, the Mass Shooting Tracker, and *Vox* suffer from selection bias due to the earlier discussed issues with the definitions used to identify the incidents. In other words, since each definition used by the respective organization is crafted specifically to support their cause or mission, the number of attacks in each database subsequently is inflated. In many instances, this is done to give the perception that the number of shootings is on the rise and something (e.g., adding restrictions for gun control or expanding rights for legal firearms owners) must be done (see also Ehrenfreund & Goldfarb, 2015; Healy, 2015; Lutz, 2012; Plumer, 2012; Wing & Stein, 2014). In reality, however, the number of mass shootings is relatively stable and has been for several decades (averaging approximately 20 attacks per year), even taking into account high-profile incidents such as Columbine, Virginia Tech, Sandy Hook, and the Pulse nightclub (Fox & DeLateur, 2014; Schildkraut & Elsass, 2016).

We do know that mass shootings are not a recent phenomenon, despite the public's misperception that the 1999 shooting at Columbine (or even the 1966 Tower shooting at the University of Texas, for some older Americans) was the first event of its kind in our nation's history. In fact, mass shootings have a long and public history in the United States, dating back to the late 1800s. They also are not specific to one particular type of location. Nearly every state has experienced some type of mass shooting attack (only five have not), and they have occurred in communities of varying shapes and sizes (e.g., urban, suburban, rural). Interestingly, despite the fact that homicides are more highly concentrated across the southern region of the nation, mass shootings have more commonly occurred in the western United States. Further, despite the common misperception that mass shootings are a uniquely American phenomenon, similar attacks have occurred on six of the seven continents.

When people think of mass shootings, they often consider those attacks that occur in schools. While this is the most common type of location and such events typically garner more attention among the media and politicians, mass shootings happen at a variety of locations. Workplaces are the second most common type of location; together with schools, such attacks account for nearly 65 percent of mass shootings. As noted earlier, these locations often are chosen as a function of opportunity, with the perpetrator being either a student or employee of the establishment. Still, mass shootings have occurred at a variety of other types of locations including, but certainly not limited to, places of worship (e.g., churches, mosques, and temples), malls, movie theaters, restaurants and bars, museums, salons, hospitals, gyms, courthouses, government buildings, post offices, and airports.

When it comes to the shooters, there also are many myths and misconceptions about who they are. Along with politicians and the media, members of the general public have adopted a "stereotype" or profile for what a mass shooter is: a young white male who brandishes an assault rifle and commits suicide after the attack (Petee, Padgett, & York, 1997; see also Healy, 2015; Hesse, 2015; Kluger, 2014; Mingus & Zopf, 2010; Wise, 2001; Xie, 2014). The reality, however, is that mass shooters do not conform to such a stereotype, and attempting to model policy around such a stereotype is doomed to fail (see, generally, Fox & DeLateur, 2014).

While the majority of perpetrators are, as believed, males, they are not so exclusively. Female offenders, though rare, still account for approximately 4 percent of shooters. Similarly, mass shooters are not all white—in fact, whites account for perpetrators in just over half (54 percent) of attacks. Shooters who are either black or Asian are overrepresented as compared to their proportion in the general U.S. population. Both the 2016 Pulse nightclub and 2007 Virginia Tech shootings, which are among the most lethal events, each were perpetrated by nonwhite attackers. Similarly, the number of victims claimed (both killed and injured) by white and nonwhite shooters is quite similar, particularly when reviewing attacks that have taken place since 2000 (Schildkraut & Elsass, 2016).

Contrary to the aforementioned stereotype, not all shooters are in their teens either. Nearly one in four shooters is under the age of 18 (which, given the fact that the greatest proportion of attacks happen in K–12 schools, is not unexpected), yet more than half of shooters are over the age of 30. In fact, the average age of a mass shooter in the United States is 33 years. Additionally, despite the perception that these shootings typically are carried out with assault rifles, the reality is that the perpetrators overwhelmingly use semiautomatic handguns in their attacks (Follman, Pan, & Aronsen, 2013; Fox & DeLateur, 2014). Finally, the belief that all shooters commit suicide at the end of their rampage equally is misplaced. In reality, more than half live through their rampages.

HOW DO WE KNOW WHAT WE KNOW ABOUT MASS SHOOTINGS?

For the majority (95 percent) of the general public, information about crime in the United States is derived from the media (Graber, 1980; Surette, 2015). That is because the majority of people in this country also are not the victims of crime; thus, their experiences are indirect. This is even more true in the context of mass shootings, which make up just a mere fraction of offenses known to law enforcement annually (Schildkraut, Elsass, & Meredith, 2017). As most people will never be the victim of a mass shooting, the media then become the main source of information on these events. Accordingly, the manner in which shootings are covered has a considerable effect on public attitudes and beliefs.

One key consideration in how perceptions are shaped by the media is the amount of coverage these events garner. When mass shooting events erupt, news stations often air live, uninterrupted coverage directly from the scene. This practice began during the Columbine shootings (Muschert, 2002) and continues in the coverage of attacks today. Beyond the initial attention, the media also will follow with a stream of stories. Matthew Robinson (2011), for example, found that Columbine was the most covered crime story during national evening news broadcasts in 1999, accounting for 319 stories aired that year. Brendan Maguire, Georgie Ann Weatherby, and Richard Mathers (2002) found that in the first week after the shooting, the three major broadcast networks—ABC, CBS, and NBC—devoted nearly four hours of airtime and 53 individual stories to covering the attack (see also Robinson, 2011). Comparatively, when looking at the collective coverage of 13 other mass shootings studied by the researchers, these cases—combined—received about as much media coverage as Columbine alone (Maguire et al., 2002). This same format has been observed with other mass shootings, including Virginia Tech, Aurora, Sandy Hook, and Pulse.

Excessive media attention of mass shootings is not solely limited to the television news format; pervasive coverage can also be observed through the newspaper medium. In her analysis of the nation's 50 most circulated newspapers, Katherine Newman (2006) found that over 10,000 articles had been written about Columbine in the year following the shooting. Of these, 170 were published by the *New York Times* alone (Chyi & McCombs, 2004; Muschert & Carr, 2006). Other shootings, such as Virginia Tech (Schildkraut, 2012) and Sandy Hook (Schildkraut & Muschert, 2014), also have been found to have been covered extensively in print, but the attention these shootings have received in terms of article counts failed to surpass that of Columbine, despite their having higher death tolls.

In addition to the extensive media attention these events often receive, another problem that impacts our collective understanding about mass shootings is which events are covered. These events are statistically rare and, therefore, theoretically all high-profile and sensational, but researchers have found that not every incident is guaranteed to be covered and of those that are, the amount of attention received can vary considerably (e.g., Elsass, Schildkraut, & Stafford, 2014; Schildkraut, 2014; Schildkraut et al., 2017). For example, 23 percent of mass shooting events that took place in the United States between 2000 and 2012 were never mentioned in the *New York Times*. In a 2017 study, Jaclyn Schildkraut and colleagues explored why this might be the case. Through statistical analyses, they determined that mass shootings were more likely to be covered (as compared to not receiving any mention) by the *Times* if the shooter committed suicide. Further, if the attack happened outside of a school, specifically at a restaurant, bar, club, or personal residence, it was less likely to be covered. When examining what led to greater amounts of coverage being devoted to a mass shooting—an important question as just 5 of the 90 cases studied accounted for 57 percent of 562 articles and 62 percent of nearly 490,000 words of text analyzed in the study—the researchers determined that incidents involving shooters of Asian or other ethnic descent, as well as those with higher victim counts and greater median incomes for the location in which the attack occurred, were significantly more likely to receive attention, both in the number and the length of articles devoted to the event. Again, those attacks occurring outside of schools were found to garner less media attention.

These are just some of the many research studies that have examined mass shootings and their complex relationship with the media (a list of additional studies can be found later in this volume). Still, there are even further-reaching consequences of misreporting on these events: inaccurate public opinions about what they mean. Columbine was the biggest news story of its year and the third most followed event of its decade (Pew Research Center for the People & the Press, 1999). Following the 2012 shooting at Sandy Hook Elementary School, a *Washington Post*–ABC News Poll (n.d.) reported that respondents indicated that the shooting was indicative of broader social problems in the nation. Conversely, these same respondents indicated that other mass shootings that happened around the same time (e.g., a 2011 mass shooting in Tucson, Arizona, and a 2012 mass shooting in Aurora, Colorado) were isolated incidents (*Washington Post*–ABC News Poll, n.d.), despite the fact that these stories also had been rated among the most important of their respective years (Drake, 2013). Public opinion polls were conducted linking these events to broader issues, such as gun control (Carlson & Simmons, 2001; Connelly, 1999; Pew Research Center for the People & the Press, 2000, 2012, 2014; Saad, 1999, 2012; Smith, 2002; Swift, 2014). As public opinion is instrumental in driving the policies discussed at the onset of this introduction, presenting mass shootings in their actual context becomes even more critical to deriving sound solutions.

WHY IS THIS BOOK IMPORTANT?

As noted at the beginning of this introduction, accurate and discerning research is a critical first step in creating effective responses to events like mass shootings. It is necessary to educate the public, inform the crafting and implementation of policy, and further the collective goal of reducing the frequency and severity of these events. Often, this research comes in pieces—spread across different journals or books in single articles or limited in scope to a particular issue or theme (see, for example, Muschert and Sumiala's [2012] edited volume examining the mediatization of mass shootings). While these works are extremely beneficial for reading on a focused topic, they do not encompass the broader totality of the issue at hand. This current volume, however, provides a unique hybrid approach to understanding the broader problem of mass shootings in America.

By uniting experts from a variety of disciplines, as called upon by John Harris and Robin Harris (2012), we are able to achieve this goal. This book is divided into five key sections that assess the debates, causes, and responses surrounding mass shootings. The first section offers essays from invited experts from the fields of criminal justice, criminology, sociology, and psychology. While, on their face, mass shootings might seem simple to understand, these events are actually highly complex in terms of the broader related issues. From the widely recognized causal factors of guns, mental health, and violent media to issues of gender and masculinity, to studies of warning signs and response measures, mass shootings are a complex phenomenon. These essays explore broader issues related to these events, including guns, mental health, violent media, challenges for law enforcement, gender, mass shootings as terrorism or acts of hate crime, averted rampages, and prevention strategies.

Next, there is an encyclopedia of mass shootings for 50 years (1966–2016) to provide readers with detailed accounts of individual events. Events that are included in this section meet the criteria identified in the definition proposed by Schildkraut and Elsass in *Mass Shootings: Media, Myths, and Responses* (2016), which, as noted, is used as the basis of this book. Based on this definition, exhaustive keyword searches of news media, law enforcement, and other agency websites were scoured for events that met the criteria for inclusion. It is important to note that, since no national database of events exists, nor does a universal definition for these events, it is impossible to ensure that every mass shooting event over the 1966–2016 time span is included. Still, based on the available research, it is believed that the list of events included here is as complete, inclusive, and representative of the phenomenon during this time frame as possible.

Each event entry in the encyclopedia is structured similarly. Basic information on each perpetrator, such as name and age, is included for readers to cross-reference for additional information they may seek independently. Similarly, a basic timeline of events and information on the day of the shooting is offered along with the number of fatalities and injuries from the attack. In the event that the shooter was taken into custody by law enforcement, as opposed to dying at the scene (either by suicide or being killed by responding police), verifiable details related to the trial, outcome, sentence, and punishment (e.g., location of incarceration) are also included. All information related to incarceration has been verified through the respective state's department of corrections offender locator website.

The reader may find that many of the entries are a bit short in length. This is due to the limited information released and/or the minimal coverage of these events (see, for example, the discussion of selection bias in the coverage of mass shootings by the media in this introduction). Those events that are more high-profile in nature typically yield more information, which is reflected here in various entries. These specific entries are emphasized to stand out for the reader. They also link back to the broader issues related to mass shootings that were discussed earlier in the volume in the essays in the section "Understanding Mass Shootings in America."

As this encyclopedia only includes information that can be cross-referenced, and any discussion of shooters' motivation is purely speculative or anecdotal commentary, such information has been omitted from the individual entries. It is particularly rare for shooters to leave behind information that directly speaks to their motivation (the Columbine shooters, via their videos entitled *The Basement Tapes*, are a notable exception; these videos, however, have never been made public and were subsequently destroyed by the Jefferson County Sheriff's Office in 2011). As such, this information has been omitted.

We also have elected, in an effort to reduce the sensationalism of these events and the glorification of the perpetrators, to minimize the use of the shooters' names in accordance with the No Notoriety campaign (www.nonotoriety.com). Therefore, most entries only list the perpetrator's name once and readers may use this to seek additional information beyond this book. Similarly, the make and model of the weapon(s) used by the shooters will not be listed; rather, only the general type of weapon (e.g., handgun, shotgun, rifle) is included. This information often is available in the media, or you may review investigatory reports, such as the Columbine Review Commission and Virginia Tech Review Panel reports (excerpts of which can be found later in this volume in the Pivotal Documents section), or police reports, which can be obtained through Freedom of Information Act (FOIA) requests.

After the encyclopedia portion of the book, a second collection of essays is offered featuring experts weighing in on specific key issues and debates related to these events, including whether gun control is an appropriate response to mass shootings, how best to study mass shootings and develop corresponding policy, and different aspects of prevention efforts. While the authors of the essays in the opening section of this book, "Understanding Mass Shootings in America," are considered experts in their respective disciplines, their contributed works address broad issues related to mass shootings. Yet there also are specific, more pointed questions that often linger in the minds of citizens, both in and out of academia, regarding mass shooting events. This section features explorations of some of these specific discussion points with other experts in the field. These articles seek to offer well-crafted arguments surrounding a particular hypothesis and engage experts with competing points of view. Further, while the earlier chapters are grounded in academic literature and therefore more neutral in tone, the essays in this section reflect personal and, at times, controversial opinions of the contributors, which can add important and much needed insights to the discussion of mass shootings.

Subsequent to that section, the reader will find a section of pivotal documents that provide additional context to understanding the broader issues—including gun control, mental health, and violent media—surrounding mass shootings. An important asset in any type of research is official documentation, and the study of mass shootings is no exception. Official documentation may come in the form of investigatory or review reports, official government assessments, legislation (either introduced or passed), notable speeches and remarks from lawmakers, or statements and testimony from congressional hearings. This section gives a sample of documents that are among the go-to sources in this area of research. Each pivotal document includes an excerpt from the respective source, as well as a reference to retrieve the full record for further review.

Finally, a list of further references is offered to help readers continue their research exploration in understanding the complex issue of mass shootings in America. This section includes a variety of sources, including peer-reviewed academic journal articles, books, government reports, and other essential works. Complete citations have been included so that interested readers can retrieve the source through their school or public libraries. Additional works also can be found with a simple Google Scholar or Google Web search.

REFERENCES

Altheide, D. L. (2009). The Columbine shooting and the discourse of fear. *American Behavioral Scientist, 52*(10), 1354–1370.

Bernard, T. (1999). Juvenile crime and the transformation of juvenile justice: Is there a juvenile crime wave? *Justice Quarterly, 16*(2), 337–356.

Bjelopera, J. P., Bagalman, E., Caldwell, S. W., Finklea, K. M., & McCallion, G. (2013). *Public mass shootings in the United States: Selected implications for federal public health and safety policy*. Washington, D.C.: Congressional Research Service. Retrieved from http://fas.org/sgp/crs/misc/R43004.pdf

Blair, J. P., & Schweit, K. W. (2014). *A study of active shooter incidents, 2000–2013*. Washington, D.C.: U.S. Department of Justice, Federal Bureau of Investigation. Retrieved from http://www.fbi.gov/news/stories/2014/september/fbi-releases-study-on-active-shooter-incidents/pdfs/a-study-of-active-shooter-incidents-in-the-u.s.-between-2000-and-2013

Burns, R., & Crawford, C. (1999). School shootings, the media, and public fear: Ingredients for a moral panic. *Crime, Law & Social Change, 32*(2), 147–168.

Carlson, D. K., & Simmons, W. W. (2001, March 6). Majority of parents think a school shooting could occur in their community. *Gallup*. Retrieved from http://www.gallup.com/poll/1936/Majority-Parents-Think-School-Shooting-Could-Occur-Their-Community.aspx

Centers for Disease Control. (2014). *School-assisted violent death study*. Washington, D.C.: Centers for Disease Control. Retrieved from http://www.cdc.gov/ViolencePrevention/youthviolence/schoolviolence/SAVD.html

Chyi, H. I., & McCombs, M. E. (2004). Media salience and the process of framing: Coverage of the Columbine school shootings. *Journalism and Mass Communication Quarterly, 81*(1), 22–35.

Columbine Review Commission. (2001). *The Report of Governor Bill Owens' Columbine Review Commission*. Denver, CO: State of Colorado. Retrieved from http://trac.state.co.us/Documents/Reports%20and%20Publications/Columbine_2001_Governor_Review_Commission.pdf

Connelly, M. (1999, August 26). Public supports stricter gun control laws. *New York Times*. Retrieved from http://partners.nytimes.com/library/national/082699poll-watch.html

Donohue, E., Schiraldi, V., & Ziedenberg, J. (1998, July). *School house hype: School shootings and the real risks kids face in America*. Washington, D.C.: Justice Policy Institute. Retrieved from http://www.justicepolicy.org/uploads/justicepolicy/documents/98-07_rep_schoolhousehype_jj.pdf

Drake, B. (2013, September 17). Mass shootings rivet national attention, but are a small share of gun violence. *Pew Research Center*. Retrieved from http://www.pewresearch.org/fact-tank/2013/09/17/mass-shootings-rivet-national-attention-but-are-a-small-share-of-gun-violence/

Ehrenfreund, M., & Goldfarb, Z. A. (2015, June 18). 11 essential facts about guns and mass shootings in the United States. *Washington Post*. Retrieved from http://www.washingtonpost.com/blogs/wonkblog/wp/2015/06/18/11-essential-facts-about-guns-and-mass-shootings-in-the-united-states/

Elsass, H. J., Schildkraut, J., & Stafford, M. C. (2014). Breaking news of social problems: Examining media effects and panic over school shootings. *Criminology, Criminal Justice, Law & Society, 15*(2), 31–42.

Everytown for Gun Safety. (2014). *Analysis of school shootings: December 15, 2012– December 9, 2014.* Retrieved from http://everytown.org/documents/2014/10 /analysis-of-school-shootings.pdf

Follman, M., Pan, D., & Aronsen, G. (2013, February 27). A guide to mass shootings in America. *Mother Jones.* Retrieved from http://www.motherjones.com/politics /2012/07/mass-shootings-map

Fox, J. A., & DeLateur, M. J. (2014). Mass shootings in America: Moving beyond New-town. *Homicide Studies, 18*(1), 125–145.

Graber, D. A. (1980). *Crime news and the public.* Chicago, IL: University of Chicago Press.

Harris, J. M., & Harris, R. B. (2012). Rampage violence requires a new type of research. *American Journal of Public Health, 102*(6), 1054–1057.

Healy, M. (2015, June 19). It's not just a perception: Mass shootings have become more frequent, data show. *Los Angeles Times.* Retrieved from http://www.latimes.com /science/sciencenow/la-sci-sn-mass-shootings-more-frequent-data-20150618 -story.html

Hesse, J. M. (2015, June 23). Why are so many mass shootings committed by young white men? *Vice.* Retrieved from http://www.vice.com/read/why-are-so-many-mass -shootings-committed-by-young-white-men-623

Investigative Assistance for Violent Crimes Act of 2012, H.R. 2076, 112th Cong., 1st Sess. (2013). Retrieved from https://www.congress.gov/112/plaws/publ265/PLAW -112publ265.pdf

Kalish, R., & Kimmel, M. (2010). Suicide by mass murder: Masculinity, aggrieved entitle-ment, and rampage school shootings. *Health Sociology Review, 19*(4), 451–464.

Kluger, J. (2014, May 25). Why mass killers are always male. *Time.* Retrieved from http:// time.com/114128/elliott-rodgers-ucsb-santa-barbara-shooter/

Larkin, R. W. (2007). *Comprehending Columbine.* Philadelphia, PA: Temple University Press.

Larkin, R. W. (2009). The Columbine legacy: Rampage shootings as political acts. *Ameri-can Behavioral Scientist, 52*(9), 1309–1326.

Lutz, A. (2012, December 14). Why mass shootings have become more common in the U.S. *Business Insider.* Retrieved from http://www.businessinsider.com/why -shootings-have-become-more-common-2012-12

Maguire, B., Weatherby, G. A., & Mathers, R. A. (2002). Network news coverage of school shootings. *The Social Science Journal, 39*(3), 465–470.

Mingus, W., & Zopf, B. (2010). White means never having to say you're sorry: The racial project in explaining mass shootings. *Social Thought & Research, 31*(1), 57–77.

Morton R. J., & Hilts, M. A. (Eds.). (2006). *Serial murder: Multi-disciplinary perspectives for investigators.* Washington, D.C.: National Center for the Analysis of Violent Crime (NCAVC). Retrieved from https://www.fbi.gov/stats-services/publications /serial-murder

Muschert, G. W. (2002). *Media and massacre: The social construction of the Columbine story.* (Unpublished doctoral dissertation). University of Colorado at Boulder, Boulder, CO.

Muschert, G. W. (2007). The Columbine victims and the myth of the juvenile superpreda-tor. *Youth Violence and Juvenile Justice, 5*(4), 351–366.

Muschert, G. W., & Carr, D. (2006). Media salience and frame changing across events: Coverage of nine school shootings, 1997–2001. *Journalism and Mass Communica-tion Quarterly, 83*(4), 747–766.

Muschert, G. W., & Larkin, R. W. (2007). The Columbine High School shootings. In S. Chermak & F. Y. Bailey (Eds.), *Crimes and trials of the century* (253–266). Westport, CT: Praeger.

Muschert, G. W., & Sumiala, J. (Eds.). (2012). *School shootings: Mediatized violence in a global age*. Bingley, UK: Emerald Publishing.

Newman, K. S. (2006). School shootings are a serious problem. In S. Hunnicutt (Ed.), *School shootings* (10–17). Farmington Hills, MI: Greenhaven Press.

Petee, T. A., Padgett, K. G., & York, T. S. (1997). Debunking the stereotype: An examination of mass murder in public places. *Homicide Studies, 1*(4), 317–337.

Pew Research Center for the People & the Press. (1999, December 28). *Columbine shooting biggest news draw of 1999*. Retrieved from http://people-press.org/report/48/columbine-shooting-biggest-news-draw-of-1999

Pew Research Center for the People & the Press. (2000, April 19). *A year after Columbine public looks to parents more than schools to prevent violence*. Retrieved from http://www.people-press.org/2000/04/19/a-year-after-columbine-public-looks-to-parents-more-than-schools-to-prevent-violence/

Pew Research Center for the People & the Press. (2012, July 23). *Colorado shootings capture public's interest*. Retrieved from http://www.people-press.org/2012/07/23/colorado-shootings-capture-publics-interest/

Pew Research Center for the People & the Press. (2014, December 10). *Growing public support for gun rights*. Retrieved from http://www.people-press.org/2014/12/10/growing-public-support-for-gun-rights/

Plumer, B. (2012, December 14). Why are mass shootings becoming more common? *Washington Post*. Retrieved from http://www.washingtonpost.com/blogs/wonkblog/wp/2012/12/14/why-are-mass-shootings-becoming-more-frequent/

Robinson, M. B. (2011). *Media coverage of crime and criminal justice*. Durham, NC: Carolina Academic Press.

Saad, L. (1999, April 23). Public views Littleton tragedy as sign of deeper problems in country. *Gallup News*. Retrieved from http://www.gallup.com/poll/3898/public-views-littleton-tragedy-sign-deeper-problems-country.aspx

Saad, L. (2012, December 27). Americans want stricter gun laws, still oppose bans. *Gallup*. Retrieved from http://www.gallup.com/poll/159569/americans-stricter-gun-laws-oppose-bans.aspx

Schildkraut, J. (2012). Media and massacre: A comparative analysis of the reporting of the 2007 Virginia Tech shootings. *Fast Capitalism, 9*(1). Retrieved from http://www.uta.edu/huma/agger/fastcapitalism/9_1/schildkraut9_1.html

Schildkraut, J. (2014). *Mass murder and the mass media: An examination of the media discourse on U.S. rampage shootings, 2000–2012*. (Unpublished doctoral dissertation). Texas State University, San Marcos, TX.

Schildkraut, J., & Elsass, H. J. (2016). *Mass shootings: Media, myths, and realities*. Santa Barbara, CA: Praeger.

Schildkraut, J., Elsass, H. J., & Meredith, K. (2017). Mass shootings and the media: Why all events are not created equal. *Journal of Crime and Justice*. https://doi.org/10.1080/0735648X.2017.1284689

Schildkraut, J., & Hernandez, T. C. (2014). Laws that bit the bullet: A review of legislative responses to school shootings. *American Journal of Criminal Justice, 39*(2), 358–374.

Schildkraut, J., & Muschert, G. W. (2014). Media salience and the framing of mass murder in schools: A comparison of the Columbine and Sandy Hook school massacres. *Homicide Studies, 18*(1), 23–43.

Smith, T. W. (2002). Public opinion about gun policies. *The Future of Children, 12*(2), 154–163.

Soraghan, M. (2000). Colorado after Columbine: The gun debate. *State Legislatures, 26*(6), 14–21.

Springhall, J. (1999). Violent media, guns, and moral panics: The Columbine High School massacre, 20 April 1999. *Paedagogica Historica, 35*(3), 621–641.

Surette, R. (2015). *Media, crime, & criminal justice: Images and reality* (5th ed.). Pacific Grove, CA: Brooks/Cole.

Swift, A. (2014, October 31). Less than half of Americans support stricter gun laws. *Gallup.* Retrieved from http://www.gallup.com/poll/179045/less-half-americans -support-stricter-gun-laws.aspx

U.S. Department of Homeland Security (DHS). (2008). *Active shooter: How to respond.* Washington, D.C.: DHS. Retrieved from http://www.dhs.gov/xlibrary/assets/active _shooter_booklet.pdf

U.S. Secret Service, National Threat Assessment Center. (2002). Preventing school shootings: A summary of a U.S. Secret Service Safe School Initiative report. *NIJ Journal, 248*, 10–15. Retrieved from https://www.illinois.gov/ready/plan/Documents /PreventingSchoolShootingsSecretService.pdf

Vossekuil, B., Fein, R. A., Reddy, M., Borum, R., & Modzeleski, W. (2002). *The final report and findings of the Safe School Initiative: Implications for the prevention of school attacks in the United States.* Washington, D.C.: United States Secret Service and United States Department of Education. Retrieved from https://www2.ed.gov /admins/lead/safety/preventingattacksreport.pdf

Washington Post–ABC News poll. (n.d.). *Washington Post politics.* Retrieved from http:// www.washingtonpost.com/wp-srv/politics/polls/postabcpoll_20121216.html

Wing, N., & Stein, S. (2014, June 10). If it's a school week in America, odds are there will be a school shooting. *Huffington Post.* Retrieved from http://www.huffingtonpost .com/2014/06/10/school-shootings-since-newtown_n_5480209.html

Wise, T. (2001). School shootings and white denial. *Multicultural Perspectives, 3*(4), 3–4.

Xie, T. (2014, June 19). Mass shooters have a gender and a race. *Political Research Associates.* Retrieved from http://www.politicalresearch.org/2014/06/19/mass-shooters -have-a-gender-and-a-race/#sthash.bHg5mJqG.dpbs

Understanding Mass Shootings in America

The Role of Firearms in Mass Shootings

Jack Levin

In December 2000, an employee at Edgewater Technology in Wakefield, Massachusetts, shot to death seven of his coworkers. Owing a good deal of money to the IRS for nonpayment of federal taxes, the killer had learned that his wages would be garnished by his employer. Waiting for the optimal moment to strike, he hid his semiautomatic weapons under his desk and opened fire the next day on the employees who worked in human resources and the company's payroll office—the two groups at his workplace that he blamed for reducing his income. None of his other coworkers were targeted.

Mass killers tend to be like the assailant at Edgewater Technology, at least in one respect: they are quite selective in their choice of victims. Firearms allow killers to aim their violence at the particular targets they associate with causing their miseries in life—at certain family members, coworkers, classmates, or members of a despised outgroup. Relatively few mass killers are bent on revenge against all of the residents of a particular community or against human beings generally. In most cases, they have experienced some catastrophic loss—the loss of a job, income, or relationship with their spouse and children—and they lash out to get even.

Thus, firearms are rarely employed by political terrorists to massacre civilians in countries outside of the United States, where gun control laws are strict and terrorists seek to take as many lives as possible. Bombs are more likely than guns—even high-powered semiautomatic weapons—to maximize the carnage, causing terror to spread among local residents and bringing a terrorist organization all of the publicity that it seeks. In April 2017, for example, a 22-year-old suicide bomber from the Central Asian country of Kyrgyzstan planted a bomb on the metro in St. Petersburg, Russia, killing 13 and hospitalizing at least 50. He was sending a message of terror to Russian civilians and government officials, but he was not interested in taking the lives only of those individuals who organized against his cause (Levin, 2006).

ACTIVE "SHOOTER" EVENTS

Guns are particularly lethal weapons. They are more likely than knives to leave a trail of death and destruction, and they are more reliable than explosives. Almost 78 percent of all mass killings are committed with a rifle or a handgun; fewer than 11 percent are committed with a knife (Fox & Levin, 2015). In addition, attacks with firearms enable an assailant to carry out lethal attacks from a distance, whereas stabbing represents an up close and personal method of attack. Many people who can easily fire a gun to end someone's life would not—as a result of deep-rooted empathy—be able to plunge a knife into the body of another human being. Moreover, in order to commit a mass killing, the victims cannot be given an opportunity to leave the scene. Knives are more often used to kill one victim at a time; guns (especially semiautomatics) can target numerous victims almost simultaneously. Most mass shootings take only a few minutes to commit. By the time that authorities arrive at the crime scene, the killer has amassed a large body count and may also have taken his own life (Blair & Schweit, 2014).

In part because of the availability of firearms, mass stabbings have rarely occurred in the United States—and when they do, they seldom yield a large number of deaths, although mass injuries sometimes occur. In April 2014, for example, 22 people—21 students and a security guard—were injured when a 16-year-old student went on a stabbing rampage at a Pennsylvania high school near Pittsburgh. The assailant ran from classroom to classroom and down a corridor, stabbing and slashing as many of his schoolmates as possible. Finally, he was tackled by a security guard and an assistant principal who held him down until the police arrived. The student's mass stabbing was meant to kill; the result, however, was to inflict many injuries but no deaths.

In contrast, semiautomatic firearms, whether rifles or handguns, have been responsible for causing massive death and destruction (Duwe, Kovandzic, & Moody, 2002; Fox & Levin, 2015). In December 2012, for example, 20 children and 6 adults at Sandy Hook Elementary School in Newtown, Connecticut, were shot to death by a 20-year-old former student using a semiautomatic rifle, who had been bullied from the first grade on at that same school. In the wake of this attack, it was suggested that his victims served as surrogates for the first graders who had humiliated him years earlier (Lysiak & Shapiro, 2013). Coincidentally, on the same day as the Sandy Hook massacre, a 36-year-old man, using a knife, attacked primary school children at Chenpeng Village in the southern Chinese province of Guangxi. He injured 22 children and 1 adult. None of his victims were wounded seriously; none lost their lives. If the assailant had used a gun rather than a knife, he most likely would have left a trail of deadly destruction.

This potential for extreme violence can be seen in the largest mass shooting in modern American history. In June 2016, 49 people lost their lives when a "lone wolf" killer opened fire on patrons at a gay nightclub in Orlando, Florida. The Orlando massacre was perhaps both an act of terrorism as well as a violent hate crime. The perpetrator seemed to be inspired by radical Islam, but he also apparently despised gays and lesbians (see the chapters "Mass Shootings as Hate Crimes" and "Mass Shootings as Acts of Terrorism" later in this volume).

Guns have also served as effective weapons of mass destruction when an assailant's original list of victims does not satisfy his quest for bloodshed. In such cases, the distinction between family and public massacres breaks down. The assailant might start his killing spree by specifically targeting those members of his family he blames for his personal miseries but then decide also to punish coworkers, classmates, or humanity in general. In July 1999, for example, a 44-year-old stock market day trader, having suffered huge financial losses over a two-month period, bludgeoned to death his wife and two children as they slept in their beds. A day later, he shot to death nine employees in two Atlanta stock market firms and then took his own life. His weapons: a .45-caliber and a 9-millimeter handgun. A note that the shooter left behind indicated that he held his wife responsible for his failures in life.

ARGUMENT FOR CONCEALED CARRYING OF GUNS

Gun advocates have argued that civilians carrying concealed weapons would be able to stop a mass killer before he amasses a large body count. State "right to carry" laws vary as to whether, and under what conditions, they sanction carrying concealed firearms in public places.

In October 1991, a 35-year-old man rammed his pickup truck through the plate glass window of a crowded Luby's Cafeteria in Killeen, Texas, as the patrons inside were having lunch. Thinking the driver had had an accident, many customers rushed to assist him. Instead, the driver got out of his truck and immediately opened fire on the crowd, killing 23 people.

One Luby's restaurant customer, Suzanna Hupp, helplessly watched as her mother and father were gunned down. Reasoning that she might have saved her parents' lives, she later expressed remorse for having left her handgun in her vehicle outside of the restaurant at the very time that it was most needed. In Texas, state law prohibited residents from carrying guns concealed inside their clothing or pocketbooks. Hupp was a law-abiding citizen, so she complied with the law.

Even if Hupp is correct that more lenient concealed carry laws might have prevented or limited the Luby's massacre, it is less than clear that outlawing guns in public places would, in general, reduce the number of mass shootings. Researchers are seriously at odds when it comes to being for or against so-called "gun-free zones." Grant Duwe and his associates (2002) have found virtually no support for assertions that restrictive gun control laws increase vulnerability to mass shootings. These researchers determined that only 13 percent of mass public shootings perpetrated between January 2009 and July 2015 occurred in gun-free zones. Using county-level data, Charles Phillips and his colleagues (2015) similarly concluded that concealed handgun licensing is independent of crime rates. That is, the rate at which concealed licenses are issued does not influence violent crime, and violent crime does not influence concealed handgun licensing.

Other researchers, however, argue that mass shootings are more likely to happen in "gun-free zones" where a killer is aware that he is unlikely to confront armed opposition (Lott, 1998). This disagreement may be, in part, a result of differences in definitions of gun-free zones and mass shootings as well as variations in sampling. If the almost 50 percent of mass murders that happen in residences are included, then the influence of gun-free zones becomes sharply reduced. If schools and college campuses are included, then there will be a major increase in the presence of mass murder located in gun-free zones.

Some perpetrators may actually look for victims who are easy to overcome. In Aurora, Colorado, on the evening of July 20, 2012, for example, a gunman opened fire during a midnight showing of *The Dark Knight Rises* at the Century Aurora 16 Multiplex Theater. The assailant killed 12 audience members and injured another 58 (12 others sustained various injuries not caused by gunfire in the attack). John Lott suggests that the killer looked for an easy target and selected the Century Aurora Theater because it was the only cinema in the area that advertised being a gun-free zone.

On the other side of the argument, some researchers believe that the widespread availability of firearms may actually increase the potential for carnage in situations like Aurora. Like many other patrons, the gunman had entered the cinema in costume. The theater was dark. Audience members were confused as to who was the killer and who was an innocent victim. If customers had been carrying, they might easily have shot one another and not the rampaging killer.

The difficulty of identifying killers in the heat of the moment is suggested in the aftermath of school shootings in many locations, where law enforcement requires students to file out of buildings on campus holding their hands over their heads. In many cases, the authorities believe that two killers were involved, and only one is in custody. This almost always turns out not to be true.

Still, Hupp may be correct in asserting that lives might have been saved if some of the Luby's diners had been carrying firearms. In 2007, a church security volunteer stopped a 24-year-old gunman who had already killed four people at a megachurch in Colorado Springs. The killer was aiming his firearm to shoot more innocent victims when Jeanne Assam opened fire on him until he was down and disarmed. Assam had served as a police officer in Minneapolis during the 1990s and was subsequently a security guard in Colorado. She had been professionally trained in the use of a firearm and was able to confront the killer without excessive anxiety or trepidation. Her intervention clearly saved the lives of at least some of the thousands of worshippers who were attending the church service. Unfortunately, the same cannot necessarily be said about ordinary citizens who carry a concealed firearm but who lack the training and skill required to stop a mass killer.

If almost everybody in town is packing heat, then you would potentially be safer doing the same. Certainly, a bank robber might think twice about pulling a loaded gun if he is aware that all the customers and employees have one. But just the opposite may be true in settings where relatively few citizens carry firearms and the real problem is not murders committed by strangers, but by friends and family members who have a temper tantrum and impulsively shoot one another. A liberal concealed weapons law might add to the murder rate in a particular location by providing more citizens with a lethal means for resolving everyday arguments, not only at home but also in bars and on the job, not to mention on the roads in and out of town during commuting hours.

THE AUSTRALIAN EXPERIENCE

In the United States, the evidence for a legal approach to reduce mass murder is mixed and inconclusive. The Australian experience represents what is perhaps the most definitive evidence we have confirming the efficacy of a firearm ban on the prevalence of multiple homicide.

In April 1996, a 28-year-old man who suffered from a profound intellectual deficit shot and killed 35 people in the popular Australian tourist destination of Port Arthur, located on the island of Tasmania. The so-called Port Arthur Massacre was the deadliest mass shooting in Australian history. It inspired a sweeping series of gun control laws known as the National Firearms Agreement, which, beginning in June 1996, banned semiautomatic rifles and established a set of hurdles—passing a safety test, showing a history of moral character, and waiting at least 28 days—for potential gun owners to meet in order to purchase a firearm. Also under the agreement, Australia enacted a mandatory gun-buyback program that resulted in the purchase and destruction of more than 650,000 firearms (Chapman, Alpers, & Jones, 2016).

From 1979 up to and including the Port Arthur massacre in 1996, Australia had experienced 13 mass shootings in which at least five victims were killed. By contrast, after the National Firearms Agreement came into force, there were no shootings involving five or more fatalities from 1997 to 2016 (Chapman et al., 2016). However, the enactment of tough Australian gun laws in 1996 apparently had little, if any, effect on the reduction in gun homicides generally. According to Samara McPhedran, Jeanine Baker, and Pooja Singh (2011), New Zealand has more relaxed gun control laws than Canada or Australia, yet its gun murders declined more than in either of the other countries.

THE BRADY LAW

The inconsistency of Australia's gun ban with respect to its effectiveness in reducing mass versus single-victim murder cannot be overemphasized as a general principle. Certain gun control laws can be expected to reduce only certain types of gun violence.

In February 1994, for example, the Brady Handgun Violence Prevention Act, or Brady Act as it is commonly known, established a five-day waiting period for the purchase of firearms (for an excerpt of the legislation, see the Pivotal Documents section later in the book). The National Rifle Association (NRA) spent millions of dollars to defeat the bill, but it was not able to overcome support for the law in both houses of Congress. The NRA did win one concession, however: the final version of the legislation provided that beginning in 1998, the five-day waiting period for handgun sales would be replaced by an instant computerized background check that involved no waiting period. Moreover, the law stipulated that background checks would apply only to transactions with federally licensed gun dealers and not cover the unregulated market (gun shows and private sales), which accounted for an estimated 30 percent to 40 percent of all sales. Those who sought to avoid a background check could thus do so by purchasing their firearm from a friend or relative or by making their purchase on the Internet. Further, school rampage shootings in particular are often committed by teenagers who secure their weapons from their own homes, unbeknownst to parents who purchased firearms after passing background checks.

There is some evidence that the waiting period established by the Brady Act helped to reduce certain suicides. A 2000 study found that the implementation of the Brady Act was associated with reductions in the firearm suicide rate for persons aged 55 years or older (Ludwig, Cook, & Rosenfeld, 2000). It did nothing, however, to decrease the valence of mass murder. Most mass killers apparently do not mind waiting. They are likely to plan their attacks well in advance.

For example, in December 1993, a 59-year-old Jamaican immigrant boarded a Long Island Railroad commuter train and opened fire on riders, killing six of them. In April 1993, more than eight months prior to his deadly rampage, the killer had moved to California in search of new career opportunities. He purchased a Ruger semiautomatic pistol in Long Beach for $400, after waiting the 15-day period required under California law. Like so many other mass killers, the shooter saw himself as a law-abiding individual who was only interested in taking the lives of his enemies. In this case, he felt that racism was to blame for all of his failures and he sought to get even with white Americans.

Most mass killers are like the Long Island commuter rail gunman in at least one important respect. They have typically planned their attack for weeks or months before opening fire in a crowded train, cinema, shopping mall, or school. A waiting period would therefore do almost nothing to reduce the possibility of these kinds of massacres. It certainly would not have stopped the Virginia Tech shooter from executing 32 students and faculty on campus on April 16, 2007. More than two months earlier, in early February, he bought a semiautomatic handgun on the Internet from a Green Bay, Wisconsin, dealer. One month later, he purchased a second semiautomatic pistol from a local firearms dealer. The law mandated a waiting period of 30 days between the purchases of two guns, so the shooter obeyed the law.

Although it probably failed to make a dent in the prevalence of mass shootings, the Brady Law's five-day waiting requirement may have been effective in providing a cooling-off period for enraged lovers and friends who might otherwise have killed themselves or others if they had easier access to a loaded gun at the time.

THE U.S. BAN

The Public Safety and Recreational Firearms Use Protection Act, more commonly known as the Federal Assault Weapons Ban, which outlawed semiautomatic weapons, was passed as part of the Violent Crime Control and Law Enforcement Act by the U.S. Congress in September 1994 (an excerpt from this legislation is available in the Pivotal Documents section). The American version, unlike its Australian counterpart, only included a prohibition on firearms defined as "assault rifles and handguns" as well as certain "large capacity" ammunition magazines. Also different from the Australian version, the American law had a 10-year life span, meaning that it would expire in 2004 if Congress failed to reauthorize it. Moreover, the ban applied only to firearms manufactured after the law's enactment, leaving numerous semiautomatic weapons to be bought and sold during the years when the prohibition was in effect. Assuming that the ban would soon be a reality, some firms increased their manufacturing of assault weapons during the period before the law was enacted, placing larger numbers of semiautomatic rifles and handguns on the market. Finally, the law specified certain features of semiautomatic rifles and pistols with detachable magazines and named only particular firearms as assault weapons. Many weapons of mass destruction were excluded from the scope of the ban because they lacked all of the mandatory features thought to constitute "assault weapons" or simply were not on the banned list. As a result of all these exceptions and loopholes, the ban's capacity to take preferred weapons of mass murder off the streets and out of the hands of angry individuals was limited.

For the above-mentioned reasons and others, the effect of the U.S. ban was, according to many observers, minimal at best. Moreover, a rash of school rampage shootings occurred while the ban was in effect, including the infamous Columbine High School massacre as well as multiple murders in Moses Lake, Washington; West Paducah, Kentucky; Pearl, Mississippi; and Springfield, Oregon. In most of these incidents, the weapons were originally purchased legally by adults. In the case of the deadly school rampage in Littleton, Colorado, one of the shooters' firearms—the IntraTec TEC-DC9—was explicitly listed on the federal assault weapons ban, but he was still able to acquire it through a private seller. At Columbine High, 12 students and a teacher were killed before the shooters committed suicide.

THE IMPACT OF GUN CONTROL

Does gun control actually reduce mass murder? The truth will satisfy almost nobody because it lies in the gray area between gun-control zealots and gun fanatics. In reality, it depends on what type of control measure is being advocated and on what kind of killing is being examined.

Most of the large-scale massacres have been committed with semiautomatic rifles and handguns (Fox & Levin, 2015). Get rid of high-powered firearms and you would almost definitely reduce the massive body counts, if not the prevalence, of mass killings. It is often said that if we make guns difficult to obtain, then only the criminals will be able to get them. This argument makes the dubious distinction between the good guys without guns and the bad guys who use them on the good guys. Actually, most lethal injuries are inflicted not by outlaws but by people who accidentally shoot one another, leave their guns in places accessible to children, or lose their cool.

When it comes to mass murder, this distinction is even more unclear. Murders of entire families have been committed by dedicated but emotionally disturbed husbands and fathers who carry out their deeds under twisted justifications that they must protect their wives and children from their miserable existence. The killer believes that his family members would be better off dead. In other cases, the killer is convinced that his spouse is responsible for all of his miseries and deserves to die. He is not, in his own mind, taking the lives of innocent victims but guilty villains. Or a man who shoots his boss and coworkers after being terminated from a job might feel that he has helped build the company, made it the success it is to-day, and what does he get in return? He is fired! Or a child who has been bullied and humiliated at school might decide to get even with his nasty schoolmates through the barrel of a gun. Many mass killers in families, workplaces, and schools have no criminal record and no formal psychiatric history. Until the time they go on a rampage, they look and act like humane, law-abiding people, not criminals (Fox & Levin, 2015; Levin & Fox, 1985).

Few Americans favor a total ban on firearms, but many recognize the need to limit the availability of high-powered firearms in order to reduce the prevalence of mass killings. A majority—55 percent—supports stricter gun control laws. Some 64 percent express their opposition to carrying guns in public places such as schools and college campuses (see, for example, Wolfson, Teret, Azraek, & Miller, 2017). At the other end of the continuum, a smaller number believes that restrictions of any kind on the purchase of firearms constitutes an abridgement of their Second Amend-ment constitutional rights. They also are often convinced that stricter gun control measures would have no effect on the rate of extreme violence (Jacobs, 2002).

Rather than continue to debate a false and divisive all-or-nothing issue, we should now focus on determining which gun control measures are both constitu-tional and effective and which ones are a waste of our time (Schildkraut & Elsass, 2016). There is much common ground in the gun control argument, but only if we get beyond the extreme positions on both sides of the issue.

REFERENCES

Blair, J. P., & Schweit, K. W. (2014). *A study of active shooter incidents, 2000–2013.* Washington, D.C.: U.S. Department of Justice, Federal Bureau of Investigation.

Chapman, S., Alpers, P., & Jones, M. (2016). Association between gun law reforms and intentional firearm deaths in Australia, 1979–2013. *JAMA, 316*(3), 291–299.

Duwe, G., Kovandzic, T., & Moody, C. E. (2002). The impact of right-to-carry concealed firearm laws on mass public shootings. *Homicide Studies*, *6*(4), 271–296.

Fox, J. A., & Levin, J. (2015). *Extreme killing: Understanding serial and mass murder.* Thousand Oaks, CA: Sage.

Jacobs, J. B. (2002). *Can gun control work?* Oxford: Oxford University Press.

Levin, J. (2006). *Domestic terrorism.* New York: Chelsea House.

Levin, J., & Fox, J. A. (1985). *Mass murder: America's growing menace.* New York: Plenum Books.

Lott, J. R. (1998). *More guns, less crime.* Chicago: University of Chicago Press.

Ludwig, J., Cook, P. J., & Rosenfeld, R. (2000). Homicide and suicide rates associated with implementation of the Brady Handgun Violence Prevention Act. *Journal of the American Medical Association, 284*(5), 585–591.

Lysiak, M., & Shapiro, R. (2013, April 7). Adam Lanza's murder spree at Sandy Hook may have been "act of revenge." *New York Daily News.* Retrieved from http://www.nydailynews.com/news/national/lanza-article-1.1309766

McPhedran, S., Baker, J., & Singh, P. (2011). Firearm homicide in Australia, Canada, and New Zealand: What can we learn from long-term international comparisons? *Journal of Interpersonal Violence, 26*(2), 348–359.

Phillips, C. D., Nwaiwu, O., Lin, S., Edwards, R., Imanpour, S., & Ohsfeldt, R. (2015). Concealed handgun licensing and crime in four states. *Journal of Criminology,* 1–8.

Schildkraut, J., & Elsass, H. J. (2016). *Mass shootings: Media, myths, and realities.* Santa Barbara: CA, Praeger.

Wolfson, J. A., Teret, S. P., Azraek, D., & Miller, M. (2017). US public opinion on carrying firearms in public places. *American Journal of Public Health, 107*(6), 929–937.

Mass Shooters and Mental Illness

Jennifer Johnston

When teenagers are surveyed about the motives of school shooters, many cite mental illness as a leading factor. Where did they get this idea? None of these teens personally know a perpetrator of mass murder nor have they studied the anatomy of a criminal mind. Their opinions likely are formed by public discourse, what they hear friends and family discussing, and stories of mass shooters as reflected in the media. We often attribute the problems and mistakes of others to their "bad character," yet we forgive ourselves easily for our own transgressions and believe that circumstances are more likely to blame. This is known as the *fundamental attribution error*—a classic theory in social psychology. So, our tendency to assume that mass shooters must be bad apples down to the core or deeply disturbed individuals with mental illnesses that we can only shudder to imagine (and sometimes we merge the two) is a common psychological tendency. It serves to distance us from thinking we too are capable of "evil," protecting our self-esteem and preserving a holistic "good" sense of self. The media further reinforces these ideas.

WHAT DOES THE MEDIA SAY?

Mental illness has frequently been presented to the public as a key cause of mass shootings. This phenomenon was documented by Emma McGinty, Daniel Webster, Marian Jarlenski, and Colleen Barry (2014) in a study that found an increase in media coverage of mass shootings in newspaper articles and TV news report transcripts over time. They randomly sampled 25 percent of more than 5,000 stories about mass shootings collected from 1997 to 2012, specifically looking for themes of whether the media assigned blame for the violence to the mental health of the shooters or gun laws. The researchers also analyzed how long each story stayed in the news (about two weeks on average). They found that schizophrenia and psychosis were mentioned more often than any other serious mental illness in stories that mentioned mental illness (26 percent and 29 percent, respectively). Depression was mentioned half as often. Bipolar disorder and personality disorder were also infrequently mentioned. Overall, in the stories that mentioned the causes of gun violence, mental illness was mentioned as a primary cause 22 percent of the time, whereas lax gun laws were mentioned 14 percent of the time.

In another content analysis, Jaclyn Schildkraut (2014) analyzed hundreds of newspaper articles on mass shootings over 12 years. Mental illness was mentioned as a major cause of the shooting in 65 percent of the articles until 2008, and then that dropped to about 35 percent of the articles from 2008 to 2012. Clearly, the news media and the general public believe that mental illness is a primary cause of mass shootings.

WHAT DO MENTAL HEALTH EXPERTS SAY?

Psychological disorders, which can involve psychosis, like schizophrenia, delusional disorder, major depressive disorder, and bipolar disorder, are not associated with violent behavior. Substance use, when combined with one of these other disorders, has been linked to increased violence. However, experts believe it is the substance use that is to blame, not the mental disorder (Rosenberg, Rosenberg, Ellefson, & Corrigan, 2015). Even most of the personality disorders, excluding antisocial personality disorder (APD), are not associated with violence. Although APD is generally an unfortunate consequence of severe attachment problems and intense adversity in childhood, its sufferers are usually mentally capable and have violated the rights of others and social norms for much of their lives, unlike most school or mass shooters.

As an example, the Sandy Hook shooter was in and out of mental health treatment for many years, and during that time his clinicians did not see any aggressive tendencies that would specifically predict his later crimes (Bonanno & Levenson, 2014). J. Reid Meloy and colleagues (2004) found that only 25 percent of the adolescent mass shooters they examined had a history of any kind of mental health treatment. In one of the most comprehensive reports on mental health and murder, Robert Fein and Bryan Vossekuil (1999) examined mental health records of 83 fame-motivated assassins and found that almost all had no contact with a mental health professional in the year before their attack. More than 75 percent showed no evidence of hallucinations or delusions that might be indicative of schizophrenia or other serious mental illness. Even of those who were delusional, fewer than 10 percent had any history of violence while delusional. In fact, those who were actively delusional most often did not succeed in their attack. They approached and retreated or they were apprehended.

Years later, Fein continued to contend that fame-seeking, or becoming a "somebody," is the primary motivator for most killers (Fein, 2014; Fein, personal communication, November, 2015). For example, the delusions of killers are not persecutory, grandiose, or somatic (the most common types of delusion), but instead are narcissistic (they will become famous, they can save the world, their target personally hurt them/denied them, and/or they could get close to a celebrity they believe might love them). That said, in his study, 40 percent of offenders did have a history of psychiatric hospitalization, usually for suicidal thoughts or behavior, a year or more before the attack (Fein & Vossekuil, 1999). The tendency toward serious depression and suicidality emerges as the most important mental illness signpost of potential mass shooters.

Most shooters resent and blame their victims/targets for their problems. This is not an aspect of mental illness. Instead, the field of psychology uses highly unscientific yet appropriate terms for this: bad behavior and wrong thinking—what we might call "aggrieved entitled" thinking, as Rachel Kalish and Michael Kimmel (2010) name it. Aggrieved entitlement is "feeling wronged by the world" or a particular group, and believing the world or that group owes you something. Research carried out by James Alan Fox and Monica DeLateur (2014) and Fox and Jack Levin (2015) indirectly supports the aggrieved entitlement hypothesis. They note that mass murderers generally do not want psychological help. Instead, they believe their problems stem from someone else. They believe themselves to be "victims of injustice" and want their "fair share" of attention, money, or status, all of which have been denied them through, according to their perceptions, no fault of their own. Both Fox and DeLateur (2014) and Jonathan Metzl and Kenneth MacLeish (2015) argue that there is no clarity that mental illness leads to mass murder; however, it is clear that people diagnosed with mental illness are almost twice as likely to be assaulted or killed by the non–mentally ill. As Jeffrey Swanson, professor of psychiatry and leading expert in mental health and violence, suggests, we should not be linking the terms "mental illness" and "homicide." We should instead speak of "behavioral risk indicators" when it comes to violence, such as two key indicators: depression and substance abuse (Swanson, McGinty, Fazel, & Mays, 2015).

Psychosis. In an analysis of mass shooters by Mayors Against Illegal Guns (2013), there was evidence of mental health concern for only 11 percent of the 93 shooters from 2009 to 2013. To be fair, among adolescent shooters, it is harder to determine psychosis or psychopathy, especially personality disorder, since those diagnoses require longer time periods for verification, such as more than six months of ongoing psychotic symptoms for a diagnosis of schizophrenia and at least one year of symptoms beyond the age of 18 for a diagnosis of antisocial personality disorder (APD)—a condition known to the layperson as sociopathy (American Psychiatric Association, 2013). In fact, in one case of a very young shooter (age 14) who survived, he later developed schizophrenia, living out his sentence in prison (Newman, Fox, Harding, Mehta, & Roth, 2004). Individuals with psychosis are only slightly more likely to commit violence than the average person with no psychological disorder. Olav Nielssen and colleagues (2009), based on their multicountry meta-analysis of stranger murder and mental illness, estimate only about 25 stranger murders in the United States are committed by people with psychological illness each year. The researchers did not include mass murder in their analysis. As discussed above, if 10 percent to 20 percent of mass shooters who are believed to have psychosis are added, the total number would be only 35 to 45 individuals annually. Even then, as the authors conclude, murder by a stranger with psychosis is exceptionally rare. Since almost all attacks involve careful planning that precludes serious psychosis or other debilitating mental illness, the motives and "leakage" of the intentions of the individuals are much more important to identify than their mental health status (Fein & Vossekuil, 1999).

Depression and suicidality. Depression has been mentioned frequently as common among mass shooters. Obviously, depression is a mental illness, although people do not often think of it that way. It is the most commonly suffered mental disorder, so sometimes it is written off as nonconsequential. About one-third of people will experience depression in their lifetime (American Psychiatric Association, 2013). However, there are varying levels of severity, and feeling suicidal or planning suicidal actions is the most severe form. So, just speaking of depression, there is a preponderance of that type of mental illness among mass shooters, and it deserves our attention.

Among school shooters and mass shooters, depression is listed by many expert profilers and researchers as a major predisposing factor (Fein & Vossekuil, 1999; Meloy et al., 2004; Newman et al., 2004; O'Toole, 2000; Wike & Fraser, 2009). The percentage of suicides that occur as part of the resolution of an attack is also significant, and although almost always linked to depression, the motives for suicide can vary and warrant additional consideration (see Lankford, 2014, for a thorough discussion). Adam Lankford's (2015) analysis of 185 mass shooters found that 48 percent committed suicide after the crime or engaged in "suicide-by-cop," which he linked to direct evidence of the shooters' underlying or prior depressive behaviors, statements, or writing.

The mental health status of shooters is a causal factor in the incidence of mass shootings, but the specter of psychosis is not to blame, as many people imagine. Old-fashioned depression, combined with a penchant for narcissism, is the most common culprit (Johnston & Joy, under review). It is important to remember that social context is likely a more important causal variable than mental health status (Kalish & Kimmel, 2010). The predominant climate of bullying in most schools and social settings, when boys do not fit the gender stereotype of athlete/tough guy, can influence boys on the losing end to embrace that stereotype and end up "overconforming" to it by seeking stereotypical male, violent revenge against those who hurt or humiliate them. Evidence of their targeted attacks on tormentors comes from the locations of their rampages (Schildkraut & Elsass, 2016).

Despite being diagnosed with autism spectrum disorder many years before, the Sandy Hook shooter was not assessed by mental health professionals to be a danger to others. His writings and free-time activities indicated an interest in violence, but individuals with autism are so rarely violent and are often incapable of the detailed planning involved in mass shootings that the professionals who cared for him never became sufficiently alarmed to warn parents, school professionals, or law enforcement about his potential for committing acts of violence.

PSYCHOLOGISTS' DUTY TO WARN

According to ethics of mental health professionals surrounding confidentiality, homicidal ideation is not reported outside of the therapeutic relationship unless a clear victim has been named and intent to kill is explicitly stated or plainly evident in behavior, a requirement known as Tarasoff's rule. Clinicians do not warn a potential victim or alert authorities about the dangerousness of their clients unless these two factors are present: identified victim and clear intent. However, several court cases have set a precedent to expand Tarasoff. For example, courts have ruled that even unnamed victims connected to a threat should be told to authorities (American Psychological Association, 2013; Kring & Johnson, 2016, p. 439).

Normally, mental health patients are allowed to freely express mild desires to do harm or indulge fantasies of bad behavior as a part of the therapeutic process. Why? This works by identifying and working on negative impulses and thoughts during treatment sessions, without fear of retribution. We have all had very angry thoughts, and sometimes even murderous thoughts, but we may want to feel free to speak with a therapist about it so that we can change the negative or violent thinking while not worrying that the therapist will immediately report us to the police. In fact, researcher David Buss estimated that 90 percent of men and more than half of women have had vivid fantasies about committing murder, but few consider seriously acting on the fantasies (Buss, 2005).

The case of the Aurora, Colorado, shooting that took place on July 20, 2012, illustrates how even referral to mental health professionals and accurate assessment of threat may not lead to involuntary commitment or protection of the public. The shooter sought professional help in the months before the shooting and revealed his desire to harm others. It was reported to campus police and the shooter's mother because the psychiatrist followed Tarasoff's rule. However, when the authorities interviewed the shooter, they were unsure if he needed to be committed, so they asked the psychiatrist her opinion. She erred on the side of least restrictive intervention—outpatient therapy (McGhee, 2013). Instead of completing treatment, he mercilessly killed strangers.

Tragically, the University of Colorado, where this shooter attended graduate school and where he sought mental health services, had a detailed and actionable behavioral and threat assessment plan at the time of the incident that many schools would envy. Further, the mental health staff and police followed it, but to no avail. The shooter's mental health assessment would not have made it into the National Instant Criminal Background Check System (NICS) system (Federal Bureau of Investigation, n.d.) to prevent him from buying guns, and because the psychiatrist reported that his threats were nonspecific and no clear plan was told to her, she did not feel she could warn any particular person or have her patient committed (Nussbaum, Steffan, & Ingold, 2015).

THE MENTALLY ILL AND ACCESS TO GUNS

The NICS system that grew out of the 1993 Brady Handgun Violence Prevention Act (an excerpt of which is available in the Pivotal Documents section later in this volume) was set up to prevent the purchase of guns by people who might not be able to safely use guns. The only provision of NICS that safeguards against guns being purchased by people who may suffer from mental illness, however, applies to three very rare instances: people who have been involuntarily committed to a mental institution at some point in their lives, people who were accused of a crime but could not stand trial due to mental incapacitation or being deemed guilty by reason of insanity, and people assigned a permanent legal guardian because of mental disability or psychological incapacitation. The incidence of loss of legal autonomy or involuntary commitment, even for brief periods, is quite rare. The American legal system leans heavily on the side of assisting people in keeping their rights, taking responsibility for their actions, and deciding for themselves what treatment they want. Temporary commitments are a little more common, such as 3- to 30-day treatment. Generally, both the mental health field and the courts attempt the least restrictive interventions first, and only if all of those fail do they move toward permanent legal decisions.

This practice does well to protect patients' rights, but sometimes people who are dangerous are not identified, so the NICS system does not flag them or prohibit them from purchasing guns. The NICS is also dependent upon appropriate and timely reporting by state psychologists and courts that have knowledge of patients or convicted criminals who have lost their legal rights. There is evidence that only since 2013 have states improved reporting practices (Rosenberg et al., 2015; Schildkraut & Elsass, 2016). Further, the NICS system cannot stop someone from buying a gun at a gun show, due to a loophole in the Brady Act, or from purchasing a gun illegally. As Swanson wisely asserts, "I don't think we're ever going to live in a world [without] troubled, confused, isolated young men. But we shouldn't live in a world where men like that have very easy access to semi-automatic handguns" (in Beckett, 2014).

AN OUNCE OF PREVENTION . . .

Given all this somewhat disheartening information, are there any bright spots? Many experts believe that the following steps can prevent mass shootings from happening in many, if not most, instances:

1. Reduce social triggers of mass shooting like bullying (Bonanno & Levenson, 2014; Kimmel & Mahler, 2003; Levin & Madfis, 2009; Newman et al., 2004). Do not engage in any form of bullying and stand up or stand with bystanders who counter bullying.

2. Take suicidal ideation seriously because it is a common characteristic of shooters (Fox & Levin, 2015; Kalish & Kimmel, 2010; Lankford, 2014; Vossekuil, Fein, Reddy, Borum, & Modzeleski, 2002). Never assume someone is joking if he or she discusses suicide; tell a trusted adult or mental health professional. They will follow up and know the right questions to ask. Crisis intervention training reminds us that homicide and suicide are two sides of the same coin, and we should be assessing for both when someone suicidal is referred.

3. Take depression seriously, especially in teenagers (Meloy et al., 2004; O'Toole, 2000). Ask questions, show concern, and connect people who suffer to resources.

4. Report "leakage" or warnings that hint or directly suggest a person is planning a mass shooting to law enforcement or school authorities immediately (O'Toole, 2000; Weisbrot, 2008).

A person who has committed a number of violent acts in the past is more likely to commit violence in the future. However, this is not usually true of mass shooters. They seem to reach a social breaking point and become willing to carry out plans that were mostly fantasy until then. Telling someone about their desire or intent to harm is another predictor of actually carrying it out, so all such claims should be taken seriously. Finally, carrying weapons or transporting oneself to a leaked location is a sure sign that intent has become actionable. Emergency personnel should immediately be deployed (Blair, Nichols, Burns, & Curnutt, 2013).

Of the 114 children who were referred over nine years to Deborah Weisbrot, a clinical psychiatrist, for evaluation after some "leakage" occurred, none went on to commit mass shootings. She recommends that mental health professionals assess the severity (realistic execution) of the threat, amount of preoccupation with the threat, target of the threat, and access to weapons. She further notes that she always thoroughly assesses depression, suicidal thinking, reality testing, as well as collects data on any previous mental health concerns and asks family about past trauma and peer relationships, all of which she finds very pertinent to effective intervention (Weisbrot, 2008).

CONCLUSION

Mass shootings are on the rise, and even though the threat is exceptionally rare to most Americans, we are all understandably concerned. Although the media frames psychosis as a major cause of mass shootings, depression and substance abuse are much more common in shooters. Many have almost no history of violence, unlike other types of murderers. However, a specific social context of bullying, isolation, and perceived entitlement seems to fuel them to cross the line. We have evidence that interventions such as duty-to-warn laws and threat assessment plans catch some shooters before they act, but not all. Also, the criteria for NICS registration is very stringent and not always timely. Therefore, we must also consider prevention opportunities such as early identification of suicidality, serious bully prevention, and reduction of male entitlement, and gun access based on proving an earned responsibility to carry, rather than an automatic right to carry.

REFERENCES

American Psychiatric Association. (2013). *Diagnostic and statistical manual of mental disorders* (5th ed.). Washington, D.C.: Author.

American Psychological Association. (2013). *HIPPA, what you need to know now: The privacy rule*. Washington, D.C.: American Psychological Association Practice Organization. Retrieved from http://www.apapracticecentral.org/business/hipaa /hippa-privacy-primer.pdf

Beckett, L. (2014, June 10). What we actually know about the connections between mental illness, mass shootings, and gun violence. *Pacific Standard.* Retrieved from https://psmag.com/social-justice/actually-know-connections-mental-illness-mass-shootings-gun-violence-83103

Blair, J. P., Nichols, T., Burns, D., & Curnutt, J. R. (2013). *Active shooter events and response.* Boca Raton, FL: CRC Press.

Bonanno, C. M., & Levenson, Jr., R. L. (2014). School shooters: History, current theoretical and empirical findings, and strategies for prevention. *Sage Open, 4*(1), 1–11.

Buss, D. M. (2005). *The murderer next door: Why the mind is designed to kill.* New York, NY: Penguin Books.

Federal Bureau of Investigation. (n.d.). National Instant Criminal Background Check System (NICS). Retrieved from https://www.fbi.gov/services/cjis/nics/about-nics

Fein, R. A. (2014). "Assassins of rulers" (MacDonald, 1912). *Journal of Threat Assessment and Management, 1*(4), 225–227.

Fein, R. A., & Vossekuil, B. (1999). Assassination in the United States: An operational study of recent assassins, attackers, and near-lethal approachers. *Journal of Forensic Sciences, 44*, 321–333.

Fox, J. A., & DeLateur, M. J. (2014). Mass shootings in America: Moving beyond Newtown. *Homicide Studies, 18*(1), 125–145.

Fox, J. A., & Levin, J. (2015). *Extreme killing: Understanding serial and mass murder.* Los Angeles, CA: Sage.

Johnston, J. B., & Joy, A. (Under review). Mass shootings and the media contagion effect. *Media Psychology.*

Kalish, R., & Kimmel, M. (2010). Suicide by mass murder: Masculinity, aggrieved entitlement, and rampage school shootings. *Health Sociology Review, 19*(4), 451–464.

Kimmel, M. S., & Mahler, M. (2003). Adolescent masculinity, homophobia, and violence: Random school shootings, 1982–2001. *American Behavioral Scientist, 46*(10), 1439–1458.

Kring, A. M., & Johnson, S. L. (2016). *Abnormal psychology: The science and treatment of psychological disorders* (13th ed.). Hoboken, NJ: Wiley.

Lankford, A. (2014). Précis of the myth of martyrdom: What really drives suicide bombers, rampage shooters, and other self-destructive killers. *Behavioral and Brain Sciences, 37*(4), 351–362.

Lankford, A. (2015). Mass shooters in the USA, 1966–2010: Differences between attackers who live and die. *Justice Quarterly, 32*(2), 360–379.

Levin, J., & Madfis, E. (2009). Mass murder at school and cumulative strain: A sequential model. *American Behavioral Scientist, 52*(9), 1227–1245.

Mayors Against Illegal Guns. (2013). *Analysis of recent mass shootings.* New York: Author. Retrieved from http://libcloud.s3.amazonaws.com/9/56/4/1242/1/analysis-of-recent-mass-shootings.pdf

McGhee, T. (2013, January 15). Theater shooting victim's wife sues Holmes' psychiatrist. *Denver Post.* Retrieved from http://www.denverpost.com/breakingnews/ci_22378331/theatershooting-victims-wife-sues-holmes-psychiatrist/

McGinty, E. E., Webster, D. W., Jarlenski, M., & Barry, C. L. (2014). News media framing of serious mental illness and gun violence in the United States, 1997–2012. *American Journal of Public Health, 104*(3), 406–413.

Meloy, J. R., Hempel, A. G., Gray, B. T., Mohandie, K., Shiva, A., & Richards, T. C. (2004). A comparative analysis of North American adolescent and adult mass murderers. *Behavioral Sciences & the Law, 22*(3), 291–309.

Metzl, J. M., & MacLeish, K. T. (2015). Mental illness, mass shootings, and the politics of American firearms. *American Journal of Public Health, 105*(2), 240–249.

Newman, K. S., Fox, C., Harding, D. J., Mehta, J., & Roth, W. (2004). *Rampage: The social roots of school shootings.* New York: Basic Books.

Nielssen, O., Bourget, D., Laajasalo, T., Liem, M., Labelle, A., Häkkänen-Nyholm, H., Koenraadt, F., & Large, M. M. (2009). Homicide of strangers by people with a psychotic illness. *Schizophrenia Bulletin, 37*(3), 572–579.

Nussbaum, M., Steffan, J., & Ingold, J. (2015, June 16). Aurora theater shooting gunman told doctor: "You can't kill everyone." *Denver Post.* Retrieved from http://www.denverpost.com/2015/06/16/aurora-theater-shooting-gunman-told-doctor-you-cant-kill-everyone/

O'Toole, M. E. (2000). *The school shooter: A threat assessment perspective.* Quantico, VA: Critical Incident Response Group, FBI Academy, National Center for the Analysis of Violent Crime. Retrieved from https://www.fbi.gov/file-repository/stats-services-publications-school-shooter-school-shooter

Rosenberg, J., Rosenberg, S., Ellefson, S., & Corrigan, P. (2015). Public mental health stigma and mass shootings. *SAJ Forensic Science, 1*(1), 1–6.

Schildkraut, J. (2014). *Mass murder and the mass media: An examination of the media discourse on U.S. rampage shootings, 2000–2012.* (Unpublished doctoral dissertation). Texas State University, San Marcos, TX.

Schildkraut, J., & Elsass, H. J. (2016). *Mass shootings: Media, myths, and realities.* Santa Barbara, CA: Praeger.

Swanson, J. W., McGinty, E. E., Fazel, S., & Mays, V. M. (2015). Mental illness and reduction of gun violence and suicide: Bringing epidemiologic research to policy. *Annals of Epidemiology, 25*(5), 366–376.

Vossekuil, B., Fein, R. A., Reddy, M., Borum, R., & Modzeleski, W. (2002). *The final report and findings of the "Safe School Initiative": Implications for the prevention of school attacks in the United States.* Washington, D.C.; United States Secret Service and Department of Education. Retrieved from https://www2.ed.gov/admins/lead/safety/preventingattacksreport.pdf

Weisbrot, D. M. (2008). Prelude to a school shooting? Assessing threatening behaviors in childhood and adolescence. *Journal of the American Academy of Child and Adolescent Psychiatry, 47*(8), 847–852.

Wike, T. L., & Fraser, M. W. (2009). School shootings: Making sense of the senseless. *Aggression and Violent Behavior, 14*(3), 162–169.

Violent Media and Video Game Effects

Sven Smith and Christopher J. Ferguson

On July 24, 2016, the *New York Times* reported that a teenage gunman killed nine people in a rampage in Munich. The *Times* explained that the gunman had been treated for paranoia and depression and appeared to have been planning the attack for over a year. Quoting an investigation source, the *New York Times* article described the shooter as a "a mentally disturbed teenager obsessed with mass shootings and first-person-shooter video games" (Eddy, 2016). Of course, many teens enjoy (or are "obsessed with," whatever that may mean) action-oriented video games. Was observing this in the current case a meaningful clue as to the chain of events leading to his crime, or was it more akin to something unrelated, such as noticing that he sometimes wore sneakers, just as many law-abiding teens do?

THE HISTORY OF THE RELATIONSHIP BETWEEN MODERN MASS SHOOTINGS AND VIOLENT MEDIA

Since the 1990s, political activists have attempted to link mass murders to violent video games, films, song lyrics, and other elements of popular culture, despite strong evidence to the contrary. Public discussions parallel this trend. The increase in graphic violence of video games in the mid-1990s triggered increasing amounts of political scrutiny on video games. This, in conjunction with the concurrent reported increase in school shooting incidents of the 1990s, sparked hearings on violent entertainment in the U.S. Senate. The Entertainment Software Ratings Board was created in 1994 in order to thwart the alleged dangers of video games and violent media, as were international ratings boards like the Pan European Game Information (PEGI) and British Board of Film Classification. At least 10 states and municipalities in the United States attempted to pass legislation regulating the sale of violent games to minors (Ferguson, Coulson, & Barnett, 2011). Several activists expressed views on the proposed dangers inherent in video games. For example, Florida attorney Jack Thompson implicated video games as the causal agent in school shootings such as the Virginia Tech massacre in 2007 (Benedetti, 2007), although it later was revealed that the shooter was not a video game player (Virginia Tech Review Panel, 2007).

Particular scholars became involved, drawing causal connections between violent media, video game violence, and school shootings (Anderson, 2004). They suggested a three-part mechanism to explain the causality between violent video games and aggression. First, violent video game exposure increases aggression-related knowledge structures. Second, this exposure decreases feelings of empathy for victims and decreases negative emotional reactions to violent thoughts, images, and scripts. Third, combining the first two proposed mechanisms, when there is provocation of some kind, the increased accessibility of aggressive thoughts increases the likelihood that the event will be perceived as hostile. For example, an individual gets bumped in a school corridor. If he or she is a gamer, the thinking goes that the individual is more likely to interpret the bump as intentional and retaliate aggressively. As a result, aggressive response options will more likely be prevalent in the mind of the violent video gamer and selected for action as a response to provocation. In this way, the individual is developing an aggressive personality (Anderson, 2004).

The claims about violent media effects fit well with the efforts by some politicians and antimedia activists to regulate media, and these groups worked with some scholars to create a narrative in which video games could be "linked" to school shootings (see Anderson, 2004 as an example from academia). As a result, the news media became increasingly fascinated with the theory that video game violence was a "cause" of mass murders or youth violence more generally (see Ferguson, 2015a; Kutner & Olson, 2008 for discussions). In the political arena, this became most notable when then-governor of California Arnold Schwarzenegger (ironically a star of violent action movies popular with youth, both before and after his term as governor) signed legislation attempting to regulate the sale of violent video games to minors. The U.S. Supreme Court would ultimately strike down this legislation as both unconstitutional and lacking scientific justification (*Brown v. EMA*, 2011).

In many cases, the information put forward by some scholars and activists appeared to selectively neglect an increasing pool of research indicating that violent video games and other media were not causally implicated in aggression or violent crime (Anderson, 2004; Bushman & Anderson, 2001). In this sense, the "science" may have been manipulated to fit a preexisting social narrative about the "harms" of violent media and its proposed link to societal violence including mass homicides. This may also help explain why news media selectively attend to video games and media only in the case of younger but not older mass homicide perpetrators (the latter of whom do not likely play violent video games) or mistakenly persist in identifying some shooters (e.g., Virginia Tech, Sandy Hook) as frequent violent video game players, despite evidence from official investigation reports that suggest they were not motivated by such games. For instance, in the case of the Sandy Hook shooting from 2012, although several violent action games were recovered from the shooter's home, these were old and outdated versions of the game, suggesting a lack of recent use. Further, the official investigation reported that witnesses could only remember the shooter playing nonviolent games such as Super Mario Brothers and Dance, Dance Revolution (State's Attorney for the Judicial District of Danbury, 2013).

THE FEDERAL GOVERNMENT AND SCHOOL SHOOTINGS: THE SSDE AND CRS REPORTS

Although much speculation persists regarding the role of violent video games and school shootings, statements claiming a causal relationship between these are seldom based on factual evidence. Information gathering about mass killings is also hindered by the fact that so many perpetrators are killed or commit suicide during the events. This reduces available methods for study, rendering such empirical research on mass murders limited.

At present, there have been two attempts by the federal government to analyze mass killers. In 2002, the U.S. Secret Service and Department of Education issued the SSDE Report, which researched 37 school shootings between 1974 and 2000, as well as the respective 41 attackers involved; investigators also interviewed the 10 surviving attackers and reviewed the school, mental health, and court records of all 41 known attackers (Vossekuil, Reddy, Fein, Borum, & Modzeleski, 2002). Contrary to expectations that school shooters would be avid consumers of violent media, consumption of violent media by the attackers was reported by the SSDE as lower than normal for typical youth of similar age. Although the majority of young males consume at least some violent media (Ferguson et al., 2011), only 15 percent of shooters (after eliminating several early cases where the perpetrator likely had very little opportunity to play violent games; see Ferguson, 2008) displayed "some interest" in violent video games. In addition, 59 percent displayed "some interest" in violent media of any kind. This is considerably lower than for nonshooter males from other studies, although it should be noted that the SSDE did not create a comparison group of nonshooters to compare with the actual shooters they were profiling. The largest exposure to "media violence" for school shooters (37 percent) was the shooter's own writings. In other words, rather than video games or movies, some of the youth became obsessed with their own hateful writings and rage-filled diaries.

In the federal government's second analysis of mass killers, the Congressional Research Service (CRS) carried out a study that broadened the focus of mass killings to include other public and private spaces in addition to schools (Krouse & Richardson, 2015). Although the report attempted to profile mass killers, asserting that most were white males between their 30s and 40s who are quite often mentally ill, the CRS report did not mention violent media as a cause and does not mention video games. The report's only mention of media is how, as mentioned above, it exaggerates the effect of mass killings and how it exacerbates public anxiety over mass killings.

INDIVIDUAL RESEARCH STUDIES

Most research studies are not on school shootings, of course. Rather, we have college students or teens play different games or watch different movies and see how they respond to prompts to carry out various measures of mild aggression. For example, participants may be asked to give bursts of annoying white noise to opponents in a competitive game or administer spicy hot sauce to another person. Evidence from such studies have been mixed. Some studies do indicate that exposure to violent media may increase aggression (e.g., Scharrer & Leone, 2008), but others do not find this effect (Przybylski, 2014). Nor has evidence supported the notion that certain "at-risk" groups of youth may be particularly prone to violent media effects (Engelhardt, Mazurek, Hilgard, Rouder, & Bartholow, 2015; Ferguson & Olson, 2014).

Other studies may track youth over time, administering surveys about their media use at one time point and, in essence, waiting to see who gets into trouble or arrested. Generally, such studies suggest that, while issues such as family environment, genetics, and mental health may predict negative outcomes, television, movie and video game exposure does not (e.g., Breuer, Vogelgesang, Quandt, & Festl, 2015). Two meta-analyses of such studies concluded that the impact of media such as video games or television on youth violence is negligible (Ferguson, 2015a; Savage & Yancey, 2008). As such, overall research studies have not provided encouraging evidence in support of the contention that violent media is a cause of violence in society.

Further, despite the fact that American popular media inarguably has grown more violent, youth violence has declined by over 80 percent over the past few decades (see Ferguson, 2015b). Several additional analyses have even suggested that the release of popular violent video games such as *Grand Theft Auto* are associated with immediate declines in societal violence (Cunningham, Engelstätter, & Ward, 2016; Markey, Markey, & French, 2015).

CONFIRMATION BIAS

At present, there is little data to suggest that violent video games or other violent media contribute to mass homicides. Research data from experimental studies of video game violence and aggression have returned mixed results at best and there are significant controversies about the reliability and validity of many such studies. No evidence has emerged to indicate that perpetrators of school shootings or other mass homicides are particularly prone to consuming violent media. The perceived correlation between mass homicides and violent media seems to be a classic case of "confirmation bias."

Confirmation bias occurs when people pay attention to cases that fit their prejudices and ignore those that do not. If people believe that video games and mass shootings are linked, for example, they may focus only on cases in which a shooter may have played video games and ignore cases where the shooter did not. This allows the perception of an association to persist even when it does not. A vast majority of young men play violent video games (Kutner & Olson, 2008). Thus, discovering that a young male who committed a horrible crime also happened to play violent video games is no more surprising than discovering that he sometimes wore sneakers or liked to eat sweets. Yet people may consider this information a confirmation of their preexisting beliefs. At the same time, relatively few people over the age of 45–50 play video games. So when a mass shooter is older, and the average age of shooters is about 40 (Lankford, 2013), people ignore video games altogether. Noting that older shooters do not play games might challenge the belief that a correlation between games and mass violence exists, so people ignore the inconvenient cases.

For instance, when the Columbine killers turned out to have played the violent video game Doom, people perceived this as confirmation of their prejudices. However, when a female professor in her forties fired on her tenure committee, as happened at the University of Alabama, no one mentioned video games or media at all. In some cases (e.g., Virginia Tech and Sandy Hook), people may persist in believing the shooters were avid violent video game players even after the official investigation reports concluded they were not. People only attend to evidence that supports their beliefs and ignore that which does not.

TRAINING MASS SHOOTERS

The issue of confirmation bias may also play into the belief that, even if video games don't motivate mass shootings or other acts of violence, perhaps they make shooters more accurate. This belief was reinforced by a 2011 shooting and bombing in Oslo, Norway, that killed 77. In this case, the perpetrator had written a 1,500-page manifesto detailing his views. Most of the 1,500 pages detailed his beliefs about a Muslim takeover of Europe dating back to the Ottoman Empire. In that sense, the shooter seems to have been influenced mainly by history books, but few people called for banning those. Instead, many commentators focused on about 2–3 pages where the shooter mentioned using World of Warcraft (WoW) to excuse the long periods of isolation he used to prepare for his attack (in other words, he told people he was playing WoW rather than building bombs). He also suggested that playing shooter games made him more of a marksman. But do video games really train shooting accuracy? The mechanics of firearms and game controllers are actually rather different. And research evidence suggests that, in general, learning in video games does not transfer to real life (Simons et al., 2016). One study, perhaps influenced by the Oslo shooting, did try to link violent video games to greater handgun accuracy (using a pellet gun) and the tendency to take head shots. However, this study ultimately had to be retracted due to unexplainable problems with the data (Whitaker & Bushman, 2014). Thus, at present, there is no evidence to support the Oslo shooter's claims that playing video games improved his ability to kill people.

Society may be beginning to move past the fear that mass murder is a new phenomenon necessarily connected to smartphones, violent media, or video games. Empirical evidence has identified that the majority of scholars (Quandt et al., 2015), clinicians (Ferguson, 2015b), and the general public (Przybylski, 2014) are skeptical of claims linking violent video games to violence in society. Increasingly, research evidence on violent video games and broader areas of violent crime, such as youth violence, have suggested an absence of a clear link (Ferguson et al., 2011). This is not to say that the debate is over. However, mental health experts and law enforcement may be better served by focusing on the stronger associations gleaned from the aforementioned government reports (CRS and SSDE). If school shootings are indicative of all mass public murders, the SSDE report provides further guidance on the most predictive and type-specific characteristic associated with public shooters. The SSDE reports that 81 percent of the perpetrators informed another uninvolved person of their intent to commit a school attack. The SSDE further explains that 93 percent of school shooters engaged in other behaviors that caused alarm in peers, parents, teachers, or mental health professionals. These include fantasizing about violence, particularly toward innocent targets. Such findings indicate that such behaviors are probably a better indicator of their potential for committing violent acts than their video game preferences.

REFERENCES

Anderson, C. A. (2004). An update on the effects of playing violent video games. *Journal of adolescence, 27*(1), 113–122.

Benedetti, W. (2007, April 20). Were video games to blame for massacre? Pundits rush to judge industry, games in the wake of the shooting. *NBCNews.com*. Retrieved from http://www.nbcnews.com/id/18220228/#.WUpsTGjyuUl

Breuer, J., Vogelgesang, J., Quandt, T., & Festl, R. (2015). Violent video games and physical aggression: Evidence for a selection effect among adolescents. *Psychology of Popular Media Culture, 4*(4), 305–328.

Brown v. Entertainment Merchants Association, 564 U.S. 786 (2011). Retrieved from http://www.supremecourt.gov/opinions/10pdf/08-1448.pdf

Bushman, B. J., & Anderson, C. A. (2001). Media violence and the American public: Scientific facts versus media misinformation. *American Psychologist, 56*(6–7), 477–489.

Cunningham, S., Engelstätter, B., & Ward, M. R. (2016). Violent video games and violent crime. *Southern Economic Journal, 82*(4), 1247–1265.

Eddy, M. (2016, July 24). Munich gunman portrayed as having planned attack for a year. *New York Times*. Retrieved from http://www.nytimes.com/2016/07/25/world/europe/munich-gunman-portrayed-as-having-planned-attack-for-a-year.html

Engelhardt, C. R., Mazurek, M. O., Hilgard, J., Rouder, J. N., & Bartholow, B. D. (2015). Effects of violent-video-game exposure on aggressive behavior, aggressive-thought accessibility, and aggressive affect among adults with and without autism spectrum disorder. *Psychological Science, 26*(8), 1187–1200.

Ferguson, C. J. (2008). The school shooting/violent video game link: Causal relationship or moral panic? *Journal of Investigative Psychology and Offender Profiling, 5*(1–2), 25–37.

Ferguson, C. J. (2015a). Do angry birds make for angry children? A meta-analysis of video game influences on children's and adolescents' aggression, mental health, prosocial behavior, and academic performance. *Perspectives on Psychological Science, 10*(5), 646–666.

Ferguson, C. J. (2015b). Does movie or video game violence predict societal violence? It depends on what you look at and when. *Journal of Communication, 65*(1), 193–212.

Ferguson, C., Coulson, M., & Barnett, J. (2011). Psychological profiles of school shooters: Positive directions and one big wrong turn. *Journal of Police Crisis Negotiations, 11*(2), 141–158.

Ferguson, C. J., & Olson, C. K. (2014). Video game violence use among "vulnerable" populations: The impact of violent games on delinquency and bullying among children with clinically elevated depression or attention deficit symptoms. *Journal of Youth and Adolescence, 43*(1), 127–136.

Krouse, W. J., & Richardson, D. J. (2015). *Mass murder with firearms: Incidents and victims, 1999–2013.* Washington, D.C.: Congressional Research Service. Retrieved from http://www.fitgny.com/uploads/7/5/7/0/75709513/congressional_research_paper_mass_shootings.pdf

Kutner, L., & Olson, C. (2008). *Grand theft childhood: The surprising truth about violent video games and what parents can do.* New York, NY: Simon & Schuster.

Lankford, A. (2013). A comparative analysis of suicide terrorists and rampage, workplace, and school shooters in the United States from 1990 to 2010. *Homicide Studies, 17*(3), 255–274.

Markey, P. M., Markey, C. N., & French, J. E. (2015). Violent video games and real-world violence: Rhetoric versus data. *Psychology of Popular Media Culture, 4*(4), 277–295.

Przybylski, A. K. (2014). Who believes electronic games cause real world aggression? *Cyberpsychology, Behavior, and Social Networking, 17*(4), 228–234.

Quandt, T., Van Looy, J., Vogelgesang, J., Elson, M., Ivory, J. D., Consalvo, M., & Mäyrä, F. (2015). Digital games research: A survey study on an emerging field and its prevalent debates. *Journal of Communication, 65*(6), 975–996.

Savage, J., & Yancey, C. (2008). The effects of media violence exposure on criminal aggression: A meta-analysis. *Criminal Justice and Behavior, 35*(6), 772–791.

Scharrer, E., & Leone, R. (2008). First-person shooters and the third-person effect. *Human Communication Research, 34*(2), 210–233.

Simons, D. J., Boot, W. R., Charness, N., Gathercole, S. E., Chabris, C. F., Hambrick, D. Z., & Stine-Morrow, E. L. (2016). Do "brain-training" programs work? *Psychological Science in the Public Interest, 17*(3), 103–186.

State's Attorney for the Judicial District of Danbury. (2013). *Report of the state's attorney for the judicial district of Danbury on the shootings at Sandy Hook Elementary School and 36 Yogananda Street, Newtown, Connecticut on December 14, 2012.* Danbury, CT: Office of the State's Attorney for the Judicial District of Danbury. Retrieved from http://www.ct.gov/csao/lib/csao/Sandy_Hook_Final_Report.pdf

Virginia Tech Review Panel. (2007). *Mass shootings at Virginia Tech April 16, 2007: Report of the review panel.* Arlington, VA: Governor's Office of the Commonwealth of Virginia. Retrieved from http://www.governor.virginia.gov/TempContent/techpanelreport.cfm

Vossekuil, B., Reddy, M., Fein, R., Borum, R., & Modzeleski, W. (2002). *The final report and findings of the Safe School Initiative: Implications for the prevention of school attacks in the United States.* Washington, D.C.: U.S. Secret Service and U.S. Department of Education. Retrieved from https://www2.ed.gov/admins/lead/safety/preventingattacksreport.pdf

Whitaker, J. L., & Bushman, B. J. (2014). "Boom, headshot!": Effect of video game play and controller type on firing aim and accuracy. *Communication Research, 41*(7), 879–891.

School Shootings

Glenn W. Muschert

INTRODUCTION

School shootings, including the quintessential 1999 Columbine shootings, are notable as a topic of public concern in the early 21st century. However, prior to the last two decades, this was not the case. While shootings in schools have happened as far back as the 18th century, it was not until the final years of the 20th century that school shootings became recognized as a coherent phenomenon, rather than isolated events in educational settings. School shootings first attracted concentrated media attention in the late 1990s, and since then, they have been recognized as an ongoing and significant social problem.

This chapter provides a typology of school shooting incidents, including five types that range from the commonly known rampage attacks and school invasion attacks to other, less common forms of school shootings. The chapter then examines the causes of school shootings at the individual/interpersonal, community, and societal levels. The chapter concludes by examining the tendency for extreme cases of school violence to drive antiviolence policy, a phenomenon known as the Columbine Effect.

TYPOLOGY

School shootings are events in which perpetrators use firearms, sometimes in conjunction with other weapons, to attack fellow students, school personnel, or school buildings. Muschert (2007) described five types of school shootings, which vary based on the characteristics of the shooters, type(s) of victims, and motivations for the attacks. These types are (1) school rampage attacks, (2) school-related mass murders, (3) targeted attacks at schools, (4) terrorist attacks on schools, and (5) government shootings at schools. The most publicized cases in the 1990s and later fit within the first category, though a longer view reveals a variety of types of school shootings have happened in a variety of settings. The varieties of shootings described in this typology are what Max Weber (1997) called "ideal types," generalized categories used for the sake of analytical clarity. Actual cases may, of course, be more complex and sometimes difficult to categorize.

Rampage school shootings are expressive attacks on schools and/or school members. The term *rampage* was coined by Newman, Fox, Harding, Mehta, and Roth (2004) as an

> institutional attack [that] takes place on a public stage before an audience, is committed by a member or former member of the institution, and involves multiple victims, some chosen for their symbolic significance or at random. This final condition signifies that it is the organization, not the individuals, who are important. (p. 231)

The rampage shooter is a member or former member of the school, such as a student, faculty member, or administrator, who chooses victims for their symbolic importance and who carries out the attack for the purposes of exacting revenge, seeking pleasure, or a combination of the two.

Rampage shootings are expressive events and, as such, they are often used as vehicles to send messages. Thus, it is important to understand what is conveyed, regardless of whether we accept the validity of the messages themselves. Muschert and Ragnedda (2010) clarified that the *performative script* in rampage school shootings involved the use of lethal or near-lethal violence on the part of a (typically male) student or former student who perceives that he or she has been unjustly subordinated in the school social hierarchy. The attacker directs hostility toward the entire school or toward those deemed responsible for his or her loss of social status, or those who he or she believes are generally behind their marginalization. The rampage shooter attempts to express frustration with the school and its pecking order.

In the late 1990s, a number of rampage-type shootings took place across the United States in places such as Pearl, Mississippi (1997); Paducah, Kentucky (1997); Bethel, Alaska (1997); Jonesboro, Arkansas (1998); and Springfield, Oregon (1998). Given the backdrop of the apparent string of school shootings in the two previous years, and given its severity, the 1999 Columbine High School shootings in Littleton, Colorado, has become a cultural touchstone for rampage-type school shootings. School rampage shootings are often described as being "Columbine-type" or "Columbine-style" attacks. North Americans had already commonly used the term "going postal" for cases when a person carries out a random shooting in a public place or workplace. That term was coined after a string of post office shootings occurred in the 1980s and 1990s across the United States (Ames, 2005). Its use spread to describe workplace shootings. Use of the terms "going Columbine" or "pulling a Columbine" have been adopted for describing school rampage attacks, comparable to the use of the term "going postal" to describe workplace attacks.

A second variety of school shootings, the school-related mass murder, shares many characteristics with the rampage type. The victims tend to be chosen at random or for symbolic importance, and the motivation tends to be expressive, involving the desire to seek revenge, gain power, or convey a message. The key distinction between school-related mass murders and rampage attacks is that in mass murders at schools, the shooters do not share any affiliation with the school, nor have they ever shared such an affiliation. Though less common than rampage-type shootings, school-related mass murders also generate noted media attention and generate public anxiety about violence in schools. Varieties include those known as school invasions and sniper attacks on schools. A school invasion is when an outsider enters a school building or grounds and targets the students, personnel, or building in the attack. Similar to rampage shootings, these events also generate significant media coverage and public concern, such as increased fear of violence in schools.

A third type of school shootings is targeted attacks on individuals in schools. Typically, these are carried out by insiders (e.g., students, faculty, administration, or staff) against other individuals who are also insiders. For example, students may shoot other students with whom they have a dispute, or students may shoot faculty members or administrators. Targeted attacks are by far the most commonly observed form of shooting incidents at schools, though they often fail to generate media attention and public outcry beyond their local setting. The violence seems to be limited to actions between individuals or group members who have specific grievances, and this variety of school shooting does not generate widespread fear and concern, especially when compared to the anxiety generated by rampage- or mass murder–type school shootings.

A fourth type of school shootings is terror attacks, which occur when a school building, its personnel, or students are targeted as symbolic victims, and to draw attention to the attacker's political motives or messages. Symbolically, children and schools represent the future hopes of a community, culture, or nation, and a terror attack on a school or school children does great symbolic damage to its targeted community. The terror-type school shootings sometimes stretch the definition of school shootings, as many also involve forms of assault other than guns, such as bombs or chemical attacks. To date, this type of attack has occurred more commonly outside the United States, with the 2004 school siege in Beslan, Russia, being among the most noteworthy.

A final type of school shooting is the government shooting, where government agents, such as police or military, shoot students, faculty, and/or staff. Though government shootings at schools occur less frequently than the other types, they have nonetheless been a feature of social life for decades. Typical cases involve the use of police or military personnel to respond to student protest or riot behaviors. Motives for government attacks are unclear, though at times the attacks seem to erupt spontaneously as tensions build between protesters and social control agents. In other cases, government attacks might suggest deliberate attempts to suppress opposition movements or a crisis of authority within the society. Quintessential cases include the iconic 1970 Kent State massacre, in which unarmed college students protesting the Vietnam War were gunned down by National Guard soldiers, and the 1968 Orangeburg shooting of civil rights demonstrators by South Carolina Highway Patrol officers.

CAUSES

The etiology or analysis of school shootings is complex. Despite difficulties involved in studying school shootings, social scientists can provide clarity about the varieties of factors that contribute. Perhaps the best metaphor for understanding school shootings is that of the plane crash (Henry, 2000). Like airline accidents, school shootings tend to involve a variety of contributing causes converging in the worst of combinations, resulting in a case of extreme violence. What makes it even more difficult to identify causes is that many of the identified factors are commonly present in social life without causing extreme violence. Thus, no single cause or set of causes seems in and of itself sufficient to cause a school shooting. When examining the cases of school shootings that have occurred over the past decades, empirical studies of the contributing causes exist on a variety of analytical levels, including the individual/interpersonal level, the community and school level, and the large-scale sociocultural level. The following section explores these levels and clarifies some limitations in determining the causes of school shootings.

A number of individual or interpersonal factors appear as proximate contributing factors. Nearly all school shooters are male, and many are white. As a necessary prerequisite, these shooters must have personal access to firearms, whether legally or illegally. Individual access to guns is in fact the only necessary cause and the only factor that appears in all school shooting incidents (Newman et al., 2004). Many school shooters appear to suffer from mental health conditions, including suicidal ideation or personality disorders. Many seem to have intricate fantasy lives, often involving violent ideation, are fixated on weapons, or are obsessed with violent media such as films or video games. Interpersonally, many attackers have troubled social lives and numerous school shooters have experienced romantic rejection prior to their attacks. Many are socially marginalized in their peer groups and many are victims of bullying. Finally, some school shooters come from troubled home situations or have been the victims of familial neglect or abuse, including sexual abuse.

When examining the community- and school-level circumstances of places that have experienced school shootings, a number of factors emerge. The youth social dynamics of communities experiencing school shootings are often exclusionary, meaning that students who are different are ostracized. Similarly, shootings more commonly take place in communities that are generally intolerant of difference. Some communities exhibit high levels of intergroup conflict, whether along lines of social class, racial/ethnic group, or youth clique. Many of the schools have environments characterized by poor relations between students and faculty or a crisis of authority for the faculty, administration, and other disciplinarians. School shootings have occurred in tightly knit communities that may suppress delinquency, but also in uprooted communities that are incapable of responding to delinquency by informal means.

When examining the wider sociocultural factors that may operate as backdrops, social scientists have identified a number of factors. The occurrence of school shootings may suggest crises in youth culture or in the culture of educational institutions, like public schools. Similarly, school shootings might reflect wider political or cultural conflicts, as incidents in the United States have occurred more frequently in politically conservative states or those with religiously conservative populations. Researchers also have observed that most school shooters are male, and that there is evidence that suggests that broader cultural expectations of masculinity play a part in driving their actions, as masculine roles provide a trope or script for violent behaviors in boys. In some cases, girls or women have been specifically targeted. Finally, such events happen within what sociologists refer to as a wider culture of violence, one that provides acceptance of the use and availability of firearms. Similarly, the widespread portrayal, and at times even glorification, of violence in media might spark copycat crimes.

Of the causes identified, availability of guns on the individual level is the sole factor that is present in all school shootings, and thus stands out as the only essential factor. All other causes appear (or fail to appear) in various cases and in varying intensity. Therefore, it is difficult to identify a set of causes, or even a subset of causes, that can absolutely clarify the etiology of school shootings. Beyond this, there is no theory of school shootings per se, and the study of cases or the phenomenon in general has proceeded from the ground up. As an example, Levin and Madfis (2009) suggested school shootings are caused by a buildup of cumulative strain. The essential nature of gun access in school attacks is a tricky issue, as schools have also been victimized by rampage attacks with knives. Although such attacks do not technically qualify as school shootings, they share many characteristics with rampage-type school shootings. The newly emergent issue of lethal violence in schools involving knives needs greater examination, particularly when the attacks take place in contexts where gun ownership is rare and the attacks appear to have a rampage-like motivation.

THE COLUMBINE EFFECT

School shootings of all types are highly undesirable events that require preventive action and development of response protocols. Despite their rarity, such events exert a disproportionately high rhetorical leverage on discourse about school violence. The tendency for intense fear and public concern about school shootings to drive the development and expansion of school antiviolence policies has become known as the Columbine Effect (Muschert, Henry, Peguero, & Bracy, 2014; Muschert & Peguero, 2010). School shooters have become the poster children for violent youth offenders and school antiviolence policies often address worst-case scenarios. Though not exclusively so, control responses in the United States tend to be punitive in the form of zero tolerance policies, use of police, and surveillance practices. Such punitive responses are in contrast to the restorative/integrative measures available, including mediation programs, conflict resolution, and anti-bullying programming. Those who criticize the use of punitive measures in schools claim that such measures may do more harm than they prevent, introducing a prison-like atmosphere to schools, socializing youth into compliance with police and other agents of social control, and potentially undermining the primary goals of learning institutions (Muschert et al., 2014; Muschert & Peguero, 2010).

Still, something must be done about risks of extreme violence. The initial response to these events, particularly of the rampage type, was the search for a profile of the typical school shooter. In the popular media, one heard about potential youth superpredators living in our midst, although it was rarely mentioned that there are millions of school-aged children who would never commit such atrocities, and that the latter youths needed encouragement and reassurance. Instead of encouraging people to join in solidarity with youth in their families, schools, or communities, it seemed that the initial response was to increase anxiety about troubled youth or even about youth in general. The result was that so many youths fit the popular image of the potential school shooter that such a profile was impractical, as its use could stigmatize a large number of youth while still failing to identify even a small number of potential shooters. The U.S. Secret Service (see Vossekuil, Reddy, Fein, Borum, & Modzeleski, 2002) advocates the use of a threat assessment technique in which all threats to safety in schools are taken seriously, but subject to investigation in order to separate credible threats from those that are noncredible. In a practical sense, most schools now utilize crisis management plans for shooters and other threats, and law enforcement and school administrators cooperate in preparedness drills. Finally, many police units actively practice the tactics and scenarios they may need in an active shooter situation on campus.

CONCLUSION

Researchers, crisis managers, and response teams have made great strides in learning about school shootings. These insights have been applied to prevention efforts that have helped create an environment in which the number of averted shootings outnumber those that are carried out. This is good news; however, there remains the challenge that school environments are complicated social locations that in practice cannot be securitized to the level of preventing all possible attacks. This means that school shootings, though some may be averted and/or reduced in severity, likely will continue to happen from time to time. In our media-saturated world, those events will continue to generate great notoriety. While there are types of school shootings that are absent from the North American context, prevention and response experts are wise to concentrate on mitigating the various contributing causes of all school shooting types. Although there is evidence of the Columbine Effect (the tendency for extreme cases to drive school antiviolence policies, often resulting in punitive measures), researchers have observed that there are countercurrents in any social trend (see Kupchik, 2012). In the search for evidence-based violence control practices, some school administrators, districts, and researchers are also adopting peacemaking and restorative measures to prevent school violence.

REFERENCES

Ames, M. (2005). *Going postal: Rage, murder, and rebellion: From Reagan's workplaces to Clinton's Columbine and beyond.* Brooklyn, NY: Soft Skull Press.

Henry, S. (2000). What is school violence? An integrated definition. *Annals of the American Academy of Political and Social Science, 567*(1), 16–29.

Kupchik, A. (2012). *Homeroom security: School discipline in the age of fear.* New York: New York University Press.

Levin, J., & Madfis, E. (2009). Mass murder at school and cumulative strain: A sequential model. *American Behavioral Scientist, 52*(9), 1227–1245.

Muschert, G. W. (2007). Research in school shootings. *Sociology Compass, 1*(1), 60–80.

Muschert, G. W., Henry, S., Peguero, A. A., & Bracy, N. L. (2014). *Responding to school violence: Confronting the Columbine effect.* Boulder, CO: Lynne Rienner.

Muschert, G. W., & Peguero, A. A. (2010). The Columbine effect and school anti-violence policy. In M. Peyrot & S. L. Burns (Eds.), *New approaches to social problems treatment (Research in social problems and public policy, volume 17)* (117–148). Bingley, UK: Emerald Publishing Group.

Muschert, G. W., & Ragnedda, M. (2010). Media and violence control: Communication in school shootings. In W. Heitmeyer, H-G. Haupt, S. Malthaner, & A. Kirschner (Eds.), *The control of violence in modern society: Multidisciplinary perspectives, from school shootings to ethnic violence* (345–361). New York: Springer.

Newman, K., Fox, C., Harding, D., Mehta, J., & Roth, W. (2004). *Rampage: The social roots of school shootings.* New York: Basic Books.

Vossekuil, B., Reddy, M., Fein, R., Borum, R., & Modzeleski, W. (2002). *The final report and findings of the Safe School Initiative: Implications for the prevention of school attacks in the United States.* Washington, D.C.: U.S. Secret Service and U.S. Department of Education. Retrieved from https://www2.ed.gov/admins/lead/safety/preventingattacksreport.pdf

Weber, M. (1997). *The methodology of the social sciences.* E. A. Shils & H. A. Finch (Eds.). New York: Free Press.

School Security Responses after Mass Shootings

Lynn A. Addington

INTRODUCTION

This chapter considers reactions to mass shootings at elementary and secondary public schools in the United States. Specific responses vary but share goals of trying to calm fears and prevent future violence. A common approach is to consider increasing levels of school security. School security encompasses a range of measures including formats visible to students as well as ones that operate behind the scenes, such as teacher training, schoolwide safety plans, and classroom alarms. This chapter focuses on visible security measures such as security cameras, security personnel, metal detectors, student and staff identification badges, visitor sign-in requirements, and locked entrances. To understand the use of visible security measures as a response to school shootings, this chapter covers the following issues: the popularity of relying on security measures as a policy option, the trends in the use of school security, the effectiveness of these measures, and the costs of additional school security.

THE POPULARITY OF THE SCHOOL SECURITY RESPONSE

Using security measures to address school crime is not a new practice. The presence of metal detectors and guards can be traced back to urban high schools in the 1970s (Addington, 2009). What has changed is the increased use of security across all locations and grade levels and the expansion in the use of new technologies, including surveillance cameras and biometric identification. The deadly shootings at Columbine High School in 1999 prompted a great deal of conversation about school safety and proposals for new security and safety measures (Addington, 2009, 2014). Many of the actual policies implemented were responses not only to the Columbine shootings, but also to address what was perceived as a growing epidemic of school violence, especially deadly violence (Muschert & Peguero, 2010). The proposed security measures suggested immediately after Columbine included the use of surveillance devices (such as metal detectors and cameras), requirements for identification of students and staff (including ID badges and uniforms), and the employment of security personnel (such as law enforcement officers in general, specially trained school resource officers, and private security agents). Immediate changes actually adopted resulted in greater use of security cameras and security personnel (Addington, 2009).

Adding security personnel and cameras was not only a popular policy response after the shootings at Columbine, but also after other acts of deadly school violence. While school administrators guide their district's policies pertaining to security, state and federal policymakers can issue their own recommendations. After the December 2012 mass shooting at Sandy Hook Elementary School in Connecticut, for example, the Obama White House advocated for the increased use of security personnel in schools nationwide as well as the need to fund 1,000 more officers (White House, 2013).

While these policy responses are clear, the motivations behind them are not as apparent. As will be discussed below, little evidence exists to indicate their effectiveness in preventing school violence, especially deadly violence. Researchers have hypothesized other possible explanations for this continued reliance on security measures as a response to mass school shootings despite the lack of evidence-based support that they prevent violence. One suggested reason is that administrators may feel pressured to act (and act quickly in a visible way) in the wake of an act of serious school violence, especially widely publicized, fatal school violence (Addington, 2009; Na & Gottfredson, 2013). Increased security likely resonates with parents, who often demand immediate actions to ensure their children's safety. In this context, choosing to install cameras or hire guards may be appealing as it is a tangible action that demonstrates a fast and decisive change to calm parents and students (Addington, 2014). Similarly, school administrators may view these security measures as necessary tools to combat crime (Kupchik & Monahan, 2006). These beliefs, though, typically are based on personal perceptions or conventional wisdom rather than relying on evidentiary support. Finally, these decisions may at least be pragmatic responses to monetary incentives. In the years since Columbine, schools have received federal grant support specifically earmarked for hiring and training school resource officers (SROs). SROs are specially trained law enforcement personnel. SRO programs received federal support via both policy initiatives and hundreds of millions of dollars in COPS grants (Finn, McDevitt, Lassiter, & Rich, 2005).

TRENDS IN THE USE OF SCHOOL SECURITY MEASURES

To appreciate the reliance on security measures at school as a prevention policy, it is important to look at their current use as well as trends over time. The U.S. Department of Education and its federal partners started collecting information on the prevalence of school security in the late 1990s. Since the shootings at Columbine High School, these data collections have added more details. These data are based on reports by both school administrators and students about the types of security used at their schools.

Security measures vary in the frequency of their use by schools. The most common ones involve controlling access to the school building such as locking doors, requiring visitors to sign in, using staff identification badges, and enforcing a dress code. Data from school administrators (collected in 2013–2014) and students (collected in 2015) indicate that 93 percent of schools limit access to the building, 90 percent require visitors to sign in, 68 percent require staff to wear IDs, and 58 percent enforce a dress code (Musu-Gillette, Zhang, Wang, Zhang, & Oudekerk, 2017). These security measures all share the goal of limiting campus access to those with a reason to be there. They also are similar in that they do not cost much money and are relatively easy to implement, which likely contributes to their popularity.

Other security measures frequently used at schools require greater financial investments to implement. These include employing security personnel, adding security cameras, and purchasing metal detectors. In addition to incurring a substantial monetary cost, these measures focus on identifying activity that violates the law or school rules. Other examples of security that focus on rule violations are the use of locker checks and dog sniffs to check for drugs. The school administrator and student data noted above indicate that 70 percent of schools use security personnel, 75 percent employ security cameras, and 12 percent feature metal detectors (Musu-Gillette et al., 2017). About half of schools (52 percent) check lockers and a quarter (24 percent) use dog sniffs (Musu-Gillette et al., 2017).

These numbers speak to the use of security measures in schools generally. Variations occur across school levels and locations. Secondary schools use security measures more frequently than middle or elementary schools (Addington, 2014). With regard to location, schools in cities use security cameras the least and metal detectors the most as compared to schools in nonurban environments (Robers, Zhang, Morgan, & Musu-Gillette, 2015). In addition, metal detectors are more commonly used in high-poverty schools (no matter where the school is located) than in low-poverty schools (Addington, 2014).

To appreciate the use of security as a response to mass school shootings, it is useful to consider trend data. Here the fatal shootings at Columbine can serve as a starting point to consider change over time. Research examining overall trends indicates that measures such as security cameras and security personnel have increased the most since Columbine and that this pattern is consistent across school levels (Addington, 2014). Between 1999 and 2013, the use of security personnel increased from 54 percent to 70 percent (Robers et al., 2015). Similar increases are observed for security cameras, which increased in use from 39 percent to 77 percent between 2001 and 2013 (Robers et al., 2015).

THE EFFECTIVENESS OF SCHOOL SECURITY MEASURES

If school security measures are implemented to reduce violence and fear, their effectiveness should be assessed by their ability to accomplish these goals. The most rigorous program evaluations require the use of experimental designs, such as randomized control trials. Researchers have not conducted these types of studies with regard to school security, but they have investigated the association between school security and certain outcomes using quasi-experimental tests as well as statistical models. A review of this work found that using security had either no effect or arguably negative effects on the school (Addington, 2016). Specifically, that review found that the presence of security measures, particularly SROs, did not reduce school crime (and a few studies found an increase in crime), did not reduce student fear (and may increase it), may negatively affect views of the school environment, and did not benefit academic performance (and may negatively affect it) (Addington, 2016). In addition, these effects appear to be particularly acute for schools serving low-income, inner-city students and schools where a majority of students are of a minority racial or ethnic group (Addington, 2016).

THE COSTS OF SCHOOL SECURITY MEASURES

A related consideration in assessing effectiveness of school security is the cost of implementing these measures. Policy decisions often have costs associated with them, but ideally these costs are offset by benefits obtained from implementing the program. Effective policies seek to minimize these costs. For school security, two examples of costs are monetary ones and unintended consequences.

With regard to monetary costs, school administrators must decide how to allocate finite financial resources and ensure their schools provide safe learning environments. Ineffective programs not only waste money and divert resources from successful ones, but also may create a false sense of security, which can be harmful (Addington, 2014). The variation of costs across school districts is another relevant consideration. One study found that urban schools not only spend more money on school security but disproportionately spend more of their budgets on security (DeAngelis, Brent, & Ianni, 2011). Schools can vary in their actual needs for security, but disproportionate spending is a concern since more money allocated for things like security means fewer dollars available for other purposes (DeAngelis et al., 2011).

Monetary costs are relatively straightforward to envision. While unintended consequences can be more difficult to conceptualize, they are important to identify as these represent harms that arise from the school's decision to add security measures. Examples include greater levels of student fear and crime at school, a negative school climate, an increase in students caught in the school-to-prison pipeline, and detrimental effects on students' civic engagement and views of their civil liberties.

A clear unintended consequence of school security is if these measures increase the behaviors they are meant to lower such as students' fear and school violence. Several studies that examined associations between school security and student fear as well as levels of crime indicate this negative outcome. Specifically, the presence of SROs and metal detectors are associated with increased student fear as well as greater amounts of crime at school (Addington, 2016). A related unintended consequence is creating a negative school climate (Cook, Gottfredson, & Na, 2010). School climate is important to consider, as a positive school climate supports learning and student academic achievement while a negative one hinders these aims. Security measures can contribute to a negative school climate indirectly by increasing fear and crime as well as directly. For example, the combined use of police, security cameras, and metal detectors can foster a prison-like atmosphere for the school (Mayer & Leone, 2007).

Another unintended consequence of school security measures concerns the increased criminalization of violations of school rules. Incidents such as fights that traditionally were addressed within the school context now are eligible to be treated as a crime if law enforcement officers are present at the school (French-Marcelin & Hinger, 2017). As a result, students are at greater risk of contact with the juvenile and criminal justice system. This connection between security personnel, especially police in school, has been dubbed the "school to prison pipeline" (Redfield & Nance, 2016; Wald & Losen, 2003). The long-term effects of these school-based arrests as well as increased use of suspensions and expulsions are not clear, but likely could include contact with the criminal justice system as well as implications for students' education and employment (Theriot, 2009). Contributing to this concern are two related patterns. One is the disproportionate use of school security in urban school districts, especially those serving majority minority student populations (Addington, 2014; Gastic, 2011; Tanner-Smith & Fisher, 2016). The second is the fact that African American and Latino male students are more likely to be ensnared by the school to prison pipeline (French-Marcelin & Hinger, 2017).

Unintended consequences do not need to be immediately felt. While few studies have directly considered the long-term consequences of the use of school security on students, researchers have identified negative repercussions on civic engagement as well as views of civil liberties as areas of concern. Students' civic engagement could be negatively affected by attending schools that utilize various security measures such as metal detectors, SROs, and security cameras. Researchers have hypothesized that students who attend such schools may view themselves as lacking power, as these students often have little say in their school governance (Addington, 2016; Kupchik & Catlaw, 2015). This lack of power and voice may lead to decreased interest as adults in civic activities such as voting, community involvement, and volunteering. Another long-term consequence of using security measures is the effect on students' views of their civil liberties and expectations of privacy (Addington, 2009, 2014; Muschert & Peguero, 2010). When students are subjected to regular surveillance they may accept this monitoring as normal and not question such behaviors later in life as adult citizens.

CONCLUSION

A common policy response to mass school shootings has been to rely on additional school security measures, especially security personnel and cameras. While these measures are popular, they are not the only option. Evidence-based programs exist that incorporate whole-school or other holistic approaches to addressing school violence (see Muschert & Peguero, 2010). These programs incorporate proactive ways to deter conflicts from escalating into violence through antibullying programs and conflict resolution classes, the creation of more positive and inclusive communities, and promotion of a school atmosphere where all have a stake in safety and a responsibility to maintain a secure school (Gagnon & Leone, 2001; Greene, 2005; Juvonen, 2001; Peterson, Larson, & Skiba, 2001). Many of these programs have initial support from evaluation research studies that indicate their effectiveness (e.g., CrimeSolutions.gov). Other responses are specifically tailored to address deadly school violence by using threat assessment techniques (Borum, Cornell, Modzeleski, & Jimerson, 2010). This threat assessment approach is specifically designed to minimize profiling and alienating students while assessing the danger of an identified threat. An open question is why school administrators are reluctant to adopt measures that have more evidence to support their effectiveness as compared to visible security measures.

Mass school shootings evoke fear as well as a desire to prevent future tragedies. Greater attention is needed to provide administrators with effective responses. More research is needed to identify not only effective approaches to preventing school violence but also to ensure evidence-based programs that minimize unintended consequences are used.

REFERENCES

Addington, L. A. (2009). Cops and cameras: Public school security as a policy response to Columbine. *American Behavioral Scientist, 52*(10), 1426–1446.

Addington, L. A. (2014). Surveillance and security approaches across public school levels. In G. W. Muschert, S. Henry, N. L. Bracy, & A. A. Peguero (Eds.), *Responding to school violence: Confronting the Columbine effect* (71–88). Boulder, CO: Lynne Rienner.

Addington, L. A. (2016). *The use of visible security measures in public schools: A review to summarize current literature and guide future research.* Invited White Paper. Washington, D.C.: U.S. Department of Justice.

Borum, R., Cornell, D. G., Modzeleski, W., & Jimerson, S. R. (2010). What can be done about school shootings? A review of the evidence. *Educational Researcher, 39*(1), 27–37.

Cook, P. J., Gottfredson, D. C., & Na, C. (2010). School crime control and prevention. *Crime and Justice, 39*(1), 313–440.

DeAngelis, K. J., Brent, B. O., & Ianni, D. (2011). The hidden cost of school security. *Journal of Education Finance, 36*(3), 312–337.

Finn, P., McDevitt, J., Lassiter, W., & Rich, T. (2005). Case studies of 19 school resource officer (SRO) programs. Washington, D.C.: U.S. Department of Justice, National Institute of Justice. Retrieved from https://www.ncjrs.gov/pdffiles1/nij/grants/209271.pdf

French-Marcelin, M., & Hinger, S. (2017). *Bullies in blue: The origins and consequences of school police.* New York: American Civil Liberties Union. Retrieved from https://www.aclu.org/sites/default/files/field_document/aclu_bullies_in_blue_4_11_17_final.pdf

Gagnon, J. C., & Leone, P. E. (2001). Alternative strategies for school violence prevention. *New Directions for Youth Development, 2001*(92), 101–125.

Gastic, B. (2011). Metal detectors and feeling safe at school. *Education and Urban Society, 43*(4), 486–498.

Greene, M. B. (2005). Reducing violence and aggression in schools. *Trauma, Violence & Abuse, 6*(3), 236–253.

Juvonen, J. (2001). *School violence: Prevalence, fears, and prevention.* Rand Issue Paper. Retrieved from http://www.rand.org/pubs/issue_papers/2006/IP219.pdf

Kupchik, A., & Catlaw, T. J. (2015). Discipline and participation: The long-term effects of suspension and school security on the political and civic engagement of youth. *Youth & Society, 47*(1), 95–124.

Kupchik, A., & Monahan, T. (2006). The new American school: Preparation for post-industrial discipline. *British Journal of Sociology, 27*(5), 617–631.

Mayer, M. J., & Leone, P. E. (2007). School violence and disruption revisited: Equity and safety in the school house. *Focus on Exceptional Children, 40*(1), 1–28.

Muschert, G. W., & Peguero, A. A. (2010). The Columbine effect and school antiviolence policy. *Research in Social Problems and Policy, 17,* 117–148.

Musu-Gillette, L., Zhang, A., Wang, K., Zhang, J., & Oudekerk, B. A. (2017). *Indicators of school crime and safety: 2016* (NCES 2017-064/NCJ 250650). Washington, D.C.: U.S. Department of Education and U.S. Department of Justice. Retrieved from https://nces.ed.gov/pubs2017/2017064.pdf

Na, C., & Gottfredson, D.C. (2013). Police officers in schools: Effects on school crime and the processing of offending behaviors. *Justice Quarterly, 30*(4), 619–650.

Peterson, R. L., Larson, J., & Skiba, R. (2001). School violence prevention: Current status and policy recommendations. *Law & Policy, 23*(3), 345–371.

Redfield, S. E., & Nance, J. P. (2016) *School-to-prison pipeline: American Bar Association preliminary report.* Chicago, IL: American Bar Association. Retrieved from https://www.americanbar.org/content/dam/aba/administrative/diversity_pipeline/stp_preliminary_report_final.authcheckdam.pdf

Robers, S., Zhang, A., Morgan, R. E., & Musu-Gillette, L. (2015). *Indicators of school crime and safety: 2014.* Washington, D.C.: U.S. Department of Justice. Retrieved from http://nces.ed.gov/pubs2015/2015072.pdf

Tanner-Smith, E. E., & Fisher, B. W. (2016). Visible school security measures and student academic performance, attendance, and postsecondary aspirations. *Journal of Youth and Adolescence, 45*(1), 195–210.

Theriot, M. T. (2009). School resource officers and the criminalization of student behavior. *Journal of Criminal Justice, 37*(3), 280–287.

Wald, J., & Losen, D. J. (2003). Defining and redirecting a school-to-prison pipeline. *New Directions for Youth Development, 2003* (99), 9–15.

White House. (2013). Now is the time: The president's plan to protect our children and communities by reducing gun violence. Retrieved from https://obamawhitehouse.archives.gov/sites/default/files/docs/wh_now_is_the_time_full.pdf

Gender and Mass Shootings

Melissa J. Tetzlaff-Bemiller

While incidents of mass shootings are not particularly new, the study of these events is still relatively young. Mass shootings often are thought of in the broader, albeit slightly, context of mass murder, which is defined by the Federal Bureau of Investigation (FBI) (2008) as a multiple homicide incident in which at least four victims are murdered within one event and in one or more locations in close geographical proximity. The main difference between these two types of events is that a mass murder can be accomplished with many different types of weapons, whereas a mass shooting is specifically accomplished with the use of a firearm.

With the technological advances in weaponry and the increase in media attention, mass shootings have become a central topic for the public and researchers alike. According to an FBI (2014) report on active shooters (see the Pivotal Documents section later in this volume for an excerpt), instances of mass shootings have increased over the past several years, but when also acknowledging the population change, trends have been stable (see also Schildkraut & Elsass, 2016). Although such events are statistically rare (Schildkraut & Elsass, 2016), the magnitude and mystery about the motivation behind them has resulted in widespread attention (Langman, 2009).

It is important to note that while mass shootings discussed in the media usually revolve around schools and the workplace, mass shootings can happen elsewhere. Lin Huff-Corzine and colleagues (2014) suggest that they can also occur in a private location, such as the residence or home, or in other public areas, such as a church (see also Schildkraut & Elsass, 2016). Regardless of where mass shootings occur, research shows that the vast majority of offenders are male (FBI, 2008; Fox, Levin, & Quinet, 2012; Huff-Corzine et al., 2014; Schildkraut & Elsass, 2016). When discussing mass shootings specifically, between the years of 1880 and 2014 there were only 10 attacks committed by solo female shooters (Schildkraut & Elsass, 2016). This total represented slightly less than 4 percent of all mass shooting perpetrators. Two additional female offenders were present, each of whom committed their rampages with their husbands, during the shootings in 2014 in Las Vegas, Nevada, and 2015 in San Bernardino, California. The low prevalence of female offenders mirrors research findings related to mass murderers. Specifically, when using the Supplemental Homicide Report and the National Incident-Based Reporting System, Huff-Corzine and colleagues (2014) found that from 2001 to 2010, only 8 percent of mass murder offenders were female.

The fact that these violent events are predominantly male-perpetrated mirrors patterns found in the broader context of crime in the United States. Accordingly, it is important to understand not only the gender gap among the perpetrators, but also why such a divide may exist. This gender disparity among mass shooters and violent criminals more generally also is examined through theoretical lenses that may cast light on why such a gap exists.

THE GENDER GAP IN CRIME IN THE UNITED STATES

When considering crime in its broader context, scholars agree that gender is a persistent and a major correlate of crime (Gottfredson & Hirschi, 1990). In fact, research has indicated that males are more likely than females to be both the offender and the victim. Michael Gottfredson and Travis Hirschi (1990) claim that "gender differences appear to be invariant over time and space." When males and females are involved in crime, they are both more likely to be involved in property and substance abuse offenses rather than in violent crime (Schwartz & Steffensmeier, 2007). However, males commit crime, particularly violent crime, at higher rates than females. According to Callie Rennison (2009) and Jennifer Schwartz and Darrell Steffensmeier (2007), the gender gap in crime is greatest for serious crime (such as murder and rape) and smallest for mild forms of lawbreaking behavior (such as property crime).

According to the Uniform Crime Reports compiled by the Federal Bureau of Investigation for 2015 (the most recent completed official data at the time of this writing), males were arrested more than twice as often as females, with 5,603,363 and 2,086,392 apprehensions respectively. Concerning homicide more specifically, 62.3 percent of offenders and 78.8 percent of victims were male. When examining the Uniform Crime Reports 10-year arrest trends (2006 to 2015) compiled by the Federal Bureau of Investigation (2015), the data indicate that arrests rates are decreasing: there has been a 25.6 percent decrease for males and an 11.8 percent decrease for females. Specifically concerning homicide arrests, there were 6,904 males and 842 females arrested in 2006; these figures decrease to 5,875 and 765, respectively, in 2015. It is important to note, however, that for homicide offenses, these statistics indicate that the *frequency* of arrests is decreasing. When it comes to mass shootings, however, approximately half of the perpetrators commit suicide (Kalish & Kimmel, 2010; Schildkraut & Elsass, 2016); thus, arrest records are not the best measure to determine actual trends related to the phenomenon. With official crime data showing such a difference and researchers pointing out how few women are the perpetrators of mass shootings, it becomes evident that gender is important and should be discussed.

THEORETICAL DEVELOPMENTS

Many mass shootings researchers and media outlets alike have focused on social factors, such as bullying and harassment. In addition, media usage—such as violent television shows, violent video games, or types of music listened to—has also been considered as a potential causal factor for these events. Further, many government-supported investigations of mass shooters have focused on the psychological and cultural backgrounds of the perpetrators. Some of the broader focus pertaining to these events has been on drugs and alcohol usage, father absences, parental neglect, child abuse, socially disorganized communities, failing grades, mental illness, and crime rates in the perpetrators' neighborhoods. Peter Langman (2009) declares that such factors alone cannot explain mass shootings because many people are harassed, listen to/watch violent-themed media, or come from similar backgrounds or geographically disorganized areas and never perpetrate a rampage. In fact, all of these explanations fail to account for one of the most significant findings about mass shooters: the simple fact that they are mostly perpetrated by males. The following discussion includes traditional criminological theories that are applicable to the gender differences in crime perpetration and will be followed by a relatively new explanation for the gender difference among mass shooters.

When exploring possible explanations of why males are more likely to be mass shooters than females, some criminological theories can be utilized. These theories can help to describe the difference between the genders when it comes to offending in general, and, in several cases, disparities among perpetrators of violent crime. They also provide background information on some newer ideas regarding gender. While some criminologists argue that traditional theories are in fact gender-specific models and are not well suited to explain female crime, others suggest that some of the approaches can be applied to female criminality (Schwartz & Steffensmeier, 2007).

First, the environment has been examined. Crime can be attributed to social disorganization, which occurs when a community cannot properly supervise and control deviance. The usual methods of social control, such as supervision of juveniles, parental guidance, and strong government, are not evident in these areas, resulting in higher levels of deviance and lawless acts (Akers & Sellers, 2009). Individuals who reside in areas that are characterized by impoverished conditions, evidenced by decaying housing, broken families, low income and education levels, substance abuse, and a normalcy of violence and crime, among other issues, are more likely to experience deviance, regardless of gender. These issues have been addressed by researchers and while they correlate to mass shootings in general, they do not specifically speak to why males perpetrate while females rarely do. Other theories may offer a better explanation for this disparity.

To begin, the organization of gender (expectations) and structural arrangements that determine gender differences in norms, morals, values, and social controls produce greater differences in opportunities, motivations, and contacts for criminal behavior. The social control perspective explains that a greater female socialization toward bonding behavior leads to more established self-control and subsequently less crime (Schwartz & Steffensmeier, 2007). Socialization is an important process in the development of a law-abiding citizen, with males and females tending to be socialized differently. Elizabeth Cauffman (2008) adds that aspects of the family environment influence both male and female antisocial behavior. In fact, gender expectations are put forth many times before the child is even born, as evidenced in differences among colors, clothes, and toys chosen.

Both as children and adults, females are more closely supervised and their misbehavior discouraged through negative sanctions (Schwartz & Steffensmeier, 2007). Attachments to conventional peers and adults are nurtured for females, which may be due to the difference in socialization for them as compared to males. In addition, certain risk-taking behaviors, such as speaking out of turn, taking a more aggressive approach to situations (e.g., fighting), promiscuity, and the use of drugs and alcohol, are rewarded among boys yet censored among girls (Schwartz & Steffensmeier, 2007). It is the social bonds (integration into society) that protect individuals from committing criminal acts. Weak or broken social bonds with members of conventional society will increase the likelihood of criminal involvement (Hirschi, 1969). This socialization process sets up the gender expectations, which in turn follow individuals throughout their lives.

Adolescence can be a difficult time for many. Adolescents are increasingly affected by peer group socialization (Seidman, 2003). Peers can be strict regulators of behavior, which can affect one's identity. A person who finds it difficult to fit in may endure insults and stigma. Since the peer group is such a dominant regulating force, stigma from them can be damaging (Kalish & Kimmel, 2010). Labeling theory explains crime as a consequence of negative stereotypes and behavioral characterization (Schwartz & Steffensmeier, 2007). If an individual does not satisfy what the peer group deems appropriate, that individual is likely to receive ridicule, which subsequently can produce strain that leads to criminal responses.

It is suggested that crime and deviance are the most likely to occur when the strain results in anger (Agnew, 1992; Broidy & Agnew, 1997). While it is likely that both males and females respond to strain with anger, this anger is handled differently. Females are more likely to internalize the anger (and the anger is accompanied by emotions such as depression, guilt, anxiety, and shame), while males externalize it and are more conducive to violence (Broidy & Agnew, 1997). Nicole Piquero and Miriam Sealock (2006) have found that males are more likely to engage in aggressive behavior than females. These responses to anger are presumed to be due to gender differences in social support and coping styles, as well as differences in opportunities for crime, social control, and the disposition for crime (Broidy & Agnew, 1997).

In a separate study by Rachel Kalish and Michael Kimmel (2010), the lack of support that males perceive may be a contributing factor in their violent behavior. This study focused on suicide ideation among mass shooters and examined how males may feel that the rampage and suicide culminated due to the perception that they do not have a place to go for support of their grievances. These same males felt that school authorities and parents would be unresponsive to their plight and therefore felt as though they had nowhere to express their emotions. "It was not because they were deviants, but rather because they were over-conformists to a particular normative construction of masculinity, a construction that defines violence as a legitimate response to a perceived humiliation" (Kalish & Kimmel, 2010, p. 461).

Another explanation concerning the overrepresentation of male mass murder perpetrators combines the above socialization and reaction theories and focuses on one key concept: masculinization. The main idea here is that the socialization that creates gender expectations defines what it is to be masculine. When a male's masculinity is challenged (even if it is only perceived), he is supposed to do something to prove he is adequate. Furthermore, young men are socialized to behave in a way that asserts their masculinity and taught to use violence if their manhood is threatened (Kimmel, 2008). Such an attack can cause an individual to feel humiliated. Kalish and Kimmel (2010) suggest that this aggrieved feeling is common in adolescence, but it is a sense of entitlement and the use of violence against others to enact pain that transforms this humiliation into mass shootings or other extreme episodes. Karen Tonso (2009) further notes that this humiliation may also emerge from perceptions of loss of privilege by way of the school and administration and not just the offender's peers.

A key word used in many situations where masculinity is challenged is the word "gay," which in that context is wielded as a term of insult and emasculation. In Michael Kimmel and Matthew Mahler's (2003) study, they discussed how many of their subjects had been gaybaited. It is important to understand that gaybaiting here does not necessarily imply homosexuality, but rather that the males were seen simply as different and less manly than the others—a geek, nonathletic, academically focused, or the like. As they note, "homophobia—being constantly threatened and bullied as if you are gay as well as the homophobic desire to make sure that others know that you are a 'real man'—plays a pivotal and understudied role in these school shootings" (Kimmel & Mahler, 2003, p. 1449). Individuals who are the targets of gaybaiting recognized that they are being attacked for failure to "be a man." The application of such a stigma, coupled with a culture that often normalizes and even glorifies violence, teaches males that it is appropriate to retaliate when provoked in order to reclaim their manhood. This dynamic has been cited as one factor why males are more likely to be the perpetrators of mass shootings.

While males are most likely to be the perpetrators of mass shootings, females still have committed similar acts. One such example is the mass shooting that occurred in San Diego, California, at Grover Cleveland Elementary School on January 29, 1979. The perpetrator was a 16-year-old who opened fire on the elementary school from her home across the street. She killed two people, principal Burton Wragg and custodian Michael Suchar, and wounded eight children and one policeman. She then barricaded herself in her home before surrendering to police six hours later. She later was tried as an adult and pleaded guilty to two counts of murder and assault with a deadly weapon. She became eligible for parole in 1993 but has been continuously denied at each hearing. Her next possibility for a parole hearing is in 2019.

When trying to understand why this perpetrator committed her act, several potential explanations have been offered. One journalist who communicated with the shooter claimed that she said, "I don't like Mondays" when asked why she shot the children (Daly, 2014). During her later parole hearings, the shooter also claimed that she was under the influence of drugs and alcohol at the time of the attack, despite tests indicating that her system was clean. She also claimed that her father had physically and sexually abused her, and that the attack was another failed attempt at suicide (Daly, 2014). Many of these justifications align with the mitigating excuses used to downplay female criminality.

Conversely, when a male shooter opened fire on a school of the same name, located less than 500 miles up the coast, nearly 10 years later on January 17, 1989, his actions were reasoned to be the result of his hatred toward Asians. The perpetrator, a 24-year-old male, had been described as an angry person frustrated with blocked employment opportunities. The shooter blamed his struggles on immigrants who were taking jobs that he would otherwise have been able to fill. He also had been found in possession of white supremacist literature two years prior to the shooting during a separate arrest, and he was described as both mentally ill and dangerous during a mental health evaluation. These findings not only were offered as justification for the rampage, but also align with aggravating circumstances typically linked to male mass shooters.

CONCLUSION

As the data show, a gendered difference exists in both general and violent crime, with males being more likely to commit homicide than females and to do so with a firearm. The gender gap further extends to mass shooters (Fox et al., 2012; Huff-Corzine et al., 2014; Hough & McCorkle, 2017; Schildkraut & Elsass, 2016). The differences in propensity for crime may be due to the socialization process and the differences between males and females throughout their lives, how these individuals are labeled by their peers, the impact of family dynamics, and even the social and physical environments within which perpetrators are raised.

There is not a single theory that will account for all motivations for mass shootings or explain why it is predominately a male-perpetrated phenomenon. It is important to acknowledge that each shooter will have his or her own stories and motivations. Thus, it is imperative that scholars continue to engage in individual offender case studies, as well as examinations of the phenomenon of mass shootings as a whole, in order to further the knowledge base about these events and facilitate both proactive and reactive responses to such tragedies.

REFERENCES

Agnew, R. (1992). Foundation for a general strain theory of crime and delinquency. *Criminology, 30*(1), 47–87.

Akers, R. L., & Sellers, C. S. (2009). *Criminological theories: Introduction, evaluation, and application.* New York, NY: Oxford University Press.

Broidy, L., & Agnew, R. (1997). Gender and crime: A general strain theory perspective. *Journal of Research in Crime and Delinquency, 34*(3), 275–306.

Cauffman, E. (2008). Understanding the female offender. *The Future of Children, 18*(2), 119–142.

Daly, M. (2014). The first modern school shooter feels responsible for the rest. *The Daily Beast.* Retrieved from: http://www.thedailybeast.com/the-first-modern-school-shooter-feels-responsible-for-the-rest

Federal Bureau of Investigation. (2008). Crime in the United States, 2008. Washington, D.C.: Department of Justice. Retrieved from https://ucr.fbi.gov/crime-in-the-u.s/2008

Federal Bureau of Investigation. (2014). Crime in the United States, 2014. Washington, D.C.: Department of Justice. Retrieved from https://ucr.fbi.gov/crime-in-the-u.s/2014/crime-in-the-u.s.-2014

Federal Bureau of Investigation. (2015). Crime in the United States, 2015. Washington, D.C.: Department of Justice. Retrieved from https://ucr.fbi.gov/crime-in-the-u.s/2015/crime-in-the-u.s.-2015

Fox, J. A., Levin, J. A., & Quinet, K. (2012). *The will to kill: Making sense of senseless murder* (4th ed.). Upper Saddle River, NJ: Pearson Education.

Gottfredson, M. R., & Hirschi, T. (1990). *A general theory of crime.* Stanford, CA: Stanford University Press.

Hirschi, T. (1969). *Causes of delinquency.* Berkeley, CA: University of California Press.

Hough, R. M., & McCorkle, K. D. (2017). *American homicide.* Thousand Oaks, CA: Sage.

Huff-Corzine, L., McCutcheon, J. C., Corzine, J., Jarvis, J. P., Tetzlaff-Bemiller, M. J., Weller, M., & Landon, M. (2014). Shooting for accuracy: Comparing data sources on mass murder. *Homicide Studies, 18*(1), 105–124.

Kalish, R., & Kimmel, M. (2010). Suicide by mass murder: Masculinity, aggrieved entitlement, and rampage school shootings. *Health Sociology Review, 19*(4), 451–464.

Kimmel, M. (2008). *Guyland: The perilous world where boys become men.* New York: HarperCollins.

Kimmel, M. S., & Mahler, M. (2003). Adolescent masculinity, homophobia, and violence: Random school shootings, 1982–2001. *American Behavioral Scientist, 46*(10), 1439–1458.

Langman, P. (2009). Rampage school shooters: A typology. *Aggression and Violent Behavior, 14*(1), 79–86.

Piquero, N. L., & Sealock, M. D. (2006). Generalizing general strain theory: An examination of an offending population. *Justice Quarterly, 17*(3), 449–484.

Rennison, C. M. (2009). A new look at the gender gap in offending. *Women and Criminal Justice, 19*(3), 171–190.

Schildkraut, J., & Elsass, H. J. (2016). *Mass shootings: Media, myths, and realities.* Santa Barbara, CA: Praeger.

Schwartz, J., & Steffensmeier, D. (2007). The nature of female offending: Patterns and explanation. In R. T. Zaplin (Ed.), *Female offenders: Critical perspectives and effective interventions* (43–76). Sudbury, MA: Jones and Bartlett Learning.

Seidman, S. (2003). *The social construction of sexuality.* New York: W. W. Norton.

Tonso, K. L. (2009). Violent masculinities as tropes for school shooters: The Montréal Massacre, the Columbine attack, and rethinking schools. *American Behavioral Scientist, 52*(9), 1266–1285.

Mass Shootings as Hate Crimes

Marc Settembrino

INTRODUCTION

After a mass shooting, people typically may ask, "Why did this happen? Why would he do this?" Often, the media portrays mass shooters as irrational, unstable, or mentally ill. For most Americans, such explanations make sense, as we cannot imagine ourselves perpetrating such violence. Since 2010, there have been several mass shootings that have been motivated by the shooter's bias against his victims. This means that although we may conclude that the shooter acted irrationally, in reality, the shooting was rooted in the logic of the perpetrator's ideology.

WHAT IS A HATE CRIME?

There are various laws enacted by the federal, state, and local governments that define hate crimes. Depending on where you live, there may be different protected categories and enhanced penalties for hate crimes. The Federal Bureau of Investigation's (FBI) Civil Rights Division is tasked with investigating and compiling annual reports on the prevalence of hate crimes in the United States. The FBI (n.d.) defines hate crimes as criminal offenses "against a person or property motivated in whole or in part by an offender's bias against a race, religion, disability, sexual orientation, ethnicity, gender or gender identity." Thus, hate crimes are different from traditional offenses because they are motivated by bias. This means that the perpetrator is motivated by negative attitudes toward the victim because of certain characteristics, such as race, religion, gender, or sexual orientation. Such motivation differs from crimes of "passion" or "desperation," wherein the victim can be considered to have been "in the wrong place at the wrong time." As such, a wide range of offenses—including property crimes like vandalism, theft, or arson, and violent crimes such as armed robbery, assault, or rape—may be classified as hate crimes, depending on the motivations of the per-petrators. Hate crimes also differ from traditional offenses because they carry enhanced penalties. This means individuals convicted of hate crimes may receive longer prison sentences compared to offenders who commit similar offenses without bias.

PERSPECTIVES ON HATE CRIMES

There are different perspectives on the necessity and effectiveness of hate crime laws. The liberal perspective suggests that offenders who commit hate crimes need longer sentences to reflect on their crimes. Additionally, this viewpoint argues that hate crime laws keep dangerous people off the streets and may deter others from committing similar offenses (Segura, 2014). For liberals, hate crimes laws send the message that our society values the lives of minority groups. Conversely, some conservatives argue that hate crimes laws are redundant and unnecessary. Particularly, they argue that all crimes should be treated equally in sentencing (Segura, 2014). Typically, these conservatives believe that all crimes should carry tougher sentences. Departing from both liberal and conservative opinions, prison abolitionists argue that hate crime laws should be abandoned because they only increase the size of the prison industrial complex (Nair, 2014). Further, abolitionists argue that prison does little to reform violent offenders. Instead, abolitionists advocate for broader reforms in society and the criminal justice system to create a society that values all human beings and seeks to treat lawbreakers humanely (Nair, 2014).

MASS SHOOTINGS AS HATE CRIMES

Since 2010, there have been a number of mass shootings that can also be classified as hate crimes. These shootings have targeted a wide range of minority groups across the country. Several shootings, for example, have targeted religious minorities. These include anti-Semitic shootings, such as the 2006 attack on the Seattle Jewish Community Center, a 2009 shooting at the National Holocaust Museum, and the 2014 shooting at the Overland Park Jewish Community Center. Additionally, Islamophobia and nativism has resulted in several attacks targeting Muslims and Middle Eastern and South Asian immigrants. For example, a 2012 shooting killed six people and injured four others at the Sikh Temple of Wisconsin. It should be noted that Sikhs are not Muslims.

In this chapter, specific consideration is given to the Charleston church shooting, which targeted African Americans, and the Pulse nightclub massacre, which targeted Latinx and LGBTQ people. These shootings are compared and contrasted to examine their relationship to historical patterns of violence against minority groups in the United States and to demonstrate the complexity associated with labeling a particular mass shooting as a hate crime.

THE CHARLESTON CHURCH SHOOTING

On the evening of June 17, 2015, news broke that there had been a mass shooting at the Emanuel African Methodist Episcopal (AME) Church in Charleston, South Carolina. At the time, the shooter was on the run and described as a "21-year-old, clean-shaven, white male with sandy blond hair" ("9 Dead in Shooting," 2015). The description of the shooter led many to believe that this shooting was not a typical mass shooting—many news and social media commentators called it a hate crime, even in early coverage. Speaking at around 1:00 a.m. on June 18, the Charleston police chief announced that the shooting would be investigated as a hate crime.

This was not the first time that Emanuel AME Church had been the target of hate-motivated violence. According to the National Park Service (n.d.), the Emanuel AME Church was burned down in 1822 by a mob of whites angry over the pastor's involvement in organizing a slave rebellion. In fact, African American churches have long been targets of white supremacist violence. This was especially true during the civil rights movement of the 1950s and 1960s, when African American churches throughout the South were routinely burned and bombed by individuals associated with the Ku Klux Klan (KKK). For example, the 16th Street Baptist Church in Birmingham, Alabama, was bombed during Sunday services on September 15, 1963. Twenty-two people were injured and four girls—Addie Mae Collins (age 14), Cynthia Wesley (age 14), Carole Robertson (age 14), and Carole Denise McNair (age 11)—were killed in the terrorist attack.

On the morning of June 18, 2015, the Charleston shooter was arrested without incident. Days later, investigators discovered a website owned by the shooter that outlined his white supremacist views. The website included pictures of the shooter posing with guns and Confederate flags, as well as blogs he had authored condemning African Americans and other minorities. The site further expressed views honoring Hitler, neo-Nazis, and the KKK. According to reports, the website also included a manifesto that explained the shooter's motivation. In it, he wrote that African Americans are "stupid and violent" and "the biggest problem for Americans," and he compared them to dogs (in Bernstein, Horwitz, & Holley, 2015). Each of these statements represents the ideology of white supremacy. Thus, the shooter, in his own words, declared his attack as being motivated by his racist biases.

Following the revelation of this manifesto, some commentators and activists declared that the shooting should be considered an act of domestic terrorism, rather than simply a hate crime (Gladstone, 2015). However, the FBI did not classify the shooting as terrorism and the shooter was indicted on 33 counts in federal court, including 9 counts of murder and 24 civil rights violations (Berman, 2015). He was also charged with 9 counts of murder, 3 counts of attempted murder, and possession of a firearm during the commission of a felony at the state level. On December 15, 2016, a federal jury found the shooter guilty on all counts. On January 11, 2017, he was sentenced to death by lethal injection (Blinder & Sack, 2017). On March 31, 2017, the shooter pleaded guilty to the charges he faced in South Carolina, thus avoiding a second murder trial.

The Charleston church shooting is a clear example of hate-motivated violence. The shooter was not only prejudiced against African Americans, but he actively wrote and published essays rooted in the ideology of white supremacy. Furthermore, he published a manifesto explaining that his actions were the result of his white supremacist views. Finally, the shooter was captured alive, meaning he could be interrogated for additional information beyond what was published online. Unfortunately, roughly half of mass shooters do not live to explain their actions, nor do they publish manifestos providing insights into their actions (Ferro, 2013; Schildkraut & Elsass, 2016). In cases such as the Pulse nightclub massacre, for example, this means that we may never fully understand the true motives of the shooter. This uncertainty can, in some cases, lead to painful disagreements between survivors, the community, law enforcement, and the news media.

PULSE NIGHTCLUB MASSACRE

On June 12, 2016, Omar Mateen changed the way that society views antigay violence in America. At around 2:00 a.m., he entered Pulse armed with a semiautomatic rifle and semiautomatic pistol and opened fire on the patrons inside. The massacre continued for nearly three hours before police stormed the building and killed the shooter. In total, 49 people were killed—38 of whom were pronounced dead at the scene; another 58 people were injured (Santora, 2016). In the first minutes and hours of the shooting, local news stations were reporting the attack. By daybreak, the story was a national headline.

Since the middle of the 19th century, LGBTQ Americans have experienced various forms of homophobic and/or transphobic violence. During the Red Scare, the U.S. government banned gays and lesbians from working in federal jobs and from serving in the military. The FBI conducted investigations into the lives of suspected homosexuals to uncover closeted gay and lesbian federal workers. Medical doctors and psychologists considered homosexuality to be an illness and employed brutal techniques, such as electroshock therapy and chemical castration, as potential cures. Additionally, state and local governments passed laws criminalizing homosexuality and police forces routinely targeted gay bars and their patrons.

In addition to institutionalized discrimination and violence, LGBTQ people also suffered at the hands of other citizens. Historically, however, antigay violence had been limited to attacks on individuals or small groups. For example, one of the most well-known victims of homophobic violence was Matthew Shepard of Laramie, Wyoming. On October 6, 1998, Matthew met two straight men at a bar and accepted a ride home from them. Instead of taking him home, the two took Matthew to a pasture outside of town, where they beat him and tied him to a fence, leaving him to die. The two perpetrators later were arrested, tried, and convicted of Matthew's murder. While this high-profile case generated national attention, countless other LGBTQ people have suffered from various forms of intimidation and violence simply because of their sexual orientation or gender identity.

In the hours that followed the shooting, more was learned about the perpetrator. At around 9:30 a.m., news outlets began reporting that he was Muslim and an

"ISIS sympathizer." From that moment on, the news media shifted their coverage to link this shooting with "radical Islamic terrorism" (Tsukayama, Berman, & Markon, 2016). The FBI investigated the shooter and his family. Ultimately, the agency concluded the shooter was not biased against LGBTQ people. Furthermore, they determined there was no evidence that the shooting was an attack on the LGBTQ community (Goldman, 2016). Therefore, they did not classify the shooting as a hate crime. They instead classified the shooting as an act of domestic terrorism.

Classifying the Pulse shooting as domestic terrorism, rather than a hate crime, conflicts with earlier media reports and has caused confusion within the community. For instance, the shooter's father reportedly claimed that he was extremely homophobic. He cited an incident only a few days before the massacre when the shooter had a negative reaction to a public display of affection between two gay men (Hanks, 2016). However, other media reports conflict with both the hate crime and terrorism narratives. Instead, such reports claimed that the shooter himself was gay and was a regular patron of the Pulse nightclub (Hennessy-Fiske, Jarvie, & Wilber, 2016). Of course, such inconsistencies may be attributed to fast-paced reporting in 24-hour news cycles. However, they have caused many unanswered questions.

Unlike the Charleston gunman, the Pulse shooter did not publish essays denigrating the LGBTQ community. The FBI did uncover some evidence indicating the shooter had sympathized with various terrorist groups, including ISIS and Al Qaeda; however, he did not leave behind a manifesto explaining his motives. The fact remains, however, that the deadliest mass shooting in modern American history took place at a gay bar during Gay Pride Month. For many in the LGBTQ community, that is not a coincidence; rather, it is further evidence of systemic discrimination against LGBTQ people (Lang, 2016).

PREVENTING HATE CRIMES AND MASS SHOOTINGS

Along with the Overland Park Jewish Center shooting, the Charleston church shooting and the Pulse nightclub massacre represent a new and terrifying phenomenon in mass shootings: mass shootings as hate crimes. However, mass shootings represent just one tactic—albeit a particularly horrifying one—used to perpetrate violence against minorities. Most hate crimes are property crimes, such as vandalism for example, when perpetrators write epithets on the victims' property. However, violent crimes, such as murder and mass shootings, receive more attention because they are more severe (Schildkraut & Elsass, 2016). As such, it is alarming that hate-motivated offenders are using mass shootings as a tactic.

Strategies to reduce or eliminate hate-motivated mass shootings are predicated on confronting the ideologies that produce and foster hate-motivated violence. Hate is an emotion that is characterized by intense or passionate dislike. As such, offenders subsequently may be overcome by their emotions and act irrationally. Thus, such shooters often are dismissed as being flawed, ignorant, or mentally ill. However, it is important to remember that hate crimes specifically target minority groups, such as African Americans, Muslims, people with disabilities, and lesbian, gay, bisexual, or transgender people. Social sciences research suggests that negative attitudes about minorities do not come out of thin air. Rather, they are produced by the norms and values within a society (Blumer, 1958; Herek, 2004). This means that in order to understand hate crimes, the influences of institutionalized oppression in our society must be examined, including white supremacy, negative attitudes, and discrimination against racial and ethnic minorities and homophobic and transphobic attitudes, actions, policies, and laws hostile toward LGBTQ people.

The shootings at the Pulse nightclub and the Emanuel AME Church are intensified versions of the daily physical, emotional, and financial violence perpetrated against LGBTQ people and people of color. Each day, lesbian women are assaulted by men who think that they can "turn them straight." Feminine boys are teased, bullied, beaten, and humiliated, sometimes to the point at which they kill themselves, and transgender people cannot even use the bathroom without fear of persecution and prosecution. Such violence usually is considered as being inflicted by strangers, but for many LGBTQ people, this violence starts in their own homes. Mass shootings and terrorism need to be discussed. Simultaneously, however, the homophobia, transphobia, and white supremacy that exist in our daily lives also must be examined. The truth is that many Americans are complicit in violence against LGBTQ people and people of color. If we truly want to end mass shooting hate crimes, we also need to end discrimination against and abuse of minorities in the United States.

REFERENCES

Berman, M. (2015, July 22). Dylann Roof, accused Charleston church gunman, indicted on federal hate crime charges. *Washington Post.* Retrieved from https://www.washingtonpost.com/news/post-nation/wp/2015/07/22/dylann-roof-accused-charleston-church-gunman-has-been-indicted-on-federal-hate-crime-charges/?utm_term=.944a005bc52e

Bernstein, L., Horwitz, S., & Holley, P. (2015, June 20). Dylann Roof's racist manifesto: "I have no choice." *Washington Post*. Retrieved from https://www.washingtonpost.com/national/health-science/authorities-investigate-whether-racist-manifesto-was-written-by-sc-gunman/2015/06/20/f0bd3052-1762-11e5-9ddc-e3353542100c_story.html?utm_term=.178210b89a81

Blinder, A., & Sack, K. (2017, January 10). Dylann Roof is sentenced to death in Charleston church massacre. *New York Times.* Retrieved from https://www.nytimes.com/2017/01/10/us/dylann-roof-trial-charleston.html

Blumer, H. (1958). Race prejudice as a sense of group position. *Pacific Sociological Review, 1*(1), 3–7.

Federal Bureau of Investigation. (n.d.). *Hate crimes.* Retrieved from https://www.fbi.gov/investigate/civil-rights/hate-crimes

Ferro, S. (2013, September 12). How often do mass shooters die in their attacks? *Popular Science.* Retrieved from http://www.popsci.com/science/article/2013-09/how-often-do-mass-shooters-die-their-attacks

Gladstone, R. (2015, June 18). Many ask, why not call church shooting terrorism? *New York Times*. Retrieved from https://www.nytimes.com/2015/06/19/us/charleston -shooting-terrorism-or-hate-crime.html

Goldman, A. (2016, July 16). FBI has found no evidence that Orlando shooter targeted Pulse because it was a gay club. *Washington Post*. Retrieved from https://www .washingtonpost.com/world/national-security/no-evidence-so-far-to-suggest-orl ando-shooter-targeted-club-because-it-was-gay/2016/07/14/a7528674-4907-11e6 -acbc-4d4870a079da_story.html?utm_term=.aa7f9a5c9a48

Hanks, D. (2016, June 12). Orlando shooter's father points to men kissing in Miami to explain son's anger. *Miami Herald*. Retrieved from http://www.miamiherald.com /news/local/community/miami-dade/article83329252.html

Hennessy-Fiske, M., Jarvie, J., & Wilber, D. Q. (2016, June 13). Orlando gunman had used gay dating app and visited LGBT nightclub on other occasions, witnesses say. *Los Angeles Times*. Retrieved from http://www.latimes.com/nation/la-na-orlando -nightclub-shooting-20160613-snap-story.html

Herek, G. M. (2004). Beyond "homophobia": Thinking about sexual prejudice and stigma in the twenty-first century. *Sexuality Research and Social Policy*, *1*(2), 6–24.

Lang, N. (2016, June 13). Call the Orlando massacre a hate crime: This was an attack on the LGBT community—and that matters. *Salon*. Retrieved from http://www.salon .com/2016/06/13/call_the_orlando_massacre_a_hate_crime_this_was_an_attack _on_the_lgbt_community_and_that_matters/

Nair, Y. (2014). Why hate crime legislation is still not a solution. In R. Conrad (Ed.), *Against Equality: Queer Revolution, Not Mere Inclusion* (199–204). Edinburgh: AK Press.

National Park Service. (n.d.). *Emanuel A.M.E. Church*. Retrieved from https://www.nps .gov/nr/travel/charleston/ema.htm

9 dead in shooting at Charleston AME church (2015, June 17). *Herald-Journal*. Retrieved from http://infoweb.newsbank.com/resources/doc/nb/news/15609DB08203F9D8? p=NewsBank

Santora, M. (2016, June 12). Last call at Pulse nightclub, then shots rang out. *New York Times*. Retrieved from https://www.nytimes.com/2016/06/13/us/last-call-at -orlando-club-and-then-the-shots-rang-out.html

Schildkraut, J., & Elsass, H. J. (2016). *Mass shootings: Media, myths, and realities*. Santa Barbara, CA: Praeger.

Segura, L. (2014). Do hate crime laws do any good? In R. Conrad (Ed.), *Against Equality: Queer Revolution, Not Mere Inclusion* (185–192). Edinburgh: AK Press.

Tsukayama, H., Berman, M., & Markon, J. (2016, June 13). Gunman who killed 49 in Orlando nightclub had pledged allegiance to ISIS. *Washington Post*. Retrieved from https://www.washingtonpost.com/news/post-nation/wp/2016/06/12/orlando -nightclub-shooting-about-20-dead-in-domestic-terror-incident-at-gay-club/?utm _term=.168556b4b9d3

Mass Shootings as Acts of Terrorism

Jeff Gruenewald

INTRODUCTION

Though neither terrorism nor mass shootings are new in the United States, high-profile terrorist attacks occurring around the turn of the 21st century awoke Americans to two harsh realities. First, mass casualty terrorism was not just a threat to foreign nations. This was evidenced in 1995 when an antigovernment terrorist detonated a truck bomb in Oklahoma City, Oklahoma, partially demolishing a federal office building and killing 168 people. Six years later, Al Qaeda's terrorist attacks on September 11, 2001, killed nearly 3,000 victims and forever changed the public's understanding of terrorism. Second, American's perceptions of schools as a safe place for children was fundamentally altered with the mass shooting at Columbine High School in Littleton, Colorado, which killed 13 people. To date, terrorists and mass shooters have generally been viewed as two distinct social threats by researchers and other experts. Importantly, though, an increase in terrorists using firearms to carry out high-casualty attacks in furtherance of religious, political, and other social objectives has blurred the definitional boundaries between terrorism and mass shootings.

DEFINING TERRORIST SHOOTERS

There has yet to be consensus among government agencies and criminologists regarding how to define mass shootings and terrorism. The Federal Bureau of Investigation (FBI) defines a mass murder as an incident involving four or more murder victims in a single time and place (Douglas, Burgess, Burgess, & Ressler, 2006; FBI, 2008). Others have narrowed this definition specifically to mass murders committed with firearms in public places, or public mass shootings (Krause & Richardson, 2015). In one study, Jaclyn Schildkraut and H. Jaymi Elsass (2016) suggest that existing definitions have inhibited a comprehensive understanding of mass murder by excluding shootings involving less than four murder victims. They assert that with a more inclusive definition that considers cases involving multiple victim incidents where individuals survive their injuries, more can be learned about mass shootings. Like others studying mass shootings, Schildkraut and Elsass exclude cases motivated by ideology from their definition. As for defining terrorism, a consensus definition has also yet to be determined (Silke, 1996; Weinberg, Pedahzur, & Hirsch-Hoefler, 2004). Surveying political scientists on how they personally define terrorism, terrorism experts Alex Schmid and Albert Jongman (1988) discovered over 100 various definitions in use. Similar to studying mass murder, many researchers and practitioners look to the FBI's definition of terrorism for guidance, which generally defines domestic terrorism as

> the unlawful use, or threatened use, of force or violence by a group or individual based and operating entirely within the United States or Puerto Rico without foreign direction committed against persons or property to intimidate or coerce a government, the civilian population, or any segment thereof in furtherance of political or social objectives. (FBI, 2005, p. v)

Two important points regarding definitions are worth noting. The first point is that definitions of mass shootings usually exclude acts of terrorism, possibly due to differences in disciplinary backgrounds and the interests of researchers. Second, though terrorism is usually associated with bombings, definitions of terrorism encompass mass shootings when offenders are motivated by political or social aims. For these reasons, mass shootings and terrorism research literatures have evolved along separate tracks with their intersections remaining largely unexplored. This has possible implications for practitioners who train for and face active shooter situations involving offenders motivated by terrorist ideologies. Are intervention and response strategies the same for all mass shooters? What can terrorism researchers learn from empirical mass shootings studies? To examine these questions, this draws from elements of the FBI's (2005) definition of terrorism and Schildkraut and Elsass's (2016) definition of mass shootings to define a terrorist shooting *an incident of violence by one or more persons against multiple victims (fatal and nonfatal gunshot wounds) at one or more public or populated locations within a 24-hour period and with the aim of intimidating or coercing a government, the civilian population, or any segment thereof in furtherance of political or social objectives.*

WHO ARE FAR-RIGHT TERRORIST SHOOTERS?

The Oklahoma City bombing in 1995 by a far-right extremist remains the second deadliest act of terrorism in American history, though it is shootings committed by far-right extremists that arguably continue to pose the biggest threat to American communities (Gruenewald, 2011). Discriminatory violence against minorities has evolved in America, stemming back to Ku Klux Klan attacks on blacks in the early and mid-20th century to more recent far-right shootings of victims targeted because of their race, faith, sexual orientation, or gender. The belief systems of far-right terrorists are multifaceted, encompassing political and social grievances that are often interweaved with personal issues into conspiratorial narratives driving them toward violence. While succinctly capturing such beliefs is challenging, Joshua Freilich and colleagues (2014) define far-right extremists as

> fiercely nationalistic, anti-global, suspicious of federal authority and reverent of individual liberties, especially their right to own guns and be free of taxes. They believe in conspiracy theories involving imminent threats to national sovereignty or personal liberty and beliefs that their personal or national "way of life" is under attack. Sometimes such beliefs are vague, but for some the threat originates from specific racial or religious groups. They believe that they must be prepared to defend against this attack by participating in paramilitary training or survivalism. (p. 380)

Over the last few decades, far-right shooters have justified their killings based on their belief that social minorities are a threat to white America. One important contributor to modern far-right violence is the infusion of neo-Nazism, specifically a desire to eradicate Jews, into America's skinhead counterculture movement. Though originally a nonviolent movement that promoted working-class values and a unique style (e.g., steel-toe boots, shaved heads), narratives of anti-Semitism and white supremacy infiltrated the skinhead subculture and music scene during the 1980s and 1990s (Cotter, 1999; Futrell, Simi, & Gottschalk, 2006; Hamm, 1993). Also shaping far-right violence is the alternative religious ideology of Christian Identity, which maintains that whites of European heritage are the true "Chosen People" described in the Bible, while Jews are the spawn of Satan and non-Aryan races are considered pre-Adamic, subhuman "mud people." As with neo-Nazism, Christian Identity beliefs have permeated extreme far-right ideology and provided scapegoats for the grievances of disenfranchised white Americans. Christian Identity ideology also promotes conspiracy theories suggesting that the U.S. government is occupied by Jewish, globalist elites who wish to establish a "New World Order" whereby a single world governing body would control international financial institutions and the media. Followers often contend that the end of days, or Armageddon, is imminent and will be sparked by a war between whites and armies of Jews and nonwhites who are supported by the one world government. Importantly, many members of the extreme far right look forward to this apocalyptic war, as they believe that whites will ultimately be triumphant over all other races.

The threat posed by far-right shooters was realized on June 17, 2015, when six female and three male parishioners were massacred during an evening Bible study at the Emanuel African Methodist Episcopal (AME) Church in Charleston, South Carolina. The shooter, a 21-year-old neo-Nazi who also held Christian Identity beliefs, reportedly targeted the church in part because of its historical significance to the American civil rights movement (Sanchez & Payne, 2016). Unaffiliated with a formal terrorist group, the far-right shooter was radicalized by consuming extremist materials on the Internet, where he also communicated with other like-minded white supremacists and propagated cultural myths about black men raping and killing white women. After the incident, the far-right shooter claimed that he intended his shooting to ignite the much anticipated "race war."

The morning after the terrorist shooting, law enforcement released surveillance footage of the far-right shooter and a description of his car. Within hours, he was spotted while driving and arrested. The shooter was later indicted on 9 counts of capital murder, attempted murder, and a weapons charge in South Carolina. He was also charged with 9 counts of using a firearm to commit murder and 24 civil rights violations, including federal hate crime charges, in federal court. After making a full confession that was later used as evidence in his trial, he was found guilty on all 33 federal charges. On January 10, 2017, he was sentenced to death by lethal injection.

Despite the social and political goals of this shooting, the far-right shooter was not charged with terrorism. This decision reflects the definitional ambiguities in official classifications of mass shootings and terrorism. In fact, FBI director James Comey initially stated that he did not view the shooting as a political act, though he later acknowledged the shooter's desire to start a race war (Reilly, 2015). Moreover, U.S. attorney general Loretta Lynch described discriminatory violence like that committed in Charleston as "the original domestic terrorism" (Johnson, 2015). Regardless of how the attack was officially classified, the broader impact of the terrorist shooting was almost immediate. During the sensationalized coverage of the attack, images of the far-right shooter posing with guns and the Confederate flag circulated on popular media outlets. While viewed as a symbol of Southern heritage by some, the flag has also been used as a symbol of racial prejudice by white supremacist groups. Heeding the calls by advocacy groups and prominent politicians, South Carolina removed the Confederate flag from the Capitol State House (McCrummen & Izadi, 2015).

WHO ARE GLOBAL JIHADI TERRORIST SHOOTERS?

Mass shootings in America committed by jihadi terrorists have also posed a persistent threat to homeland security since the 9/11 attacks. Research from the United Extremist Crime Database has found that over 50 percent of murders committed by jihadi terrorists in the United States involved firearms rather than some form of explosive (Gruenewald, Klein, Freilich, & Chermak, 2016). While the 9/11 attacks involved a large conspiracy, approximately 60 percent of deadly jihadi attacks in the United States were perpetrated by lone actors. These terrorists blame the United States and other Western nations for the oppression of Muslims around the world and for exploiting the resources of Muslim nations through the guise of war. Though multiple definitions of "jihad" exist, terrorist leaders have promoted an interpretation that demands the eradication of all those who threaten Islam.

Especially troubling is a series of mass casualty attacks by jihadi shooters pledging allegiance to the terrorist group known as ISIS (Islamic State of Iraq and Syria), a media-savvy splinter group of Al Qaeda. Jihadi shooters in America are often Muslim converts with no tangible ties to ISIS or any terrorist organization. Instead, they view anti-American terrorist propaganda on the Internet and become self-radicalized. One such case occurred in the early morning hours of June 12, 2016, when a jihadi shooter entered the Pulse gay nightclub in Orlando, Florida, armed with a handgun and an assault rifle that he used to kill 49 people and wound 58. This was the deadliest mass shooting in American history, the most lethal act of terrorism since the 9/11 terrorist attacks, and was a direct attack on the lesbian, gay, bisexual, and transgender (LGBT) community. The jihadi shooter was a 29-year old, college-educated, married father who was working as a security guard. Though he did not have a criminal record, he had twice been investigated by the FBI for proclamations of ties to terrorism (Wilbur, 2016). Because no solid connections to terrorism could ever be substantiated, he maintained his gun licenses. As the shooting nightmare unfolded, the jihadist called 9-1-1 and pledged his allegiance to ISIS, despite having had no actual known contact with ISIS (Callimachi, 2016). He claimed that his shooting was in retaliation for airstrikes targeting ISIS in Syria and Iraq. Why he chose to target a gay nightclub remains unclear, though many Islamic extremists decry Westerners for their acceptance of homosexuality and advocacy for equal rights (Alter, 2016).

After a three-hour standoff, police officers shot and killed the jihadi shooter. The nation watched in horror as the casualty count continued to rise. Classifying this attack proved challenging as well because it encompassed elements of mass shootings, terrorism, and hate crimes (FBI, 2014). Signaling that some mass shootings can also be acts of terrorism (and hate crimes), President Obama referred to the shooting as an "act of terror and an act of hate" during his visit to Orlando (Bradner, 2016). The shooting also served as political fodder for presidential candidates Hillary Clinton, who called for tighter restrictions on gun purchases (Hook, Reinhard, & Epstein, 2016), and Donald Trump, who capitalized on the shooting to support a proposed immigration ban.

CONCLUSION

In sum, terrorism and mass shootings have usually been considered distinct social problems by researchers and other experts. Mass shootings are thought to stem from personal grudges, while terrorism is often associated with politically motivated bombings. Since 9/11, however, several high-profile terrorist shootings by far-right and jihadi shooters have blurred the definitional lines between these two forms of violence. To understand the complex nature of the threats posed by terrorist shooters, conventional definitions of terrorism or mass shootings should be expanded to carefully explore their intersections.

REFERENCES

Alter, C. (2016, June 15). Ex-wife says Orlando shooter might have been hiding homosexuality from his family. *Time.* Retrieved from http://time.com/4369577/orlando-shooting-sitora-yusufiy-omar-mateen-gay/

Bradner, E. (2016, June 12). Obama on Orlando shooting: "An act of terror and an act of hate." *CNN.com.* Retrieved from http://www.cnn.com/2016/06/12/politics/orlando-shooting-obama-response/

Callimachi, R. (2016, June 12). Was Orlando shooter really acting for ISIS? For ISIS, it's all the same. *New York Times*. Retrieved from https://www.nytimes.com/2016/06/13/us/orlando-omar-mateen-isis.html

Cotter, J. M. (1999). Sounds of hate: White power rock and roll and the neo-Nazi skinhead subculture. *Terrorism & Political Violence, 11*(2), 111–140.

Douglas, J. E., Burgess, A. W., Burgess, A. G., & Ressler, R. K. (2006). *Crime classification manual: A standard system for investigating and classifying violent crime* (2nd ed.). Hoboken, NJ: Jossey-Bass.

Federal Bureau of Investigation (2005). *Terrorism 2002–2005*. Washington, D.C.: Department of Justice.

Federal Bureau of Investigation. (2008). *Serial murder: Multi-disciplinary perspectives for investigators*. Behavioral Analysis Unit. National Center for the Analysis of Violent Crime. Washington, D.C.: U.S. Department of Justice.

Federal Bureau of Investigation. (2014). *Hate crime statistics, 2013—Methodology*. Washington, D.C.: Department of Justice. Retrieved from https://ucr.fbi.gov/hate-crime/2013/resource-pages/methodology/methodology_final.pdf

Freilich, J. D., Chermak, S. M., Belli, R., Gruenewald, J., & Parkin, W. S. (2014). Introducing the United States Extremist Crime Database (ECDB). *Terrorism & Political Violence, 26*(2), 372–384.

Futrell, R., Simi, P., & Gottschalk, S. (2006). Understanding music in movements: The White Power music scene. *Sociological Quarterly, 47*(2), 275–304.

Gruenewald, J. (2011). A comparative examination of far-right extremist homicide events. *Homicide Studies, 15*, 177–203.

Gruenewald, J., Klein, B. R., Freilich, J. D., & Chermak, S. (2016). American jihadi terrorism: A comparison of homicides and unsuccessful plots. Published online first in *Terrorism & Political Violence*. https://doi.org/10.1080/09546553.2016.1253563

Hamm, M. S. (1993). *American skinheads: The criminology and control of hate crime*. Westport, CT: Praeger

Hook, J., Reinhard, B., & Epstein, R. J. (2016, June 13). Orlando shooting widens Hillary Clinton, Donald Trump divide. *Wall Street Journal*. Retrieved from https://www.wsj.com/articles/hillary-clinton-calls-for-reinstatement-of-assault-weapons-ban-after-orlando-shooting-1465826332

Johnson, K. (2015, June 24). Attorney General Lynch: "Hate crimes are the original domestic terrorism." *USA Today*. Retrieved from http://www.usatoday.com/story/news/nation/2015/06/24/loretta-lynch-baptist-church-birmingham/29238615/

Krause, W. J., & Richardson, D. J. (2015). Mass murder with firearms: Incidents and victims, 1999–2013. *Congressional Research Service*. Retrieved from https://fas.org/sgp/crs/misc/R44126.pdf

McCrummen, S., & Izadi, E. (2015, July 10). Confederate flag comes down on South Carolina's statehouse grounds. *Washington Post*. Retrieved from https://www.washingtonpost.com/news/post-nation/wp/2015/07/10/watch-live-as-the-confederate-flag-comes-down-in-south-carolina/?utm_term=.a16eb71eb60d

Reilly, R. (2015, July 9). FBI director James Comey still unsure if white supremacist's attack in Charleston was terrorism. *Huffington Post*. Retrieved from http://www.huffingtonpost.com/2015/07/09/james-comey-charleston-terrorism-n_7764614.html

Sanchez, R., & Payne, E. (2016, December 16). Charleston church shooting: Who is Dylann Roof? *CNN.com*. Retrieved from http://www.cnn.com/2015/06/19/us/charleston-church-shooting-suspect/

Schildkraut, J., & Elsass, H. J. (2016). *Mass shootings: Media, myths, and realities*. Santa Barbara, CA: Praeger.

Schmid, A. P., & Jongman, A. J. (1988). *Political terrorism: A new guide to actors, authors, concepts, databases, theories and literature*. Amsterdam: North-Holland.

Silke, A. (1996). Terrorism and the blind men's elephant. *Terrorism & Political Violence*, *8*(3), 12–28.

Weinberg, L., Pedahzur, A., & Hirsch-Hoefler, S. (2004). The challenges of conceptualizing terrorism. *Terrorism & Political Violence*, *16*(4), 777–794.

Wilbur, D. Q. (2016, July 14). The FBI investigated the Orlando mass shooter for 10 months—and found nothing. Here's why. *Los Angeles Times*. Retrieved from http://beta.latimes.com/nation/la-na-fbi-investigation-mateen-20160712-snap-story.html

Issues and Challenges for Law Enforcement Responding to Mass Shootings

Amanda L. Farrell

Shots fired. Active shooter. Multiple casualties. That is the radio broadcast that no chief, no agency, no officer, or other first responder wants to hear. While the media would have citizens believe these incidents happen all too often and are increasing in frequency, reality and research tells us that these are actually very rare events (Paparazzo, Eith, & Tocco, 2013; Schildkraut & Elsass, 2016), with most citizens having a very low risk of being a victim. Rare as they may be, however, communities and institutions (schools, business offices, police departments) have recognized the need to prepare for such events. Such preparations are particularly urgent for law enforcement officers (LEOs). In modern times, LEOs must train and plan to respond to the unthinkable because the worst approach is to believe that it can never happen in your community. To add further fuel to this fire, these shootings are, by and large, high-profile events that are subject to intense and ongoing media, public, and professional scrutiny, and under the intense spotlight of public opinion, inadequate responses and errors are magnified. In short, deliberate indifference or negligence is *not* an option.

LESSONS LEARNED FROM PREVIOUS MASS SHOOTINGS

The mass shooting at Columbine High School in Colorado on April 20, 1999, was a watershed moment for a variety of reasons (Altheide, 2009; Kalish & Kimmel, 2010; Larkin, 2007, 2009; Muschert, 2007; Muschert & Larkin, 2007), including its lasting impact on American culture, news media, and concepts of safety and security. It also signaled a shift in law enforcement response to and planning for these types of events. In the intervening years since Columbine, the law enforcement community has learned some lessons and adapted their responses to mass shooting incidents. There are now active shooter protocols in place in most jurisdictions and the focus on evidence-based policy (EBP) has led to the refinement of these policies based on research and data. The law enforcement response to mass violence incidents is often very rapid, with one study finding that the average response time to active shooter events is approximately three minutes (Blair, Martaindale, & Nichols, 2014). Yet a rapid response to the scene is only a small portion of the overall protocol. The "what if" and preparation are even more critical, meaning that thinking about a plethora of scenarios that could happen and having both physical training and tabletop exercises that address as many potentialities as possible provides the foundation for a coordinated, unified, and strong response. Preparation also involves regular and continued communication among stakeholders and coordinated efforts in the forms of threat assessment initiatives, mental health awareness, education, and others.

Many people are not aware or do not wish to acknowledge that mass shootings and the prevention and addressing of such incidents (Blair & Martaindale, 2013; Goldman, 2013; Jarvis & Scherer, 2015; Schildkraut & Elsass, 2016; Schweit, 2013) are not the sole responsibility of any one group or institution or agency. Specifically, this is not just a law enforcement problem. Other community groups increasingly recognize this, contributing to multifaceted prevention and response strategies, as well as a multifaceted approach to threat assessment. This point was driven home in December 2016 when Sandy Hook Promise, a national nonprofit formed after the 2012 shooting, released its "Know the Signs" public service announcement (Shellbourne, 2016). Most people had to watch the nationally televised public service announcement (PSA) more than once, as they missed the signs at first viewing, paying more attention to the blossoming flirtation between two high school students written on the library table than to the behavioral warning signs of a potential shooter displayed by a classmate, all of which were taking place in the background. This television ad was thought-provoking, but also empirically supported, based on research that found that in over 90 percent of incidents of targeted school shootings, the perpetrator exhibited concerning behaviors prior to the event—and that in over 80 percent of incidents, someone was aware of the perpetrator's plans beforehand (Drysdale, Modzeleski & Simons, 2010; Pollack, Modzeleski, & Rooney, 2008; Schweit, 2013). This research matters to law enforcement because it underscores how preventing violence can negate the need to respond to it. Jarvis and Scherer (2015) emphasize preparation, communicating with community partners (e.g., school boards, threat assessment teams, religious organizations, victims' services agencies, mental health providers, and others), creating and managing threat management teams, educating the public, debunking the myths of mental illness, and conducting tabletop exercises with community partners. In reaching out to community partners, establishing lines of communication, and establishing mechanisms to address concerning behaviors and potential threats, it allows all these stakeholders to work toward prevention and makes it very clear that mass violence is not just a law enforcement problem.

EVIDENCE-BASED IMPROVEMENTS IN TRAINING AND RESPONSE

Although prevention is the favorable resolution for these incidents, preventing all incidents is unlikely to happen. While efforts at cooperative strategies for prevention have increased, law enforcement has also focused on how to respond to active shooter events with sound best practices. For example, early tactics required officers to hold and stage to enter—in other words, first responders were told not to enter an active shooting, but were to instead wait for backup to arrive and assemble a full entry team—when an active shooter scenario emerged. Yet researchers found that over half of active shooter situations are over before law enforcement arrives. In addition, researchers documented that the majority of active shooter situations required some form of force or confrontation to end the incident (Blair & Martaindale, 2013; Schweit, 2013). It was thus determined that waiting to stage and enter as a team poses a greater risk for more violence and more casualties in an incident. In short, protocol changed to focus on swift intervention, even if only by a single officer, to stop the threat as soon as possible, possibly at a much greater risk to the individual officer's safety. Another thing that people do not typically understand about crime scenes in general, especially active ones, is that they tend to be chaotic. In a mass shooting, that chaos is magnified a thousandfold. There may be multiple jurisdictions responding, as well as people fleeing, and, depending on the speed of media coverage, both the media and concerned citizens may be rushing to the scene. This is why preparation, especially training with fellow first responders, is so essential. Tabletop exercises and scenario-based training (e.g., having a campus shooter drill on a campus with all responding parties to run through what would happen, or talking through various scenarios from different perspectives) help identify issues, such as problems synching radio communications across jurisdictions (ICSC, 2013), *before* there is a crisis.

That said, in addition to planning and preparation, training has advanced since Columbine and other shooting incidents on multiple fronts. In 2013, the Advanced Law Enforcement Rapid Response Training (ALERRT) Center was recognized by the Federal Bureau of Investigation (FBI) as the national standard for active shooter training and has set the bar for training since then (ALERRT, 2017). ALERRT is research-based, so as active shooter events occur, they are able to gather data, analyze trends, and effectively alter training to meet emergent needs. This ability to adapt can and does save lives. One specific example relates to the Active Threat Integrated Response Course (ATIRC) offered. Traditional responses to any shooting scene dictate that LEOs must clear the scene and ensure that it is safe before other first responder counterparts (Fire and Rescue) enter. Due to the scope and nature of active shooter/mass shooting incidents, this process can take quite a bit of time—imagine having to clear an entire school or a mall or an office building—to ensure that the threat has either been neutralized or is no longer on scene. In the intervening hours between shooting and clearing a large scene, some victims may die from shock and blood loss because emergency medical services (EMS) cannot safely enter the scene to get to them (Blair et al., 2014). In the 2012 Clackamas Mall shooting (please see the entry on this shooting in the encyclopedia portion of this book for a synopsis of this and other events), even though first responders were on scene almost 1 minute into the event, it took almost 12 hours to clear the mall (ICSC, 2013). At Columbine, meanwhile, teacher Dave Sanders died in the school from gunshot wounds because EMS personnel could not get to him for more than 3 hours (Columbine Review Commission, 2001). Thus, ALERRT was able to develop this integrated course, which includes tactical medical training for LEOs so that they can address and provide critical care for the wounded while clearing the scene.

WHAT NEXT? THE MISSING DISCUSSION ABOUT INVESTIGATIVE NEEDS

As much as training and preparation have improved, there has been a lack of research and follow-through dedicated to looking at what happens after the threat has been stopped. One of the questions that is consistently echoed in the aftermath of any tragedy, and especially in the aftermath of a mass shooting, is "why?" Answers can sometimes be found by conducting a thorough investigation. Most reactive investigations follow a similar pattern of how they are conducted, insofar as what steps are taken, but the existing research largely fails to account for the specific issues that arise when facing the daunting task of investigating a mass shooting. As Timothy Keel (2014) noted at the 2014 International Homicide Investigators' Association Seminar, there is often insufficient consideration of the extensive use of resources and coordination necessary to conduct investigations in the days, weeks, and months following a mass shooting incident. Even the preliminary investigation may be problematic, as multiple jurisdictions' EMSs may be transporting victims to various medical facilities. Just as first responders' resources and capabilities may be taxed in a mass shooting incident, hospitals, morgues, medical examiners' offices, victims' services/advocates, medical and forensic labs, forensic units, mental health providers, funeral homes, local hotels for media, and others all may also have their capabilities/resources overwhelmed, making it difficult to coordinate and gather necessary information in an investigation.

In the aftermath of the Clackamas Mall shooting, one of the investigative suggestions that emerged was to create two command posts—one to deal specifically with the incident and its immediate response, and one to address the wider investigation of the event (ICSC, 2013). Investigators will be challenged by the number of personal items left behind and sorting those from the evidence, as well as establishing a protocol to return personal items, like purses, wallets, and phones, to their rightful owners if they are not taken into evidence. They will also be challenged with collecting all surveillance footage and social media posts with photos and time stamps to identify witnesses and victims, to recreate the timeline of events, and to develop a better understanding of what happened, when, and in what order. These tasks are often monumental in scale following a mass shooting and require a team of investigators, especially in cases such as the 2015 San Bernardino shooting, where the specter of terrorism adds additional impetus to rule out subsequent and connected planned terroristic activities. Additionally, if LEOs did use force against the suspect, whether they missed, shot, or killed the assailant, many jurisdictions have to devote additional resources to an officer-involved shooting investigation.

Another of the formidable investigative challenges that is not typically discussed in the research and literature is the forensics associated with these scenes. These investigations will likely require multiple forensic teams to cover the incident location, the shooter's home and/or vehicle, and any other secondary scenes. These scenes will take days to process. For example, the Sandy Hook videos released with the report note that processing completed at around 8 p.m. on December 20—six days after the event (Connecticut State Police, 2013). This means extended manpower (both forensics—including additional personnel and rotating shifts—and security for the scene) is needed. Smaller jurisdictions may not have the supplies or equipment necessary to process scenes of this magnitude—especially in terms of evidence packaging and collection materials. Also, outdoor scenes may require tents, generators, and other equipment that some agencies do not have readily available. Secured storage space for evidence may also be lacking or inadequate, and these events may also overwhelm the lab in terms of equipment, supplies, training, experience, and manpower. The good news is that, while not often considered in the literature, federal assistance is available in these instances under the Investigative Assistance for Violent Crimes Act of 2012, which applies to violence and shootings in areas of public use and to mass killings (Schweit, 2013). Regardless of this assistance, more focus needs to be directed to developing EBP and specific investigative models and protocols for these incidents because although most investigative processes are similar in terms of goals and procedures, mass shootings are vastly larger in scale and scope, and they require significant resources that many jurisdictions may not have available or be able to afford.

THE VICTIMS WE RARELY TALK ABOUT: LEOs AND THE IMPACT OF A MASS SHOOTING

The second topic that is typically overlooked in discussions of mass shooting incidents is also a question of resources, but in a different context. Mass shooting events often take a heavy toll on the mental and emotional health of first responders, especially in smaller communities where it is likely that those first responders know one or more of the victims. Adequately training and preparing LEOs for these events is vital, especially given research indicating that 15 to 30 percent of active shooter incidents will involve responding officers being shot (Blair et al., 2014; Schweit, 2013). How will having a friend and colleague shot during this incident impact other first responders, even those who were not even immediately on scene for the event?

Mental health in first responders is a topic that, while being more openly discussed within the last decade, is still rife with stigma and an issue that many members of the first responder community are reluctant to address (Farrell, 2014). It is often perceived to be a weakness if a first responder has difficulty coping with the events he or she sees on the job. Yet the trauma of responding to mass shooting events can be overwhelming, even for LEOs who see more trauma in their first three years on the job than most people see in an entire lifetime (Kamena, Gentz, Hays, Bohl-Penrod, & Greene, 2011; Kirschman, 2007). Mass shooting incidents most certainly meet the criteria for trauma, as well as provide ample opportunity for vicarious or secondary trauma (Office for Victims of Crime [OVC], n.d.). Secondary or vicarious trauma, as defined by OVC (n.d.), is trauma experienced through exposure to the traumatic experiences of others and is particularly important to keep in mind when dealing with first responders. Just as the physical and financial resources of a responding agency can be overwhelmed, it must be remembered that the emotional and mental resources of first responders are also likely overwhelmed. These individuals see the true carnage of these scenes and must cope with things like the incessant ringing of cell phones, knowing that friends and family are desperately trying to reach loved ones who may be injured, dying, or dead (Pearson, 2013).

These experiences can haunt LEOs in numerous ways. Critical incident stress encompasses physical and psychological reactions that may persist for two days to one month after the incident (Kirschman, 2007). Post-traumatic stress disorder (PTSD), meanwhile, may manifest itself with mild to extreme reactions starting just after the trauma is experienced. These symptoms can range in intensity and severity, and they may include things like nightmares, preoccupation with the incident, and social isolation. Without recognition and treatment, PTSD may last for years and negatively impact large portions of the LEO's personal and professional life (Farrell, 2014). Not only must agencies recognize that mass shootings will likely be traumatic to their personnel, they need to include this knowledge in their planning and prevention strategies. Knowing how and when to incorporate critical incident stress management (CISM) teams, chaplains, employee assistance programs (EAPs), having prepared and accessible lists of culturally competent clinicians and counselors, and other such resources will be critical in terms of providing quick and early intervention, which may avoid long-term trauma symptoms. The initial focus in a mass shooting may be providing services to victims and witnesses, as well as the overall community, but first responders must not be overlooked, as the lasting impacts of critical incidents that are not addressed can develop into PTSD and may lead to the loss of the employee due to resignation, medical retirement, or suicide.

CONCLUSION

Since the tragic events at Columbine, law enforcement has made great strides in responding to mass shooting incidents, developing policy and protocols that are based on and responsive to evidence and data. The focus on active training and prevention, as well as the demonstrated importance of multifaceted partnerships to address these issues, have helped equip LEOs facing a mass shooting to respond quickly and efficiently, and likely heightened their abilities to save lives. However, to this point the research focus has largely overlooked the "what next?" aspects of mass shooting incidents, particularly the investigative challenges and the impact these events have on the mental and emotional well-being of LEOs. As researchers and first responders move forward and continue to collect data and refine policy based upon empirical evidence, these aspects must be included as a consideration and essential part of planning and prevention strategies.

REFERENCES

ALERRT. (2017). *Advanced law enforcement rapid response training.* Retrieved from https://alerrt.org/

Altheide, D. L. (2009). The Columbine shooting and the discourse of fear. *American Behavioral Scientist, 52*(10), 1354–1370.

Blair, J. P., & Martaindale, M. H. (2013). *United States active shooter events from 2000 to 2010: Training and equipment implications.* San Marcos: Texas State University, Advanced Law Enforcement Rapid Response Training (ALERRT).

Blair, J. P., Martaindale, M. H., & Nichols, T. (2014, January). Active shooter events from 2000 to 2012. *FBI Law Enforcement Bulletin.* Retrieved from https://leb.fbi.gov/2014/january/active-shooter-events-from-2000-to-2012

Columbine Review Commission. (2001). *The report of Governor Bill Owens' Columbine Review Commission.* Denver: State of Colorado. Retrieved from http://trac.state.co.us/Documents/Reports%20and%20Publications/Columbine_2001_Governor_Review_Commission.pdf

Connecticut State Police. (2013). *Sandy Hook Elementary School shooting reports.* Middletown: State of Connecticut. Retrieved from http://cspsandyhookreport.ct.gov

Drysdale, D. A., Modzeleski, W., & Simons, A. B. (2010). *Campus attacks: Targeted violence affecting institutions of higher education.* Washington, D.C.: U.S. Secret Service; Office of Safe and Drug-Free Schools; Federal Bureau of Investigation. Retrieved from https://www2.ed.gov/admins/lead/safety/campus-attacks.pdf

Farrell, A. L. (2014). *Exploring police shootings and officer survivability: A case study.* (Unpublished doctoral dissertation). Old Dominion University, Norfolk, VA.

Goldman, R. (2013, November 5). Active shooter events have spiked in recent years. *ABC News.* Retrieved from http://abcnews.go.com/US/active-shooter-incidents-spiked-recentyears/print?id=20790333

ICSC (Director). (2013). Active shooter at the mall: Lessons learned, lessons shared. [Motion Picture].

Jarvis, J., & Scherer, J. (2015) *Mass victimization: Promising avenues for prevention.* Washington, D.C.: Federal Bureau of Investigation. Retrieved from http://www.sameshield.com/PDF/nps76-062116-01.pdf

Kalish, R., & Kimmel, M. (2010). Suicide by mass murder: Masculinity, aggrieved entitlement, and rampage school shootings. *Health Sociology Review, 19*(4), 451–464.

Kamena, M., Gentz, D., Hays. V., Bohl-Penrod, N., & Greene, L. W. (2011). Peer support teams fill an emotional void in law enforcement agencies. *Police Chief, 78*(8): 80–84.

Keel, T. (2014, June). *Investigating mass murders.* Paper presented at the annual symposium of the International Homicide Investigators Association, Philadelphia, PA.

Kirschman, E. (2007). *I love a cop: What police families need to know.* New York: Guilford Press.

Larkin, R. W. (2007). *Comprehending Columbine.* Philadelphia, PA: Temple University Press.

Larkin, R. W. (2009). The Columbine legacy: Rampage shootings as political acts. *American Behavioral Scientist, 52*(9), 1309–1326.

Muschert, G. W. (2007). The Columbine victims and the myth of the juvenile superpredator. *Youth Violence and Juvenile Justice, 5*(4), 351–366.

Muschert, G. W., & Larkin, R. W. (2007). The Columbine High School shootings. In S. Chermak & F. Y. Bailey (Eds.), *Crimes and trials of the century* (253–266). Westport, CT: Praeger.

Office for Victims of Crime (OVC). (n.d.). *The vicarious trauma toolkit.* Retrieved from https://vtt.ovc.ojp.gov/

Paparazzo, J., Eith, C., & Tocco, J. (2013). *Strategic approaches to preventing multiple casualty violence: Report on the national summit on multiple casualty shootings.* Washington, DC: U.S. Department of Justice, Office of Community Oriented Policing Services. Retrieved from https://www.fletc.gov/sites/default/files/imported _files/publications/summits-on-preventing-multiple-causality-violence/e02131 1546_MultiCasualty-Violence_v508_05APR13.pdf

Pearson, M. (2013). Eerie sounds of cell phones amid disaster adds to first-responder toll. *CNN.com.* Retrieved from http://www.cnn.com/2013/01/28/health/cell-phones -death/index.html

Pollack, W. S., Modzeleski, W., & Rooney, G. (2008). *Prior knowledge of potential school-based violence: Information students learn may prevent a targeted attack.* Washington, DC: United States Secret Service and United States Department of Education. Retrieved from https://rems.ed.gov/docs/DOE_BystanderStudy.pdf

Schildkraut, J. & Elsass, H. J. (2016). *Mass shootings: Media, myths and realities.* Santa Barbara, CA: Praeger.

Schweit, K. W. (2013, May). Addressing the problem of the active shooter. *FBI Law Enforcement Bulletin.* Retrieved from http://leb.fbi.gov/2013/may/addressing-the -problem-of-the-active-shooter

Shellbourne, M. (2016, December 3). Gun group releases shocking school shooting PSA. *The Hill.* Retrieved from http://thehill.com/homenews/308629-gun-group-releases -shocking-psa-on-school-shooting

Insight from Averted Mass Shootings

Eric Madfis

This chapter will explain the phenomenon of averted rampage and discuss the ways in which previous mass killing attacks have been prevented. Despite common misperceptions, mass killers do not suddenly snap out of nowhere and these events are not entirely unavoidable (Levin & Madfis, 2009), as recent empirical work on averted events proves extremely useful for future prevention efforts.

Despite the breadth of research and theorizing on mass shootings and other rampage attacks where multiple victims are targeted, far fewer studies have examined attacks that have been planned but have not come to fruition. While mass shooting incidents that result in numerous fatalities are generally explored extensively by various parties in government, academia, media, and the justice system, there is far less information about "near misses" (Verlinden, Hersen, & Thomas, 2000, p. 28). The few studies that have explored these cases (such as Daniels et al., 2007, 2010; Larkin, 2009; Madfis, 2014a, 2014b; Mongan, 2013) have almost exclusively entailed looking at averted incidents in school settings (but see Sarteschi, 2016 and White-Hamon, 2000 for notable exceptions). Though understudied, research on averted rampage attacks has clear practical significance. By learning from the instances in which rampage threats were thwarted, there exists the potential for future interventions and policies to be modeled on prior successes.

First, it is vital to note that the notion of an averted rampage leaves room for a wide range of severity between various cases wherein a plotter's genuine desire to complete a rampage attack is perhaps problematically assumed. For example, scrawling a vague threat referencing the 1999 Columbine mass shooting on a school bathroom wall and stockpiling an arsenal of weaponry next to a diary full of lengthy notes on who one wishes to kill where and in what order are both actions that could be classified as evidence of an averted rampage (both are cases described by Madfis, 2014a), though the actual level of threat present in these two scenarios varies a great deal (Reddy et al., 2001). Dewey Cornell and colleagues (2004) distinguished between "transient" threats made carelessly in jest or in a moment of anger and the more serious "substantive" threats where genuine harm is intended, and so it is important to recognize this distinction when considering the phenomenon of averted rampage. In particular, this issue presents a problem when attempting to quantify averted incidents. Eric Madfis (2014a, 2014b) located 195 cases of averted school rampage attacks that occurred in the United States from 2000 to 2009, but he did not quantify the level of threat in each of these cases beyond the 11 incidents that he explored in depth. Among those 11 cases, he classified 6 (55 percent) as very serious substantive threats, as they were death threats with actionable and detailed plans and/or the weapons necessary to carry out the threat. Likewise, Christine Sarteschi (2016) identified 57 cases of mass homicide attempts that occurred in the United States between January 1993 and June 2014, and she found that 35 threats (61 percent) in her sample were deemed to be substantive threats with significant specificity.

In one of the first studies to explore averted attacks, Jeffrey Daniels and his colleagues (2007) studied 30 potential rampage attacks at schools in 21 states that were averted between 2001 and 2004. From analyzing newspaper reporting, these authors discovered information about the details of the rampage plot, how this plan was discovered, and the steps that were taken by school and law enforcement officials to respond to the plot after it was revealed. They reported that most violent plots targeted public high schools, though some were aimed at public middle and elementary schools and one targeted a private school. In 50 percent of incidents, just one student acting by him/herself was implicated, while the other 50 percent of cases entailed two to six accused students. The most common weapons for plotters were guns, though knives, bombs, and even swords were mentioned in some news coverage of incidents. Most plotters (65 percent) expressed their deadly plans to other people, with 30 percent doing so through paper notes or email, 20 percent informing people verbally, and 15 percent admitting guilt under police questioning.

In addition, this study found rampage plots to have been uncovered in numerous ways. Students coming forward to inform police or school officials about the threat was the most common form. Often, this resulted from student plotters informing—and in some cases unsuccessfully recruiting—other student peers. However, students who had themselves been personally threatened or who had overheard various rumors also came forward. Other rampage plots were thwarted by alert school administrators whose suspicions were aroused by irregular student behavior, rumors, or even overhearing conversations of plotters. Other potential attacks were prevented by police officers alerted to rumors, notes, or emails that revealed the threat (Daniels et al., 2007).

Jeffrey Daniels and his colleagues (2010) also conducted interviews with school officials at four schools where mass shootings were prevented. These researchers found that the school personnel they interviewed believed antibullying programs to be the most significant method to avert rampages in the future. Many school officials stated that strong and supportive relationships between students and school staff encourage students to come forward when they have been exposed to information about threats, and that formal crisis plans dictating specific roles for school staff members help to prevent and respond to these potentially fatal events.

In his interviews with school administrators, counselors, security and police officers, and teachers directly involved in thwarting rampage attacks at 11 Northeastern public schools, Madfis (2014a, 2014b) similarly found that it was fellow students coming forward with knowledge about a potential school rampage that consistently preempted these nearly fatal occurrences. However, even in many of these successfully averted incidents, numerous student bystanders exposed to threats still did not come forward (Madfis, 2014a, 2014b). This finding is consistent with cases of completed rampage attacks, such as the 2005 massacre at a school in Red Lake, Minnesota, where "nearly 40 people [who] had advanced warning that [the killer] might shoot up the school" nevertheless did not alert authorities to the threat (Robertson, 2006, para. 3).

Further, Madfis found that the students who did come forward were often not close associates or confidants of the accused students, but were often acquaintances, targets, and even co-conspirators. Many of the adolescents exposed to vital information who were the closest to the students accused of plotting attacks did not in fact come forward to authorities. In nearly all cases, there were far more students who had some knowledge about their peers' rampage threat and still did not come forward than the number of students who did in fact speak up about the threat (Madfis, 2014b). This represents a longstanding aversion on the part of young people to engage in positive bystander behavior, a term employed to describe active intervention to keep dangerous or harmful events or situations from further deteriorating or escalating. From an early age, children are urged not to be "tattletales" and not to "snitch" on their peers. However, by comparing the divergent disciplinary practices at these schools, Madfis (2014a) suggests that a persistent student "code of silence," which discourages students from coming forward with vital information about the dangerous intentions of their peers, may be explained in part due to the increasingly punitive nature of school environments, zero tolerance policies, and increased security and surveillance, which increases student distrust in school officials and their fear of being punished themselves if they come forward and expose potential threats. In contrast, positive school climates where students trust teachers and school administrators and the school emphasizes restorative disciplinary practices that focus on resolving student conflicts and issues are much more likely to see students report the problematic behavior of peers (McCluskey et al., 2008; Morrison, 2007; Sherman & Strang, 2007).

In one of the only attempts to explore averted rampages outside of school settings, Sarteschi (2016) found that plots were most commonly discovered by the friends, family, and acquaintances of threateners and members of the general public (such as a gun dealer, a drugstore clerk, and other people with little connection to the plotter). However, she also found some incidents that had been identified via law enforcement and mental health professionals.

These scholars have gleaned substantial new information about foiled rampage attacks through content analyses of media and via interviews with police and school officials. In contrast, few studies have been conducted through interviews with offenders of foiled rampage plots. This gap also exists in research on completed mass murders in schools and more generally. Only a few researchers (see

Mullen, 2004 and Vossekuil, Fein, Reddy, Borum, & Modzeleski, 2002) have conducted multiple interviews with killers who have successfully carried out a rampage attack.

As the studies described above indicate, empirical research on averted and completed school rampages has begun to locate a key preventive factor present in almost every case. A landmark study of targeted school shootings discussed the importance of the concept of "leakage" that occurs when "a student intentionally or unintentionally reveals clues to feelings, thoughts, fantasies, attitudes, or intentions that may signal an impending violent act. These clues could take the form of subtle threats, boasts, innuendos, predictions, or ultimatums" (O'Toole, 2000, p. 14) (for an excerpt of her report, please see the Federal Bureau of Investigation's report entitled "The School Shooter: A Threat Assessment Perspective" in the Pivotal Documents section later in this volume). Vossekuil and colleagues (2002, p. 25) found that at least one person had some previous knowledge about the plans of offenders in 81 percent of targeted school shooting incidents, while numerous individuals were aware in 59 percent of their sample. Of those people who possessed this crucial knowledge, 93 percent were the peers of student perpetrators, such as siblings, schoolmates, or friends (Vossekuil et al., 2002, p. 25). Thus, it is crucial that people exposed to leakage make that information known to school and police officials, and accordingly, that bystander prevention programs that encourage students to be more active about reporting problematic behaviors are widely implemented (Lodge & Frydenberg, 2005; Twemlow, Fonagy, & Sacco, 2004).

Averted mass shooting attacks outside of the school setting warrant far more scholarly attention. It would be enormously valuable for future researchers to explore whether or not other forms of attempted rampage (such as family annihilators, workplace avengers, and/or disgruntled citizens) were prevented by the same or similar means as those of school attacks. It is unclear how often adult mass killers display leakage and inform other people about their homicidal thoughts and goals. While adults who have been informed about the deadly plans of a would-be mass killer may not be influenced by a student code of silence, many may still demonstrate distrust in law enforcement and/or view "snitching" as an improper violation of the "code of the street" that remains powerful in many disadvantaged communities (Anderson, 1999; Morris, 2010; Rosenfeld, Jacobs, & Wright, 2003). Thus, much insight could be gleaned by comparing the role that intervention by the confidants of adult mass killers has played in thwarting attacks to that of school massacres averted by adolescent confidants who have come forward. Similarly, though adults are not assessed and monitored systematically in the manner that schools do to their students, adults with well-developed and achievable plots to harm many people generally also engage in leakage and/or raise concerns among their friends, family members, mental health providers, coworkers, or other acquaintances (Meloy & O'Toole, 2011; Sarteschi, 2016). This suggests that there may well be substantial preventive utility in more seriously and thoroughly investigating the role of leakage and bystander behavior among mass shooting events that occur outside of the school setting.

REFERENCES

Anderson, E. (1999). *Code of the street: Decency, violence and the moral life of the inner city*. New York: Norton.

Cornell, D., Sheras, P., Kaplan, S., McConville, D., Douglass, J., Elkon, A., McKnight, L., Branson, C., & Cole, J. (2004). Guidelines for student threat assessment: Field-test findings. *School Psychology Review*, *33*(4), 527–546.

Daniels, J., Buck, I., Croxall, S., Gruber, J., Kime, P., & Govert, H. (2007). A content analysis of news reports of averted school rampages. *Journal of School Violence*, *6*(1), 83–99.

Daniels, J., Volungis, A., Pshenishny, E., Gandhi, P., Winkler, A., Cramer, D., & Bradley, M. (2010). A qualitative investigation of averted school shooting rampages. *Counseling Psychologist*, *38*(1), 69–95.

Larkin, R. W. (2009). The Columbine legacy: Rampage shootings as political acts. *American Behavioral Scientist*, *52*(9), 1309–1326.

Levin, J., & Madfis, E. (2009). Mass murder at school and cumulative strain: A sequential model. *American Behavioral Scientist*, *52*(9), 1227–1245.

Lodge, J., & Frydenberg, E. (2005). The role of peer bystanders in school bullying: Positive steps toward promoting peaceful schools. *Theory into Practice*, *44*(4), 329–336.

Madfis, E. (2014a). *The risk of school rampage: Assessing and preventing threats of school violence*. New York: Palgrave Macmillan.

Madfis, E. (2014b). Averting school rampage: Student intervention amid a persistent code of silence. *Youth Violence and Juvenile Justice*, *12*(3), 229–249.

McCluskey, G., Lloyd, G., Kane, J., Riddell, S., Stead J., & Weedon, E. (2008). Can restorative practices in schools make a difference? *Educational Review*, *60*(4), 405–417.

Meloy, J., & O'Toole, M. (2011). The concept of leakage in threat assessment. *Behavioral Sciences and the Law*, *29*(4), 513–527.

Mongan, P. (2013). *Rampage school shootings: A context analysis of media and scholarly accounts of perpetration factors associated with the phenomenon*. (Unpublished doctoral dissertation). University of Kentucky, Lexington, Kentucky.

Morris, E. (2010). "Snitches end up in ditches" and other cautionary tales. *Journal of Contemporary Criminal Justice*, *26*(3), 254–272.

Morrison, B. (2007). *Restoring safe school communities: A whole school response to bullying, violence and alienation*. Sidney: Federation Press.

Mullen, P. (2004). The autogenic (self-generated) massacre. *Behavioral Sciences and the Law*, *22*(3), 311–323.

O'Toole, M. E. (2000). *The school shooter: A threat assessment perspective*. Quantico, VA: Critical Incident Response Group, National Center for the Analysis of Violent Crime, FBI Academy. Retrieved from https://www.fbi.gov/file-repository/stats-services-publications-school-shooter-school-shooter

Reddy, M., Borum, R., Berglund, J., Vossekuil, B., Fein, R., & Modzeleski, W. (2001). Evaluating risk for targeted violence in schools: Comparing risk assessment, threat assessment, and other approaches. *Psychology in the Schools*, *38*(2), 157–172.

Robertson, T. (2006, January 30). Prosecutor: Dozens knew school shooter's plan. *Minnesota Public Radio*. Retrieved from http://news.minnesota.publicradio.org/features/2006/01/30_robertsont_redlake/?refid=0

Rosenfeld, R., Jacobs, B., & Wright, R. (2003). Snitching and the code of the street. *British Journal of Criminology*, *43*(2), 291–309.

Sarteschi, C. (2016). An examination of thwarted mass homicide plots and threateners. *Aggression and Violent Behavior, 30*(1), 88–93.

Sherman, L. W., & Strang, H. (2007). *Restorative justice: The evidence.* London: Smith Institute.

Twemlow, S., Fonagy, P., & Sacco, F. (2004). The role of the bystander in the social architecture of bullying and violence in schools and communities. *Annals of the New York Academy of Sciences, 1036,* 215–232.

Verlinden, S., Hersen, M., & Thomas, J. (2000). Risk factors in school shootings. *Clinical Psychology Review, 20*(1), 3–56.

Vossekuil, B., Fein, R., Reddy, M., Borum, R., & Modzeleski, W. (2002). *The final report and findings of the safe school initiative: Implications for the prevention of school attacks in the United States.* Washington, D.C.: U.S. Secret Service and U.S. Dept. of Education. Retrieved from https://www2.ed.gov/admins/lead/safety/preventing attacksreport.pdf

White-Hamon, L. (2000). *Mass murder and attempted mass murder: An examination of the perpetrator with an empirical analysis of typologies.* (Unpublished doctoral dissertation). California School of Professional Psychology, Fresno, CA.

Responses to Mass Shootings

Jaclyn Schildkraut, Kristina Anderson, and Michele Gay

In the aftermath of targeted mass shootings, there often is a demand for action among the public, politicians, and pundits alike in order to prevent similar events from occurring again in the future. Often, these responses are discussed in the form of what Jaclyn Schildkraut and Glenn Muschert (2013) call "the usual suspects"—guns, mental health, and violent media. Certain groups, for example, advocate for stricter gun control measures, while others argue in favor of an expansion of gun rights. Discussion of the need for an increase in resources for mental health care also comes into play, particularly when perpetrators of mass shootings, such as the shootings at Virginia Tech (2007), Tucson, Arizona (2011), and Aurora, Colorado (2012), which claimed the innocent lives of 32, 6, and 12 people, respectively, have been determined to have symptoms of depression, social anxiety, paranoia, or other mental health issues that likely may have contributed to their predisposition for violence. Even mass media—including popular movies, music, and video games—has been accused of influencing shooters in the planning and execution of their rampages (Schildkraut & Elsass, 2016; Schildkraut & Muschert, 2013).

While they are easily identifiable and understandable as potential causal factors, focusing solely on these issues can be short-sighted. Often, the acquisition of firearms by the perpetrators occurs either through theft, access through family members, or through legal means. The latter is of importance as it highlights issues of systems failure rather than a need to introduce new restrictions, which largely target law-abiding gun owners (see, generally, Kleck, 2009; Schildkraut & Hernandez, 2014). In instances where weapons are acquired through theft (e.g., the 1998 Westside Middle School gunmen in Jonesboro, Arkansas) or indirect means (such as with the Columbine shooters), any regulations passed on the sale or transfer of weapons would be irrelevant in preventing the attacks.

In the same vein, over 43 million U.S. citizens (or approximately one in every five adults) experiences some form of mental illness each year (National Alliance on Mental Illness, n.d.; Substance Abuse and Mental Health Services Administration,

2016). Millions of people also consume the various forms of media that have been suggested to influence mass shooters (Fox & DeLateur, 2014; Schildkraut & Elsass, 2016). In both cases, however, the vast majority of these individuals never engage in *any* violent episodes, including a mass shooting. Thus, the age-old adage of "correlation does not equal causation" is particularly applicable.

Mass shootings are a complex and multifaceted problem, and attempting to focus on just one or a few potentially related issues still fails to adequately address the issue. Furthermore, the responses outlined to this point, as well as the flurry of legislation that often accompanies mass shootings (Schildkraut & Hernandez, 2014; Soraghan, 2000), emphasize a reactive strategy to addressing these events. In order to prevent mass shootings—or mitigate the loss of life and injury in the event that one occurs—a more sustained proactive approach emphasizing training and education is needed.

LESSONS FROM TRAGEDY: IDENTIFYING OPPORTUNITIES FOR IMPROVEMENT

A number of best practices that currently are in use across the country are informed by lessons learned in the tragic aftermath of mass shootings. The need for school- and community-based threat assessment models, for example, was recommended following the 1999 Columbine shootings, when it was determined that the perpetrators had spent a considerable amount of time planning their attack (O'Toole, 2000; Vossekuil, Fein, Reddy, Borum, & Modzeleski, 2002). While threat assessment and management procedures are beneficial in identifying and assessing the potential of an individual to commit harm against self or others, a pillar of a team's success relies upon the community willingness to openly communicate safety concerns and information. Through various means and investigatory practices, the process to determine if an individual poses a threat is accomplished through a team approach that seeks to evaluate all knowable information, often through sources internal to a community. As a small percentage of attacks are committed by perpetrators with no prior ties to an organization or institution, which may never be discussed or knowable through a threat management process, emergency response and preparedness protocols are critical. When it comes to a would-be mass shooter, there also is the opportunity for overprediction, meaning that others may share similar traits but never be capable of planning nor executing an attack. As such, a related shift in safety protocols emphasizes planning and preparedness.

Active shooter and related lockdown/lockout drills are currently conducted at schools and workplaces across the nation. While there are different versions of these programs, the general premise behind each is to teach individuals what to do and how to respond in the event of an active shooter. Depending on which model is used, the mode of teaching instruction can vary from instructional PowerPoint presentations to interactive, simulation-based exercises. Some versions also may combine different instructional modalities into a single training package. It is important to note that there is no "one size fits all" program, and individuals and organizations must choose that which best fits their particular needs.

Having a plan in place, however, is not wholly sufficient in and of itself. In order to be effective, such drills must be conducted routinely to identify areas of improvement needed. Safe and Sound Schools (2017a), an organization developed after the 2012 Sandy Hook Elementary School shooting, advocates for a "Straight 'A' model," one in which safety practices exist on a continuum, rather than a single point in time (see also Morris, 2014). In this design, drills and other related protocols are examined in three phases: assess, act, and audit.

Assess refers to determining a safety plan that is best tailored to the organization and individuals at hand, as such solutions are not "one size fits all." Different location types (e.g., schools versus workplaces or malls) will have different needs that need to be considered when determining the best model to be utilized. Once a plan is developed, it must be *acted* upon, meaning that it is put into practice at the organization, often through the sharing of educational information about the procedures. Finally, these protocols continually must be *audited*, or tested and revised as needed to ensure compatibility with the needs of the organizations and individuals. The auditing process often is accomplished by conducting active shooter or lockdown/lockout drills, which allows the organization to identify weaknesses or gaps in their protocols and adjust procedures as needed. This three-phase process is not linear; instead, it continues through a cycle and is continually improved upon and amended in each wave (Greenberg, 2007).

When emergency plans are practiced, it is imperative that all potential stakeholders—including (but not necessarily limited to) students (if a school), employees, and law enforcement and other first responders—be involved (see, generally, Koshka Foundation, n.d.). In the event of an actual shooting, individuals from these various sectors will be involved in some manner; thus, coordinating their efforts in advance can improve the implementation of the emergency response plan and help to minimize the loss of life (Fox & Savage, 2009; Greenberg, 2007; Morris, 2014). Further, as most events are over before law enforcement arrives on scene (Blair, Nichols, Burns, & Curnett, 2013), it is particularly important to prepare individuals within the organization to respond in a number of different ways, including how to respond during a shooting and in the minutes after (e.g., first aid) (Greenberg, 2007; Morris, 2014).

Even in cases where such drills are conducted routinely, where organizations are considered to be models of doing everything right, vulnerabilities still can present themselves. The shooting at Sandy Hook is one such event. Though the school routinely practiced lockdown drills (Lupkin, 2012; McCormack, 2012), other deficiencies—such as the ease of access through the building's entryway and the inability for doors to be secured quickly—proved to be areas in need of improvement (Safe and Sound Schools, 2017b). While these concerns were addressed in the construction of the new school (Altimari, 2016; Sisson, 2016), many other schools across the nation share similar vulnerabilities but are not rebuilt to meet these updated needs.

In response, a flurry of consumer products touted as solutions has entered the market. Companies have introduced bullet-resistant products, including whiteboards, security blankets, backpacks, and building materials such as glass. Other products introduced include various designs for lockdown or lockout systems, panic buttons, and gunfire detection systems (Schildkraut & Elsass, 2016). Yet despite the perceived potential effectiveness of these objects, their actual ability to affect the outcome of a mass shooting remains untested; thus, their touted capabilities rely on people's fear of such events and willingness to buy into the solution's performance.

Conversely, research has found that during mass shootings, perpetrators have never been able to break secured door hardware (Blair et al., 2013). In fact, both the Columbine Review Commission (2001) and Sandy Hook Advisory Commission (2015) reports identified that individuals who were able to secure their locations were able to survive their respective attacks (for additional recommendations from each report, please see the Pivotal Documents section later in the volume). Due to building regulations and ADA compliance, such as those related to exit doors in public places or fire codes, however, certain lock types cannot be outfitted to secure a location (Schildkraut & Elsass, 2016; Schneider, 2010b; see also Partner Alliance for Safer Schools, n.d.). Accordingly, new solutions aimed at securing doors quickly (and cost-effectively) also have entered the consumer market (Schildkraut & Elsass, 2016). One example of this is the Sleeve, a device that was designed to slide over the door's control arm joint, requiring just a few seconds to install in place. Able to withstand over 550 pounds of force due to its design and made of carbon steel material, the Sleeve has a greater potential to effectively keep a shooter out of a location (Reinwald, 2014). Still, the use of such devices must be incorporated into the planning and practicing of active shooter response protocols, as even the simplest of solutions might be misused in times of crisis.

Finally, in the event of a mass shooting, people within a particular location must be made aware of the situation and provided with additional information about how to respond. This commonly is accomplished through the use of a mass emergency notification system, which can be utilized by organizations not only for information about mass shootings, but other emergencies as well (e.g., weather). Though email and text messages often are the most common way in which notifications are transmitted, the potential for technological problems to arise in times of crisis (such as occurred during the 2007 mass shooting attack at Virginia Tech) must be considered. Organizations are encouraged to adopt multimodal systems with other forms of communication available to serve as backup in case primary methods of communicating during emergencies fails (Mastrodicasa, 2008; Schneider, 2010a). Further, like other response protocols related to mass shootings, people must not only be made aware of the technology, but the use of these systems also must be practiced so that people know what to expect in the event of their employment during an emergency situation (Elsass, McKenna, & Schildkraut, 2016; Schildkraut, McKenna, & Elsass, 2017).

MOVING PREVENTION AND RESPONSES FORWARD

Most of the strategies discussed here have developed out of mass shooting incidents in schools. While such solutions can be applicable to other types of locations, such as offices, malls, movie theaters, restaurants, or places of worship, each has its own specific set of challenges. Schools, for example, often maintain tight control over who can enter the building and at what time, whereas office buildings may have a more open-door, come-and-go policy that makes it difficult to control access. Locations such as malls and similar establishments can have upwards of 10,000 individuals at a location at one time, with hundreds of exits and separate stores that would require securing, making the issue of lockdowns all the more challenging. Even within the education sector alone, the challenges are fundamentally different in important respects for K–12 schools and colleges and universities. The former, for example, often are housed in a single building, whereas the latter may be spread out over multiple buildings and more physical space (Fox & Savage, 2009). Similarly, there are developmental and capability differences within and between K–12 students and those enrolled in colleges and universities. In sum, while all organizations can (and should) have an emergency response plan, each must be tailored to the organization's specific goals and needs.

Further, one of the biggest impediments to safety as it relates to a mass shooting is complacency. People often say, "It could never happen here" or "Not in my community." In reality, however, the communities in which mass shootings have taken place are so varied that nearly every type of setting is encompassed. These perceptions of mass shootings as someone else's problem can provide a false sense of security. While mass shootings remain statistically rare events (Fox & DeLateur, 2014; Fox & Savage, 2009; Schildkraut & Elsass, 2016), schools, businesses, and individuals must have a plan in place in the event that such a crisis develops.

The lessons learned from previous mass shootings highlight several important takeaways. First, emergency preparedness is a task that requires all stakeholders to be active participants in safety preparations by providing ongoing, audience-appropriate training on school preparedness and workplace violence prevention (Koshka Foundation, n.d.). Second, such plans must consistently be assessed, practiced, and revised to ensure that they meet the needs of all involved (Safe and Sound Schools, 2017a). Finally, any preparedness plan must include solutions and strategies that are based upon empirical research rather than emotion, fear, and a knee-jerk reaction to another event (Schildkraut & Elsass 2016; Schildkraut & Hernandez, 2014).

REFERENCES

Altimari, D. (2016, July 31). A sparkling new Sandy Hook school arrives, with high-tech features and security "second to none." *Los Angeles Times*. Retrieved from http://www.latimes.com/nation/la-na-new-sandy-hook-school-20160730-snap-story.html

Blair, J. P., Nichols, T., Burns, D., & Curnett, J. (2013). *Active shooter events and response*. Boca Raton, FL: CRC Press.

Columbine Review Commission. (2001). *The report of Governor Bill Owens' Columbine Review Commission*. Denver: State of Colorado. Retrieved from http://trac.state.co.us/Documents/Reports%20and%20Publications/Columbine_2001_Governor_Review_Commission.pdf

Elsass, H. J., McKenna, J. M., & Schildkraut, J. (2016). Rethinking crisis communications on campus: An evaluation of faculty and staff perceptions about emergency notification systems. *Journal of Homeland Security and Emergency Management, 13*(3), 329–349.

Fox, J. A., & DeLateur, M. J. (2014). Mass shootings in America: Moving beyond Newtown. *Homicide Studies, 18*(1), 125–145.

Fox, J. A., & Savage, J. (2009). Mass murder goes to college: An examination of changes on college campuses following Virginia Tech. *American Behavioral Scientist, 52*(10), 1465–1485.

Greenberg, S. F. (2007). Active shooters on college campuses: Conflicting advice, roles of the individual and first responder, and the need to maintain perspective. *Disaster Medicine and Public Health Preparedness, 1*(1), S57–S61.

Kleck, G. (2009). Mass shootings in schools: The worst possible case for gun control. *American Behavioral Scientist, 52*(10), 1447–1464.

Koshka Foundation. (n.d.). *About us.* Retrieved from http://koshkafoundation.org/about-us/

Lupkin, S. (2012, December 16). School safety experts disagree on lock down procedures after Newtown shooting. *ABC News.* Retrieved from http://abcnews.go.com/US/school-safety-experts-disagree-lockdown-procedures-newtown-shooting/story?id=17978485

Mastrodicasa, J. (2008). Technology use in campus crisis. *New Directions for Student Services, 2008*(124), 37–53.

McCormack, D. (2012, December 14). Murdered principal's haunting pictures of Sandy Hook children practicing their evacuation drill—just days before massacre. *Daily Mail.* Retrieved from http://www.dailymail.co.uk/news/article-2248426/Connecticut-massacre-Heart-breaking-pictures-Sandy-Hook-Elementary-School-just-days-shooting.html

Morris, L. (2014). Three steps to safety: Developing procedures for active shooters. *Journal of Business Continuity & Emergency Planning, 7*(3), 238–244.

National Alliance on Mental Illness. (n.d.). *Mental health by the numbers.* Retrieved from https://www.nami.org/Learn-More/Mental-Health-By-the-Numbers

O'Toole, M. E. (2000). *The school shooter: A threat assessment perspective.* Quantico, VA: Critical Incident Response Group, FBI Academy, National Center for the Analysis of Violent Crime. Retrieved from https://www.fbi.gov/file-repository/stats-services-publications-school-shooter-school-shooter

Partner Alliance for Safer Schools. (n.d.). *Toolkits.* Retrieved from http://passk12.org/toolkits/

Reinwald, C. (2014, June 10). Muscatine teachers' invention could save your child's life. *WQAD 8.* Retrieved from http://wqad.com/2014/06/10/muscatine-teachers-invention-could-save-your-childs-life/

Safe and Sound Schools. (2017a). *The straight "A" safety improvement model.* Retrieved from https://www.safeandsoundschools.org/resources/straight-a-safety-improvement/

Safe and Sound Schools. (2017b). *Our story.* Retrieved from https://www.safeandsoundschools.org/about-us/our-story/

Sandy Hook Advisory Commission. (2015). *Final report of the Sandy Hook Advisory Committee.* Hartford, CT: Sandy Hook Advisory Committee. Retrieved from http://www.shac.ct.gov/SHAC_Final_Report_3-6-2015.pdf

Schildkraut, J., & Elsass, H. J. (2016). *Mass shootings: Media, myths, and realities.* Santa Barbara, CA: Praeger Books.

Schildkraut, J., & Hernandez, T. C. (2014). Laws that bit the bullet: A review of legislative responses to school shootings. *American Journal of Criminal Justice, 39*(2), 358–374.

Schildkraut, J., McKenna, J. M., & Elsass, H. J. (2017). Understanding crisis communications: Examining students' perceptions about campus notification systems. *Security Journal, 30*(2), 605–620.

Schildkraut, J., & Muschert, G. W. (2013). Violent media, guns, and mental illness: The three ring circus of causal factors for school massacres, as related in media discourse. *Fast Capitalism, 10*(1). Retrieved from http://www.uta.edu/huma/agger /fastcapitalism/10_1/schildkraut10_1.html

Schneider, T. (2010a). Mass notification for higher education. *National Clearinghouse for Educational Facilities*. Retrieved from http://files.eric.ed.gov/fulltext/ED508002 .pdf

Schneider, T. (2010b). School securities technologies. *National Clearinghouse for Educational Facilities*. Retrieved from http://files.eric.ed.gov/fulltext/ED507917.pdf

Sisson, P. (2016, August 28). New Sandy Hook Elementary School design finds safety, security in openness. *Curbed*. Retrieved from https://www.curbed.com/2016 /8/1/12341054/sandy-hook-elementary-school-design-security-safety

Soraghan, M. (2000). Colorado after Columbine: The gun debate. *State Legislatures, 26*(6), 14–21.

Substance Abuse and Mental Health Services Administration. (2016). *Key substance abuse use and mental health indicators in the United States: Results from the 2015 national survey on drug use and health*. Rockville, MD: Substance Abuse and Mental Health Services Administration. Retrieved from https://www.samhsa.gov/data /sites/default/files/NSDUH-FFR1-2015/NSDUH-FFR1-2015/NSDUH-FFR1 -2015.pdf

Vossekuil, B., Fein, R.A., Reddy, M., Borum, R., & Modzeleski, W. (2002). *The final report and findings of the Safe School Initiative: Implications for the prevention of school attacks in the United States*. Washington, D.C.: United States Secret Service and United States Department of Education. Retrieved from https://www2.ed.gov /admins/lead/safety/preventingattacksreport.pdf

Encyclopedia of Mass Shooting Events, 1966–2016

1960s

August 1, 1966: University of Texas, Austin, TX

After killing his mother and wife in their shared home, 25-year-old architectural engineering student Charles Whitman arrived at the main building of the University of Texas at Austin. The former Marine sharpshooter was armed with seven different firearms (primarily shotguns and rifles), a machete, three knives, and over 700 rounds of ammunition he brought in a footlocker along with other provisions, such as food, toiletries, and a radio. As he made his way up to the observation deck of the building, more commonly known as the Tower, he encountered several people, including the observation deck's receptionist. The gunman killed three and injured two others before continuing up to the deck.

Once he made his way to the observation deck approximately 230 feet above street level, the shooter began firing at people on the ground. Over the next 96 minutes, the gunman continued his shooting spree, striking people as far away as 500 yards (1,500 feet). The first responding policeman was shot and killed by the sniper; additional officers soon arrived on scene and attempted to engage the shooter from the ground. Civilians also fired up at the shooter alongside the police, forcing him to stay low on the deck and fire through the storm drains.

As people on the ground engaged the shooter, two officers and a former Air Force tail gunner made their way to the building through the school's underground tunnels and then up to the observation deck, stopping to check on the injured along the way. The two police officers made entry to the deck and rounded the corner. The first officer, Ray Martinez, fired at the shooter but missed. The other officer, Houston McCoy, hit the shooter twice with bullets from his shotgun; Martinez then took the weapon and fired the final shot at point-blank range, ending the rampage. A total of 15 people had been killed (excluding the shooter's family) and an additional 31 suffered nonfatal injuries.

During the investigation following the shooting, police found a suicide note at the shooter's home that stated he had killed his wife and mother to spare them the humiliation of his impending act. Prior to the shooting, the gunman also had sought professional help for violent fantasies, including thoughts of shooting people from the tower. During the autopsy of the shooter (which he had requested in his suicide note), a small tumor was found at the base of his brain. Though initially considered to have no effect on the shooter, later reports suggested that the location of the tumor may have pressed on the shooter's amygdala, triggering anxiety or a flight-or-fight response that led to the rampage.

The Second Wave of Mass Murder in the United States

The shooting at the University of Texas (UT) marks an important shift in the broader discussion of mass murder in the United States. Researchers such as Grant Duwe (Minnesota Department of Corrections) propose that there are actually two significant yet distinct waves of mass murder. The first occurred in the 1920s and 1930s, when farmers and others in industrial-type sectors struggled during the Great Depression. Unable to take care of their families, many resorted to familicides—that is, they killed their entire family rather than not being able to provide for them. Many times, these individuals also committed suicide as part of their act. The second wave of mass murder, beginning with the UT shooting, marks a shift to more public episodes of mass killing. In fact, the UT shooting was the first of its kind to have footage of the attack aired on television for viewers to get a first-hand look at the events of August 1, 1966.

October 5, 1966: Grand Rapids High School, Grand Rapids, MN

Armed with a pistol and hunting knife, 15-year-old David Black entered Grand Rapids High School. He first approached a group of students inside the school, opening fire and shooting one of his classmates in the chest. When the school's principal arrived, the gunman shot him in the abdomen before fleeing the scene of the crime. Police found the gunman a few streets away from the school, and both sides exchanged fire before he ultimately surrendered and was taken into custody. The principal died eight days later at the local hospital, while the student survived his injuries. The shooter, set to be tried as an adult, pleaded guilty to third-degree murder and aggravated assault just prior to trial and was sentenced to a maximum of 25 years in a Minnesota prison. He was released in 1976, though he was returned to prison just four months later after being arrested for criminal sexual conduct. He was released on that charge in 1980.

November 12, 1966: Rose-Mar College of Beauty, Mesa, AZ

Early in the morning, 18-year-old Robert Benjamin Smith walked into the Rose-Mar College of Beauty with a bag filled with a pistol, plastic sandwich bags, nylon cord, tape, and a hunting knife. He ordered the five women and two children in the room to go to the back room and lie down in a circle. When they complied, he opened fire at them. Four of the women and one of the children were killed, while the other two were wounded but survived. Once having finished, the shooter walked out of the building and freely surrendered to police, who arrived on the scene. During the investigation, the shooter stated he did it to make a name for himself. He was tried and found guilty on five counts of first-degree murder and was sentenced to death. Four years after the trial, the shooter was granted another hearing due to testimony being unreliable in the initial trial. He subsequently pleaded guilty and was sentenced to life in prison and incarcerated at the Red Rock Correctional Center in Eloy, AZ, where he currently remains.

October 23, 1967: Hammermill Paper Company, Lock Haven, PA

Armed with two pistols, 40-year-old Leo Held entered the Hammermill Paper Company plant, where he worked, and opened fire on his coworkers. Five were killed, and four others were injured in the attack. Several minutes after he began shooting, the gunman left the building and drove to the Lock Haven Airport, where he shot and wounded one of his neighbors. He then drove to his neighborhood, where he broke into the house of one of his neighbors and shot the couple. The husband was killed, while his wife was wounded but survived her injuries. The shooter then ran from the home but was followed by police. A shootout began and the gunman was wounded; he died later at a nearby hospital.

May 22, 1968: Drew Junior High School, Miami, FL

Following being disciplined by school officials, 15-year-old Ernest Lee Grissom left the Drew Junior High School principal's office and returned a few minutes later with a firearm. He opened fire on the room of administrators, wounding one before running into the hallway and shooting at a group of students, hitting one of them. He then ran home, where he was later apprehended by police. The teacher and student who were shot both survived their injuries. The shooter was tried and subsequently found guilty of second-degree murder and aggravated assault. He was sentenced to 20 years of incarceration. The shooter later appealed the conviction and sentence, citing a due process violation related to his competency hearing, but the trial court's actions were reaffirmed on appeal.

January 17, 1969: University of California, Los Angeles, CA

As a meeting regarding a black studies program concluded, a man entered the UCLA classroom in which the meeting was taking place and opened fire. Two students, who were members of the Black Panther Party, were killed. The suspected shooter, a 21-year-old black man named Claude Hubert, then fled the scene, but never was apprehended. Two other men were convicted of conspiracy to commit murder related to the incident and were sentenced to life in prison; they later escaped from their facility in 1974. One of the men surrendered after fleeing to Suriname, where he hid for 20 years; the other man never was found.

1970s

November 11, 1971: Gonzaga University, Spokane, WA

Armed with a rifle, a sledgehammer, and a pickax, 21-year-old Larry Harmon walked into the St. Aloysius Roman Catholic Church, located on the Gonzaga University campus. He first shot and killed a custodian who was working, and then proceeded to use the sledgehammer to break many of the church statues, windows, and a railing. The shooter then moved outside and opened fire on anyone passing by, wounding four others. Police arrived on the scene and shot the gunman, killing him.

June 21, 1972: Key Personnel, Inc., Cherry Hill, NJ

After being denied a job with Key Personnel, 33-year-old Edwin James Grace entered the heritage building where the Key Personnel office was located armed with two rifles. He began to shoot at employees in one office before moving on to another office. Six were killed, while six others were wounded but survived. The shooter then made his way down to the basement of the building where he shot himself. He was found by police and taken to the Cherry Hill Medical Center, later dying as a result of his injuries.

January 17, 1974: Barton Elementary School, Chicago, IL

Following expulsion from school, 14-year-old Steven Guy entered the Barton Elementary School armed with a pistol and a revolver, both of which he had stolen from his father, a police officer. He first encountered the assistant principal and the school's security guard, shooting them when they questioned him. The shooter then made his way to the principal's office, where he shot and killed the school's principal before leaving to search for a former teacher. While fleeing the scene, the teacher fell down a flight of stairs, sustaining minor injuries. The shooter returned to the principal's office, where he attempted to shoot another teacher, but was tackled and disarmed when his guns jammed. Both the assistant principal and security guard survived their injuries. The shooter was charged with murder, but found not guilty by reason of insanity. As a result, he was committed to the Illinois Department of Mental Health and Developmental Disabilities.

December 30, 1974: Olean High School, Olean, NY

While the school was closed for winter break, 18-year-old Anthony Barbaro drove to Olean High School armed with three rifles and entered through a side door of the building. He first made his way to the third floor of the building, where he broke into one of the classrooms, set off a smoke bomb in the hall, and shut the door behind him. When a school custodian approached the room to gain access, the gunman shot and killed him. The shooter then moved to the window and opened fire on people passing by the school, killing 2 people and wounding 11 others. Police arrived and made their way up to the third floor, where the shooter had tied the door shut, and forced their way inside. The shooter was taken into custody and charged with second-degree murder and first-degree assault. He later committed suicide while awaiting trial.

February 24, 1975: St. James Regional Grammar School, Penns Grove, NJ

Early in the morning, 24-year-old David Gary entered the St. James Regional Grammar School, carrying a shotgun. He entered one of the classrooms and began shooting at the teacher in the room. Upon hearing the gunfire, the school principal approached the room to investigate, where he met the shooter. The principal was shot before the shooter fled from the building. The shooter was found by police a few streets from the school and arrested. The principal ultimately died, while the teacher was treated and survived. The shooter was convicted of murder and assault, and sentenced to life in prison, where he died in 2014.

September 11, 1975: U.S. Grant High School, Oklahoma City, OK

James Briggs, a 15-year-old student, entered U.S. Grant High School armed with a firearm. After getting into a fight with another student, the shooter retrieved his gun and opened fire. One student was killed and another was wounded in the attack. The shooter was convicted of first-degree man-slaughter by an Oklahoma County juvenile court jury and was institutionalized until his 18th birthday.

July 12, 1976: California State University, Fullerton, CA

Armed with a semiautomatic rifle, 37-year-old Edward Charles Allaway arrived at work at the library on the California State University campus in Fullerton and opened fire. Seven people were killed and two others injured before the shooter left the building and drove to his ex-wife's place of work, where he called police and surrendered. Upon investigation, witnesses noted that during the shooting, the gunman had been shouting about all of them messing around with his wife. He was charged with murder, but found not guilty by reason of insanity. He was placed in Patton State Hospital, where he currently remains due to denial of several petitions for release.

July 27, 1976: Marvin Glass and Associates, Chicago, IL

Albert Keller, a 33-year-old employee of Marvin Glass and Associates, entered his workplace with a firearm and opened fire on his coworkers. Three were killed, and two others were seri-ously injured but survived. The gunman then shot and killed himself.

February 14, 1977: Neptune Worldwide Moving Company, New Rochelle, NY

Following a two-week suspension from work, 34-year-old Frederick Cowan returned to his employer armed with an automatic rifle and four handguns. He then opened fire with the rifle. Four people were killed and two wounded inside the building as the shooter searched for his supervisor. When the first police officer arrived on the scene, he was shot and killed by the gun-man. As more police arrived, the shooter shot at them from a second-story window, wounding three. Throughout the day, the gunman held hostages in the building, letting them leave one by one. Several hours after the shooting had begun, the shooter went to the second floor of the building and committed suicide. Four of the five who were wounded survived their injuries; one of the workers who had been wounded inside the building, however, died several weeks later at a nearby hospital.

February 22, 1978: Everett High School, Lansing, MI

Armed with a pistol, 15-year-old Roger Needham arrived at Everett High School and opened fire following an altercation. Two students were shot, one fatally, before the shooter handed the gun over to a teacher. The shooter was arrested, and the subsequent investigation revealed that he had a considerable fascination with Adolf Hitler and Nazi culture. The shooter was charged with first-degree murder, to which he pleaded no contest. He spent four years in a secure juvenile detention facility, where he had been ordered to undergo psychiatric treatment, before being released. He has since received several degrees, including his PhD in mathematics, and went on to teach at City College of New York before working in the computer industry, having never reoffended.

January 29, 1979: Grover Cleveland Elementary School, San Diego, CA

Early on a Monday morning, 16-year-old Brenda Spencer opened fire on Cleveland Elementary School, which was located across the street from her home. The school's principal and a custodian both were killed in the attack, and eight students were wounded. When a police officer arrived, she also shot and wounded him. Another officer and a security guard from a neighboring high school drove a garbage truck in front of the school to block the school from the shooter's sight, and they were able to get inside her home and arrest her. When asked why she did it, the shooter said that she did not like Mondays and that the shooting livened up the day. Tried as an adult, she pleaded guilty to two counts of first-degree murder, as well as assault with a deadly weapon, and was sentenced to 25 years to life in prison. She remains incarcerated at the California Institution for Women in Chino, California, and will be eligible for parole again in 2019, having already been denied on four separate incidents.

October 6, 1979: University of South Carolina, Columbia, SC

Armed with a pistol, 19-year-old student Mark Houston walked into a fraternity party during homecoming weekend on the University of South Carolina campus and opened fire, killing one person and wounding four others. The shooter then moved outside and shot two students passing by before fleeing. He was found at Allen University and freely surrendered after speaking with his parents. Of the two students shot outside the fraternity house, one died the next morning while the other survived. The shooter pleaded guilty to murder and was given two life sentences. In 1994, he killed another inmate with a homemade knife while serving his sentence. He currently remains in prison at the McCormick Correctional Institution in McCormick, South Carolina, and is ineligible for parole.

1980s

March 19, 1982: Valley High School, Las Vegas, NV

Following an argument with a teacher, 17-year-old Patrick Lizotte left Valley High School that morning and returned shortly after, armed with a pistol. He made his way to his teacher's classroom and shot him. The teacher later died at the hospital. The gunman then ran from the building, shooting at and wounding two students (both of whom survived) as he fled. Police caught him several blocks from the school and shot him when he pulled out his weapon. He was wounded but survived, and later was found guilty of murder and attempted murder. Initially, the shooter was sentenced to life in prison without the possibility of parole; however, following a change in Nevada law, he became eligible for parole in 2015. He was granted release on March 7, 2017.

August 9, 1982: Multiple Locations, Grand Prairie, TX

After encountering problems with his supervisors at Western Transfer Company, 49-year-old John Parish arrived at work early in the morning, armed with two pistols and a rifle. He first shot his supervisor and then two other workers, all three of whom died. The shooter then left the building and stole a truck before driving to another Western Transfer office a few blocks away. There, he opened fire again, shooting three others. One person died of his injuries, while the other two were injured but later recovered. The gunman then made his way to the Jewel-T discount store, which Western Transfer contracted with. He shot three more people, two of whom died from their injuries. In a final act, the shooter stole a tractor trailer and crashed it into a police barricade, continuing to exchange gunfire with the officers as he climbed from the vehicle. He was hit several times as he made his way inside a nearby building, where he later was found to have died from his wounds.

August 20, 1982: Bob Moore's Welding and Machine Service Inc., Miami, FL

Following a dispute with workers at Bob Moore's Welding and Machine Service, 51-year-old Carl Brown armed himself with a shotgun and returned to the business the next day. He first opened fire on those inside the building, killing six. The shooter then moved outside, where he shot five more individuals, killing two of them. He then rode away from the scene of the crime on his bicycle. A witness to the shooting stopped a car driving by, and both men pursued the gunman in the vehicle. When the shooter turned the gun toward the vehicle, the men ran him over with the car. The shooter died later from his injuries.

September 25, 1982: Multiple Locations, Wilkes-Barre, PA

Early in the morning, 40-year-old George Banks opened fire in his own home with a rifle, shooting and killing eight people. The shooter then made his way outside, shooting two neighbors. One of the men was killed, while the other was wounded but survived. The shooter then drove to an ex-girlfriend's home in Jenkins Township and entered the mobile home, where he shot and killed four more individuals. He then fled the scene of the crime, arriving at his mother's home the next day. She got in contact with the police, and the shooter then fled to an abandoned home nearby, where police later found him. After a standoff with police, the shooter surrendered and was taken into custody. Seven of the 14 victims were children, 5 of whom were his own. He was found guilty on 12 counts of first-degree murder and 1 count of third-degree murder and was sentenced to death. In 2011, the shooter was ruled incompetent to aid his counsel in petitioning for a pardon and was therefore not able to be executed. He currently remains on death row at SCI Graterford in Pennsylvania.

January 20, 1983: Parkway South Junior High, Manchester, MO

David Lawler, a 14-year-old student, arrived at Parkway South Junior High School armed with two pistols. After an altercation with another student, the shooter pulled out one of his firearms and shot two students. He then committed suicide. One of the students later died at the hospital, while the other was in critical condition but survived.

August 19, 1983: Johnston Post Office, Johnston, SC

Perry Smith, who had resigned from the Johnston Post Office several months prior, entered the building early in the morning armed with a shotgun and threatened to open fire. When workers began to run from the building, the 56-year-old gunman followed and began to shoot at those fleeing. He shot two workers in the parking lot, wounding both. He then chased the postmaster back inside the building, where he shot and killed him. The shooter then went back outside, where he encountered a police officer. He shot and wounded the officer, who then proceeded to fire back at him. The shooter then surrendered and was taken into custody without further incident. Though initially deemed incompetent to stand trial, the shooter was later found fit for trial after receiving treatment in a state mental facility. His conviction at his first trial was reversed and remanded and the second trial resulted in a mistrial. At a third trial, however, he was found guilty of murder and assault and battery with intent to kill and sentenced to life in prison plus 10 years.

December 2, 1983: Anniston Post Office, Anniston, AL

Following a dispute with management at the Anniston Post Office, 53-year-old postal worker James Howard Brooks arrived at his place of employment armed with a shotgun. He shot and killed the Anniston postmaster and wounded a superintendent. He was arrested at the post office and subsequently charged with first-degree murder and first-degree assault. Though his first hearing ended in a mistrial, the federal government retried and convicted the shooter. He was sentenced to life in prison without the possibility of parole, the mandatory punishment for the homicide, plus the maximum of 10 years for the assault. He was incarcerated in a federal penitentiary until his death in 2012.

February 24, 1984: 49th Street Elementary School, Los Angeles, CA

Tyrone Mitchell, a 28-year-old who was under the influence of drugs at the time of the attack, opened fire from his home on a schoolyard located directly across the street. He killed 2 people and wounded 12 others. The gunman remained barricaded in his home after the shooting. Several hours later, police entered his home to find that he had committed suicide.

June 29, 1984: Ianni's Restaurant and Club, Dallas, TX

After a woman denied his advances, 39-year-old Abdelkrim Belachheb left Ianni's Club and retrieved his pistol from his vehicle. He went back inside and opened fire, killing six individuals and wounding one other. The shooter then fled the scene of the crime. Police found him at a friend's home a few hours later and arrested him. He was found guilty of murder and sentenced to life in prison; he currently is incarcerated at the Clements Unit in Potter County, Texas.

July 18, 1984: McDonald's Restaurant, San Ysidro, CA

After parking his vehicle in the parking lot of a San Diego–area McDonald's near his apartment, 41-year-old James Huberty entered the restaurant armed with a semiautomatic pistol, a submachine gun, and a shotgun, as well as hundreds of rounds of ammunition for each weapon. Over the next 78 minutes, the shooter methodically made his way through the restaurant, shooting many of the 45 patrons and employees who were inside; a number of individuals were struck multiple times by the gunfire.

Unaware of what was taking place at the restaurant, several individuals approached the scene. Three 11-year-old boys who had ridden their bikes to the McDonald's were shot multiple times when they froze; two died shortly thereafter. An elderly couple who arrived moments later also were shot; the wife was killed after being struck multiple times, though the husband survived. Approximately 15 minutes into the attack, a young family approached the restaurant. The shooter approached their car and continued firing, wounding all three, including a four-month-old infant.

The shooter then returned inside the restaurant, pausing to change the radio station, before resuming his shooting. He first searched the kitchen area, discovering several employees attempting to hide, and fired his guns at them. He then returned to the main dining area, where he continued shooting. Finding several victims still alive, the gunman fired several more shots, killing them.

At approximately 5:17 p.m., a SWAT sniper who had positioned himself atop the post office across from the restaurant shot and killed the gunman. Investigators later determined that the gunman had fired 245 rounds over the course of the rampage. A total of 21 people were killed and 19 others injured in the attack. Ten days after the shooting, the restaurant was demolished; a portion of the land later was used for a permanent memorial to the victims. The San Ysidro McDonald's shooting was the deadliest mass shooting until the 1991 Luby's Cafeteria shooting.

January 21, 1985: Goddard Junior High School, Goddard, KS

James Alan Kearbey, a 14-year-old student, entered Goddard Junior High School armed with a rifle and a pistol and headed toward the school cafeteria. On the way there, he passed by the teachers' lounge and the principal's office. The shooter turned and opened fire, shooting the principal and a teacher who had come to question him before continuing down the hall. He then shot at another teacher and a student who had approached as he continued walking. The school's principal died later at a nearby hospital, while the two teachers and the student survived. The shooter then ran from the school and was arrested walking through a field a few miles away. He was found guilty of murder and aggravated assault, but was charged as a juvenile and was released in 1991. He was convicted in 2002 on a firearms charge, but was released again in 2003.

March 6, 1985: Atlanta Post Office, Atlanta, GA

Steven W. Brownlee, a 30-year-old employee, entered the Atlanta Post Office armed with a handgun. He first made his way to the mail-sorting area of the office and began firing at his coworkers. Two were killed and one was wounded. One of the shooter's coworkers grabbed the gun from him and began to get people out of the building as they waited for police. The shooter was arrested and charged with murder and aggravated assault. At the trial, he was found not guilty by reason of insanity and was remanded to the Georgia Regional Hospital.

November 26, 1985: Spanaway Junior High School, Spanaway, WA

Following a breakup with her boyfriend, 14-year-old Heather Smith arrived at Spanaway Junior High School armed with a rifle and immediately began to search for her ex-boyfriend. After convincing another classmate to retrieve the ex-boyfriend, he and a friend exited the school gym. At that point the shooter shot and killed both of them. She then left the school but returned later, where she was confronted by police. They attempted to get her to drop her weapon, but she shot herself and died the next day at the local hospital.

December 10, 1985: Portland Junior High School, Portland, CT

During a conversation with the school principal, 13-year-old Floyd Warmsley became upset and left the office. He returned shortly after, armed with a semiautomatic pistol belonging to his father. After threatening everyone in the room, he began shooting, wounding the principal and a secretary before leaving the office. The shooter then made his way to the second floor, where he shot and killed the school custodian and then took another student hostage. He surrendered shortly after the father and aunt of the hostage pleaded with him over the school's intercom system. The shooter was charged as a juvenile with murder and kidnapping. Following his conviction, he was sentenced to four years in a juvenile correctional facility, but was released for good behavior after serving only three years.

August 20, 1986: Edmond Post Office, Edmond, OK

Following an unsatisfactory performance review, 44-year-old postal employee Patrick Sherrill returned to his workplace, where more than 75 employees were working. Armed with three handguns, he entered through the building's back door. He opened fire on his coworkers without warning, shooting at anyone he saw moving. Over the next 15 minutes, the gunman shot 20 people, killing 14 of them. Police quickly arrived on scene and attempted to make contact with the shooter, but to no avail. At the end of the rampage, the gunman committed suicide.

"Going Postal"

Though there were several incidents of postal shootings prior to the Edmond, Oklahoma, massacre, this particular event was the catalyst for the adoption of the phrase "going postal." The phrase was used to describe incidents where employees become extremely angry and resort to violence against those in their workplace. In addition to the Edmond attack, other similar incidents occurred in post offices across the nation, including in Ridgewood, New Jersey (1991), Royal Oak, Michigan (1991), Dearborn, Michigan (1993), Dana Point, California (1993), and Goleta, California (2006).

December 5, 1986: Fergus High School, Lewistown, MT

After earning a poor grade on an exam, 14-year-old Kristofer Hans arrived at Fergus High School armed with a handgun. He made his way to his teacher's classroom, and when the woman substituting for his regular teacher came to open the door, the shooter opened fire and killed her. He then ran from the school, continuing to shoot on his way out. Three people were wounded but survived. The shooter later was found at home and was arrested. He was convicted of deliberate homicide, attempted deliberate homicide, aggravated assault, and two weapons charges. He was given two 100-year sentences for the homicide charges plus an additional 180 months total for the assault and weapons charges. He was paroled on June 5, 2015, and currently is under community supervision in Nebraska.

April 16, 1987: Murray-Wright High School, Detroit, MI

Michael Schofield, a 14-year-old student, first opened fire in the school gymnasium, shooting and wounding a fellow student. He then ran from the gym, wounding another student on his way outside. Once in the parking lot, the gunman shot and killed another classmate before being taken into custody. He was charged as a juvenile and found guilty of second-degree murder and assault.

He was put in a training school for two years, and then in another program until he turned 19, when he was placed in a rehabilitation program. In 2003, the shooter killed four people during the commission of a robbery and then took his own life.

April 23, 1987: Multiple Locations, Palm Bay, FL

William Cruse left his home armed with a rifle and a handgun. The 60-year-old first opened fire on two teenagers across the street, wounding one of them, before getting in his car and driving away. As he was driving, he continued to shoot out the window, killing two others. The shooter stopped at a Publix Supermarket and shot and killed a woman who was leaving. He then crossed the street to a Winn-Dixie Supermarket and continued shooting, killing five more people, including two police officers. He then ran into the Winn-Dixie store, locking himself inside, and continued to shoot at customers. The shooter took one woman hostage who was inside the building, but let her go and surrendered after police shot tear gas into the store. Overall, 6 people were killed and 10 others were wounded. The gunman was tried and convicted of six counts of murder and was sentenced to death. He died in 2009 while awaiting execution.

February 11, 1988: Pinellas Park High School, Pinellas Park, FL

Accompanied by his friend James McCoy, 15-year-old Jason Harless arrived at Pinellas Park High School armed with a revolver. When school administrators approached the boys in the cafeteria, an argument occurred and the shooter opened fire. He shot two assistant principals and a student teacher. The teacher and one of the administrators were wounded, while the other assistant principal later died at the local hospital. The shooter then ran from the school, firing at police when he encountered them. He was wounded, disarmed, and arrested. After being convicted of second-degree murder, he was given a 17-year sentence. He was granted parole after spending 8 years in prison. The shooter's friend was convicted of third-degree murder and sentenced to 6 years in prison; he was released after just 2.

February 16, 1988: Electromagnetic Systems Labs, Inc., Sunnyvale, CA

After a coworker filed stalking charges against him, 39-year-old Richard Farley walked into the Electromagnetic Systems Lab plant armed with a shotgun, a rifle, and two automatic pistols. He began shooting once employees approached and began questioning him, and continued to shoot at everyone he saw as he made his way through the plant. Seven were killed and four others wounded, including the woman who had pressed charges against him. After negotiating with a police officer, the shooter surrendered and was arrested. He was found guilty of murder and attempted murder and was sentenced to death. He currently remains on death row at California's San Quentin prison.

May 20, 1988: Hubbard Woods School, Winnetka, IL

With a prior history of threatening people, 30-year-old Laurie Dann entered the Hubbard Woods School with a firearm and began shooting. Six children were shot, one of whom was killed. She then ran from the school and let herself into someone else's home, holding the residents hostage. She shot and wounded one of the men, and then committed suicide. Prior to the rampage, she had set fire to a home where she previously babysat and dropped off poisoned food and drinks to several other families for whom she had worked, as well as several fraternity houses at Northwestern University.

September 23, 1988: Multiple Locations, Chicago, IL

Clemmie Henderson entered the Comet Auto Parts store armed with a pistol and opened fire. The 40-year-old killed two employees before making his way outside, where he shot and killed a garbageman. The gunman then walked to the Montefiore School and continued firing, killing a school custodian outside. He then made his way inside and encountered two police officers, who had already been on the scene for a separate incident. He shot both officers, killing one of them, and then retreated to a classroom where he reloaded before returning to the hallway. Both the gunman and the other officer exchanged gunfire, during which the shooter was shot and killed.

September 26, 1988: Oakland Elementary School, Greenwood, SC

Armed with a pistol belonging to his grandfather, 19-year-old James William Wilson entered Oakland Elementary School and made his way to the cafeteria, where he wounded a teacher and three students before going into a women's bathroom to reload his weapon. When another teacher came inside to try to stop him, the gunman shot and wounded her as well. He then made his way to a classroom, where he opened fire again, wounding five more students and killing one other. He then dropped his gun and waited for police, who arrested him upon arrival. One of the students who had been wounded died at the local hospital a few days later. The gunman was charged with murder, assault, battery with intent to kill, aggravated assault, and carrying a gun on school property. He pleaded guilty but mentally ill on all charges and was sentenced to death. He still remains on death row at the Lieber Correctional Institution in Ridgeville, South Carolina, pending appeals to prevent his execution due to mental illness.

December 14, 1988: New Orleans Post Office, New Orleans, LA

Following a dispute with a coworker, 39-year-old Warren Murphy pulled a shotgun out of a bag he had brought to work with him and opened fire. He shot and wounded three coworkers and held two women hostage for more than 13 hours. Police later entered the building and began searching for the gunman, whom they found in a small room on the first floor. The gunman shot at police, but eventually surrendered and was taken into custody. The shooter was found guilty of kidnapping and three counts of assault with intent to kill. He was sentenced to a 200-month imprisonment term, which he served at a federal penitentiary until his release in 2003.

December 16, 1988: Atlantic Shores Christian School, Virginia Beach, VA

Following an argument in which racial slurs were exchanged with another student, 16-year-old Nicholas Elliott entered the school armed with a semiautomatic pistol. When a teacher attempted to stop him, he shot and killed her and continued walking through the hallway. He went into a classroom and shot another teacher, wounding him. The shooter chased another teacher out of the room, but missed when firing at her. He made his way into another classroom and continued shooting. His firearm jammed before anyone was hit, and the teacher in the classroom tackled and disarmed him. The gunman was arrested and charged on 14 separate counts, all of which he pleaded guilty to. He was sentenced to life in prison. Though eligible for parole several times, all petitions have been denied and he currently remains incarcerated at the Nottoway Correctional Facility in Burkeville, Virginia.

January 17, 1989: Cleveland Elementary School, Stockton, CA

Patrick Purdy walked onto the school grounds armed with a rifle and two handguns. The 24-year-old opened fire on students outside during recess, killing 5 children and wounding 32 others. The shooter then committed suicide on the school's grounds.

August 10, 1989: Orange Glen Postal Station, Orange Glen, CA

John Merlin Taylor, a 52-year-old employee of the Orange Glen Postal Station, entered his workplace armed with a semiautomatic rifle. He shot and killed two coworkers who had been sitting outside on the loading dock before moving inside. Continuing to fire, he wounded another coworker, who managed to flee the building to safety. The gunman then shot himself and later was pronounced brain-dead at the local hospital. During the rampage, police arrived at the shooter's home after receiving a call and discovered that he had shot and killed his wife earlier in the morning. Several weeks after the incident, it was found that the gunman had left a suicide note for his children.

September 14, 1989: Standard Gravure Corporation, Louisville, KY

After reaching a settlement on a case involving discrimination accusations with the company he worked for, 47-year-old James T. Wesbecker entered the Standard Gravure Corporation plant armed with an assault rifle. He shot and killed 8 workers and wounded 12 others. He then committed suicide at the scene.

1990s

June 18, 1990: General Motors Acceptance Corporation, Jacksonville, FL

Following his vehicle being repossessed, 42-year-old James E. Pough entered the General Motors office armed with a semiautomatic rifle and a revolver. He began shooting indiscriminately at individuals, including those who had taken cover underneath their desks. Nine workers were killed and four others were wounded. When there was no one else left for him to shoot, the gunman committed suicide. During a police investigation, it was discovered that he also had shot and killed two individuals who had been walking past his house the day before.

October 10, 1991: Ridgewood Post Office, Ridgewood, NJ

After being fired from his job at the Ridgewood Post Office, 35-year-old Joseph Harris entered the post office armed with a handgun, a machine gun, a samurai sword, three hand grenades, and several homemade bombs. He opened fire, shooting and killing two mail handlers. Shortly thereafter, he left the basement of the building and surrendered to the SWAT team. It later was discovered that the shooter had broken into the home of his former supervisor and stabbed her to death. He then shot her boyfriend before going to the post office. Upon further investigation, it was found that the gunman also was responsible for a murder that had occurred three years earlier. He was tried and convicted for all of these murders and was sentenced to death plus 160 years. In 1996, he had a stroke and died while awaiting execution.

October 16, 1991: Luby's Cafeteria, Killeen, TX

During a crowded time at the Luby's restaurant, 35-year-old George Hennard drove his pickup truck through the eatery's front windows into the crowd. As patrons rushed to his aid, the gunman exited the vehicle armed with two pistols and began firing. He circled through the restaurant, shooting at patrons, many of whom were killed with point-blank shots to their heads. During the rampage, one customer threw a table through a window, creating a pathway for some to escape as the gunman continued to shoot at people in the restaurant. Law enforcement quickly responded to the report of shots fired. When they arrived at the restaurant, they quickly engaged the shooter in an exchange of gunfire; he was wounded during this time. The shooter then retreated to a bathroom in the restaurant, where he committed suicide. By the time the shots had subsided, 23 people had been killed and another 27 were wounded.

Changing the Face of Texas Law

One of the earliest victims of the shooting was Suzanna Gratia Hupp. While wounded in the attack, Suzanna also had to watch as the gunman shot and killed her parents, Al and Ursula, with whom she was having lunch in the restaurant that day. A registered concealed handgun license (CHL) holder, she had left her gun in her car in order to comply with Texas law at the time that prohibited carrying concealed weapons in a private space. In testimony given after the event, she noted that if she had been armed, she might have been able to save the lives of her parents. Suzanna went on to be a leading gun-rights advocate, speaking in support of such laws across the nation. Her testimony was crucial in helping pass legislation in Texas that permitted licensed CHL holders to carry in public; the law was enacted in 1995 by then governor George W. Bush. In 1996, she was elected to the Texas House of Representatives on behalf of the 54th District, where she served six terms before stepping down in 2006.

November 1, 1991: University of Iowa, Iowa City, IA

After not receiving a dissertation prize from his university, 28-year-old Gang Lu walked into an academic building on the University of Iowa campus. Armed with a revolver and a handgun, he opened fire, killing two professors. He also shot and killed a former roommate. The shooter then made his way down the stairs to the office of the Physics Department chair, killing him. He left the building and crossed the campus to the administration building, where he shot the associate vice president of academic affairs as well as a receptionist. The vice president later died at the local hospital; the receptionist was wounded but survived. The shooter then moved upstairs in the administration building and committed suicide.

November 14, 1991: Royal Oak Post Office, Royal Oak, MI

Following being fired from his job at the Royal Oak Post Office, 31-year-old Thomas McIlvane entered the building through the loading dock, armed with a rifle. He roamed around the building, shooting at those he encountered. Three supervisors were killed and six other workers were injured. He then shot himself and was declared brain-dead the next day.

February 26, 1992: Thomas Jefferson High School, Brooklyn, NY

Khalil Sumpter, a 15-year-old student, entered the high school armed with a pistol. He approached two fellow students, shooting and killing both. He then ran from the scene, with school security guards following him; he was arrested two blocks away. The shooter was charged as an adult with second-degree murder but was convicted of manslaughter. He was sentenced to $6^2/_3$ to 20 years in prison. After serving less than six years, he was released in 1998.

May 1, 1992: Lindhurst High School, Olivehurst, CA

Eric Houston, a 20-year-old former student of Lindhurst High School, returned to the school armed with a shotgun and a rifle. He first made his way to the classroom of a former teacher who had failed him. He opened fire, shooting and killing his teacher and a student in the classroom. He then left the room and went to the next classroom, shooting and killing another student. The gunman continued to make his way down the hallway, shooting at people as they passed. He killed another student and wounded 10 other individuals. He then entered another classroom with 30 students inside and held them as hostages, occasionally having one of them gather more students. By the end of the rampage, the gunman had taken 70 students hostage in the classroom, keeping them there for several hours. He surrendered to police after being told he would only receive five years in prison. He was convicted of first-degree murder and was sentenced to death. He currently remains on death row at California's San Quentin prison.

May 14, 1992: Silverado Middle School, Napa, CA

John McMahan, a 14-year-old student, entered Silverado Middle School armed with a pistol. He pulled the weapon out of his bag during science class and opened fire, wounding two students. He continued to threaten everyone in the classroom before making his way outside and shooting at a bush. He was convinced to surrender by a group of teachers and was taken into custody by responding law enforcement. The shooter was charged with two counts each of attempted murder and bringing a gun onto school property.

September 11, 1992: Palo Duro High School, Amarillo, TX

Amidst a fight with another student, 17-year-old Randy Earl Matthews pulled a handgun out of his bag and opened fire. He first shot at the student with whom he was fighting, critically wounding him (the student later recovered at the local hospital). The gunman continued to move through the school, firing at students who were leaving a school pep rally. Five other students were wounded as he attempted to clear his way out of the building. He fled the scene and was caught and arrested several blocks away by a police officer who had been at the school. The gunman was convicted of five counts of aggravated assault and unlawfully carrying a weapon on school grounds. He was sentenced to eight years in prison and was released in 2001. Since then, he has been rearrested twice on controlled substance charges. He is currently serving a 26-year sentence for possession at the Dalhart Unit in Dalhart, Texas; in 2015, his petition for parole was denied.

October 15, 1992: Schuyler County Child Support Unit, Watkins Glen, NY

After a lengthy history of failure to pay child support and frustrated over the garnishment of his wages, 50-year-old John T. Miller entered the Schuyler County building armed with a semiautomatic pistol. He opened fire on women working in the child support unit, shooting and killing four of them. When police arrived, the shooter was standing in the middle of the office with his weapon raised to his head. He committed suicide as the police were trying to convince him to surrender.

December 14, 1992: Simon's Rock College of Bard, Great Barrington, MA

Wayne Lo, an 18-year-old student, arrived at the Simon's Rock College of Bard campus armed with an assault rifle he had purchased that morning. He first shot and wounded the security guard working at the front gate and then killed a professor who had pulled onto the campus in his car. Next, the shooter made his way to the college's library, continuing to fire his weapon. One student was killed and another wounded before the shooter left the library and moved to a dormitory. While in the lobby, he shot and wounded two other students. The gunman next went to the student union building, set down his weapon, and called police to surrender. He was arrested and charged with murder and assault with a deadly weapon. He was found guilty and sentenced to life in prison without the possibility of parole. He is currently incarcerated at MCI Norfolk, a medium security prison.

January 18, 1993: East Carter High School, Grayson, KY

Scott Pennington, a 17-year-old student, arrived at East Carter High School with a revolver belonging to his father in his bag. He retrieved the firearm during class and fired at the teacher, killing her. The school's custodian ran into the room upon hearing the gunfire and also was fatally shot. The shooter then shut the door, holding the rest of the students present as hostages. Within 15 minutes, however, the shooter had released all the students and surrendered to police. He was tried as an adult and convicted of murder and kidnapping. He pleaded guilty but mentally ill to the charges and was sentenced to life without the possibility of parole for 25 years. In 2014, he assaulted a food service employee at the prison where he was incarcerated. After being indicted on first-degree assault, the shooter was transferred to Kentucky's State Reformatory. He will be eligible for parole on January 8, 2035.

May 6, 1993: Dearborn Post Office, Dearborn, MI

After being passed over for a position, 45-year-old Larry Jasion arrived at work at the Dearborn Post Office armed with a handgun and a shotgun, and began to shoot. He shot and killed a coworker and wounded two others. One of those wounded was the woman who had gotten the position he had wanted. The shooter then went to the garage, where he committed suicide.

May 6, 1993: Dana Point Post Office, Dana Point, CA

After stabbing his mother to death and killing her dog at her home, 38-year-old Mark R. Hilbun entered the Dana Point Post Office where he had previously worked. Armed with a revolver, he opened fire, killing a letter carrier and wounding a clerk. He then left the building and drove away from the scene, continuing to shoot at people as he drove; three others were wounded in the attack. Police found the shooter the next day sitting in a sports bar several miles away from where the crime was committed. He was tried and convicted of murder and sentenced to life in prison without the possibility of parole. He currently is incarcerated at the Richard J. Donovan Correctional Facility in San Diego. The shooting in Dana Point came just hours after the post office shooting in Dearborn, Michigan (above).

July 1, 1993: Pettit and Martin Law Firm, San Francisco, CA

Following a bankruptcy filing, 55-year-old Gian Luigi Ferri entered the Pettit and Martin Law Firm, where he previously had been a client. Armed with three semiautomatic pistols and a revolver, he first opened fire on two individuals in a conference room, killing both. He then moved out of that room and fired at another worker, killing that person before moving down to lower floors. As he made his way throughout the building, he killed five more individuals and wounded six others. When police arrived, they shut down the elevators and locked stairwell doors, trapping the shooter inside the building. As he saw police approaching, he ran in the opposite direction, ultimately committing suicide with the revolver.

August 6, 1993: Luigi's Restaurant, Fayetteville, NC

Kenneth Junior French, a 22-year-old soldier at Fort Bragg, walked a mile from his Army post to Luigi's restaurant armed with two shotguns, a rifle, and a bag of ammunition. He opened fire, killing four, including the restaurant's two owners. Six customers also were wounded. Hearing the gunshots, a nearby off-duty police officer ran to the scene; he shot and wounded the perpetrator, who was able to get back up. The shooter continued to fire until another officer arrived minutes after, shooting and disabling him. He was arrested and charged with four counts of first-degree murder, eight counts of assault with a deadly weapon with intent to kill, and one count of discharging a firearm in an occupied building. He was found guilty on several different charges and sentenced to life in prison. He currently is incarcerated at Scotland Correctional Institution in Laurinburg, North Carolina, and continues to face disciplinary troubles while in prison.

September 17, 1993: Central Middle School, Sheridan, WY

Following a less-than-honorable discharge from the Navy, 29-year-old Kevin Newman approached the football field of Central Middle School armed with a rifle and a pistol. He fired at students who were outside for gym class. Four students were wounded before the gunman shot himself. He died at a nearby hospital several hours later.

December 2, 1993: State Employment Development Department Office, Oxnard, CA

After having struggled to find a job for seven years, 33-year-old Alan Winterbourne entered an unemployment office in Oxnard armed with a pistol and a shotgun and opened fire. He shot only at employees, not targeting individuals in the waiting area. Three people were killed and four others wounded before the gunman fled the building, exchanging gunfire with police as he ran. An officer was shot and killed before the shooter drove away in his vehicle. He was stopped outside another unemployment office in a nearby town, and when he emerged from his vehicle with one of his weapons, the officers who had been chasing him shot and killed him.

December 7, 1993: Long Island Rail Road (Merillon Avenue Station), Garden City, NY

After boarding the Long Island Rail Road train at the Jamaica station in Queens, 35-year-old Colin Ferguson took a seat at the back of the third car. Armed with a handgun and 160 rounds of ammunition, the shooter stood up and drew his weapon as the train approached the Merillon Avenue station in Garden City. He opened fire, walking up the aisle of the train car and turning side to side, shooting at passengers in both directions. After emptying two 15-round magazines, the shooter stopped to reload, at which time several passengers tackled him and held him down until law enforcement could arrive on scene and take him into custody. By that time, 6 people had been killed and 19 others were wounded.

The shooter initially was charged with 93 separate counts, ranging from weapons violations to first-degree murder charges. Though a court-appointed psychologist found that he suffered from paranoid personality disorder, the shooter was declared competent to stand trial. After issues with several of his appointed and selected counsel representatives, the shooter elected to represent himself in court. In February 1995, he was convicted of murder and attempted murder and was sentenced to 315 years and eight months to life in prison. He currently is incarcerated at the Upstate Correctional Facility in Malone, New York, where he was transferred after attempting to start a riot at Attica prison in 2011.

A Platform for Change

Among the victims of the Long Island Rail Road massacre were Dennis and Kevin McCarthy. Dennis was killed in the shooting, while Kevin was severely injured. Carolyn

McCarthy, Dennis's widow and Kevin's mother, used the shooting as a call to action. After launching a stringent gun-control campaign, she used the momentum to earn a position in Congress, serving as the U.S. House of Representatives member for New York's 4th District. During her 18 years in office, Representative McCarthy was a fierce lobbyist for gun control measures, particularly after mass shooting episodes, including Columbine and Virginia Tech. One of her most successful pieces of legislation was the NICS Improvement Amendments Act of 2007, signed into legislation after the Virginia Tech shooting, that dedicated federal funding to states to improve reporting of mental health records to the national criminal background check system. Citing poor health, she left office in 2015.

December 14, 1993: Chuck E. Cheese, Aurora, CO

Following being fired from Chuck E. Cheese a week prior, 19-year-old Nathan Dunlap entered the business armed with a semiautomatic handgun as the employees were closing for the night. He first shot and killed two teenage employees near the entrance, and then fired at another worker in the hallway. Next, he shot another employee, wounding him, but the victim was able to run from the building to get help. The shooter moved on to the back office where the manager was working and proceeded to shoot and kill her. Police arrived shortly after the first shots were fired and took the gunman into custody. He was charged with four counts of first-degree murder, among a host of other charges, and was found guilty on all counts. He was sentenced to death plus 113 years. He currently is incarcerated at the Colorado State Penitentiary awaiting execution.

December 17, 1993: Chelsea High School, Chelsea, MI

At a grievance hearing, 39-year-old Stephen Leith left the building and went home. He returned shortly after, armed with a semiautomatic handgun. He returned to the meeting, opening fire on those who were present. The school's superintendent was killed, while the principal and a teacher were wounded. The shooter then left his gun on the table and went to his office, where police found him grading papers. He was arrested and charged with first-degree murder. Following his conviction, he was sentenced to life in prison without the possibility of parole, a term he currently is serving at the Carson City Correctional Facility.

March 1, 1994: Kemper Military School and College, Boonville, MO

Dante Hayes entered the Kemper Military School and College cafeteria armed with a shotgun. The 33-year-old claimed he was going to talk things through with his wife, an employee at the school. He shot at a worker as she ran into the kitchen but missed. He then shot and killed a manager and another worker. After leaving the building, the gunman took two teenage hostages in a nearby apartment. Over the next few hours, the shooter released each of them one at a time, and then surrendered to police. He was charged with two counts of first-degree murder, as well as counts related to burglary and kidnapping. After reaching a deal in which prosecutors would not seek the death penalty, the shooter pleaded guilty. He received a sentence of life without the possibility of parole, which currently is being served at the Jefferson City Correctional Facility.

March 14, 1998: Extron Electronics, Santa Fe Springs, CA

After being fired for unsatisfactory performance, 29-year-old Tuan Nguyen entered Extron Electronics armed with a pistol. He shot and killed one man in the equipment test area and fatally wounded another. He then traveled to the southwest side of the building, where he shot and killed another person before committing suicide. Another worker, who was shot in the attack, was taken by helicopter to a nearby hospital, where he was later pronounced dead.

June 20, 1994: Fairchild Air Force Base, Spokane, WA

Following his discharge from the military, 20-year-old Dean Mellberg entered the Fairchild Air Force Base hospital armed with a rifle. He opened fire on the two psychiatrists who had found him unfit for duty; both were killed. He continued firing as he made his way into the hospital's waiting room, shooting indiscriminately. His final actions led him to the hospital's parking lot, where he continued firing until a responding military officer shot and killed him. A total of 4 people were killed and another 23 people were wounded.

November 7, 1994: Wickliffe Middle School, Wickliffe, OH

Keith Ledeger, a 37-year-old former student, entered Wickliffe Middle School armed with a shotgun. In a span of three-and-a-half minutes, the shooter fired 10 times, killing a custodian and wounding two of the school's staff members and a responding police officer. The gunman was shot by officers and taken to the hospital for treatment before being transferred to the jail for processing. The shooter, diagnosed as a paranoid schizophrenic, pleaded guilty and was sentenced to life in prison with the possibility of parole in just under 41 years. The shooter died in prison in 2011 of natural causes.

January 12, 1995: Garfield High School, Seattle, WA

A 15-year-old freshman (whose name was not released due to his juvenile status) was being teased by classmates prior to a Martin Luther King Day assembly. He went home and armed himself with a handgun that he had stolen from his grandfather. He returned to the assembly and opened fire. Two students were wounded before the shooter was arrested. He was tried as a juvenile for first-degree attempted murder and first-degree assault. He pleaded guilty and served five years in the King County juvenile detention system. He was released on his 21st birthday.

April 3, 1995: Walter Rossler Company, Corpus Christi, TX

After quitting his job at the Walter Rossler Company, 28-year-old James Simpson entered his former workplace armed with a pistol and a revolver. He shot and killed five employees, including his former boss and his boss's wife. No others were wounded. The shooter left through the back door and committed suicide. According to police, the shooter's depression played a role in the attack.

July 19, 1995: Piper Technical Center, Los Angeles, CA

Following a series of poor performance reviews, 42-year-old electrician Willie Woods entered Piper Technical Center armed with a pistol. After arguing with his supervisors, the shooter retrieved the pistol and started firing. Four of the company's supervisors were killed; no other individuals were wounded. He was arrested by police officers, who had stopped by the company to pick up supplies. He was convicted on three counts of first-degree murder and one count of second-degree murder and was sentenced to life in prison without the possibility of parole. He currently is incarcerated at the Wasco State Prison in Wasco, California.

October 12, 1995: Blackville-Hilda High School, Blackville, SC

Following suspension from the school for making an obscene gesture and facing his second expulsion, 16-year-old Anthony Sincino returned to Blackville-Hilda High School armed with a revolver. He shot two math teachers, killing one and wounding the other, before committing suicide. No others were wounded in the attack.

November 15, 1995: Richland High School, Lynnville, TN

Angered by his poor grades, 17-year-old James Ellison Rouse entered Richland High School armed with a semiautomatic rifle. He confronted two teachers, shooting both in the head. He then aimed his weapon at the football coach and fired, but missed; the bullet struck a student in the throat. One of the teachers and the student both died from their injuries; the other teacher survived. The shooter was taken down by the football coach and a student and taken to the office, where police took him into custody. The shooter was convicted as an adult on one count each of first-degree murder, second-degree murder, and attempted murder. He was sentenced to life in prison without the possibility of parole and currently is serving his punishment in the state's South Central Correctional Facility.

February 2, 1996: Frontier Junior High School, Moses Lake, WA

Barry Loukaitis, a 14-year-old student, entered Frontier Junior High School armed with a rifle and two handguns that belonged to his father. He made his way to his algebra classroom and opened fire. Two students and the teacher were killed; another student was wounded in the attack but survived. The shooter held the rest of the class hostage until another teacher entered the room and subdued him until police arrived on scene. A year and a half after the shooting, the gunman was convicted of 2 counts of first-degree murder, 1 count of second-degree murder, 1 count of first-degree attempted murder, and 16 counts of aggravated kidnapping. He initially was sentenced to two life sentences plus an additional 205 years without the possibility of parole. Due to a 2012 Supreme Court ruling, which declared that life sentences could not be given to individuals under the age of 16 at the time of the crime, the shooter's case was resentenced in 2017. He now is serving a 189-year term at the Coyote Ridge Corrections Center in Connell, Washington.

February 8, 1996: Mid-Peninsula High School, Palo Alto, CA

After having problems with his girlfriend and a history of depression, 16-year-old Douglas Bradley drove to Mid-Peninsula High School armed with a handgun. He stopped near an outside basketball court and threw fake money at his classmates. When they came closer, he started firing. He wounded three students before committing suicide.

February 9, 1996: Fort Lauderdale Beach, Fort Lauderdale, FL

Following his termination from his city job for failing a drug test, 41-year-old Clifton McCree returned to Fort Lauderdale Beach armed with a pistol. He opened fire, killing five coworkers and wounding a sixth. The shooter then committed suicide.

April 24, 1996: Jackson Fire Station, Jackson, MS

After shooting his wife, 32-year-old Kenneth Tornes entered the Jackson Fire Station, where he was a nine-year veteran. Armed with a rifle, he opened fire on his supervisors. Four people were killed and two others were wounded. After leading police on a 10-mile chase that ended with a shootout, the gunman and one police officer were wounded. The shooter was tried and convicted and sentenced to death, but has since died in prison.

August 15, 1996: San Diego State University, San Diego, CA

After having his thesis rejected once, 36-year-old Frederick Davidson returned to his former school to meet with a panel of professors to defend his thesis again. Prior to the meeting, the shooter stored a handgun in the classroom. He retrieved the gun as the meeting began and opened fire, killing three professors. The shooter then called 9-1-1 and waited for police. When they arrived on scene, he begged them to kill him; when they would not, he surrendered without further incident. The shooter was convicted under a plea bargain that removed the death penalty as a sentencing option. He was sentenced to three consecutive life terms without possibility of parole, which he currently is serving at the California State Prison for Los Angeles County, located in Lancaster, California.

September 17, 1996: Penn State University, State College, PA

Suffering from a long list of psychiatric disorders, 19-year-old Jillian Robbins arrived at Penn State University armed with a knife and a rifle that she received as a gift from her father. She fired at students on the campus lawn; one was killed while a second was injured. Another student wrestled the gun away from the shooter and she retaliated with the knife. She stabbed herself in the leg, creating the opportunity for the student to disarm her and hold her until responding law enforcement could take her into custody. The shooter spent six months in a mental institution and was convicted of murder in the third degree, which carries a 30- to 60-year sentence. She currently is incarcerated Women's State Correctional Facility in Muncy, Pennsylvania.

February 20, 1997: Bethel Regional High School, Bethel, AK

After being bullied by peers and enduring various forms of abuse at home, 16-year-old Evan Ramsey entered Bethel Regional High School armed with a shotgun. He approached the student commons area and opened fire. One student was killed and two others were injured. He then entered the main lobby, where he shot and killed the principal. After firing his weapon at police, the shooter surrendered. The shooter was tried as an adult and convicted on two counts of first-degree murder, one count of first-degree attempted murder, and seven counts of third-degree assault. Originally sentenced to 210 years, the shooter appealed the convictions in 2004; the conviction for attempted murder was reversed and his sentence was reduced to 198 years. He currently is serving his sentence at the Wildwood Correctional Center in Kenai, Alaska, and will be eligible for parole in 2066.

February 23, 1997: Empire State Building, New York, NY

Seeking revenge against the United States for supporting Israel, 69-year-old Ali Abu Kamal entered the Empire State Building armed with a handgun. He opened fire on the observation deck, killing one and wounding six others before committing suicide. The shooter had arrived in the United States in 1996 from Gaza.

June 5, 1997: Omni Plastics Plant, Santa Fe Springs, CA

Daniel Marsden, a 38-year-old employee of Omni Plastics, felt that he was being taunted by his coworkers about his sexual orientation. After an argument with a coworker, he left the plant and returned a short time later armed with a gun. He began firing indiscriminately, killing two workers and wounding four others. The shooter later committed suicide.

September 15, 1997: R. E. Phelon Company, Aiken, SC

After being fired from the company, 43-year-old Hastings Arthur Wise returned to his former workplace armed with a semiautomatic pistol. He first shot and wounded a security guard outside of the facility. The shooter then entered the building and fatally shot the man who had fired him. He continued to move throughout the building, firing at individuals he saw. In total, four workers were killed and three others were wounded. After a failed suicide attempt, the shooter was arrested by police. He was convicted of all murders and sentenced to death. In 2005, he was executed by lethal injection.

October 1, 1997: Pearl High School, Pearl, MS

After stabbing his mother to death at their home, 16-year-old Luke Woodham entered Pearl High School armed with a rifle he concealed in his coat. He fatally shot two female students, one of whom was his former girlfriend. He continued to fire indiscriminately, wounding seven others. The school's principal retrieved a gun from his car and was able to detain the shooter at gunpoint until the police arrived and took him into custody. Over three trials, the shooter was tried and convicted of three counts of murder and seven counts of attempted murder. He is currently serving three life-term sentences plus an additional 140 years at the Mississippi State Penitentiary in Parchman, Mississippi. He will be eligible for parole in 2046.

October 7, 1997: ProtoCall, San Antonio, TX

Charles Lee White entered the ProtoCall paging company armed with a rifle. The 42-year-old shooter opened fire, killing both his ex-girlfriend, an employee at the store, and another worker. A third employee was hospitalized with a gunshot wound to the head. The shooter then committed suicide.

December 1, 1997: Heath High School, West Paducah, KY

Suffering from alleged bullying from classmates, 14-year-old Michael Carneal went to Heath High School armed with several firearms. He opened fire, shooting indiscriminately toward a group of students who had gathered in a prayer circle. Three students were killed and another five were wounded. The shooter then surrendered to the school principal. Following the shooting, the shooter was diagnosed with paranoid schizophrenia. He pleaded guilty to murder, criminal attempted murder, and first-degree burglary and received a life sentence with the possibility of parole in 2022. He initially was housed at the Northern Kentucky Youth Development Center, a juvenile justice facility. Upon his 18th birthday, he was transferred to the Kentucky State Reformatory in LaGrange, Kentucky, where he remains today.

December 15, 1997: Stamps High School, Stamps, AR

Joseph Colt Todd, a 14-year-old student, opened fire outside of Stamps High School while hiding in the nearby woods. Two teenage students were shot and wounded. There were no other injuries before the shooter was taken into custody. He was charged as an adult, convicted of first-degree battery, and sentenced to two concurrent five-year terms. He served just half of each, with the balances being suspended, before being released from correctional custody.

December 18, 1997: CalTrans, Orange, CA

After being terminated from his job at a maintenance yard, 41-year-old Arturo Reyes Torres returned to his workplace at the California transportation department armed with an assault rifle, a shotgun, and a handgun. He opened fire, killing four workers and wounding two others. While he was attempting to escape, police arrived on scene and a shootout began. The gunman was shot and killed by police.

December 20, 1997: Milwaukee Post Office, Milwaukee, WI

After being denied a promotion, 37-year-old Anthony Deculit showed up for his night shift at the post office armed with a handgun. He opened fire on his coworkers, killing one and wounding two others. The shooter then committed suicide. Among the wounded was a supervisor who had disciplined the shooter for sleeping on the job.

March 6, 1998: Connecticut Lottery Headquarters, Newington, CT

Following a medical leave and being demoted, 35-year-old Matthew Beck arrived to work at the lottery headquarters armed with a handgun and knife. Thirty minutes into his shift, the shooter left his office and headed for the executive suites. He opened fire, fatally shooting four people before committing suicide. No others were wounded in the attack.

March 24, 1998: Westside Middle School, Jonesboro, AR

After stealing his mother's van, 13-year-old Mitchell Johnson drove himself and 11-year-old Andrew Golden to Golden's grandfather's house. There, they proceeded to steal nine guns, including two semiautomatic rifles, a bolt-action rifle, and six handguns. They then proceeded to Westside Middle School, where both were students. As the older perpetrator set up their weapons in a wooded area adjacent to the school, the younger entered the building where classes were in session and pulled the fire alarm, then retreated back outside to the woods. Complying with the fire alarm, students and teachers made their way out of the school, at which time the shooters opened fire. Four students and 1 teacher were killed; an additional 10 people were injured in the attack. The shooters fled into the woods but were captured by responding law enforcement officers. Each was tried as a juvenile and convicted on several murder and attempted murder charges. They were incarcerated until their respective 21st birthdays, when they were released.

The Extended Juvenile Jurisdiction Act (EJJA)

At the time of the Westside Middle School shooting, the state of Arkansas had a mandatory minimum waiver age of 14, meaning that a juvenile had to be at least 14 years old at the time of the crime in order to qualify for being tried as an adult. Furthermore, state law excluded any provision that would have allowed a juvenile offender to serve a life sentence. Accordingly, when the two shooters were sentenced, they were given the maximum penalties allowed under the law—confinement in a juvenile detention center until the age of 18. The presiding judge was able to add an additional three years to each shooter's sentence based on federal weapons violations, which kept them incarcerated until they were 21, having been transferred to federal prison on their 18th birthdays.

When they turned 21, however, both shooters were released from prison with sealed records and no criminal history. Within two years of his release, the older shooter had been rearrested after a vehicle stop produced drugs and a loaded gun. He was later convicted of possession of marijuana and using a stolen credit card. He was reincarcerated for all offenses, ultimately being granted probation in 2015 to attend a drug rehabilitation program in Texas. The younger shooter was never rearrested, though records indicate that he did apply for a firearm permit but was denied due to misinformation on the purchase application.

In response to the Westside Middle School shootings, Arkansas passed the EJJA, which revised a number of different legal codes pertaining to juveniles. Among the changes was a provision allowing for a juvenile, regardless of age, to be charged with capital or first-degree murder. It also permitted the records of a juvenile to be transferred or consolidated with his or her adult records, which would help to disqualify individuals committing offenses as a juvenile from later acquiring firearms legally. The state also passed legislation requiring its Department of Corrections to establish separate housing facilities for juvenile offenders in their institutions.

April 24, 1998: Nick's Place, Edinboro, PA

Andrew Wurst arrived at Nick's Place, a banquet hall where Parker Middle School was having their dance, armed with a pistol that he had taken from his father. Twenty minutes before the dance was scheduled to end, the 14-year-old student shot and killed one of his teachers on an outdoor patio. He entered the banquet hall and continued firing, wounding another teacher and two students. The owner of the banquet hall confronted the shooter with his own weapon, ordering him to drop his gun, and held him until police arrived and took him into custody. As part of a plea agreement, the shooter pleaded guilty to third-degree murder and attempted murder, which allowed him to avoid a sentence of life in prison as well as a trial. He was sentenced to 30 to 60 years and is currently incarcerated at SCI Forest in Marienville, Pennsylvania. He will be eligible for parole in 2029.

May 21, 1998: Thurston High School, Springfield, OR

Following an expulsion for bringing a firearm to school the prior day, 15-year-old Kip Kinkel entered the Thurston High School campus armed with two pistols, a rifle (the primary weapon in the attack), and two knives. He first opened fire on the patio and then moved into the cafeteria, where he continued shooting. Two students were killed and an additional 25 others were wounded in the attack. As he tried to reload his firearm, the shooter was tackled and restrained by students until he was subsequently taken into custody. An investigation at the shooter's home also revealed that the evening prior to the rampage, he shot and killed both of his parents. The shooter later plead guilty to murder and attempted murder charges prior to a trial and was sentenced to 111 years in prison without the possibility of parole. Originally housed in an Oregon youth correctional facility, he was transferred to the state's Department of Corrections when he turned 25. He currently remains incarcerated at the Oregon State Correctional Institution in Salem, Oregon.

June 15, 1998: Armstrong High School, Richmond, VA

Following an argument with another juvenile, 14-year-old Quinshawn Booker opened fire at the school with a handgun. He wounded a basketball coach and volunteer aide before being chased down by police and arrested. He pleaded guilty to five charges in a deal with prosecutors that spared him from adult prison. He will remain at a school for troubled boys until he completes its program. He will then be required to finish high school and further his education, either in college, at a trade school, or in the military.

July 24, 1998: United States Capitol, Washington, DC

Russell E. Weston Jr., a 41-year-old paranoid schizophrenic, arrived at the Capitol building armed with a pistol. Two United States Capitol police officers were shot and killed. Another officer and a female tourist were injured before the gunman was taken into custody. The shooter was found incompetent to stand trial on multiple occasions. He since has been committed to a psychiatric hospital at the Butner Federal Correctional Institution in Butner, North Carolina.

January 13, 1999: Triad Center, Salt Lake City, UT

De-Kieu Duy arrived at the Triad Center armed with a newly purchased handgun. The 24-year-old asked for access to the KSL newsroom but was denied; she then pulled her weapon. After firing at the receptionist's feet, the shooter took the elevator to the fourth floor, where she shot and killed an AT&T employee. As she attempted to continue shooting, the firearm jammed and she was wrestled to the floor before being taken into custody. The shooter was diagnosed a paranoid schizophrenic and committed to a mental hospital. She remains incompetent to stand trial and has yet to face charges for the shooting.

March 18, 1999: Law Office of John D. Goodin, Johnson City, TN

Following the death of his ex-wife and an alleged error in her will, 71-year-old Walter K. Shell arrived at his ex-wife's lawyer's office armed with a firearm. He opened fire, killing an attorney and an insurance agent who happened to be in the office. The shooter turned himself in and was charged with two counts of first-degree murder. He later was declared incompetent to stand trial and was committed to a mental institution, where he was ordered to remain until he was found competent to stand trial or until his death.

April 15, 1999: Mormon Family History Library, Salt Lake City, UT

Sergei Barbarin entered the Mormon Family History Library, a part of the Mormon church, armed with a pistol. The 70-year-old opened fire, killing a security guard and library patron. Five others were wounded in the attack. The shooter was wounded during a standoff with police officers. He later died while in transport to the hospital.

April 20, 1999: Columbine High School, Littleton, CO

Just after 11:00 a.m., 18-year-old Eric Harris and 17-year-old Dylan Klebold, Columbine High School students, arrived at the school, parking in separate lots adjacent to the building's cafeteria. Armed with two guns apiece and nearly 100 improvised explosive devices (IEDs) and following more than a year of planning, the pair of high school seniors walked toward the school carrying two large duffle bags, each containing a 20-pound propane tank bomb. On the way into the cafeteria, the older shooter told Brooks Brown, a classmate and friend, to leave the school. The pair then set the bags down inside the cafeteria next to tables and exited the building, heading back out to their cars.

The timers on the propane tank bombs had been set for 11:17 a.m. Prior to April 20, the shooters had determined that 11:17 was the time at which the cafeteria would be at its largest capacity for the day and thus the bombs would do the most destruction. They waited for the bombs to detonate, poised to shoot any fleeing survivors. When the devices failed to explode, the pair began to approach the school. Two minutes later, a bomb went off less than three miles away, intended to divert police away from the area of the school.

At that same moment, one of the shooters was heard yelling "Go! Go!" and both retrieved shotguns from the bags they were carrying. They opened fire on students who were eating lunch on the grassy area outside from the top of the west exterior steps, which gave them an elevated vantage point. Student Rachel Scott was the first to be killed; Richard Castaldo, who was sitting with her, was shot but survived, paralyzed from the chest down. The pair continued to fire, also setting off some of the IEDs. The school resource officer, Neil Gardner, arrived at the area where the shooting was in progress and engaged the shooters. He exchanged gunfire with the older gunman, who then retreated into the school.

Realizing the gravity of the situation, students who had hidden under cafeteria tables began to run at the urging of teacher William "Dave" Sanders, who had come to investigate the noise. He directed them to go to the east side of the building, away from the gunfire, before turning to head back upstairs. Once upstairs, he encountered the gunmen, who shot him. Students in a nearby science class dragged him inside before locking the doors, where they tried to administer first aid and keep him alive; he later died of his injuries while waiting for medical assistance to reach him. By this time, the first responding law enforcement officers had arrived on scene and were beginning to survey the situation.

The shooters continued to wander through the school, firing their weapons and detonating the IEDs. They made their way to the library hallway, where they spent several minutes, before entering the library. At the time, a total of 56 people were present. At the urging of teacher Patti Nielsen, who was on the phone with a 9-1-1 dispatcher, the students and staff in the library either had fled the room to adjoining areas (e.g., the television studio or periodical room) or took cover under the desks. Over a seven-and-a-half minute period, 10 people were killed and 12 others wounded as the shooters continued their rampage before they exited the library. The shooters then made their way back to the science wing, firing into empty rooms and throwing several pipe bombs, before returning to the cafeteria as the SWAT team set up a command post outside the school. One shooter fired his gun at one of the propane tank bombs in an attempt to detonate it, but the device failed to explode. The other shooter threw an IED at it, but was equally unsuccessful in triggering the bomb. Several minutes later, the gunmen left the cafeteria, first going to the school's office and then continuing to wander through the school. First responders aided students who were injured or who had been able to evacuate but had not yet been able to enter the school due to the area being deemed unsafe.

Just after noon, the shooters returned to the library and exchanged gunfire with responding law enforcement officers through a broken window before retreating back inside the building. At 12:08 p.m., the pair moved to the interior of the library and committed suicide. Over the nearly 50-minute-long rampage, 13 people—12 students and teacher Dave Sanders—had been killed and 21 others were wounded by gunfire. An additional three people had been injured as they attempted to escape the school.

How Did They Get Their Guns?

Many people questioned how the perpetrators were able to acquire their weapons. This question was particularly important as their journals indicated that their first three guns had been obtained the November prior—when both were under the age of 18, which thereby made them ineligible to purchase. The investigation turned to their friend and classmate, 18-year-old Robin Anderson. She had accompanied the pair to a local gun show six months prior to the shooting. While there, the shooters specifically sought private dealers who did not conduct background checks, as Anderson did not want the checks to appear on her record. At the gun show, they were able to purchase the two shotguns and a carbine rifle.

In the aftermath of the shooting, a number of pieces of legislation were introduced in an attempt to close what had been deemed "the gun show loophole." Though similar efforts had been made prior to Columbine, the revelation of how the gunmen acquired their weapons served as a catalyst for an intense national debate about the procedures for purchasing guns from private sellers. Within three weeks of the shooting, several bills had been introduced aimed at requiring background checks, establishing mandatory waiting periods for purchasers, creating greater restrictions for youth access to firearms, raising the age of handgun ownership, and holding parents responsible in the event of injury or death by a minor. Despite the emotionally charged climate, each piece of federal legislation died on the congressional floor. Many of the bills were reintroduced in subsequent legislative sessions, only to suffer the same fate. In fact, very few restrictions on firearms were able to be passed, despite the violence at Columbine. The state of Colorado was able to pass six bills related to reinstating the background check system, prohibiting straw purchases (buying a gun on another person's behalf), and including juvenile records in background checks. Nationwide, over 800 pieces of legislation were introduced in the first year after Columbine, with only approximately 10 percent of these bills being enacted into actual law.

The fourth gun used in the shooting was the IntraTec TEC-DC9, which is a semiautomatic pistol. At the time of the Columbine attack, this specific make of gun was expressly prohibited under the Federal Assault Weapons Ban of 1994, which outlined a list of firearms that were illegal to possess. An earlier model also had been used by the shooter in the 1989 Cleveland Elementary School shooting. The Columbine shooters had acquired the pistol from a friend and coworker at the pizza parlor where they worked. Despite knowing they were too young to purchase the gun, Mark Manes sold it to them for $500. He later was tried and convicted of selling a handgun to minors and was sentenced to six years in prison, as well as possessing an illegally sawed-off shotgun during target practice, for which he was sentenced an additional three years to be served concurrently (at the same time). He was released in 2001 after serving just 19 months in prison.

The Columbine Effect

Despite the number of shootings that had come before it, the shooting at Columbine High School was viewed as the first of its kind. In fact, researchers often refer to Columbine as an "archetypal case" or a "watershed moment" that changed the way America viewed mass public violence. Not only did the events of April 20 resonate with the Littleton community, they became a platform for a nationwide discourse on gun control, mental health, and violent media—what have been deemed the "usual suspects" of mass shootings.

There were many "firsts" with the Columbine shooting as well. Columbine was the first shooting in which cable news networks interrupted regular programming with live, breaking coverage from the scene. The shooting was also one of the first (though not the first) to involve multiple shooters, which is particularly rare in an already rare phenomenon. Further, the level of detail of planning and preparation conducted by the shooters was unprecedented. While mass shooters rarely snap and often employ some element of planning in their plot, the Columbine perpetrators had gone above and beyond in respect to all aspects of their attack.

When it occurred, the Columbine shooting appeared to grip the nation. According to the Pew Research Center, one of the nation's leading nonpartisan research firms, the shooting was the biggest news story of 1999. Researchers have found that in the first week alone, for example, almost four hours of total airtime from nightly news broadcasts had been dedicated to the shooting; another study found that over 319 individual stories were aired in similar broadcasts in the first year. Over 10,000 stories about the attack were published in the nation's top 50 newspapers in the same year. Columbine also was found by the Pew Research Center to be the third most closely followed news story of its decade behind the 1992 Rodney King verdict and the 1996 crash of TWA Flight 800. Even after deadlier shootings, including Virginia Tech and Sandy Hook, the coverage of Columbine remains unsurpassed.

The idea of the Columbine Effect has considerably broader impacts. Not only has the shooting been immortalized in popular culture, it also has become a measuring stick to which all other mass shootings are compared. Such events often are referred to as "Columbine at" their respective location, offering audiences a point of comparison through which to understand the current attack. Furthermore, a number of other shooters from events following Columbine typically refer back to the attack's perpetrators, either conveying sympathy toward them or using them as inspiration for their own rampages. As the 20th anniversary of Columbine approaches, the legacy of April 20, 1999 continues to wage on.

May 20, 1999: Heritage High School, Conyers, GA

Following a breakup with his girlfriend, 15-year-old Anthony "T.J." Solomon entered Heritage High School armed with a rifle and a revolver. He opened fire with the rifle, wounding six students. The shooter attempted suicide using the revolver, but was talked into surrendering by an assistant principal. He was found guilty but mentally ill. His original sentence was reduced from 40 to 20 years, and he was released on parole in 2016.

June 11, 1999: Reuven Bar-Levav & Associates, Southfield, MI

Diagnosed with paranoid schizophrenia, 27-year-old Joseph Brooks Jr. arrived at the psychiatric office where he was receiving treatment, armed with a handgun. He shot and killed his psychiatrist as well as another woman in the office before committing suicide. Four others were wounded in the shooting. The shooter had a history of refusing hospitalization and medication for his mental illness.

July 29, 1999: Momentum Securities & All-Tech Investment Group, Atlanta, GA

Angry after losing a large sum of money, 44-year-old Mark Barton armed himself with two firearms and headed to Momentum Securities, a brokerage company. He opened fire, killing 4 people. He then walked across the street to another brokerage company, All-Tech Investment Group, where he continued his rampage, killing 5 others. An additional 13 people were wounded in the attacks. The shooter fled the scene and was stopped by police at a gas station, where he committed suicide. Further investigation led police to discover that, prior to the shootings, the gunman had killed his wife and two children in their home.

August 5, 1999: Ferguson Enterprises & Post Airgas, Inc., Pelham, AL

Alan Eugene Miller arrived for his shift at Ferguson Enterprises armed with a handgun. The 34-year-old shot and killed two coworkers, who were both alleged to have received better driving routes at work than the shooter. The shooter then traveled to Post Airgas Inc., a company that had laid him off earlier that year, and opened fire, killing the assistant manager. After a high-speed chase, the shooter was apprehended by police. He was sentenced to death in 2000 and is currently incarcerated at Holman Correctional Facility in Atmore, Alabama, awaiting execution.

August 12, 1999: North Valley Jewish Community Center, Los Angeles, CA

Buford O'Neal Furrow Jr., a 38-year-old white supremacist, walked into the lobby of the community center armed with a handgun. He opened fire, wounding five people, including three children, a teenage counselor, and an office worker. He fled the scene and approached a postal worker whom he asked to mail a letter for him. The postal worker agreed, but the gunman shot and killed him. He fled to Las Vegas, where he turned himself in to the FBI. He was sentenced to life in prison without the possibility of parole in 2001 and currently is incarcerated at RRM Minneapolis, a federal correctional institution.

September 14, 1999: West Anaheim Medical Center, Anaheim, CA

Following the death of his mother, 43-year-old Dung Trinh entered the medical center where his mother had previously received treatment, armed with a gun. He arrived at the critical care unit on the second floor and opened fire. There, he fatally shot three hospital workers before being taken into police custody. The shooter believed that his mother had not received proper care at the center. He was sentenced to death in 2003 and is currently incarcerated at California's San Quentin State Prison, awaiting execution.

September 15, 1999: Wedgwood Baptist Church, Fort Worth, TX

Larry Eugene Ashbrook was armed with two handguns when he interrupted a teen prayer rally at the Wedgwood Baptist Church. The church was holding a concert that attracted hundreds of teenagers. The 47-year-old opened fire at the concert, killing seven and wounding seven others before committing suicide.

November 2, 1999: Xerox Corporation, Iwilei, HI

After allegedly being harassed at work, 40-year-old Bryan Uyesugi arrived at the Xerox Corporation armed with a pistol. He opened fire, killing his supervisor and six coworkers. He fled in a company van and engaged in a five-hour standoff with police before surrendering. He was convicted and sentenced to life in prison without the possibility of parole. He currently is incarcerated at the Saguaro Correctional Center, a private prison in Eloy, Arizona.

November 3, 1999: Northlake Shipyard, Seattle, WA

After losing his job at Northlake Shipyard, 29-year-old Kevin Cruz returned to his former place of employment armed with guns that he had stolen from a friend's house. He opened fire, killing two workers and wounding two others before fleeing the scene. Two months later, he was arrested. The shooter was convicted and sentenced to life in prison without the possibility of parole. He currently is incarcerated at the Monroe Correctional Complex in Monroe, Washington.

December 6, 1999: Fort Gibson Middle School, Fort Gibson, OK

Seth Trickey, a 13-year-old honors student at Fort Gibson Middle School, arrived at school armed with a handgun that belonged to his father. He opened fire in the school's courtyard, shooting indiscriminately. Five students were wounded before the shooter was subdued by a science teacher and ultimately taken into custody by police. A judge found him guilty of six counts of shooting with intent to kill. Though the prosecutor attempted to try him as an adult, he ultimately was tried and convicted as a juvenile and held in the custody of the state's juvenile justice system. He was released in 2004 after serving just over five years in incarceration.

December 30, 1999: Radisson Bay Harbor Hotel, Tampa, FL

Silvio Izquierdo-Leyva, a 38-year-old housekeeper at the Radisson Bay Harbor Hotel, opened fire inside the hotel. Four of the hotel's employees were killed and three others were wounded.

In an attempt to escape, he fatally shot another woman as he tried to steal her car. He subsequently was apprehended by police. He was found guilty of all five murders and sentenced to life in prison without possibility of parole. He currently is incarcerated at the annex of the Columbia Correctional Institution in Lake City, Florida.

2000s

March 30, 2000: Mi-T-Fine Car Wash, Irving, TX

After being fired from his job at Mi-T-Fine Car Wash, 28-year-old Robert Wayne Harris showed up at his former employer armed with a handgun that he borrowed from a friend. He arrived before the store opened, ordering the manager, assistant manager, and cashier to open a safe and give him money. He then fatally shot all three employees. Two other coworkers were killed and one other was wounded. The shooter was arrested, convicted, and sentenced to death. He was executed by lethal injection in 2012.

December 26, 2000: Edgewater Technology, Wakefield, MA

Michael McDermott, a 42-year-old employee, arrived at Edgewater Technology armed with various firearms. He shot and killed seven coworkers before being taken into custody by police. He was found guilty of seven counts of first-degree murder, and sentenced to seven consecutive life sentences without the possibility of parole. He currently is incarcerated at the Old Colony Correctional Center in Bridgewater, Massachusetts.

January 10, 2001: Amko Trading Store, Houston, TX

Ki Yang Park arrived at Amko Trading armed with two pistols. The 54-year-old fatally shot the owner of the wholesale firm, his wife, and their daughter before committing suicide. Further investigation led police to find the body of the shooter's wife hidden in a cooler in a convenience store that they owned together.

February 5, 2001: Navistar International Plant, Melrose Park, IL

The day before he was supposed to report to prison for his second felony conviction, 66-year-old William Baker forced his way into Navistar International Plant armed with a rifle. He was a former employee at the plant but had been fired for stealing. He opened fire, killing five people and wounding four others before committing suicide.

March 5, 2001: Santana High School, Santee, CA

Charles Andrew Williams, a 15-year-old student, arrived at Santana High School armed with a revolver. He removed the gun from his backpack in the boys' bathroom, reentered the school halls, and opened fire. He killed 2 students and wounded 13 others before surrendering to police. In an effort to avoid trial, the shooter pleaded guilty to all 28 charges against him, which included murder, attempted murder, and assault with a firearm. He was sentenced as an adult to life in prison with the possibility of parole after 50 years. He was housed in a juvenile facility until his 18th birthday; he subsequently was transferred to Valley State Prison in Chowchilla, California, where he currently remains incarcerated. He will be eligible for parole in 2052.

March 22, 2001: Granite Hills High School, El Cajon, CA

After suffering several disappointments, including being rejected by the Navy, 18-year-old Jason Hoffman, a former student at Granite Hills High School, returned to the campus armed with a shotgun. He entered the attendance office, which also housed the principal's and vice principal's offices, and opened fire. Five people were injured; no fatalities were incurred. The shooter was shot by a police officer who was present on campus and subsequently taken into custody. He pleaded guilty to six counts related to the crime. He was due to be sentenced to 27 years to life in prison when he committed suicide just eight months after the shooting. The Granite Hills High School shooting occurred in the same county as the Santana High attack just over two weeks earlier.

April 14, 2001: JB's Pub, Elgin, IL

After being kicked out of the bar for harassing female customers and employees, 42-year-old Luther Casteel returned to the bar later that night armed with several guns. He opened fire, killing a bartender and customer and wounding 16 others. He was wrestled to the ground by bar patrons and employees before being taken into custody by responding law enforcement. The shooter was found guilty of 35 different charges, including two counts of first-degree murder. He initially was sentenced to death by lethal injection, but his sentence later was reduced to life in prison without possibility of parole. He currently is incarcerated at the Menard Correctional Center in Menard, Illinois.

April 23, 2001: Laidlaw Transit Services, San Jose, CA

Armed with a semiautomatic handgun, 36-year-old Cathline Repunte arrived at the bus maintenance yard where she was employed. She opened fire, killing one person and wounding three others. A coworker then grabbed the shooter and held her until police arrived and placed her under arrest. She was charged with murder and attempted murder charges. After being diagnosed with paranoid schizophrenia, she received medication and therapy and soon was found fit to stand trial. She pleaded guilty to one count of first-degree murder and six counts of attempted murder. Sentenced to 35 years to life in prison, she currently is incarcerated at the Central California Women's Facility in Chowchilla, California.

July 23, 2001: Tony Frenchman's Creek Development, Palm Beach Gardens, FL

Keith Adams, a 28-year-old construction worker, opened fire on his coworkers with an assault rifle. Two people were struck by gunfire before the shooter was taken into custody. One of the workers died at the site; the other died at a hospital 11 days later. The shooter believed that his coworkers had urinated and defecated in his water container. When one of the workers threatened to have him fired, he began shooting. He was convicted on two counts of first-degree murdered and given two life sentences. While incarcerated in Miami, he killed another inmate and was convicted of second-degree murder for the offense. He since has been transferred to Martin Correctional Institution in Indiantown, Florida, where he currently remains.

September 9, 2001: Burns Security, Sacramento, CA

Following a breakup with his girlfriend and a suspension from work for vandalizing her car, 20-year-old Joseph Ferguson returned to Burns Security armed with a handgun and an assault weapon. He opened fire, killing five employees, including his ex-girlfriend, and wounding two others. He committed suicide the next day after being cornered by authorities.

December 6, 2001: Nu-Wood Decorative Millwork, Goshen, IN

Following an argument at work that led to his termination from the company, 36-year-old Robert Wissman returned to his place of employment later that day armed with a shotgun. He opened fire, killing one coworker and wounding six others before committing suicide.

January 16, 2002: Appalachian School of Law, Grundy, VA

After failing out of the law school for a second time, 43-year-old Peter Odighizuwa returned to the school armed with a handgun. He entered the offices of the dean and a professor, fatally shooting each at point-blank range. A female student also was killed in the attack and three others were wounded before the shooter was subdued by students and taken into police custody. He initially was found incompetent to stand trial and received treatment for three years before the case proceeded to trial. To avoid the death penalty, the shooter pleaded guilty to the murders, receiving three life sentences and an additional 28 years without the possibility of parole. He currently is incarcerated at Red Onion State Prison in Pound, Virginia.

March 22, 2002: Bertrand Products, Inc., South Bend, IN

William Lockey, a longtime employee and supervisor at the South Bend plant of Bertrand Products, arrived at work armed with a shotgun and a rifle. Four employees were killed and five others were wounded by the 54-year-old gunman, who opened fire during a meeting. He then fled the scene in a company van, continuing to fire his weapons at police who were pursuing him. At some point during the chase, while the van was still in motion, the gunman shot himself; when the vehicle came to a stop, police found him dead inside.

July 4, 2002: Los Angeles International Airport, Los Angeles, CA

Hesham Mohamad Hadayet, armed with two handguns and a knife, opened fire inside the Tom Bradley International Terminal of Los Angeles International Airport. A ticket agent and diamond importer were killed in the shooting and four others were wounded. The 41-year-old gunman was shot and killed by an airport security officer. He was not a U.S. citizen but had a green card that allowed him to work in the country.

July 8, 2002: Louis Armstrong International Airport, New Orleans, LA

Patrick Gott, a 43-year-old former Marine, opened fire with a shotgun inside Louis Armstrong International Airport. He identified himself as a practicing Muslim and opened fire when people made fun of his turban. Two people were shot, one of whom died later at the hospital. The shooter was tackled by two airline workers and a traveler and held until he could be taken into police custody. Initially charged with second-degree murder, the shooter was declared incompetent to stand trial. In 2005, a judge ruled that he could not be held criminally liable for the shooting due to his mental illness and he was remanded to a state psychiatric hospital for treatment.

October 27, 2002: Multiple Locations, Sallisaw, OK

Daniel Fears went on a killing spree in Sallisaw, Oklahoma. The 18-year-old gunman roamed through a neighborhood with a shotgun, firing indiscriminately. Two people were killed and eight others were wounded, including a 2-year-old girl, before the shooter was apprehended. He originally was convicted and sentenced to 11 life prison terms. His conviction was later overturned and he was found not guilty by reason of insanity. He was sent to the Oklahoma Forensic Center for treatment. In both 2013 and 2017, the shooter petitioned for outpatient visits; each time, his request was denied due to the judges' concerns for the danger he posed to the community.

October 28, 2002: University of Arizona, Tucson, AZ

Distraught over failing grades, 41-year-old nursing student and Gulf War veteran Robert Flores Jr. opened fire on the University of Arizona's campus. He shot and killed three of his professors before committing suicide. A suicide letter mailed by the gunman was received by the *Arizona Daily Star* after the shooting.

February 25, 2003: Labor Ready, Inc., Huntsville, AL

Emanuel Burl Patterson was looking for work at a temporary employment agency. After an argument over a CD player, the 23-year-old opened fire. Four fellow job-seekers were killed and one other was wounded. The shooter surrendered to police following a standoff at his apartment. He was charged with capital murder, convicted, and died in prison in 2012.

April 24, 2003: Red Lion Area Junior High School, Red Lion, PA

Following a breakup with his girlfriend and being disciplined by the school, 14-year-old James Sheets arrived at school armed with three guns that he had taken from his stepfather's safe. He made his way to the cafeteria and opened fire. The school's principal was killed in the attack. The shooter then committed suicide.

May 9, 2003: Case Western Reserve University, Cleveland, OH

Biswanath Halder, a 62-year-old former student at Case Western Reserve University, arrived on campus armed with a semiautomatic rifle. He opened fire as he made his way through the halls of one of the school's buildings, killing one student and wounding two others. After a gun battle with police, he was arrested. He was charged with 338 felony counts, including aggravated murder, attempted murder, and kidnapping. The shooter was convicted and sentenced to life in prison without the possibility of parole. He currently is incarcerated at the London Correctional Center in Southwest London, Ohio.

July 2, 2003: Modine Manufacturing Company, Jefferson City, MO

Jonathon Russell, a 25-year-old employee at the Modine Manufacturing Company, was on employment probation for "attendance issues." He armed himself with a concealed handgun, arrived for his shift, and opened fire. Three employees were killed, including a supervisor, and five others were wounded. He fled the scene and headed to police headquarters, where he engaged in a gun battle with two officers. He committed suicide.

July 8, 2003: Lockheed Martin Plant, Meridian, MS

Douglas Williams, a 48-year-old factory worker at the Lockheed Martin plant, was known by others as a racist. On the day of the shooting, he had to attend a mandatory ethics and diversity class with fellow employees, including several black individuals. He left the meeting and retrieved several firearms. He returned to the office where the meeting was held and opened fire. Six people, five of whom were black, were killed in the shooting and eight others were wounded. The shooter then committed suicide.

July 23, 2003: Century 21 Real Estate, San Antonio, TX

Ron Thomas, a 48-year-old real estate employee, entered his real estate office armed with a handgun. He opened fire, killing three women and critically wounding another. He later committed suicide as officers approached to take him into custody.

July 28, 2003: Gold Leaf Nursery, Boynton Beach, FL

After his estranged wife told him that she no longer loved him, 44-year-old Andres Casarrubias headed to Gold Leaf Nursery armed with a semiautomatic handgun. The shooter opened fire, killing three, including his wife and the nursery's owner, and wounding another individual. He was wrestled to the ground by two employees and was arrested by responding law enforcement. The shooter was charged with three counts of first-degree murder. He pleaded guilty to all counts in exchange for not going to trial and potentially getting the death penalty. He was handed down three life sentences without the possibility of parole. He currently is incarcerated at the Okeechobee Correctional Institution in Okeechobee, Florida.

August 19, 2003: Andover Industries, Andover, OH

After being denied vacation time for improperly filling out a form and learning that he had cancer, 32-year-old Richard Shadle returned to the Andover Industries plant after being sent home. Armed with four handguns, he opened fire, killing one coworker and wounding two others before committing suicide.

August 27, 2003: Windy City Core Supply, Chicago, IL

After being fired from his job, 36-year-old Salvador Tapia returned to the Windy City Core Supply warehouse armed with a handgun. The gunman shot and killed six former coworkers before engaging in a gun battle with police. He was fatally shot by a SWAT team member during the shootout.

September 24, 2003: Rocori High School, Cold Spring, MN

Armed with a handgun, 15-year-old student John Jason McLaughlin entered Rocori High School. As a pair of students exited the locker room, he opened fire, striking both, one of whom died instantly; the other died 16 days later at an area hospital. Following the gunfire, a gym coach confronted the shooter, who proceeded to empty his firearm; the faculty member secured the weapon and detained him until police arrived. Tried as an adult, he was found guilty of first-degree murder and second-degree murder and was sentenced to life plus 12 years, which he currently is serving at the Minnesota Correctional Facility in Stillwater, Minnesota. He will be eligible for parole in 2038. The victims' families later sued the shooter's parents, the school district, and the principal at the time of the shooting, arguing that the attack could have been prevented. The case ultimately was settled out of court.

October 5, 2003: Turner Monumental AME Church, Atlanta, GA

As churchgoers arrived at one of Atlanta's oldest black churches, 43-year-old Shelia W. Chaney Wilson opened fire from the table where she had been helping to prepare for communion. She fired her pistol toward the altar, killing the church's pastor. She then shot and killed her mother before committing suicide.

November 6, 2003: Watkins Motor Lines, West Chester, OH

After voluntarily resigning from his job in 2001, 50-year-old Joseph John Eschenbrenner (also known as "Tom West") drove through a security checkpoint at his former employer's office. Once inside the trucking company, he opened fire with two handguns. Two men were killed and three others wounded before the shooter fled in a van. He was apprehended at a truck stop approximately 50 miles away by the Indiana State Police. Initially found incompetent to stand trial, the shooter became embroiled in a legal debate over issues of forced medication. A later competency evaluation found him to be sane at the time of the shooting, and the gunman pleaded guilty in order to protect himself from the death penalty. He was sentenced to two life terms plus an additional 43 years, with no possibility of parole; he also was fined $110,000 and ordered to pay the cost of the prosecution. The shooter currently is incarcerated at the North Central Correctional Complex in Road Marion, Ohio.

April 2, 2004: North Carolina Employment Security Commission, Hendersonville, NC

William Case was in a meeting with his manager discussing the unemployment benefits he did not receive. As the conversation escalated, the 30-year-old retrieved a handgun from underneath his clothing and opened fire. Two people were shot, one of whom died at the scene. The shooter fled and was apprehended an hour later. He was convicted of first-degree murder and assault with a deadly weapon and sentenced to life in prison without the possibility of parole. He currently is incarcerated at the Pender Correctional Institution in Burgaw, North Carolina.

July 2, 2004: ConAgra Food, Inc. Meatpacking Plant, Kansas City, KS

After being teased by coworkers, 21-year-old Elijah Brown opened fire. Over the 10-minute rampage, he used two handguns to shoot seven people, five of whom died. The shooter then committed suicide at the scene.

November 18, 2004: Gateway Mall, St, Petersburg, FL

Justin Cudar entered a St. Petersburg Radio Shack electronics store armed with a handgun. Without saying a word, the 25-year-old retrieved the weapon and began firing. Two employees and a customer were struck in the attack; two of the individuals died at the hospital during surgery. The shooter then committed suicide.

December 8, 2004: Alrosa Villa Nightclub, Columbus, OH

During a Damageplan concert at the Alrosa Villa nightclub, in which more than 200 people were in the audience, 25-year-old former Marine Nathan Gale charged the stage. The gunman was armed with a rifle and began shooting through the venue. Four people were killed, including former Pantera guitarist "Dimebag" Darrell Abbott. A responding police officer shot the gunman with his service weapon, a 12-gauge shotgun. The shooter died at the scene.

January 26, 2005: Jeep Assembly Plant, Toledo, OH

Arriving mid-shift after missing work the day prior, 54-year-old Myles Meyers entered the Jeep assembly plant where he was employed. Armed with a shotgun, he entered the plant's office and took a woman hostage, ordering her to call others into the area where they were. When people entered the area, he began shooting. Two people were killed and two others were wounded before the shooter committed suicide.

February 13, 2005: Hudson Valley Mall, Kingston, NY

Entering through the mall's Best Buy store, 24-year-old Robert Bonelli Jr. opened fire on patrons with a semiautomatic rifle. As panicked customers fled into the mall, he followed, continuing to shoot until running out of ammunition. The shooter then dropped his weapon, at which time one mall employee grabbed the gun and another tackled him. He then was taken into police custody and the mall emptied. Two people were wounded in the attack; no one was killed. In order to avoid trial, the shooter pleaded guilty to an 18-count indictment, including first- and second-degree assault and criminal use of a firearm. He was sentenced to the maximum allowed under the plea deal—32 years—and will be eligible for parole in 2032. He currently is incarcerated at the Green Haven Correctional Facility in Stormville, New York.

February 21, 2005: Northrop Grumman Ship Systems, Pascagoula, MS

Upset over salary disparities, 41-year-old Alexander Lett arrived at the shipyard armed with a pistol. He opened fire on the 30 individuals who were working; two individuals were wounded in the shooting, one of whom died several days later. Other employees stopped the shooter as he was trying to leave and held him until police could take him into custody. He was charged with two counts of aggravated assault with one count upgraded to murder after the victim died. He later pleaded guilty and was sentenced to life in prison plus 20 years. He currently is incarcerated at the Southern Mississippi Correctional Institution in Leakesville, Mississippi, and will be eligible for parole in 2028.

February 25, 2005: Los Angeles Bureau of Public Works Field Office, Los Angeles, CA

Following a phone call with his supervisor about being late for work, 25-year-old Thomas Sampson traveled to the field office of the Los Angeles Bureau of Public Works. Armed with an assault rifle he had retrieved from his home on the way to the field office from where he had been working, he opened fire. Two people were killed. After leaving the field office, the shooter drove to a nearby police station, where he turned himself in. After being convicted of both first- and second-degree murder, the shooter was sentenced to life in prison without the possibility of parole. He currently is incarcerated at the Substance Abuse Treatment Facility and State Prison in Corcoran, California.

March 12, 2005: The Living Church of God, Brookfield, WI

Frustrated over a prior sermon, 44-year-old Terry Ratzmann left the service he currently was attending. He returned to the Sheraton Hotel, where the service was being held, armed with a handgun and opened fire. Within minutes, seven people, including the church's minister, had been killed and four others were wounded. The gunman then committed suicide.

March 21, 2005: Red Lake Senior High School, Red Lake, MN

After killing his grandfather and his grandfather's girlfriend at their home, 16-year-old Jeffrey Weise drove to Red Lake Senior High School on the reservation, where he previously had been a student. Armed with several weapons he had stolen from his grandfather, he entered through the school's main entrance, opening fire on two unarmed security guards, killing one. He continued to work his way through the school, firing at anyone he encountered. After police responded, they engaged in a shootout with the gunman, striking him twice. He then retreated to a vacant classroom and committed suicide. By the time the rampage ended, seven people had been killed at the school and five others injured. In the aftermath of the shootings, police arrested Louis Jourdain, the son of the tribe's chairman, on charges of conspiracy to commit murder for his communication with the shooter prior to the event. The conspiracy charges were dropped once he pleaded guilty to sending threatening messages over the Internet. Some estimates suggest that as many as 40 people knew about the rampage prior to it taking place.

August 8, 2005: Multiple Locations, Colton, CA

Armed with a handgun, 35-year-old Louis Mitchell Jr. arrived at the California Auto Specialists car dealership. He opened fire, killing two people and wounding two others. The shooter then fled the scene to an apartment complex in neighboring San Bernardino. There, he killed one person and wounded another. The day after the shooting, the gunman was seen threatening several other people with his firearm. He was taken into custody by police after they shot him in the leg. The shooter was tried and convicted on charges of capital murder and attempted murder. He was sentenced to death for the three homicides, as well as three life-in-prison terms without the possibility of parole for the attempted murder charges. He is currently awaiting execution on California's death row at San Quentin prison.

September 27, 2005: Verla International, New Windsor, NY

After being fired a year earlier for having child pornography on his work computer, 55-year-old Victor Piazza returned to the nail polish factory where he had been employed. Armed with a revolver, he opened fire. Three people were shot in the head but all survived their injuries. The shooter then retreated to the company owner's office and committed suicide.

November 8, 2005: Campbell County Comprehensive High School, Jacksboro, TN

After students notified school officials that 14-year-old Kenneth Bartley Jr. possessed a firearm on school grounds, he was called into the principal's office. Upon being questioned, the shooter retrieved the gun and opened fire. Three people were shot, one of whom died, before the shooter was disarmed by another teacher. He was initially charged as an adult for first-degree murder, but pleaded guilty to a lesser charge prior to the start of the trial and was sentenced to a total of 45 years in prison. In 2011, the plea deal was vacated after the shooter petitioned the court, citing that he had not had an opportunity to discuss the arrangement with his parents prior to accepting it. Three years later, a new trial was held and the shooter was found guilty of reckless homicide. He was released on bond but rearrested just four months later on charges of domestic assault, felony escape, and resisting arrest. He was released two days later, only to be rearrested the following month after assaulting two police deputies who were investigating a probation viola-tion. In 2015, he was allowed to relocate to Virginia to live with a counselor, but a warrant was issued after he failed to update his address with the court. A young child also died in his care while he was living with the counselor. In April 2016, he was rearrested for a probation violation but was released from jail that October.

November 20, 2005: Tacoma Mall, Tacoma, WA

Armed with a semiautomatic rifle and pistol, 20-year-old Dominick Maldonado entered the Tacoma Mall and opened fire on patrons. At one point, the shooter encountered an armed mall employee, who commanded him to put down the guns. The shooter responded by firing at him, striking him five times and leaving him paralyzed. Over the course of the attack, five other indi-viduals also were shot but all survived their injuries. He then took four people hostage in a music store before releasing them and surrendering to the responding SWAT team without further incident. He was charged with eight counts of first-degree assault, four counts of first-degree kidnapping, and two counts of unlawful possession of a firearm. Following his trial and conviction, he was sentenced to 163 years in prison. Originally housed in the Clallum Bay Corrections Center in Clallam Bay, Washington, he was transferred to the United States Penitentiary Administrative Maximum (Supermax) facility in Florence, Colorado, in 2011.

November 23, 2005: H&M Wagner and Sons, Glen Burnie, MD

After recently being fired as a driver, 54-year-old Joseph Allen Cobb returned to the restau-rant supply company. He opened fire, shooting two people, including his former supervisor; both individuals survived. The gunman then walked outside and shot himself in the head. He was pro-nounced dead several hours later at a nearby trauma center.

January 30, 2006: Santa Barbara U.S. Processing and Distribution Center, Goleta, GA

A former sorting clerk who had been placed on medical disability and had moved to New Mexico, 44-year-old Jennifer San Marco returned to the Goleta community. On the morning of the attack, she first shot and killed Beverly Graham, her former neighbor, at her house. She then drove to the mail processing plant in Goleta where she had worked, following another car through the security gates to gain access before holding an employee at gunpoint to gain access. Once inside, she opened fire with the same handgun used to kill Graham, killing six employees before turning the gun on herself.

March 14, 2006: Pine Middle School, Reno, NV

Upon arriving at school, 14-year-old James Scott Newman entered a bathroom, retrieved a re-volver he had stolen from his parents, and loaded the weapon. He then entered a hallway and fired on the first people he saw. Two people were injured before a teacher convinced the shooter to drop the gun and held him until law enforcement came. The shooter originally was charged as an adult but ultimately pleaded guilty to two charges of battery with a deadly weapon. Sentenced as a juvenile, he was placed on house arrest until the completion of 200 hours of community service.

March 25, 2006: Capitol Hill Residence, Seattle, WA

On the evening of March 24, 2006, 28-year-old Kyle Huff attended a zombie-themed rave at the Capitol Hill Arts Center. During the event, Huff was invited to an after-hours party at a local residence. While attending the party, he left the house and went to his truck, where he retrieved a shotgun and semiautomatic handgun, as well as additional ammunition. As he returned to the home, he opened fire, shooting five individuals who were outside talking. He then proceeded into the house, where he continued firing at party-goers. As a police officer arrived on scene, the shooter committed suicide. Six people had been killed and two others wounded in the attack.

April 18, 2006: Finninger's Catering Service, St. Louis, MO

Armed with a handgun, 55-year-old Herbert Chalmers Jr. arrived at his workplace. Once inside, he opened fire, killing two people, including one of the business's owners, and wounding a third. He then went outside to the parking lot and committed suicide. A further investigation revealed that prior to the rampage, he had raped one woman and then killed his ex-girlfriend with whom he shared a child. On the way to his workplace, he also had stopped to purchase more ammunition.

June 26, 2006: Safeway Distribution Center, Denver, CO

An employee at the distribution center, 22-year-old Michael Ford, entered his workplace armed with a handgun. He opened fire, shooting indiscriminately at his coworkers, killing one person and wounding five others. Responding police were able to breach the building but were ambushed as they tried to look for the shooter. One SWAT officer was injured, at which time law enforcement shot at the gunman, hitting him seven times and killing him.

July 28, 2006: Jewish Federation of Greater Seattle, Seattle, WA

Armed with two semiautomatic pistols and a knife, 30-year-old Naveed Afzal Haq forced his way into the building and gained access to the federation's offices by holding one of the employee's nieces at gunpoint. Once inside, he moved to the second floor of the building and opened fire. One person was killed and five others were injured. He then took a number of individuals hostage, holding them as police arrived on scene. Just over 15 minutes after the shooting began, the gunman dropped his weapons, exited the building, and surrendered to police. He was charged with aggravated murder, five counts of attempted murder, kidnapping, burglary, and malicious harassment. During his first trial, the jury found him not guilty on one count of attempted murder but declared itself hung on the remaining counts. The shooter was retried and convicted of all counts. He was sentenced to life in prison without the possibility of parole plus 120 years, which he currently is serving at the Airway Heights Correction Center in Airway Heights, Washington.

August 24, 2006: Essex Elementary School, Essex, VT

Armed with a handgun, 26-year-old Christopher Williams entered Essex Elementary School while teachers and staff were present for a service day (school was not in session at the time). In search of his former girlfriend, whom he never found, he opened fire, killing one teacher and wounding another. He fled the school and shot another person, who survived, at a third location before turning the gun on himself. Despite shooting himself twice in the head, the gunman survived and was taken into custody. Further investigation revealed that prior to the rampage at the school, he had shot and killed his ex-girlfriend's mother in her home, bringing the total fatalities to two. The shooter was charged with two counts each of first-degree murder and attempted murder, to which he pleaded not guilty. He later was convicted and sentenced to three consecutive life sentences; there is no possibility of parole for the gunman. He currently is incarcerated at an out-of-state facility through the Vermont Department of Corrections.

August 30, 2006: Orange High School, Hillsborough, NC

After killing his father in their home, 18-year-old Alvaro Castillo drove to Orange High School, where he had formerly been a student. After detonating a cherry bomb outside the school, he opened fire, wounding two people. Once his gun jammed, a sheriff's deputy assigned to the school and the driver's education teacher, who was a retired highway patrol officer, took the shooter into custody. The investigation of the attack revealed that prior to the shooting, the gunman sent a manifesto package to a local news station; he also emailed the principal at Columbine High School. Originally pleading not guilty to the charges, the shooter was found guilty at trial of first-degree murder, as well as multiple assault and weapons violations. He was sentenced to life in prison without the possibility of parole, which he currently is serving at the Nash Correctional Institution in Nashville, North Carolina.

October 2, 2006: West Nickel Mines School, Nickel Mines, PA

Local milk delivery man Charles Carl Roberts arrived at the West Nickel Mines School, located in Lancaster County. The 32-year-old entered the one-room schoolhouse and asked if anyone had seen a missing fastener on the road. When the room's occupants denied seeing it, he stepped outside, only to return moments later with a handgun. He ordered the male students to carry items into the schoolhouse from his truck. While he was supervising this, the school's teacher and her mother escaped and ran to a nearby farm, where the owner called 9-1-1.

Once all of the provisions had been brought inside, the shooter boarded the front door to the schoolroom shut. He then ordered all of the female students to line up against the chalkboard before allowing the boys, a pregnant woman, and three parents with infants to leave. The shooter proceeded to tie the remaining girls' legs together with plastic ties. After a brief telephone exchange with his wife and then law enforcement, who tried to negotiate a release of the girls, the gunman opened fire, shooting each of the 10 girls. As law enforcement officers approached the schoolhouse and tried to make entry, the shooter committed suicide. Five of the girls were killed, while the other 5 survived their injuries.

Within a week of the shooting, the schoolhouse had been demolished. A new building, christened the New Hope School, was built at another location within the community and opened six months after the attack. Many of the surviving children returned to continue their lessons.

A Lesson in Forgiveness

One of the main emphases in the aftermath of the shooting was that of forgiveness. Even on the day of the shooting, members of the Amish community shunned hate and thoughts of evil of the shooter. As early as several hours after the attack, one Amish neighbor had reached out to the shooter's family, offering them forgiveness and comfort over the loss of their loved one. The community set up a charitable fund to help the shooter's family. Approximately 30 members of the Amish community attended the shooter's funeral, and his widow was one of the few outsiders that was invited to the funerals of the girls who were slain in the attack.

December 9, 2006: Law Offices of Wood, Phillips, Katz, Clark, & Mortimer, Chicago, IL

Armed with a revolver, knife, and hammer, 59-year-old Joe Jackson entered the Citigroup Center and forced a security guard at gunpoint to take him to the law office. After chaining the doors to the law office shut, he opened fire, killing three people and wounding one other. After he took others hostage and engaged in a 45-minute standoff with police, a pair of SWAT snipers shot and killed the gunman, ending the rampage.

January 11, 2007: Crossroads Industrial Services, Indianapolis, IN

After being dropped off at work at Crossroads Industrial Services, a manufacturing business that works with Easter Seals to employ disabled people, 24-year-old Jason Burnam made his way to the business's cafeteria. Armed with a handgun, he stood up on one of the tables and began firing at the employees. Four people were shot and wounded before police arrived and took the shooter into custody. As a part of a plea deal, the shooter pleaded guilty to four counts of aggravated battery and was sentenced to 50 years in prison, plus 10 years on home detention and 10 years suspended to probation. He currently is serving his sentence at the Pendleton Treatment Unit in Pendleton, Indiana, and is eligible for parole in 2021.

February 12, 2007: Trolley Square Mall, Salt Lake City, UT

After arriving at the mall, 18-year-old Sulejman Talović walked toward the building, armed with a shotgun, a handgun, and a backpack full of ammunition. He shot the first two people that he encountered in the parking lot in the head before continuing into the mall. One of the individuals died; the other managed to flee and was aided by other patrons. The shooter proceeded into the mall, continuing to fire at individuals as he walked in and out of stores. Several officers in the mall were able to push the gunman into the Pottery Barn store, where an active shooter contact team had arrived and was able to confront him from behind. The team opened fire, striking the gunman 15 times and killing him. Over the six-minute rampage, five people had been killed and four others were wounded.

February 12, 2007: Zigzag Net Inc., Philadelphia, PA

Armed with an assault rifle and a handgun, 44-year-old Vincent Dortch arrived at an investors' meeting at ZigZag Net. Minutes after the meeting started, he retrieved the guns and opened fire. Three people in the meeting were killed; a fourth was wounded but managed to break free after being tied up and call police. When law enforcement arrived on scene, they exchanged gunfire with the shooter, who then ducked behind a door and committed suicide.

March 5, 2007: Kenyon Press, Signal Hill, CA

Disgruntled about a reduction in hours, 68-year-old Jose Mendez arrived at his employer's office armed with a semiautomatic handgun. He opened fire, wounding three people. The shooter then committed suicide; his body was found by law enforcement when they responded to the scene.

April 9, 2007: Gordon Advisors, Troy, MI

After being fired the week prior, 38-year-old Anthony LaCalamita returned to the offices of Gordon Advisors armed with a shotgun. He opened fire, killing one person and wounding two others. He then left the building and when his vehicle was approached by police, he engaged in a high-speed chase lasting approximately 30 miles before he was taken into custody. Following a seven-day trial, the shooter was found guilty of first-degree premeditated murder, two counts of assault with an intent to murder, and three felony firearms charges. He was sentenced to life in prison without the possibility of parole, which he currently is serving at the Saginaw Correctional Facility in Freeland, Michigan. While in jail awaiting trial for the office shooting, the gunman also had attacked a deputy, cutting his neck with a sharpened toothbrush. He was convicted of assault with the intent to murder for the incident and was sentenced to an additional 10- to 25-years in prison.

April 16, 2007: Virginia Polytechnic Institute and State University, Blacksburg, VA

At approximately 7:15 a.m., 23-year-old senior Seung-Hui Cho entered the West Ambler Johnston Hall dormitory on the campus of Virginia Tech. He made his way up to the fourth floor, where he shot and killed freshman Emily Hilscher, who had just returned to campus from a weekend away. The shooter also killed the dorm's resident advisor, Ryan Clark, who responded to the disturbance. He then returned to his dorm in the neighboring Harper Hall, where he changed his clothes, erased all files within his email account, and left his suite. At 9:01 a.m., the shooter visited a nearby post office, where he mailed a package to NBC News, later determined to contain his manifesto, 43 photographs, and approximately 10 total minutes of video. The package was received by the network two days after the shooting.

After stopping at the post office, the shooter returned to campus and proceeded to Norris Hall, the university's mechanics and engineering building, which is located on the opposite side of campus from the dormitories. At approximately 9:26 a.m., he chained the building's three main entrances shut and affixed a note to the doors indicate that bombs would detonate if anyone tried to gain access. He then made his way to the second floor, where several classes were already underway. After scoping out several of the classes, he entered Room 206, where a graduate engineering class was in session, and opened fire. The professor and nine students were killed and three other students were injured (only one student in the room was unharmed).

The shooter then moved across the hall to Room 207, where he continued firing, striking several students and the professor. Individuals in the neighboring classroom (Room 205) heard the commotion and proceeded to barricade their door; despite attempts, the shooter never was able to gain access and everyone in the room survived. Individuals in Room 211 also heard the disturbance and attempted to prevent access, but the shooter made entry before they could secure the room and he continued firing at those present. He then went back to Room 207, where several people had attempted to block the door. The shooter was able to fire through a small gap he created, but was denied full entry back inside. He returned to Room 211, continuing to fire at individuals as he methodically walked up and down the aisles of desks.

During the rampage, professor Kevin Granata ushered students from a third-floor class-room into his office and went downstairs to investigate the disruption. He was shot and killed when he encountered the gunman; none of the students secured in his office were harmed. The shooter also attempted to gain entry to Room 204, where a mechanics class had been in session. Professor Liviu Librescu, a Holocaust survivor, used his body to shield the door as he instructed students to flee out of the classroom's windows. The shooter fired through the door, killing Librescu; most of the students in the room were able to flee safely, though two were wounded by gunfire while trying to escape.

The shooter made his way back to Room 206, where he fired more rounds at the students in the room. His final move led him back to Room 211. As responding law enforcement breached the chained doors to the building, the shooter committed suicide. During his 11-minute rampage, an additional 5 faculty members and 25 students had been killed, bringing the death toll to 32; 17 others were injured in the attack.

Emergency Response and Virginia Tech

One of the major issues highlighted in the review of the events on the day of the shooting related to emergency notifications of the campus community. On April 16, the Virginia Tech community relied on email alerts to notify faculty, students, and staff of any on-campus emergencies; their text messaging system was in the process of being installed and was not in use on the day of the shooting. The initial notification about the shooting in West Ambler Johnston was not disseminated until 9:26 a.m., the precise time the shooter was in the process of chaining the doors to Norris Hall shut and well after that round of classes already had begun. The delay was caused, in part, by the belief that the initial shooting was domestic in nature—Emily Hilscher's boyfriend, with whom she had spent the weekend, was an early suspect—and this led to a delay in the convening of the campus policy group responsible for crafting and circulating such notifications.

The second notification, this one regarding the active shooter scenario at Norris Hall, was sent at 9:50 a.m. As the shooter committed suicide at 9:51 a.m., most (if not all) of his victims had been killed or injured by the time this message had been transmitted. As such, in the wake of the tragedy, many suggested that if the messages—and the initial notification in particular—had been transmitted earlier, the loss of life at Virginia Tech that day might have been lessened. The shooting led colleges and universities nationwide to implement new emergency notification systems or overhaul existing platforms to help overcome such potential issues on their campuses.

Mental Health and Virginia Tech

Another key finding of the Virginia Tech Review Panel related to the shooter's mental health leading up to the attack. Following his immigration to the United States from South Korea, the shooter struggled with mental health–related issues. During middle school, he was diagnosed with major depression and selective mutism, an anxiety disorder. Due to his struggles, he was dissuaded from going to Virginia Tech, but chose to anyway. Throughout his four years at the university, his behavior became more erratic. In his junior year, his writings became more violent and his personality more withdrawn. As his behavior in class grew more intense (including snapping photographs with his cell phone camera of female students under his desk), students stopped attending, a move that prompted one of his professors to have him removed from class, and he engaged in independent study with the English department's chair.

He also engaged in stalking of other students, which culminated on December 12, 2005, when a female student reported this behavior to the university's police department. After the police visited the shooter, he commented that he "might as well go kill [himself]" to his suitemates, which prompted them to report the threat. The shooter was detained, and during prescreening with a local mental health representative, deemed an imminent danger to himself and others and subsequently hospitalized. Following observation, he went before a judge, who reviewed the evaluations and also heard evidence from the shooter himself. The judge ruled that the shooter was in fact an imminent danger, but ordered him outpatient treatment as opposed to longer-term detention. Though the shooter kept his appointment with the counseling center immediately after his release on December 14, 2005, he never attended any follow-up sessions.

The events related to the shooter's detention and subsequent finding that he was a danger to himself were never reported to the firearms background check system. This enabled him to pass the necessary checks in order to purchase his guns, despite being disqualified under federal law from purchasing a firearm. The first pistol was purchased on February 9, 2007. The shooter followed the state-mandated waiting period of 30 days and purchased his second weapon on March 13, just over a month prior to the shooting. Both guns were used in the attack; a total of 174 rounds had been fired.

In the first days following the Virginia Tech shooting, then governor Tim Kaine passed an executive order to require outpatient orders to be grounds for disqualifications of firearms ownership and to improve reporting to the records system. At a national level, President George W. Bush signed the NICS Improvements Amendments Act into law on January 8, 2008. Among other provisions, the act designated approximately $1.3 billion in federal funding to states to help improve their reporting of mental health records to the background check system. Between its enactment and the 2012 Sandy Hook Elementary School shooting, however, just over $50 million had been appropriated by 18 states and an estimated one million records still were missing from the system.

April 27, 2007: Lode Street Wastewater Facility, Santa Cruz, CA

Armed with two handguns, 50-year-old Steven Smith arrived at the Lode Street Wastewater Facility, where he was a supervisor. He entered the plant and opened fire, killing two people, one of whom was his estranged wife who was a maintenance worker for the company. The shooter then committed suicide at the scene.

May 1, 2007: Ward Parkway Center, Kansas City, MO

After beating his next-door neighbor to death in her home, 51-year-old David Logsdon used her residence for several days before taking her car and driving it to the Ward Parkway Center. While on the way, he was stopped by a police officer who identified the car as matching the description of the neighbor's vehicle. Using a handgun, the shooter exchanged gunfire with the police officer. The officer was shot in the arm and the gunman was struck in the torso. The shooter drove off and arrived at the mall parking lot. Armed with a rifle and using ammunition he had paid for with the neighbor's credit card, he opened fire. He shot and killed two people and wounded seven others outside the mall before making his way inside, where he collapsed from blood loss attributed to the earlier shooting with the officer. Another officer arrived inside the mall and fired two shots at the gunman, killing him.

May 20, 2007: Multiple Locations, Moscow, ID

Armed with two assault rifles, 37-year-old Jason Hamilton parked his vehicle in the Latah County Courthouse parking lot. He opened fire on the sheriff's office dispatch center located across the street, killing one deputy, wounding another, and destroying several of the police cruisers. He then ran into the nearby Presbyterian Church, where he shot and killed the caretaker before turning the gun on himself. Two others were also wounded in the rampage. Prior to the shooting, the gunman also had shot and killed his wife in their home.

August 8, 2007: Liberty Transportation Company, Walbridge, OH

During a scheduled meeting with his employers regarding issues with his performance, 43-year-old Calvin Neyland Jr. retrieved a handgun and opened fire, first in the company yard and then inside. Two people were killed before the shooter fled the scene to a nearby motel, where he had a room. Several hours later, police arrested him at the motel. Originally pleading not guilty, the shooter was tried and convicted of two counts of aggravated murder; death penalty specifications related to the killings and gun specifications also were included in the convictions. He was sentenced to death, which he later appealed to the Ohio Supreme Court, along with the convictions. Both were upheld by the state's high court. In 2014, his execution was stayed so that his attorneys could pursue additional appeals. He remains incarcerated on death row at Chillicothe Correctional Institution in Chillicothe, Ohio.

August 30, 2007: Co-Op City Apartments, Bronx, NY

After being fired from his job two years earlier, 44-year-old Paulino Valenzuela returned to Co-Op City, the housing complex where he had been employed and also had resided. Armed with a pistol, he opened fire, killing one person and wounding two others. Covered in blood, he then rode the subway to the police station, where he turned himself in. The shooter was charged with murder, manslaughter, assault, and possession of a weapon. He later was convicted of second-degree murder, second-degree attempted murder, first-degree assault, and two counts of criminal possession of a weapon. He was sentenced to 90 years to life in prison; he tried to escape after the punishment was handed down. The shooter currently is incarcerated at the Five Points Correctional Facility in Romulus, New York. The shooter appealed, filing a motion for a mistrial, but this was denied by the court.

September 21, 2007: Delaware State University, Dover, DE

After running into a student with whom he had a fight in a cafeteria at Delaware State University, 18-year-old student Loyer Braden left the building. Once outside, he retrieved the handgun he had on his person and opened fire. Two individuals were hit in the attack; while one survived, the other died a month later from complications from her injuries. The shooter was arrested in his dorm room three days after the attack and subsequently was charged with attempted murder, assault, reckless endangerment, and a weapons violation. Though he initially admitted to the shooting, the case ultimately was dismissed after the prosecution failed to disclose that a witness who was with one of the victims had told investigators that the suspect actually was not the gunman.

October 4, 2007: Giordano and Giordano Law Office, Alexandria, LA

Armed with a handgun, 63-year-old John Ashley entered the law office and opened fire. Five people were shot in the rampage, two of whom died. The shooter then engaged in a 10-hour standoff with responding law enforcement, even firing his weapon at the officers, who did not fire back. In order to end the standoff after failed attempts to communicate with the shooter, police entered the building using explosives and tear gas. They exchanged gunfire with the shooter, ultimately killing him.

October 7, 2007: Private Residence, Crandon, WI

Following a heated exchange, 20-year-old Tyler Peterson, an off-duty sheriff's deputy, left and then returned to a residence where a homecoming party was taking place. Armed with an automatic rifle, he opened fire on the partygoers. Seven people were shot in the rampage, six of whom died. As he attempted to leave the party, a patrol officer responded and the two engaged in a shootout before the gunman fled. Hours later, after engaging in an exchange of fire with law enforcement, he committed suicide after attempted negotiations to surrender to the police failed. The residence where the shooting occurred was demolished in 2008.

October 8, 2007: Am-Pac Tire Pros, Simi Valley, CA

Armed with a handgun, 29-year-old Robert Becerra arrived at the Am-Pac Tire Pros store. Without saying a word, he opened fire on customers and employees. One person was killed and two others were wounded in the attack. Prior to police arriving on scene, the shooter committed suicide.

October 10, 2007: Success Tech Academy, Cleveland, OH

Armed with two handguns, three knives, and additional boxes of ammunition, 14-year-old student Asa Coon returned to the school from which he had been suspended two days earlier. He went to a bathroom on the building's fourth floor and loaded the two guns. Once he exited, he encountered another student who punched him in the face after the shooter purposefully bumped into him. The shooter then pulled his weapons and began firing. Four people (two students and two teachers) were struck by gunfire but all survived; an additional student was injured after being trampled by fleeing students. The shooter then retreated into a nearby room, where he committed suicide.

December 5, 2007: Westroads Mall, Omaha, NE

After entering and scanning the Von Maur department store at the Westroads Mall, 19-year-old Robert Hawkins exited the building and returned minutes later, armed with a semiautomatic rifle and two magazines. He took the store's elevator to the top floor and immediately opened fire once the doors opened. At the end of his six-minute rampage, eight people—six Von Maur employees and two customers—had been killed and four others were injured. The shooter then committed suicide.

December 9, 2007: Multiple Locations, Arvada and Colorado Springs, CO

After being denied overnight shelter at the Youth With A Mission training center in Arvada, CO, 24-year-old Mathew Murray opened fire with a pistol, killing two and injuring two others. Later that afternoon, he drove to the New Life Church in Colorado Springs, armed with a semi-automatic rifle and two semiautomatic pistols. He first opened fire in the parking lot, shooting four, two of whom died. He then made his way into the church, where he shot and wounded a fifth person. Jeanne Assam, a former Minneapolis Police Department officer who was also a church member, retrieved her concealed firearm and engaged the shooter, striking him several times. The shooter then committed suicide.

February 7, 2008: Kirkwood City Hall, Kirkwood, MO

Frustrated with the city government over various issues, 52-year-old Charles Thornton arrived at Kirkwood City Hall armed with a revolver. While walking to the building, he shot and killed a police officer who was picking up dinner nearby. After taking the officer's service weapon, he entered City Hall, where a council meeting had just been called to order. Moments later, he opened fire on the 30 people in attendance with the two guns. By the end of the rampage, the shooter had killed six individuals and wounded one other. Two police officers, who had heard the commotion from nearby, rushed to the building and engaged the shooter. He was hit twice and died at the scene.

February 8, 2008: Louisiana Technical College, Baton Rouge, LA

Armed with a revolver, 23-year-old student Latina Williams entered a classroom at Louisiana Technical College. She spoke briefly with the instructor and then left the room, only to return through another entrance and open fire. Two people were killed before she reloaded and committed suicide. No other students or the instructor were wounded in the attack.

February 14, 2008: Northern Illinois University, DeKalb, IL

Armed with a shotgun, three semiautomatic handguns, extra magazines, and a knife, 27-year-old former NIU graduate student Steven Kazmierczak entered Cole Hall, where he proceeded to a large auditorium. At the time, an oceanography class was in session. After arming himself and then entering the room, he made his way up to the stage at the front of the classroom, where he opened fire with the shotgun. After shooting into the crowd of students, the gunman turned and fired at the instructor, who then attempted to escape. He continued to fire the shotgun, reloading several times, before abandoning the weapon. Each time he reloaded, some of the students in the room seized the opportunity to escape; others remained in place or attempted to change their hiding positions.

The shooter then retrieved one of the handguns and continued firing. He walked off the stage and proceeded up the aisle on one side of the classroom, shooting at individuals he saw. Over six-and-a-half minutes, the shooter fired 48 rounds from the handgun and six from the shotgun. Five people had been killed and another 21 were injured (17 directly from gunfire). The shooter then committed suicide as law enforcement arrived on scene.

The Future of Cole Hall

Like other venues before, Northern Illinois University had to decide whether to reopen Cole Hall after the shooting. Previous locations, such as Columbine, had closed just the main space where the shooting occurred, opting instead to keep the building intact and memorialize the shooting location. Virginia Tech, conversely, completely renovated Norris Hall, the building in which 30 of the victims had been killed. In addition to containing offices and labs for the Department of Engineering Science and Mechanics, Norris Hall now houses the Center for Peace Studies and Violence Prevention. Similarly, Theater 9, site of the Aurora movie theater shooting, also was renovated and reopened to the public. In extreme circumstances, locations, including the original schoolhouse in Nickel Mines and Sandy Hook Elementary School, are razed completely, with entirely new buildings being erected.

The fate of Cole Hall was decided among mixed emotions. Illinois's governor at the time, Rod Blagojevich, along with the university's president, suggested that the building be demolished to prevent students from having to relive the events of February 14. This proposal received a fair amount of pushback. Nearly three months after the shooting, the decision was made that the building would be renovated completely. Construction began in 2011 and was completed the following year. The newly remodeled Cole Hall now houses the Anthropology Museum, moved from another building on campus.

March 3, 2008: Wendy's Restaurant, West Palm Beach, FL

After arriving at a West Palm Beach–area Wendy's, 60-year-old Alburn Edward Blake went into the restaurant's bathroom and came out holding a handgun. He began firing into the busy restaurant, emptying his gun and pausing only to reload. By the time the rampage was over, one person—a lieutenant for the county's fire rescue company—had been killed and four others were wounded. The shooter then committed suicide.

March 12, 2008: Regions Bank, McComb, MS

Armed with a handgun, 35-year-old Robert Lanham entered the Regions Bank where his ex-wife worked and opened fire. Two people were killed before the gunman took his ex-wife hostage and fled the building. As she tried to escape the vehicle, the car crashed and she was ejected; she died at the scene from her injuries. The shooter then committed suicide.

March 19, 2008: Black Road Auto Office, Santa Maria, CA

Armed with a semiautomatic handgun, 31-year-old Lee Isaac Bedwell Leeds arrived at his family's wrecking yard. He opened fire, first killing his father in the office and then shooting two employees and a customer outside the business. After pausing to reload his gun, the shooter fled the scene. He discarded the gun along the way, ultimately being captured and arrested as he tried to scale a fence. He was charged with four counts of first-degree murder, as well as multiple murder circumstances and gun use allegations. Despite pleading not guilty by reason of insanity, the jury convicted him of all four murder charges; he had accepted responsibility for the lesser counts prior to trial. The shooter was sentenced to four consecutive life terms without the possibility of parole plus four consecutive 25-year terms for the gun enhancements. In 2015, the shooter successfully petitioned for a new sanity hearing in relation to his father's murder. That particular hearing is still pending at the time of this writing. In 2016, the shooter filed a petition for a writ of habeas corpus, challenging the constitutionality of his detention. In 2017, the petition was denied. He currently is incarcerated at the Salinas Valley State Prison in Soledad, California.

May 25, 2008: Players Bar & Grill, Winnemucca, NV

Armed with a semiautomatic handgun, 30-year-old Ernesto Villagomez entered the bar, which had approximately 300 patrons at the time. He pulled out the gun and began firing, killing two people and wounding two others. One of the bar's patrons, a 48-year-old Marine, pulled his concealed weapon while the shooter was reloading. The patron shot and killed the gunman, ending the rampage.

June 25, 2008: Atlantis Plastics Plant, Henderson, KY

As he was being escorted out of the factory following an argument, 25-year-old Wesley Neal Higdon retrieved his semiautomatic handgun and shot his supervisor. He then went back into the plant and continued firing at employees. By the end of the rampage, five people had been killed and one injured. The shooter then committed suicide.

July 28, 2008: Tennessee Valley Unitarian Universalist Church, Knoxville, TN

During a youth performance at a local church, 58-year-old Jim David Adkisson entered the church armed with a shotgun. He opened fire on the 225 people in attendance, killing two and wounding seven others. Several of the church members were able to restrain him until police arrived, thereby ending the rampage. Following his arrest, the shooter was charged with murder and attempted murder. He pleaded guilty to two first-degree murder charges and was sentenced to life in prison without the possibility of parole. He currently is serving out his sentence at the Northwest Correctional Complex in Tiptonville, Tennessee.

August 1, 2008: Simon & Schuster Book Warehouse, Bristol, PA

Following termination for absenteeism, 32-year-old Robert Diamond arrived at his former workplace several months later, armed with a handgun. He opened fire, killing two employees, one of whom was on a temporary assignment. The shooter then surrendered at the scene without further incident. The shooter was tried and convicted of two counts of first-degree murder. He was issued a capital sentence for each of the murders. In 2015, after appeals had been exhausted, the execution warrant for the shooter was signed by the state's governor. His execution, scheduled for March 2015, was stayed; the shooter remains on Pennsylvania's death row at SCI Greene in Waynesburg, Pennsylvania.

September 2, 2008: Multiple Locations, Seattle, WA

Following release from jail on a drug offense, 26-year-old Isaac Zamora armed himself with a rifle and a handgun. He first killed a Skagit County sheriff's deputy who responded to a call to his mother's home. He continued firing throughout the neighborhood, shooting four others, before driving away. While on the road, he continued to fire at people he passed. As police responded, a high-speed chase ensued. The suspect soon ended the chase and turned himself in at the Skagit County Sheriff's Office. By the end of the rampage, six people had been killed and two others were wounded. At trial, the shooter pleaded guilty to four counts of aggravated murder; he also pleaded not guilty by reason of insanity to two additional charges of aggravated murder. He was sentenced to four life terms, which he originally began serving at Western State Hospital, a Lakewood, WA, psychiatric hospital. Citing a potential safety threat to patients and staff, the shooter was transferred to Monroe Correctional Complex in Monroe, Washington in 2012, where he currently remains incarcerated.

October 26, 2008: University of Central Arkansas, Conway, AR

Just after 9:00 p.m., the University of Central Arkansas Police Department received a call of shots fired outside of the Arkansas Hall dormitory. Two students had been killed and a third was injured. Over the course of the next day, the police identified four suspects—20-year-old Brandon Wade (the driver), 19-year-old Kelcey Perry (the suspected shooter), 19-year-old Kawin Brockman (accomplice #1), and 19-year-old Mario Toney (accomplice #2)—and took them into custody. Each were charged with two counts of capital murder, along with other felony counts including attempted murder, engaging in a terrorist act, and several weapons charges. Three of the four pleaded guilty to three counts of committing a terrorist act in exchange for the remaining charges being dismissed. The driver was sentenced to 26 years in prison with 40 years of probation. The two accomplices each were sentenced to 18 years plus the same probationary term. The three then testified against the suspected shooter, saying that that individual was the one who had fired the shots. The suspected gunman subsequently pleaded guilty and his charges were reduced from capital murder to first-degree murder; he also was convicted of first-degree battery and possession of a firearm on a public school campus and was sentenced to 45 years in prison. The shooter currently is incarcerated at the East Arkansas Regional Unit in Marianna, Arkansas, while the driver is serving his sentence at the Faulkner County Waiting List facility in Conway, Arkansas. The first accomplice was granted parole in 2016 after completing a prison vocational program. The second accomplice was released on parole after a decision in 2012, but was soon rearrested on unrelated charges.

November 14, 2008: SiPort, Inc., Santa Clara, CA

Following being terminated from the company, 47-year-old Jing Hua Wu entered the office armed with a handgun. He opened fire, killing three people, then left the building. A manhunt ensued, and the shooter was arrested several days later. Following a trial, the shooter was convicted of three counts of first-degree murder plus special circumstances of using a firearm. He was sentenced to life in prison without the possibility of parole plus an additional 75 years. He currently is incarcerated at the California State Prison Solano in Vacaville, California.

January 25, 2009: The Zone Nightclub, Portland, OR

Armed with a handgun, 24-year-old Erik Ayala arrived at the Zone, an under-21 nightclub in downtown Portland. A group of students who were part of a foreign exchange program had gathered outside the venue when, without warning, the gunman opened fire into the crowd. Two people were killed and another seven were injured. He then shot himself in the head. When police arrived on scene, the shooter still was alive; he died two days later at a local hospital.

March 10, 2009: Multiple Locations, Kinston, Sampson, & Geneva, AL

After killing relatives and their neighbors in their homes in two towns (Kinston and Samson, AL), 28-year-old Michael McLendon drove across Geneva County via Highway 52, continuing to fire his guns, which included two semiautomatic rifles, a shotgun, and a handgun. He engaged in a 24-mile-long chase with police, ending at the offices of Reliable Building Products in Geneva, where the shooter previously had been employed. He engaged in a shootout with police before retreating into the building and committing suicide.

March 24, 2009: San Diego Metropolitan Transit System, San Diego, CA

Armed with a handgun, 47-year-old Lonnie Glasco exited the employee lounge as he finished his shift at the Metropolitan Transit System complex. Once outside the building, he opened fire, shooting and killing a coworker. The other employees heard the gunfire and ran; in the attempt to escape, another employee was shot. He died later that day at the hospital. When police arrived on scene, they found the shooter holding his weapon and ordered him to drop it. When he disobeyed the command, instead raising the firearm toward the officers, they opened fire, shooting and killing the gunman and ending the rampage.

March 29, 2009: Pinelake Health and Rehabilitation, Carthage, NC

Arriving at his wife's employer, 45-year-old Robert Stewart was armed with a semiautomatic pistol, shotgun, handgun, and rifle (the latter of which he left in his vehicle during the rampage). He first opened fire in the parking lot, striking several cars and injuring a person who had just pulled into the area. That individual was able to enter the facility and warn others of the shooting. The gunman then entered the building and continued firing. Several minutes later, he was confronted by a responding police officer, who ordered him to drop his weapon. The shooter instead fired at the officer, striking him in the leg. The officer returned fire, hitting the gunman in the chest, incapacitating him and ending the rampage. Eight people had been killed and two others were injured in the attack. He was charged with and later convicted of eight counts of first-degree murder. He was sentenced to 174 years, 4 months, and 20 days in prison, which he currently is serving at the Lanesboro Correctional Institution in Polkton, North Carolina.

April 3, 2009: American Civic Association Immigration Center, Binghamton, NY

On the morning of the attack, 41-year-old Jiverly Wong, a naturalized American citizen originally from Vietnam, drove his father's vehicle to the American Civic Association building. He used the vehicle to barricade the rear door of the building before making his way around to the front. Armed with two semiautomatic handguns, he entered the immigration center where he had taken English classes earlier in the year.

Once inside, the shooter opened fire with both handguns. He first shot the center's two receptionists, one of whom died instantly. The other, shot in the stomach, faked her death until the shooter passed and then called 9-1-1. The gunman then entered a classroom just beyond the reception area, continuing to fire. After a few minutes, he took the students who were still alive hostage. As police arrived on scene, just three minutes after he began firing, the shooter committed suicide. A total of 13 people had been killed and 4 others were wounded.

The shooting at the American Civic Association is the deadliest mass killing in New York State since the September 11, 2001 terrorist attacks.

April 7, 2009: Kkottongnae Korean Retreat Camp, Temecula, CA

Armed with a handgun, 69-year-old John Chong opened fire at the religious retreat where he lived and worked as a handyman. He shot a couple, killing the wife and wounding the husband, before attempting to attack a second couple. Instead, they fought back and were able to disarm the shooter during the struggle. Both the couple and the shooter were injured before he was taken into custody. The shooter was charged with one count of first-degree murder and three counts of attempted murder; in 2011, he was convicted on all charges. He was sentenced to 136 years to life in prison, which he currently is serving at the California State Prison for Los Angeles County, located in Lancaster, California. He appealed his murder conviction in 2012, but his petition was unsuccessful.

April 17, 2009: Long Beach Memorial Hospital, Long Beach, CA

Amidst rumors of layoffs, 50-year-old Mario Ramirez arrived at the hospital where he was employed, armed with two handguns. He opened fire once inside near the emergency room, killing two people, one of whom died instantly; the other victim died several hours later while receiving treatment for his wounds. The shooter then walked outside the hospital and committed suicide.

April 26, 2009: Hampton University, Hampton, VA

A former Hampton University student, 18-year-old O'Dane Greg Maye returned to campus armed with a handgun. After entering the Harkness Hall dormitory around 1:00 a.m., the shooter opened fire, wounding two people before turning the gun on himself; he survived the self-inflicted wounds. He was charged with two counts of aggravated malicious wounding, two counts of use of a firearm in the commission of a felony, breaking and entering while armed, possession of a firearm on school grounds, and discharging a firearm in an occupied dwelling. Nearly four months after the attack, the shooter entered a conditional guilty plea to the charges of malicious wounding (two counts), using a gun in a felony (two counts), breaking and entering, and shooting into an occupied building. He was sentenced to 14 years' imprisonment with 53 years of his sentence suspended. He currently is incarcerated at the Lawrenceville Correctional Center in Lawrenceville, Virginia, and is scheduled for release in 2021. In 2011, the shooter appealed the $62,000 restitution he also had been ordered to pay, citing that the trial court abused its discretion in its order. The restitution issue was remanded back to the lower court for resolution.

May 30, 2009: Club 418, Springfield, MA

After exiting the bathroom with a semiautomatic pistol, 24-year-old Marcus Blanton opened fired on clubgoers. One person was killed and another four were injured in the shooting. A sixth person also was stabbed by the shooter. State troopers who were patrolling nearby saw people streaming out of the club and responded, taking the shooter into custody quickly after the attack began. The shooter was charged with murder and assault with a deadly weapon, as well as several other offenses. He later pleaded guilty to second-degree murder, armed assault with intent to murder, and firearms charges. He was sentenced to life in prison with the possibility of parole after 15 years. He currently is incarcerated at the Souza Baranowski Correctional Center in Shirley, Massachusetts.

June 1, 2009: U.S. Army Recruiting Center, Little Rock, AR

Armed with a semiautomatic rifle, 23-year-old Abdulhakim Mujahid Muhammad (born Carlos Leon Bledsoe) drove to a U.S. Army recruiting center in Little Rock. Several Army privates were standing outside smoking cigarettes when the shooter approached and opened fire. One of the men was killed and another was injured before the shooter sped off. He was captured eight miles from the scene and surrendered to officers without further incident. He also was in possession of a rifle, two handguns, and more than 550 rounds of ammunition, among other items. The shooter was charged with capital murder, attempted capital murder, and 10 counts of unlawful discharge of a weapon. He later pleaded guilty in exchange for prosecutors dropping the death penalty and was sentenced to life in prison without the possibility of parole for the capital murder charge. The shooter received an additional 11 life sentences plus 180 years for the remaining charges. He is incarcerated at the East Arkansas Regional Unit in Marianna, Arkansas.

June 10, 2009: U.S. Holocaust Memorial Museum, Washington, D.C.

After arriving at the museum, 88-year-old James Wenneker von Brunn entered the building armed with a rifle. A self-proclaimed white supremacist and denier of the Holocaust, the gunman opened fire, shooting a police officer, who died a short time later at a nearby hospital. Two other officers fired at the suspect, wounding him in the face, before taking him into custody. One other person was injured in the attack. The day after the shooting, the gunman was charged with first-degree murder as well as firearms violations, to which he pleaded not guilty to all counts. While awaiting trial, the shooter died of natural causes on January 6, 2010, less than seven months after the attack.

July 2, 2009: Family Dental Care, Simi Valley, CA

Armed with a semiautomatic rifle, 30-year-old Jaime Paredes opened fire in the Family Dental Care office. In under 10 minutes, law enforcement had arrived on scene and began negotiations with the shooter, who surrendered a short time later. One woman was killed and four others were injured in the attack. The shooter was charged with one count of murder, three counts of premeditated attempted murder, assault with a firearm, false imprisonment, burglary, and weapons enhancements for the lawful use of a firearm. The shooter was found incompetent to stand trial and underwent therapy for approximately seven years before being found eligible to face the court. In June 2017, just prior to the start of his trial, the shooter pleaded guilty and was sentenced to 71 years to life in prison. He also was ordered to pay $25,000 in restitution to his victims and others who were at the dental office on the day of the shooting. He currently is incarcerated at the North Kern State Prison in Delano, California.

August 4, 2009: LA Fitness, Collier Township, PA

George Sodini, a 48-year-old man, entered a fitness center with a duffle bag containing his weapons, and made his way to a women's aerobics class currently in progress. After setting the bag down, he turned off the lights, retrieved two handguns, and opened fire. Three people were killed and nine others injured before the shooter retrieved a third handgun from his bag and committed suicide. A subsequent investigation of the shooter's home revealed that he had kept a journal detailing his hatred for women; he also had the gym's schedule with the aerobics class circled. It also was revealed that a week prior to the shootings, he had brought an inert grenade on a Port Authority bus. Police questioned the shooter after another passenger reported the device but he was released and no charges were filed.

September 9, 2009: Independent Bar, Orlando, FL

After being kicked out of a downtown Orlando bar, 28-year-old Todd Buchanan returned to the bar and opened fire. Three individuals were wounded in the shooting. The shooter fled the scene and was arrested several hours later at his residence. He was charged with three counts of aggravated battery, shooting into an occupied building, and committing a felony. The jury found him guilty on two counts of attempted manslaughter, two counts of aggravated battery, and one count of shooting a deadly missile into an occupied building. He was sentenced to 105 years in prison, which he currently is serving at the Calhoun Correctional Institution in Blountstown, Florida. In 2014, the shooter appealed his sentence, calling it "vindictive"; the court affirmed the punishment.

September 12, 2009: Multiple Locations, Owosso, MI

As he drove by an abortion protest, 33-year-old Harlan James Drake opened fire, killing the demonstration's organizer. Afterward, the gunman drove to the Fuoss Gravel Co. and continued shooting; the company's owner was killed. The gunman was arrested by the authorities when he returned home after his second shooting. The shooter was charged with two counts of first-degree premeditated murder, one count of felony firearm possession, and one count of unlawful intent with a firearm. A jury later found him guilty of all charges, and he subsequently was sentenced to life in prison without parole. He currently is incarcerated at the Gus Harrison Correctional Facility in Adrian, Michigan.

November 5, 2009: Soldier Readiness Processing Center, Fort Hood, TX

Armed with a semiautomatic pistol (the weapon used in the attack) and a revolver, 39-year-old Army major Nidal Hasan entered the Soldier Readiness Processing Center, which is where service members receive treatment either prior to or following a deployment. After asking to see the major who had been working with him in preparation for deployment, the shooter opened fire. As he fired back and forth across the room, efforts were made to stop him, but each individual was killed during these efforts. Several people were able to break out a rear window of the building and escape, including the major the shooter had asked to see.

The shooter continued to move through the building, mainly shooting at uniformed personnel, before moving outside. Nurses and medics then entered the building and were able to secure it as the shooting continued just beyond the building. A civilian police sergeant responded and ordered the shooter to drop his weapon. The shooter turned and fired several rounds at the officer, and when his pistol was empty, the sergeant shot him five times as he attempted to reload. As the shooter lost consciousness, he was handcuffed and placed under arrest. By the time the attack was over, 13 people had been killed and an additional 32 people were wounded. The attack remains to date the worst mass shooting on an American military base.

In the aftermath of the attack, the shooter fell into a coma for several days but regained consciousness shortly thereafter. It also was determined that the shooter had been paralyzed from the waist down and likely would never walk again. On November 12 and December 2, 2009, the shooter was charged with 13 counts of premeditated murder and 32 counts of attempted murder under the Uniform Code of Military Justice, which made him eligible for capital punishment. On April 9, 2010, after just over six months in the hospital, the shooter was transferred to the Bell County jail until his trial.

Prior to the trial, the shooter declined to enter a plea and a request for deferment was granted. Additionally, the shooter also won the right to represent himself at trial, though his defense team remained on the case to assist if needed. Over 11 days of trial, the prosecution called nearly 90 witnesses. In addition to refusing to cross-examine any of the prosecution's witnesses, the shooter also declined calling any of his own. On August 23, 2013, the military jury found him guilty on all charges. Five days later, the jury panel recommended the death sentence. He currently remains on death row at the United States Disciplinary Barracks at Fort Leavenworth, Kansas.

A Hero Emerges

While there were many heroes on the day of the attack, one is Sergeant Kimberly Munley, a base civilian police officer. Sergeant Munley, who was washing her patrol car when she heard the news of the shooting over her radio, arrived on scene in time to encounter the shooter just outside the processing center as he was chasing a wounded soldier. She rushed toward the shooter, firing her weapon at him. He returned fire and both were injured—she was struck in the hand by shrapnel from one of his bullets, then was shot in each of her legs. As she fell to the ground, the gunman approached her and kicked away her service weapon, which had just jammed; his firearm, however, also had jammed. It was then that her partner was able to fire the shots that ended the rampage.

For her heroic actions on the day of the shooting, Sergeant Munley was awarded the Service to America Medal and the Secretary of the Army Award for Valor, both in 2010, and the Defense of Freedom Medal in 2015. Due to her injuries, Sergeant Munley had to retire from the police force. She currently serves as the president of the board for Step Up for Soldiers, a nonprofit that helps disabled veterans readjust to society, and does speaking engagements across the nation.

November 6, 2009: Reynolds, Smith & Hills, Orlando, FL

After being previously fired for poor performance, 40-year-old Jason S. Rodriguez returned to his former workplace at the Gateway Center armed with a handgun. After entering the eighth-floor office, he opened fire. One person was killed and five others were injured during the attack before the shooter fled. He was arrested several hours later at his mother's house less than 10 miles from the scene and charged with first-degree murder, as well as several other counts. In 2013, he was convicted after his insanity defense was rejected by jurors and was sentenced to six consecutive life sentences. The shooter's conviction and sentence later were overturned on appeal after discrepancies were discovered regarding jury instructions about his hallucinations. In 2015, a new trial commenced, but the shooter entered a plea deal and was sentenced to 30 years in prison. In April 2016, the shooter committed suicide in prison after being transported to Columbia Correctional Institution's protective custody.

November 8, 2009: Sandbar Sports Grill, West Vail, CO

After bothering customers and in the course of being escorted out of the restaurant, 63-year-old Richard Moreau opened fire on customers with a semiautomatic handgun he had in his possession. Within several minutes, one person had been killed and three others were injured. The shooter was taken into custody by responding law enforcement. In 2012, following a two-week trial, he was convicted of first-degree murder and seven other felonies. The shooter was sentenced to life in prison without the possibility of parole plus 80 years. He currently is incarcerated at the Sterling Correctional Facility in Sterling, Colorado.

November 10, 2009: Legacy MetroLab, Tualatin, OR

After receiving a petition for divorce, Robert Beiser, a 39-year-old man, entered a laboratory facility where his estranged wife worked. Armed with a rifle, he opened fire on employees. One person—the shooter's wife—was killed and two others were injured in the attack. He then committed suicide as law enforcement arrived on scene.

November 29, 2009: Forza Coffee Company, Parkland, WA

Out on parole for a string of other crimes, 37-year-old Maurice Clemmons entered the Forza Coffee Company shop armed with a semiautomatic handgun and a revolver. He approached four uniformed police officers, who were working on their laptops, and opened fire. One of the officers was able to fire a shot, striking the gunman, before succumbing to his injuries. Before fleeing the scene, the shooter grabbed one of the officers' service weapons. After a two-day manhunt, the shooter was spotted by a police officer, who shot the gunman as he was attempting to flee. Additional police officers arrived as backup shortly thereafter, but the shooter already had died from his injuries.

December 23, 2009: Grady Crawford Construction Co., Baton Rouge, LA

Fired several months earlier from the construction company, 53-year-old Richard Matthews returned to his former workplace armed with a revolver. He opened fire, moving between buildings; two people were killed and a third was injured in the attack. Four people were able to wrestle the shooter to the ground and hold him until law enforcement arrived and took him into custody. The shooter voluntarily pleaded guilty to two counts of first-degree murder and five counts of attempted first-degree murder. He was sentenced to two life sentences plus 250 years in prison, which he currently is serving at the Louisiana State Penitentiary in Angola, Louisiana.

2010s

January 4, 2010: Lloyd D. George U.S. Courthouse and Federal Building, Las Vegas, NV

Upset over a lawsuit related to his Social Security benefits, 66-year-old Johnny Wicks entered the Lloyd D. George Federal Courthouse armed with a shotgun. He opened fire, striking two court security officers. One of the officers died; the other survived his injuries. Seven court officers returned fire at the shooter, who fled the building. Struck in the head by one of the officers' bullets, the shooter died a short distance away. Further investigation revealed that the shooter had set fire to his apartment prior to the shooting.

January 7, 2010: ABB, Inc., St. Louis, MO

Armed with a semiautomatic rifle, a shotgun, and three handguns, 51-year-old Timothy Hendron arrived at the power plant where he was employed. He first opened fire in the company's parking lot, killing two people before moving inside. Once in the building, he continued shooting, killing a third person and wounding five others. An employee with a concealed handgun shot back at the gunman but missed; he then played dead until police arrived. Police made entry approximately two-and-a-half hours after the shooting began and found the gunman dead in an office, having committed suicide.

January 12, 2010: Penske Truck Rental, Kennesaw, GA

Former employee Jesse James Warren arrived at the truck rental facility armed with two handguns. Entering through the ground-level bay where the trucks are stored, the 60-year-old opened fire on customers and employees. Two people were killed at the scene; a third died the following day at a local hospital. Two additional people were wounded in the attack, one of whom died several years later from complications. The shooter was arrested a short distance away after fleeing the scene in his truck. The shooter was declared incompetent to stand trial and remanded to the state's custody for treatment. In 2015, an order permitting him to be forcibly medicated was reversed by the Georgia Supreme Court. He was detained at the Cobb County Adult Detention Facility in Marietta, Georgia, pending trial, until 2017 when he was transferred to a prison psychiatric hospital for indefinite commitment.

February 10, 2010: Inskip Elementary School, Knoxville, TN

After being informed that his contract would not be renewed, fourth-grade teacher Mark Stephen Foster left the school and returned with a firearm. The 48-year-old opened fire, shooting the school's principal and assistant principal, both of whom survived, before being taken into custody. The shooter later pleaded guilty to two counts of attempted murder, employing a firearm during a dangerous felony, and carrying a weapon on school property. He was sentenced to 56 years in prison, which he currently is serving at the West Tennessee State Penitentiary in Henning, Tennessee. He is eligible for parole in 2027.

February 12, 2010: University of Alabama–Huntsville, Huntsville, AL

Amy Bishop, a 44-year-old professor of biology who recently had been denied tenure, arrived on campus and went through her daily routine of teaching classes before finding herself in a department meeting in the Shelby Center for Science and Technology. After sitting there for approximately 30 to 40 minutes, she pulled out a handgun, stood up, and opened fire. Starting with the person closest to her, the shooter fired down the row, killing three people and wounding three others. When her gun clicked, either due to a jam or because it ran out of ammunition, several people in the room pushed the shooter out and blocked the door. She went outside and called her husband to pick her up, but was apprehended by police officers a few minutes later.

The shooter was charged with one count of capital murder and three counts of attempted murder for the attack. She initially pleaded not guilty. At the urging of one of the victim's families and conferring with the rest, the prosecutor elected not to seek the death penalty. The shooter then changed her plea to guilty and was sentenced to life in prison without the possibility of parole. She later tried to appeal her plea but was unsuccessful. She currently is incarcerated at Tutwiler Prison in Wetumpka, AL.

A History of Violence

Prior to the attack at the University of Alabama–Huntsville, the shooter had a well-documented history of violent episodes. In 1986, at the age of 21, she had fatally shot her 18-year-old brother. Though it initially was believed to be an accidental shooting, the case was reopened four days after the university attack. Four months later, on June 16, 2010, she formally was charged with her brother's murder. Two years later, however, the district attorney decided not to prosecute the case.

The shooter and her husband also had been suspects in a 1993 pipe bomb case. The shooter's former supervisor at the Children's Hospital Boston neurobiology lab had received a package containing two pipe bombs, which failed to detonate. Having received a negative evaluation, the shooter became a prime suspect in the incident, though the case ultimately was closed without charges being filed due to a lack of evidence. In 2002, the shooter also had been charged with punching a woman in the face at a restaurant over a booster seat, for which she received probation.

February 23, 2010: Deer Creek Middle School, Littleton, CO

Armed with a rifle, 32-year-old Bruco Eastwood returned to his former school. As the school day was coming to an end, he opened fire on students emerging after their release. Two eighth-grade students were injured before the shooter was stopped and detained by a pair of teachers and some school bus drivers. He originally was charged with four counts of attempted murder and first-degree assault, two counts of child abuse concluding in serious bodily injury, and unlawful possession of a firearm on school property; a jury later found the shooter not guilty by reason of insanity, though he was convicted of carrying a weapon on school property. He was sentenced to confinement in a state mental institution until doctors perceived that he was no longer a threat to the public. In 2015, a judge authorized limited access to the community under supervision for the shooter.

March 4, 2010: The Pentagon, Arlington, VA

Armed with two semiautomatic handguns and several additional magazines, 36-year-old John Bedell calmly approached a security checkpoint at the Pentagon's transit system station. When asked for credentials, the shooter retrieved his weapons and opened fire on the two police officers, who were wounded in the attack. A third officer responded to the sounds of shots fired. As police returned fire, they struck the shooter in the head, mortally wounding him. He died early the following morning at the hospital.

March 9, 2010: Ohio State University, Columbus, OH

Following a poor performance evaluation, 51-year-old Nathaniel Brown arrived at campus armed with two handguns. The custodial worker opened fire, killing one person and wounding two others. He then committed suicide at the scene. Further investigation discovered that the shooter had provided false information on his job application in order to hide his prior conviction. In 1979, the gunman had been convicted of receiving stolen property and served five years in prison.

April 19, 2010: Parkwest Medical Center, Knoxville, TN

Believing that a doctor had implanted a tracking chip in him during an earlier surgery, 38-year-old Abdo Ibssa returned to the facility in search of the physician. When he learned that the doctor was not at the hospital, he left and opened fire in a parking lot outside. One person was killed and two others were injured. The shooter then committed suicide at the scene.

May 17, 2010: Boulder Stove and Flooring, Boulder, CO

Frustrated by changes in the company's commission and bonus structure, 53-year-old Robert Montgomery went to the office of his employer. Armed with a handgun, he opened fire, killing two people. The shooter then committed suicide at the scene. No other individuals were reported to be injured in the attack.

June 8, 2010: Yoyito Café-Restaurant, Hialeah, FL

In the course of an argument with his estranged wife, 38-year-old Gerardo Regalado drew his handgun. He shot and killed her before entering the restaurant. Once inside, he continued shooting, killing three others and wounding three more. The shooter then left the restaurant. He was located by police several blocks from the building, having committed suicide.

July 12, 2010: Emcore Fiber Optics Corp., Albuquerque, NM

Armed with a handgun, 37-year-old Robert Reza returned to his former workplace, where his ex-girlfriend also was employed. He began shooting outside, wounding his ex-girlfriend and killing another individual before gaining access to the facility. Once inside, he continued shooting at people. In total, two people were killed and four others were injured before the shooter committed suicide.

August 3, 2010: Hartford Distributors, Manchester, CT

Armed with two semiautomatic handguns, 34-year-old Omar Thornton had arrived at a meeting to discuss accusations that he had stolen from his employer. Once video evidence was presented of the crime, he signed resignation papers and was being escorted from the building. At that time, he retrieved his weapons from his lunchbox and opened fire. Over the next few minutes, the shooter killed eight employees and injured two others. As law enforcement entered the building, he hid in a locked office and placed a call to his mother and then another to a 9-1-1 dispatcher. After terminating the 9-1-1 call, the shooter committed suicide.

August 14, 2010: City Grill Restaurant, Buffalo, NY

As patrons filed out of a restaurant that was closing for the evening, 23-year-old Riccardo McCray pulled a handgun and opened fire on the crowd. Four people were killed and three others were wounded in the shooting. The gunman fled the scene, discarding the weapon, which was never recovered. He turned himself in to the authorities 11 days after the attack. At trial, he was convicted of three counts of first-degree murder, two counts of attempted murder, and weapons possession. He was sentenced to life in prison without the possibility of parole, which he currently is serving at the Green Haven Correctional Facility in Stormville, New York. In 2014, the defendant appealed his sentence and conviction; both were upheld by the court.

September 9, 2010: Kraft Foods Plant, Philadelphia, PA

After being escorted out of her workplace following a suspension, 43-year-old Yvonne Hiller returned to the plant armed with a revolver. She first drove her car through the barricade at a security checkpoint before threatening a security officer with her weapon to gain access to the building. She made her way to the third floor break room, where she opened fire. Two people were killed and another was critically injured before the shooter was taken into custody. She was charged with two counts of first-degree murder, one count of attempted murder, and several other related offenses. After a trial, she was found guilty on the murder and attempted murder charges and was automatically sentenced to two consecutive terms of life in prison without the possibility of parole. She remains incarcerated at SCI Muncy in Muncy, Pennsylvania.

September 20, 2010: Fort Bliss Convenience Store, El Paso, TX

Steven Kropf entered a convenience store located on the Fort Bliss Army base, armed with a handgun. The 63-year-old retired Army sergeant, who was looking for the manager who was not at the shop, then opened fire. One person was killed and another was injured in the attack. He later was shot dead by Army civilian police.

September 22, 2010: AmeriCold Logistics, Crete, NE

Armed with a handgun, 26-year-old Akouch Kashoual entered a breakroom at his employer's cold-storage warehouse. The shooter opened fire on those individuals present. Three people were wounded in the attack; all survived their injuries. The shooter then went outside the plant and committed suicide before police arrived on scene.

October 4, 2010: Multiple Locations, Gainesville, FL

After killing his father in their home, 24-year-old Clifford Miller Jr. drove through his Gainesville-area neighborhood armed with a handgun. He fired indiscriminately at individuals over several blocks before driving to a nearby location and committing suicide. A total of five individuals were wounded in the shooting spree.

October 8, 2010: Kelly Elementary School, Carlsbad, CA

Armed with a revolver, gasoline can, and propane tank, 41-year-old Brendan O'Rourke arrived at the school while children were at recess on the playground. He retrieved the revolver and opened fire on a crowd of nearly 230 students, wounding two young children. As he made his way back to his truck, nearby construction workers pursued him, eventually tackling the shooter and holding him until law enforcement arrived and took him into custody. The shooter was charged with six counts of attempted murder and various weapons charges. At trial, a court-appointed psychiatrist testified that the shooter was a paranoid schizophrenic who was experiencing an episode during the shooting. The jury, however, concluded he was sane at the time of the attack and found him guilty of seven counts each of premeditated attempted murder and assault with a firearm. The shooter was sentenced to 189 years to life in prison, which he currently is serving at Mule Creek State Prison in Ione, California.

October 29, 2010: Walmart, Reno, NV

About an hour after purchasing ammunition from the Walmart store where he was employed, 45-year-old John Gillane returned to his workplace. Armed with two handguns, one of which was semiautomatic, he opened fire on his coworkers, wounding three of them. The shooter then retreated to an office in the building, barricading himself inside; he surrendered to police six hours later. He was charged with three counts of attempted murder, as well as assault with a deadly weapon and battery with a deadly weapon causing substantial harm. The shooter pleaded not guilty. After a trial, a jury convicted him on seven total counts: two counts of attempted murder with a deadly weapon, three counts of battery with a deadly weapon, one count of assault with a deadly weapon, and one count of carrying a concealed weapon. He was sentenced to 35 to 96 years in prison, which he currently is serving at the Southern Desert Correctional Center in Indian Springs, Nevada.

January 5, 2011: Millard South High School, Omaha, NE

Following a suspension from school, Robert Butler Jr., a 17-year-old senior, returned to the campus. Armed with a pistol, he first shot and killed the assistant principal, then wounded both the principal and the school nurse. The shooter then left the school, driving to a nearby parking lot. Responding law enforcement found him shortly thereafter, having died from a self-inflicted gunshot wound.

January 8, 2011: Safeway Supermarket Parking Lot, Tucson, AZ

At approximately 10:00 a.m., constituents of Congresswoman Gabrielle Giffords had gathered in the parking lot of a Safeway supermarket in Casas Adobes, AZ, part of the larger Tucson metropolitan area. Called "Congress on Your Corner," the meeting was set up so that members of the community could talk about their concerns with their representative. Minutes after the meeting began, 22-year-old Jared Loughner drew a semiautomatic pistol and opened fire. He first shot Congresswoman Giffords in the head, then turned his weapon on the crowd. Over the next five minutes, six people were killed, including federal District Court chief judge John Roll and 9-year-old Christina Taylor-Green, who had an interest in civics and politics. An additional 13 people, including Giffords, were wounded before individuals present were able to subdue the shooter and hold him until law enforcement arrived on scene.

The shooter immediately invoked his Fifth Amendment right to remain silent at arrest. He was charged in federal court with one count of attempted assassination on a member of Congress, two counts of murdering a federal employee, and two counts of attempting to murder a federal employee. Two months later, additional charges—including murder and attempted murder—were added, bringing the total to 49 counts against the shooter. He entered a plea of not guilty.

More than a year and a half after the shootings, the judge in the case declared that the gunman was competent to stand trial. In exchange for the removal of the death penalty as a possible sanction, the shooter pleaded guilty to 19 of the 49 counts. He was sentenced to seven consecutive life sentences without the possibility of parole plus an additional 140 years in prison. He also was ordered to pay the victims $19 million collectively in restitution. Due to the severity of the sentence on the federal charges, the state of Arizona declined to prosecute the case further. The shooter is presently incarcerated at FMC Rochester, a medical facility, in Rochester, Minnesota.

The Complexities of Mental Illness in the Arizona Shooting

The shooter had a long and well-documented history of mental illness that complicated the case. In 2006, after he dropped out of high school, many who knew him commented on marked changes in his personality. The shooter would fail to listen to instructions, ask questions that did not go together, and was difficult to get along with. His behavior became so erratic that his parents confiscated his shotgun and began disabling his car at night so he could not leave the house without their knowledge.

In 2010, the shooter enrolled at Pima Community College. Over just eight months as a student there, he had five separate contacts with the college's police department over behavioral issues. His professors also had complained to the administration about his disruptive behavior in class, expressing concern over potential issues of mental illness. At the end of September 2010, the college decided to suspend the shooter, ordering him to resolve his code of conduct violations and obtain a mental health clearance from a professional in the field prior to returning. He did not return to the college.

On the morning of the shooting, the gunman entered a Tucson-area Walmart store and walked to the sporting goods section. He asked a clerk for 9mm ammunition (which matched the gun used in the shooting), but his behavior was so bizarre that it alarmed the person. Even though there was ample ammunition that matched the shooter's request, the clerk told him that the store was out in an effort to not sell the bullets to him. The shooter left without further incident, purchasing additional ammunition at a different Walmart location before going to the Safeway.

After the shooting, the severity of the gunman's mental illness came to light. On May 25, 2011, the shooter was determined to be incompetent to stand trial after two medical evaluations each returned a diagnosis of paranoid schizophrenia. For more than a year, the shooter remained in medical facilities within the federal prison system, undergoing treatment and even forced medication. Nineteen months after the shooting, the gunman finally was lucid enough to face proceedings against him. He continues to receive treatment for his mental illness while incarcerated.

April 8, 2011: Minaret Temple 174, Chester, PA

As nearly 200 people gathered for a party at the Minaret Temple, 16-year-old Kanei Avery approached, armed with a semiautomatic handgun. Once inside the temple, he opened fire. Two people were killed and eight others were wounded. Hearing the commotion, a security guard approached and saw the shooter with the gun; he tackled the shooter and held him until police could place him under arrest. The shooter was charged as an adult on counts of first-degree and third-degree homicide, as well as aggravated assault and related weapons offenses. A year and half after the shooting, the prosecutors reached a plea deal with the gunman for two counts of voluntary manslaughter with the other charges withdrawn. The shooter was sentenced to seven to 14 years for the attack, which he currently is serving at SCI Pine Grove in Indiana, Pennsylvania.

September 6, 2011: International House of Pancakes Restaurant, Carson City, NV

Armed with a semiautomatic rifle, as well as a second rifle and handgun, 32-year-old Eduardo Sencion arrived at a local strip mall. He first shot a woman on a motorcycle in the parking lot before entering the restaurant. Once inside, he made his way to the back, where a group of uniformed Army National Guard troops were eating breakfast. He opened fire, shooting five of them, and continued firing on patrons as he exited the building. The gunman continued to nearby businesses, where he continued shooting, though no one was struck. When police arrived on scene, the gunman shot himself in the head. He died later at a local hospital. Four people had been killed and seven others wounded in his rampage.

October 5, 2011: Lehigh Southwest Cement, Cupertino, CA

During a safety meeting at the cement company's plant, 49-year-old Frank (a.k.a. Shareef) Allman rose and locked the door to the room. Armed with two rifles, a shotgun, and a handgun, he opened fire on his coworkers. Three people were killed and six people were wounded. The shooter then fled the plant, wounding a seventh person at the Hewlett-Packard campus several miles away as he tried to steal her car. Police located the shooter the following morning at a house in Sunnyvale. When they ordered him to come out with his hands up, the shooter showed his gun and made a threatening move, and the police officers responded by opening fire. The shooter then committed suicide.

October 12, 2011: Salon Meritage, Seal Beach, CA

Scott Evans Dekraai, armed with three handguns, entered the Seal Beach salon, where approximately 20 people were inside. The 41-year-old gunman opened fire, shooting nine people, only one of whom survived. After fleeing the scene, he was arrested approximately a half mile away without further incident. Originally charged with eight counts of murder with special circumstances plus one count of attempted murder, the shooter pleaded not guilty. Three years later, he changed his plea to guilty on all charges. The sentencing phase of the trial was postponed after the county prosecutor was removed from the case after allegations arose that he was illegally using jailhouse informants and withholding evidence in multiple cases. On September 22, 2017, the shooter was sentenced to eight consecutive life terms, one for each victim. He currently is incarcerated at the Wasco State Prison in Wasco, California.

December 16, 2011: Southern California Edison, Irwindale, CA

Following news of a possible termination, 48-year-old Andre Turner retrieved a semiautomatic handgun and opened fire at the firm's corporate office building. Two people were killed in the attack; two other individuals also were injured but survived. The shooter then committed suicide before law enforcement arrived on scene.

January 13, 2012: McBride Lumber Company, Star, NC

Armed with a shotgun, 50-year-old Robert Dean Davis arrived at work at a North Carolina–based lumber company. The shooter opened fire, killing three of his coworkers. A fourth individual was critically wounded but survived the injuries. The gunman retreated to his house, where he shot himself in an attempt to commit suicide. Police later found him there and transported him to the hospital, where he later died of his injuries.

February 27, 2012: Chardon High School, Chardon, OH

T.J. Lane, a 17-year-old student, entered his school's cafeteria while students were eating breakfast. Without saying a word, he opened fire with a semiautomatic handgun he had brought with him. He continued shooting as he fled the cafeteria, only to encounter two teachers who chased him from the school. The shooter was apprehended by police near his car nearby a short time later. Six students had been shot in the rampage, three of whom died later at a hospital in Cleveland where they had been airlifted. The shooter was charged with three counts of aggravated murder, two counts of aggravated attempted murder, and one count of felonious assault. Several months later, it was determined that the shooter would be tried as an adult for the crimes. He originally pleaded not guilty to all charges, but later changed his plea to guilty. He was sentenced to three life sentences in prison without the possibility of parole and was remanded to the Allen Correctional Facility in Lima, Ohio, to serve his sentence. In 2014, the shooter escaped from the prison with two other inmates; he was caught several hours later and returned to the facility before being transferred to the Ohio State Penitentiary in Youngstown, Ohio, a supermax facility. In 2016, he was transferred to the Southern Ohio Correctional Facility in Lucasville, Ohio, where he currently remains.

March 8, 2012: Western Psychiatric Institute and Clinic, Pittsburgh, PA

Armed with two semiautomatic handguns, 30-year-old John Shick arrived at the Western Psychiatric Institute and Clinic at the University of Pittsburgh Medical Center, where he previously had been a patient. As he entered the hospital, he opened fire. One person was killed and seven others, including a police officer, were wounded. The shooter was killed by university police who responded to the 9-1-1 calls.

March 23, 2012: J.T. Tire, Durham, NC

Armed with a handgun, 24-year-old O'Brian McNeil White entered the J.T. Tire store. He opened fire on employees and customers, killing two people. Two other individuals were wounded in the attack. The shooter fled the scene of the crime but was arrested a week later. He was charged with two counts of first-degree murder, three counts of assault with a deadly weapon, and one count of robbery with a dangerous weapon. He currently is incarcerated at the Durham County Detention Center, awaiting his trial's conclusion.

April 2, 2012: Oikos University, Oakland, CA

One L. Goh, a 43-year-old former student of the university, arrived at the campus armed with a semiautomatic handgun. During a nursing class that was in session, the shooter, who had sat in, stood up and ordered the students to line up against the wall. Once they had, he opened fire. Seven people were killed and three others were injured before the shooter fled in one of the victims' cars. He surrendered to authorities several hours later and was arrested without further incident. Following the shooting, the gunman was charged with seven counts of murder and three counts of attempted murder. He initially pleaded not guilty but was declared incompetent to stand trial after two court-appointed psychiatrists diagnosed him with paranoid schizophrenia. In 2015, after several years of receiving treatment in a mental hospital, the shooter was found competent to stand trial. In 2017, he pleaded no contest to all of the charges, which carries with it an automatic sentence of life in prison without the possibility of parole. On July 14, 2017, the shooter was sentenced to seven consecutive life terms and was incarcerated at the California Medical Facility in Vacaville, California.

April 6, 2012: Multiple Locations, Tulsa, OK

In the early morning hours, 19-year-old Jacob England and his roommate, 32-year-old Alvin Watts, drove around Tulsa. Each armed with a handgun, they opened fire at random people they saw in the streets. Three people were killed in the rampage; two others were wounded but survived their injuries. The following day, the shooters were arrested after police received a tip regarding their whereabouts. They were charged with three counts of first-degree murder, two counts of shooting with the intent to kill, and five counts of malicious harassment. Initially pleading not guilty, the pair later changed their pleas to guilty as part of a deal in order to avoid the death penalty. They both were sentenced to life in prison without the possibility of parole. The younger shooter currently is incarcerated at the Dick Conner Correctional Center in Hominy, Oklahoma, while the older shooter is serving his sentence at the North Fork Correctional Center in Sayre, Oklahoma.

May 30, 2012: Café Racer, Seattle, WA

Armed with two handguns, 40-year-old Ian Lee Stawicki entered the café from which he had previously been thrown out. Recognizing him, the staff asked him to leave; the shooter lingered for a few moments before heading for the exit. As he reached the front of the café, he retrieved one of his handguns and opened fire. Within minutes, he had killed four people and wounded one other, even as patrons tried to fight back. The shooter left the café and, a half hour later, killed a woman and stole her vehicle. Several hours later, the shooter committed suicide as police closed in.

July 17, 2012: Copper Top Bar, Tuscaloosa, AL

After shooting and wounding a person at the individual's home and setting several fires to property and equipment owned by his former employer, 44-year-old Nathan van Wilkins made his way to the Copper Top Bar. Armed with a semiautomatic rifle, he opened fire from two different positions outside the bar. By the time the shooting was over, 17 people had been wounded. The gunman fled the scene, turning himself in 10 hours later at a FedEx location in Jasper. He was charged with 19 counts of attempted murder, 19 counts of first-degree assault, 17 counts of second-degree assault, and 13 additional charges ranging from arson to fraudulent use of a credit card. As part of a plea deal, the shooter pleaded guilty to 16 of the charges—5 counts of attempted murder, 10 counts of assault, and 1 charge of arson. He was sentenced to 30 years in prison, which he currently is serving at the St. Clair Correctional Facility in Springville, Alabama. He will be eligible for parole consideration in 2027.

July 20, 2012: Cinemark Theaters, Aurora, CO

At midnight on July 20, crowds gathered at movie theaters across the nation for the premiere of the last installment of the Batman franchise—*The Dark Knight Rises*. James Holmes, a 24-year-old, entered Theater 9 of the Century 16 multiplex, where people had gathered to watch the movie. He seated himself in the front row and, approximately 20 minutes into the movie, then stepped outside through an exit at the front of the theater, propping the door open so he could regain entry. Just beyond the door, the shooter had parked his car, which contained his weapons and ballistics protective gear. After suiting up, he returned inside the theater.

Once inside, he threw two canisters into the audience, believed to contain tear gas. He then pulled out a tactical shotgun and began firing into the audience. Next, he retrieved a semiautomatic handgun that he had fitted with a 100-round drum magazine and continued firing until the gun jammed. He then abandoned that for a different handgun. Approximately six minutes later, the shooting was over. Twelve people had been killed and 58 others were wounded in the gunfire. Four additional people sustained injuries from the tear gas, while 8 were hurt in their attempt to escape.

The shooter retreated outside to where his vehicle was parked and was taken into custody without further incident. An additional firearm, not used in the shooting, was found in the car. At the time of his arrest, the shooter told police that there were explosives at his apartment. Prior to the shooting, he had rigged the dwelling with incendiary devices designed to detonate when police entered to investigate. His building and those around it were evacuated while investigators disarmed the devices using a controlled detonation. A total of 30 homemade grenades and 10 gallons of gasoline were recovered at the apartment.

Ten days after the shooting, the gunman was formally charged with 142 counts—first-degree murder (24 counts), attempted murder (116 counts), possession of explosive devices, and inciting violence. That September, additional charges were filed against the shooter, bringing the total to 165 counts. Six months later, the shooter offered to plead guilty in order to avoid the death penalty, but the prosecutors rejected the deal, stating that they would seek that punishment at trial. The shooter then entered a plea of not guilty by reason of insanity.

After a series of trial delays, jury selection finally began on January 20, 2015. A total of 9,000 potential jurors were questioned, the most in any case in U.S. history. Nearly four months later, the jury was selected. The trial began on April 27, 2015, and lasted until July 14, at which time the jury was sequestered for deliberations. After two days, the jury found the shooter guilty on all charges, as well as a sentence enhancement for a crime of violence. On August 26, 2015, the shooter was formally sentenced to 12 life terms without the possibility of parole plus an additional 3,318 years. He also was ordered to pay nearly $955,000 in restitution to the victims. Originally incarcerated at the Colorado State Penitentiary in Canon City, Colorado, he was relocated to an undisclosed facility out of state after being assaulted by another inmate before being transferred to the federal prison system, serving his sentence at a penitentiary in Allenwood, Pennsylvania.

Warning Signs and Premeditation

Despite the gunman being enrolled in a prestigious neuroscience program at the University of Colorado Anschutz Medical Campus in Aurora, warning signs predating the shooting appeared early. A year after beginning the program, his academic progress began to decline, culminating in his failing a key oral exam a month before the shooting. He had sought treatment through the campus's student mental health services, meeting with at least three different professionals. One of his psychiatrists, informed about his homicidal thoughts, considered placing him on an involuntary mental health hold but had decided against it. Another psychiatrist, Dr. Lynne Fenton, had reported to university police that the shooter also had made homicidal threats to her. The day before the shooting, he mailed a notebook to Dr. Fenton, which contained his thoughts and plans leading up to the attack, even though he had begun the process of withdrawing from the university.

A considerable amount of time went into evaluating the shooter's mental status after the attack, particularly after the court accepted his plea of not guilty by reason of insanity. At trial, a court-appointed psychiatrist, Dr. William Reid, acknowledged that the shooter was in fact mentally ill, diagnosing him with schizotypal personality disorder. Despite this, the psychiatrist reasoned that the shooter legally was sane at the time of his actions, meaning that his mental illness did not prevent him from forming the necessary intent needed to commit the crime. A second psychiatrist, Dr. Jeffrey Metzner, also concluded that the shooter was mentally ill but legally sane, but differentiated in his diagnosis, instead suggesting that he suffered from schizoaffective disorder. Both psychiatrists had evaluated the shooter for more than 20 hours each prior to giving their testimony.

Despite these diagnoses, the shooter still had engaged in a considerable amount of meticulous planning for the attack. Aside from rigging his apartment to explode, the shooter had acquired three firearms in less than two months. In the four months preceding the shooting, he had stockpiled over 6,000 rounds of ammunition for his firearms. He also had purchased head-to-toe military-grade protective gear, as well as spike strips to use against police officers who may have pursued him.

Under Colorado law, individuals cannot be held legally (not morally) responsible for their crimes if their minds are diseased to the point where they do not understand the difference between right and wrong. More specifically, the state of Colorado uses a two-prong test to determine the validity of an insanity plea:

1. "A person who is so diseased or defective in mind at the time of the commission of the act as to be incapable of distinguishing right from wrong with respect to that act"; or

2. "A person who suffered from a condition of mind caused by mental disease or defect that prevented the person from forming a culpable mental state that is an essential element of a crime charged."

The ability to distinguish right from wrong is the most important language in the first part of the test. In the second test, the mindset of the defendant is an element of the offense, meaning that there is specific intent.

Moreover, in Colorado, to be able to successfully claim the insanity defense in a case of first-degree murder, the defendant would have to be able to successfully prove that despite the premeditation, he or she lacked the mental capabilities to form the intent to kill the victim. In the case of the Aurora movie theater shooter, this intent was present and was confirmed by both court-appointed psychiatrists who evaluated him. This, coupled with the deliberate planning and premeditation leading up to the attack, led to the shooter's convictions on all counts.

August 5, 2012: Sikh Temple of Wisconsin, Oak Creek, WI

Armed with a semiautomatic pistol, 40-year-old Wade Michael Page entered the temple. As worshipers were preparing a meal for service, the shooter opened fire. Six people were killed and four others, including responding police officer Lieutenant Brian Murphy, who was shot 15 times, were wounded. Another responding officer exchanged fire with the shooter, wounding him in the stomach. The gunman then committed suicide.

August 13, 2012: Near Texas A&M University, College Station, TX

When a Brazos County constable arrived to serve him with a notice to appear in court, 35-year-old Thomas Caffall shot and killed him with a rifle. He grabbed the constable's service weapon (a semiautomatic pistol), as well as two additional rifles, and continued shooting. He first injured a neighbor and then turned his weapons on responding police, inciting a shootout. In the exchange, several police officers and bystanders were struck by the shooter's fire. Approximately 20 minutes after they arrived on scene, police shot and killed the gunman, ending the rampage. Two people had been killed and an additional four people were wounded in the attack.

August 31, 2012: Pathmark Supermarket, Old Bridge, NJ

After the completion of his shift, 23-year-old Terence Tyler returned to his workplace, armed with an assault rifle and an automatic pistol. He shot at a coworker outside the store, who ran inside to alert others about the shooter. The gunman was able to make entry into the building after they secured the door by shooting through the locks. Once inside, he continued firing his weapons, killing two people. Just before police arrived on scene, the shooter committed suicide.

September 27, 2012: Accent Signature Systems, Minneapolis, MN

After finding out he was being fired from the firm, 36-year-old Andrew Engeldinger retrieved his handgun. He began shooting, making his way through the building and firing at anyone he saw. He continued outside to the loading dock, where he killed an employee and a UPS delivery driver before returning inside the building. Once inside the basement, the shooter committed suicide. A total of six people were killed (four at the scene, one who died the next day, and one who died nearly two weeks later) and two others were injured in the attack.

October 18, 2012: Las Dominicanas M&M Hair Salon, Casselberry, FL

Hours before he was scheduled to appear in court, 36-year-old Bradford Baumet arrived at a salon where his estranged girlfriend was employed. Armed with a semiautomatic handgun, he opened fire, killing three people. His ex-girlfriend also was wounded in the attack. The shooter then fled to a friend's house nearby, where he committed suicide. Further investigation revealed that the gun used in the shooting was stolen from a man that he had killed nearly a year earlier.

October 21, 2012: Azana Salon & Spa: Brookfield, WI

Armed with a large-caliber handgun, 45-year-old Radcliffe Haughton arrived at the spa where his wife worked. He grabbed her by the hair and fired several rounds into the floor before ordering everyone in the spa to lie face down. Once they complied, he began firing at them. At one point, the shooter's gun jammed, allowing the salon's former owner to escape and notify the authorities.

By the time the attack was over, three people were killed and four others were injured. The gunman then placed a call to his brother before committing suicide. The town of Brookfield also had been the site of an earlier mass shooting in 2005.

November 6, 2012: Valley Protein, Fresno, CA

Approximately halfway through his shift at a chicken-processing plant, 42-year-old Lawrence Jones retrieved his handgun. He began firing at his coworkers. Two people were killed and an additional two were wounded in the attack. After his gun ran out of ammunition, the shooter went outside and reloaded, and then committed suicide before police arrived on scene.

December 11, 2012: Clackamas Town Center, Clackamas, OR

Armed with a semiautomatic rifle and wearing a white hockey mask, 22-year-old Jacob Roberts arrived at the Portland-area mall. After entering through the Macy's department store, he made his way to the food court area, where he opened fire. Two people were killed and another was wounded in that area of the mall. The shooter continued to run through the building, discharging his weapon until it jammed. After unblocking the weapon, the shooter made his way downstairs to the main level, where he committed suicide. At the time of the attack, it was estimated that upwards of 10,000 people were in the mall.

December 14, 2012: Sandy Hook Elementary School, Newtown, CT

Around 9:30 a.m., 20-year-old Adam Lanza drove to Sandy Hook Elementary School, less than five miles away from the home he shared with his mother. Minutes after arriving, he used a semiautomatic rifle to shoot through the school's glass entry after it had been locked down at the start of the school day. At the time, the morning announcements were in progress, so the gunshots could be heard over the intercom.

Dawn Hochsprung, the school's principal, was in a meeting with faculty members when she heard the commotion. Along with school psychologist Mary Sherlach and lead teacher Natalie Hammond, she went to investigate the noise, having not immediately recognized it as gunfire. In the hallway, the three encountered the shooter. Using a predetermined phrase, they alerted the other faculty of the situation and then attempted to stop him. Both Dawn Hochsprung and Mary Sherlach were killed; Natalie Hammond was injured but played dead until she could safely make her way back to the conference room and barricade herself in.

The school's janitor, Rick Thorne, also began to alert people of the event after ordering the shooter to drop his weapon. He went room to room, helping teachers secure their doors; one teacher was hit by a ricocheting bullet in the foot as she tried to lock her room. The shooter then made his way into the school's main office, where a number of people were hiding. Not seeing anyone, he returned to the hallway before making his way to the classrooms.

The shooter entered a first-grade classroom where Lauren Rousseau was serving as a substitute teacher, assisted by behavioral therapist Rachel D'Avino. Having heard the gunshots, the teacher and aide were trying to usher students to safety in the classroom's bathroom and were in the process of doing so when he forced entry into the room. He opened fire, killing both women and 14 of the 15 students who were in the room. One girl survived by playing dead in the corner of the bathroom until the shooting had ended; she was not wounded in the attack.

In the classroom next door to where Lauren Rousseau was teaching, Victoria Soto also was in the process of helping her students find safety with the aid of behavioral therapist

Anne Marie Murphy. The shooter then entered the room, continuing to fire, as Victoria Soto made her way to the front of the classroom to lock the door. She was killed instantly, as was Anne Marie Murphy, who died while shielding a student with her body (the young boy also was killed). When the shooter's gun jammed, nine children ran out of the room to safety. Two additional students' lives were spared when they hid in the classroom bathroom.

Within five minutes of the start of the shooting, 26 people had been killed—6 educators and 20 first-grade students (two of whom were pronounced dead once they arrived at the hospital). As police arrived on scene, the shooter committed suicide with a semiautomatic handgun while in Victoria Soto's classroom. An additional semiautomatic handgun also was found on his person. Further investigation revealed that prior to the attack at the elementary school, the gunman also had shot and killed his mother as she slept in her bed.

A Model of Doing Everything Right

School safety was a top priority for principal Dawn Hochsprung. The school routinely practiced evacuation drills. She had installed a new safety system at the school that locked the doors during the school day. Visitors would have to be buzzed through and sign in at the main office before being allowed to move about the school. She also had installed a visual monitoring system so that she could keep an eye on the school at all times. Sandy Hook Elementary School was perceived as being a model for doing everything right.

The shooting, however, revealed that no matter how prepared an organization may seem, there still are vulnerabilities to overcome. The 9-1-1 calls from teachers at the school, for example, revealed complexities of being able to secure their classrooms. The door locks required securing from the outside (in the hallway) rather than from inside the room, which would have meant that they would potentially come face-to-face with the shooter. Additionally, the glass entryway, while locked, easily was breached so the shooter could gain access.

In the wake of the shooting, the town voted to demolish the existing school and build a new structure on the same land (not in the same position, however). Many of these concerns were addressed in the design of the new building, which opened to students in July 2016. The new design features multiple security checkpoints while on the way toward the main school building. Landscaping has been used to keep unwanted people at a safe distance, while inside, the classrooms have been equipped with stainless-steel doors, bullet-resistant windows, and reinforced walls. The school also is equipped with a high-tech surveillance system, including a buzz-through system to control who gets access to the school. Despite the integrated security features, the new school was designed to create an inviting and open space for students.

Guns, Mental Health, and the Sandy Hook School Shooter

Prior to the shooting at Sandy Hook, little was known about the shooter. As a child, he briefly had attended Sandy Hook Elementary School before moving on to a local Catholic school and then Newtown High School. During high school, his mother, Nancy, removed him from the school, opting instead to educate him at home. That same year, she divorced his father, retaining primary custody over the shooter.

Mental health concerns plagued the shooter from a young age. While in elementary school, he was diagnosed with sensory-integration disorder, which refers to difficulties in organizing reactions from the senses (such as finding a fabric too itchy to wear when others do not experience the same issue). These challenges can drastically impact a person's productivity, leisure, and play. At the age of 13, the shooter was diagnosed with Asperger's syndrome, as well as an obsessive-compulsive disorder.

In looking for an explanation as to why the shooting had occurred, many people blamed his Asperger's as a causal factor. As advocates note, however, Asperger's and other forms of autism are not mental illnesses but rather brain-related development disorders. Research into Asperger's patients has found that individuals diagnosed with the syndrome rarely direct their aggression to individuals outside of their immediate family or other caregivers. Similarly, episodes of such aggression rarely are planned and almost never involve the use of weapons. In most instances, any violence engaged in by persons with Asperger's almost always is directed at themselves.

Regardless of these empirically based findings, many questioned how someone with such significant mental health concerns could easily obtain such high-powered weapons. Subsequently, the discourse of blame shifted, at least in part, from the shooter to his mother, who also was his first victim. The shooter had become increasingly more withdrawn prior to the shooting, remaining in his room, which he had blacked out with trash bags to avoid sunlight, and choosing only to communicate via email with his mother, even though they lived in the same house. In an effort to connect with her son, Nancy had shared her passion for guns with him.

A gun enthusiast, she kept many guns in the house, including those weapons that were used in the shootings (an additional shotgun, not used in the attack, was found in the shooter's car parked outside). She had taken him to the shooting range in order to teach him safe and responsible gun ownership, and she kept her weapons secured in a safe; the shooter, however, had easy access to them. She even had given him an early Christmas present prior to the attack—a check to purchase a new firearm. Though the shooter had expressed considerable fascination with guns and had exhibited concerning behavior, she never restricted his access to the weapons.

As with other school and mass shootings, the issue of gun control became a heated topic in the aftermath of the shooting at Sandy Hook Elementary School. The discourse immediately filled with calls to ban the sale of semiautomatic weapons like the rifle used in the shooting and to limit the capacity of rounds a magazine could hold. An updated version of the Federal Assault Weapons Ban, which had expired in 2004, was introduced in the first legislative session in 2013, as was a bill to expand background checks on gun purchases; both bills were defeated.

While not much traction was gained at the federal level, despite the lethality of the shooting at Sandy Hook, more movement was witnessed at the state level. Both Connecticut and Maryland expanded restrictions as part of their tougher gun laws. Connecticut expanded their list of banned assault weapons by more than 100 new gun models and required background checks on all firearm sales. Maryland also increased the number of banned gun models, but also included provisions to limit magazine capacities to 10 rounds, requiring licensing and fingerprinting for new gun owners, and banned people who had been involuntarily committed to a mental facility from purchasing a gun. The state of New York passed one of the most comprehensive and sweeping gun control packages in the nation. Known as the Secure Ammunition and Firearms Enforcement (or S.A.F.E.) Act, the bill expanded the definition of assault weapons to be banned, created a state database of pistol permits, reduced the maximum capacity of gun magazines to 7 rounds, and required universal background checks on all gun sales. Despite these states' efforts, others responded in an opposite manner. In the year after the Sandy Hook shooting, 64 percent of the 109 gun-related bills passed at the state level favored easing restrictions for gun owners.

December 15, 2012: St. Vincent's Hospital, Birmingham, AL

Upset over the care his wife was receiving, 38-year-old Jason Letts returned to the cardiac unit where she was a patient, armed with a handgun. After someone raised a concern with security, police arrived on scene. The shooter opened fire on them, wounding three, before he was killed by police.

December 21, 2012: Multiple Locations, Frankstown Township, PA

Around 9:00 a.m., 44-year-old Jeffrey Lee Michael loaded his truck with weapons. Before taking off, he went into the Juanita Valley Gospel Church, located across from his home. After firing a bullet through one of the church's windows, he went inside, where he shot and killed a woman who was volunteering there. He then approached a neighbor who was getting ready to leave to go Christmas shopping and killed him before driving off. While on the road, he intentionally rammed another vehicle, then got out and killed its driver. He continued driving, firing at police cruisers that were traveling in the opposite direction. The officers, having their vehicles struck, immediately began pursuit of the shooter. He crashed head on into one of the police cars, exited the vehicle, and fired at the officers. They returned fire, killing the shooter instantly. In addition to the three fatalities, three officers (two from gunfire) also were wounded in the attack.

January 10, 2013: Taft Union High School, Taft, CA

Armed with a shotgun, 16-year-old student Bryan Oliver made his way to one of the classrooms. He opened fire on the teacher and 28 students who were present at the time. Two people, including the teacher, were shot; both survived. The teacher and campus supervisor then persuaded the shooter to drop his weapon. When he did, they evacuated students from the room and police quickly took the shooter into custody. He was charged as an adult with two counts of attempted murder and three counts of assault with a deadly weapon. To avoid trial, the shooter took a deal, entering a plea of no contest to the two counts of attempted murder without premeditation, and was sentenced to 27 years and 4 months in prison with the possibility of parole in 13 years. He currently is incarcerated at the Kern Valley State Prison in Delano, California.

January 30, 2013: Osborn Maledon Law Firm, Phoenix, AZ

Following a mediation session, 70-year-old Arthur Harmon retrieved his handgun. He opened fire at the law firm, killing one person and wounding two others before fleeing the scene in a rental car. While trying to escape, he also shot at a person who was following him to try to get his license plate number. After a search of his home failed to produce the shooter, police located his body in the bushes in a parking lot in Mesa, a Phoenix suburb. He had committed suicide.

February 19, 2013: Multiple Locations, Orange County, CA

After killing a woman in the Ladera Ranch home he shared with his parents, 20-year-old Ali Syed fled north toward Tustin, approximately 20 miles away. Armed with a shotgun, he carjacked a vehicle at a local gas station, firing at people he saw. As he drove along the freeway, the shooter continued to fire his weapon at other vehicles. When the vehicle he had stolen was running low on fuel, he abandoned it and stole another car after killing its driver. He then drove to a nearby business, where he continued firing, killing one individual and wounding another before stealing another vehicle. Police trailed the shooter for another five miles before he got out of his vehicle at a busy intersection and committed suicide. In total, three people had been killed and three others wounded before the rampage came to an end.

March 13, 2013: Multiple Locations, Herkimer, NY

After setting his apartment on fire, 64-year-old Kurt Myers entered a Herkimer barber shop. Armed with a rifle, he opened fire on patrons. He then went to an oil change shop less than two miles away and continued shooting. In total, four people were killed and two others were injured between the two sites. The shooter then took refuge in an abandoned building nearby. After an all-night manhunt, police officers raided the building the following morning. During a shootout, they shot and killed the gunman.

April 12, 2013: New River Valley Mall, Christiansburg, VA

Armed with a shotgun, 18-year-old student Neil MacInnis arrived at the satellite campus of the New River Community College, located at a Christiansburg mall. As he approached the front desk of the college, he pulled his gun and started firing. Two people were injured before a pair of police officers and an off-duty security guard were able to subdue him. He was charged with two counts of aggravated malicious wounding and two counts of using a firearm while committing a felony. He pleaded guilty to all charges and was sentenced to 38 years in prison (a 68-year sentence with 30 years suspended), which he currently is serving at the River North Correctional Center in Independence, Virginia. Upon release, he will be placed on indefinite probation; he also has been ordered to pay restitution to both of his victims.

April 21, 2013: Pinewood Village Apartments, Federal Way, WA

After killing his girlfriend, 27-year-old Dennis Clark exited her apartment and continued firing. Three additional people were killed, including one person who was trying to contact the authorities for help. Responding police officers were able to corner the shooter at the apartments before he fled on foot. As police caught up to him, they ordered him to leave the weapon he was trying to reach for alone; when he failed to comply, the officers shot and killed him, ending the attack. No additional people were injured in the shooting.

May 26, 2013: Multiple Locations, Brady, TX

Armed with an assault rifle, handgun, and hundreds of rounds of ammunition, 23-year-old Esteban Smith began firing at cars from his moving vehicle. The North Carolina–based Marine first shot and killed a woman in the town of Eola before continuing his spree. Over a span of approximately 80 miles, he wounded five others, including a police officer. After exchanging gunfire with responding law enforcement, he was shot and killed. Further investigation revealed that prior to traveling to Texas, the shooter had killed his wife near his military base at Camp Lejeune in North Carolina.

June 7, 2013: Santa Monica College, Santa Monica, CA

After shooting and killing his father and brother and then setting their home on fire, 23-year-old John Zawahri fled. Armed with a semiautomatic rifle and handgun, he carjacked a vehicle at gunpoint and forced the driver to take him to Santa Monica College. Along the way, both from the vehicle and once on foot, the shooter continued to fire at passersby, including a city bus and police patrol car. At the college, he made his way to the library, where he continued firing upon people. Police soon arrived on scene and engaged in a shootout with the gunman, who was hit in the process. The officers brought the shooter outside, where he died of his injuries. Over the 13-minute rampage, five people had been killed and two others were wounded.

July 26, 2013: Todel Apartments, Hialeah, FL

After setting a pile of money on fire inside his apartment, 42-year-old Pedro Vargas used his semiautomatic pistol to shoot and kill the building manager and his wife, who were responding to the smoke. He then retreated back into his apartment, making his way to the unit's balcony. From there, he continued shooting at people passing by the building at street level before killing several people in a neighboring unit. Police responded to the scene, and over the next five hours, they exchanged gunfire with the shooter as he made his way through the various stairwells of the complex. In another building, the shooter kicked in a door and took the apartment's residents hostage at gunpoint. During the standoff, police attempted to negotiate the shooter's surrender, but he continued to fire his weapon at them intermittently. After three hours, during another shootout, the gunman was killed by police; the hostages were rescued without harm. A total of six people were killed in the rampage.

August 5, 2013: Ross Township Municipal Building, Saylorsburg, PA

After packing his rental car with weapons, 59-year-old Rockne Newell drove to the municipal building, where a township meeting was underway. Frustrated over issues with his property, he retrieved a rifle and opened fire. When that ran out of ammunition, the shooter returned to his car, retrieved a handgun, and went back to the building. At that time, two people who had been attending the meeting tackled him and held him down until he was taken into police custody. Three people had been killed and two others were wounded. The shooter was charged with three counts of homicide and two counts of attempted murder. Originally pleading not guilty, he later changed his plea to guilty and was sentenced to three consecutive terms of life in prison plus 61 to 122 years. He currently is incarcerated at SCI Huntingdon in Huntingdon, Pennsylvania.

August 24, 2013: Multiple Locations, Lake Butler, FL

On the morning of the shooting, Hubert Allen Jr. armed himself with a shotgun and a rifle. The 72-year-old former employee of Pritchett Trucking, Inc. fired at current employees of the company as he drove throughout town. He then retreated to his home nearby, where he committed suicide. Two people were killed and two others were injured in the attack.

September 16, 2013: Washington Navy Yard, Washington, D.C.

Just after 8:00 a.m., 34-year-old civilian contractor Aaron Alexis arrived at the Washington Navy Yard, where he had been working for several weeks. He entered the headquarters of the Naval Sea Systems Command (NAVSEA), located in Building 197. Once inside, he made his way to the fourth floor and entered a bathroom. There, he assembled the sawed-off shotgun he had brought with him to work that day.

After emerging with the gun, the shooter made his way into an area near the building's atrium that contained cubicles. He opened fire, shooting four people. He then continued firing at people along the fourth floor before making his way down a building level. There, he continued to shoot at people who were attempting to flee or hide. After shooting several others, the gunman went down to the first floor of the building.

Once downstairs, the gunman shot and killed a security officer, stealing his service weapon. He exchanged gunfire with another security guard before retreating to another area of the building. He encountered two men standing by the corner of the building and tried to shoot them. Realizing his shotgun had run out of ammunition, the shooter switched to the stolen semiautomatic pistol, killing one of them.

Though calls to 9-1-1 had been made within less than two minutes of the first shots being fired, the complex layout of the Navy Yard led to delays in law enforcement getting to the scene. When they made entry, the echoing sound of the atrium led them to believe the shooter was on the second floor, when he still was on the first. After searching for him, they located him on the third floor in a cubicle area, where he had moved after discarding the empty shotgun on the first floor. When the two officers and two NCIS agents entered the space, the shooter opened fire, hitting one of the officers.

After the other officer and the two agents helped the wounded officer out, a Washington, D.C. police officer, along with two U.S. Park Police officers, made their way into the cubicle area. The shooter emerged from his hiding spot, firing at the men and shooting the D.C. police officer in the tactical vest. The three officers returned fire, shooting the gunman in the head and bringing the rampage to an end just over an hour after it began. A total of 12 people were killed and 8 others (3 from gunfire) were injured in the attack. The Navy Yard shooting was the second deadliest mass shooting on a military installation in general and the first since the 2009 shooting at Fort Hood.

October 21, 2013: Sparks Middle School, Sparks, NV

Armed with a semiautomatic handgun, 12-year-old student Jose Reyes arrived at his middle school. He made his way to the basketball courts, where he opened fire on the students. A math teacher saw what was happening and approached the shooter to try to diffuse the situation; he was shot and killed. Two other students also were injured in the attack. The shooter then committed suicide at the scene and was found by responding law enforcement a short time later.

November 1, 2013: Los Angeles International Airport, Los Angeles, CA

After being dropped off at the airport by his roommate, 23-year-old Paul Anthony Ciancia made his way to terminal 3. He retrieved a semiautomatic rifle from a bag he was carrying and used it to shoot an officer at the TSA security checkpoint. He then bypassed the checkpoint and made his way upstairs, returning briefly to shoot the officer again when he saw him move. The shooter then returned to the concourse area, where he continued firing. When he made it to the end of the terminal, the shooter encountered airport police officers, who engaged him. The shooter was wounded in the exchange before being taken into custody. By the end of the shooting, one person had been killed and six others were injured (three from gunshots). The shooter faced both federal and state charges in conjunction with the attack but was ultimately indicted on 11 federal counts, including first-degree murder. The shooter pleaded not guilty to the charges; the federal prosecutors then announced they would seek the death penalty. Nearly three years after entering his plea, the shooter changed his plea to guilty in exchange for life in prison without the possibility of parole; he also received an additional 60 years. He currently is incarcerated at FMC Devens, a federal medical center, in Ayer, Massachusetts.

December 17, 2013: Renown Regional Medical Center, Reno, NV

Armed with a shotgun (the only weapon used in the attack) and two handguns, 51-year-old Alan Oliver Frazier arrived at the medical center. Frustrated over a previous surgery, the shooter entered the Center for Advanced Medicine and opened fire. One person was killed and two others were injured. The shooter then made his way back to the lobby, where he committed suicide as police arrived on scene.

January 14, 2014: Berrendo Middle School, Roswell, NM

Middle school student Mason Campbell arrived at his school armed with a modified shotgun. The 12-year-old shooter opened fire in the school's gym. Two students were struck in the gunfire;

both survived their injuries. A social studies teacher then intervened and was able to convince the shooter to put down his gun. He then was held against the wall by the teacher until he was taken into police custody. Due to being under 14 years old, the shooter was not eligible to be tried as an adult under state law. He was charged with three counts of aggravated assault with a deadly weapon, to which he later pleaded no contest to the charges. He was given the maximum sentence allowed by law—confinement in state custody until his 21st birthday. He currently is incarcerated with the Children, Youth, and Families Department in Santa Fe, New Mexico.

January 15, 2014: Martin's Supermarket, Elkhart, IN

Armed with a semiautomatic handgun, 22-year-old Shawn Bair arrived at the supermarket. He wandered the store for approximately 20 minutes, talking on his phone and texting, before opening fire on customers and employees. Two people were killed before the shooter took a manager hostage. When police arrived on scene, they startled the shooter, allowing the manager to escape unharmed. They then shot and killed the shooter, ending the rampage.

January 17, 2014: Delaware Valley Charter High School, Philadelphia, PA

After purchasing a gun from a former student at the school, 17-year-old Raisheem Rochwell opened fire. Two students were injured in the attack before the student fled. He surrendered to authorities a short time later after a video of the gun purchased was released. The shooter was charged with aggravated assault, reckless endangerment, and related firearms offenses. A plea deal was reached and he was sentenced to two years in a juvenile facility, which he served and was released. The former student who sold him the gun also was charged with violation of the Uniform Firearms Act, conspiracy, and related offenses. He pleaded guilty to carrying a firearm in public, possession of a weapon on school property, and reckless endangerment and was sentenced to up to 23 months incarceration followed by a maximum of five years' probation. In 2016, the supplier was rearrested on drug- and weapons-related charges.

January 25, 2014: The Mall in Columbia, Columbia, MD

Armed with a shotgun and several explosive devices, 19-year-old Darion Aguilar arrived at the mall. He first went to a retail store, Zumiez, taking a photo of himself in the dressing room and posting it to Tumblr. He then exited the dressing room, retrieved his weapon, and killed two store employees. He exited into the mall, continuing to fire his gun; five mall patrons were wounded. As police began to arrive on scene, the shooter committed suicide.

February 20, 2014: Cedarville Rancheria Tribal Office, Alturas, CA

After embezzling money during her time as tribal chairperson, 44-year-old Cherie Lash-Rhoades appeared before the council for an eviction meeting. Armed with a handgun, she opened fire, shooting the people in the room. When she ran out of ammunition, the shooter then retrieved a butcher knife to stab her victims. As police arrived on scene, an employee of the Rancheria helped to tackle the shooter; she then was taken into custody. Four people had been killed and two others were injured in the attack. The shooter was charged with four counts of murder, two counts of attempted murder, and child endangerment. She originally pleaded not guilty; a jury convicted her of all charges. She was sentenced to death for the murders, as well as 150 years to life for the attempted murder and special allegations. She also was ordered to pay $64,000 in restitution to her victims. She currently is incarcerated at the Central California Women's Facility in Chowchilla, California.

April 2, 2014: Multiple Locations, Fort Hood, TX

After his request for leave was denied, 34-year-old Ivan Lopez stepped outside of the 49th Transportation Battalion administrative office to smoke a cigarette. The Army specialist returned a short time later armed with a handgun. He reentered the building and opened fire. After shooting three people, he left and drove his vehicle toward a motor pool building where he had been assigned to work. Along the way, he continued firing at individuals as he reached the building. He then left and proceeded to the 1st Medical Brigade headquarters. Still shooting at people, he entered the building once he arrived and shot four additional people. He then drove his car to a parking lot near another building, where he encountered a military police officer. When he showed his weapon, she fired at him but missed; the shooter then committed suicide. Over nearly nine minutes, 3 people had been killed and 14 others (12 by gunfire) were wounded. The shooting was the second attack at the military base, following the 2009 rampage.

April 13, 2014: Multiple Locations, Overland Park, KS

Armed with a shotgun (the main weapon used in the shooting) and a handgun, Frazier Glenn Miller Jr., a 74-year-old former member of a Ku Klux Klan–related organization, arrived at the rear parking lot of the Overland Park Jewish Community Center. After shooting several people, the gunman drove to Village Shalom, a retirement community located just over a mile from the community center. He continued firing from the parking lot, killing one woman. Less than an hour after the shooting began, police apprehended the gunman outside a nearby elementary school. He was charged with capital murder as well as first-degree murder, three counts of attempted first-degree murder, aggravated assault, and criminally discharging a firearm at an occupied building. The shooter's attorneys attempted on several occasions to reach a plea deal but the prosecutors declined, instead announcing that they would seek the death penalty in the case. The shooter then decided that he would represent himself at trial. Within two weeks of jury selection, he had been found guilty of one count of capital murder and three counts of attempted murder, along with assault and weapon charges. The gunman was formally sentenced to the death penalty for the shootings at the recommendation of the jury. He currently is incarcerated at the El Dorado Correctional Facility in El Dorado, Kansas.

April 29, 2014: Federal Express (FedEx) Sorting Facility, Kennesaw, GA

Just before the end of his shift, 19-year-old Geddy Lee Kramer retrieved his shotgun. He first shot an unarmed security guard at an entrance gate before making his way back into the building. For the next three minutes, he continued firing; six people in total were wounded, all of whom survived. As police arrived on scene, the shooter committed suicide.

May 23, 2014: Multiple Locations, Santa Barbara, CA

Just after 6:00 in the evening, 22-year-old Elliot Rodger stabbed his three roommates to death. He then left the apartment they shared in his BMW, armed with three semiautomatic handguns and two knives. He drove to a local coffee shop, purchased a beverage, and drove back to the apartment complex. While sitting in the parking lot outside his building, the shooter uploaded a video he entitled "Retribution" to YouTube and emailed his 140-page manifesto to his parents, his therapist, and several other people. Upon receiving the email, both his mother and his therapist immediately alerted police of the shooter's impending actions, but by the time they had notified law enforcement, the rampage already was over.

Frustrated over what he perceived as slights from the female sex, the shooter drove to the Alpha Phi sorority house near the campus of the University of California–Santa Barbara. When no one answered the door, he opened fire on passersby, shooting three women who were part of the Delta Delta Delta sorority, two of whom died. The shooter then returned to his car and drove off, firing a shot into an unoccupied coffee shop nearby.

The shooter next drove to a nearby deli and continued firing his guns, killing one person inside. He then proceeded to drive down the wrong side of the road, hitting a pedestrian with his car and firing at others. He continued shooting at pedestrians as he curved around the area's loop. After proceeding a bit further and making a U-turn, the shooter exchanged fire with a sheriff's deputy, hitting two onlookers in the process.

He continued to drive recklessly through town, shooting at some people and running others over with his car. After exchanging gunfire with three other deputies, during which he was shot in the hip, the gunman fled and was pursued by police. He hit a cyclist with his car just before crashing into another vehicle near an intersection. As police approached the vehicle, they found that the shooter had committed suicide with a self-inflicted gunshot wound to the head. By the end of his rampage, 6 people had been killed and 14 others were injured.

June 5, 2014: Seattle Pacific University, Seattle, WA

Aaron Ybarra arrived at Otto Hall at the Seattle Pacific University campus, armed with a shotgun and hunting knife. After determining that students were at the building at that time, the 27-year-old parked his vehicle and began to approach. When one student did not appear afraid of his gun, the shooter opened fire, killing him. Three other students (two by gunfire) also were wounded. After making his way inside the building, the shooter's gun jammed. As he tried to clear and reload the weapon, a student security guard pepper sprayed him and held him down until law enforcement arrived and took him into custody. The shooter was charged with first-degree murder, three counts of first-degree attempted murder, and one count of second-degree assault. When his insanity plea failed, the shooter was found guilty on all charges. He was sentenced to 112 years in prison, which he is serving at the Washington State Penitentiary in Walla Walla, Washington.

June 8, 2014: Multiple Locations, Las Vegas, NV

Armed with a pistol, revolver, shotgun, and knives, 31-year-old Jerad Miller and his wife, 22-year-old Amanda Miller, approached two officers who were having lunch outside a pizzeria. Without saying a word, the shooters killed both police officers before dragging their bodies out of the booth they had been sitting in, covering one of the bodies with the Gadsen flag and a swastika, and stealing the officers' service weapons. They then fled into a nearby Walmart, where one of the shooters fired his gun into the ceiling and ordered all patrons to leave. An armed citizen drew his weapon and confronted one of the shooters, only to be shot and killed by the other. Responding police officers engaged the shooters, killing one of them in the process. The other shooter then committed suicide.

June 10, 2014: Reynolds High School, Troutdale, OR

Jared Padgett, a 15-year-old student, arrived at school armed with a semiautomatic rifle, as well as a handgun and knife. After entering the boys' locker room, he opened fire, killing one student and wounding a teacher. A police officer responded to the incident and engaged the shooter, who escaped unharmed. He then retreated into a bathroom and committed suicide as additional police and the SWAT team arrived on scene.

August 2, 2014: Hon-Dah Resort Casino and Conference Center, Pinetop, AZ

Following an argument with his wife, 28-year-old Justin Joe Armstrong retrieved his rifle and opened fire in the parking lot. A security guard came to investigate the commotion and was wounded. The shooter then moved to the middle of a nearby highway and fired at passing cars. Police quickly responded and exchanged gunfire with the shooter, who was killed. Two people, including the security guard, were wounded in the attack.

September 23, 2014: UPS Shipping Facility, Birmingham, AL

Following his termination as a driver for UPS after 21 years of service, 45-year-old Kerry Joe Tesney returned to his former employer. Armed with a handgun, he entered the shipping facility and opened fire. Two supervisors were killed in the attack before the shooter committed suicide.

October 24, 2014: Marysville Pilchuck High School, Marysville, WA

After entering the school cafeteria, 14-year-old student Jaylen Fryberg retrieved a semiautomatic handgun while sitting at a table. He approached another table where a group of students he had texted earlier were sitting and opened fire. Four students were killed and another was wounded in the shooting. The gunman then committed suicide at the scene. Approximately five months after the shooting, his father was arrested for lying on a series of applications to purchase guns, including the one used in the attack, over an 18-month period. He was found guilty of knowingly owning firearms that legally he could not possess and sentenced him to two years in prison. He appealed the conviction in 2017, but it was upheld. He was incarcerated at RRM Seattle, a residential reentry facility, until his release on November 9, 2017.

October 24, 2014: Motel 6, Sacramento, CA

After an officer responded to a call about a suspicious vehicle in a Motel 6 parking lot, 34-year-old Marcelo Marquez (real name Luis Enrique Monroy-Bracamonte) shot and killed him with a semiautomatic rifle. Along with his 38-year-old wife, Janelle Marquez Monroy, the shooter drove about a mile away, shooting another person after the individual refused to turn over his vehicle. Over the course of several more miles, the couple successfully carjacked two additional vehicles. After two deputies noticed the latest vehicle pulled over on the side of the road, they approached to speak with the driver. Both were shot at close range; one died shortly thereafter at a local hospital. After he abandoned the vehicle and fled into a nearby home, police flushed out the shooter with tear gas. His wife also was arrested separately and without incident. Both were charged with capital murder for the two officers' deaths, as well as five counts of attempted murder, two of carjacking, two of attempted carjacking, and four other felonies. The shooters' trials were expected to begin in October 2017.

November 15, 2014: Economy Inn, Springfield, MO

Believing that certain individuals were being used as police informants against him, 47-year-old Scott Goodwin-Bey entered a motel room where the men were located. Armed with a handgun, he opened fire, killing four people; a fifth individual was unharmed after he was able to flee to safety. After the shooting, the gunman went to a nearby convenience store and turned the weapon over to a clerk on duty. Police soon arrived on scene and took the shooter into custody. Four first-degree murder charges originally were filed against the shooter, but they were dropped in 2016 after a court ruling regarding the ballistics evidence. The prosecutor, however, noted that charges were expected to be refiled. The shooter still was convicted on federal gun charges stemming from the incident and was sentenced to 10 years in federal prison. He currently is incarcerated at the FCI Greenville unit in Greenville, Illinois.

November 20, 2014: Florida State University, Tallahassee, FL

Armed with a semiautomatic pistol, 31-year-old Myron May returned to his alma mater. Believing he was a targeted individual, he entered the university's Strozier Library and opened fire. Three individuals—a library employee and two students—were shot by the gunman. When police arrived on scene, the shooter exited the library and began shooting at them. The officers returned fire, killing the shooter and ending the rampage. Prior to the shooting, the gunman had mailed packages to friends and family and also had placed a number of phone calls and sent emails to various individuals.

December 20, 2014: Bedford-Stuyvesant Neighborhood, Brooklyn, NY

After shooting and wounding his ex-girlfriend in a Baltimore, MD suburb, 28-year-old Ismaaiyl Abdullah Brinsley took a bus to New York City. While en route, he posted about intending to kill police officers in anger over the deaths of Michael Brown and Eric Garner and perceived police brutality on Instagram. The Instagram posts were found by the Baltimore County Police Department, who then notified the NYPD about the threats. Minutes after the exchange of information, the shooter approached a patrol car where two officers were on duty. He pulled out his weapon and opened fire, killing both of the men. The shooter then fled, soon being chased by NYPD officers. He retreated into a subway station, where he then committed suicide.

January 26, 2015: New Hope City Hall, New Hope, MN

Armed with a shotgun, 68-year-old Raymond Kmetz arrived at a police swearing-in ceremony during a city council meeting. He retrieved his weapon and opened fire. Though no one was killed in the attack, four people, including two law enforcement officers, were injured. The shooter then was killed by police on scene. A subsequent investigation revealed that the shooter's mental illness had landed him on Minnesota's list of people prohibited from owning a gun. Despite this, the shooter still had been able to purchase ammunition for his gun on the morning of the attack.

February 7, 2015: Monroeville Mall, Monroeville, PA

On the evening of the shooting, 17-year-old Tarod Thornhill arrived at the Macy's department store at the mall. While on the store's lower level, he retrieved his semiautomatic handgun and opened fire. No one was killed but three people were wounded. The shooter fled the scene but was apprehended by law enforcement several hours later. After a trial, the shooter was found not guilty of attempted homicide but was convicted on three counts of aggravated assault. He was sentenced to 15 to 30 years in prison, which he currently is serving at SCI Pine Grove in Indiana, Pennsylvania.

February 12, 2015: Sioux Steel Pro-Tec, Lennox, SD

Following a dispute with a coworker, 51-year-old Jeffrey DeZeeuw left and returned with a handgun. He opened fire, shooting three of his coworkers, one of whom died at the scene. Another man heard the commotion and tried to intervene; he was injured when he got into a physical altercation with the shooter. The gunman then fled the building; he committed suicide three miles away in his vehicle.

March 14, 2015: Dad's Sing Along Club, San Antonio, TX

After being thrown out of the bar, 29-year-old Richard Castilleja went to his car, where he retrieved his handgun. He then waited at a nearby convenience store until the bar closed, then opened fire on patrons fleeing into the parking lot. Two people were wounded in the shooting. Responding police officers then killed the shooter, fearing he would hurt more people.

March 18, 2015: Multiple Locations, Mesa, AZ

Following an argument at a hotel that resulted in three people being shot, 41-year-old Ryan Giroux fled the scene. Armed with a handgun, he fired at a student who was eating at a restaurant across the street from the hotel at the East Valley Institute of Technology before carjacking an instructor. He then attempted to break into two apartments to hide, shooting residents in each. He was taken into police custody several hours later. In total, one person had been killed and five others were wounded in the rampage. He was charged with 23 different counts, including first-degree murder, attempted murder, and aggravated assault with a deadly weapon. Originally pleading not guilty, he later changed his plea and was sentenced to life in prison plus 83.5 years. He currently is incarcerated at the Arizona State Prison Complex Lewis in Buckeye, Arizona.

May 3, 2015: Trestle Trail Bridge, Menasha, WI

Upset over an earlier fight with his ex-fiancée, 27-year-old Sergio Valencia del Toro rode his bike to the Trestle Trail Bridge. He retrieved the two handguns he had brought with him and opened fire on the crowd of approximately 100 people who were at the bridge. Three people were killed and one other was injured in the attack. The shooter then shot himself as law enforcement arrived on scene; he died several hours later from his wounds.

May 26, 2015: Walmart Supercenter, Grand Forks, ND

Armed with a handgun, 21-year-old Marcell Willis arrived at the retailer in the early morning hours. After entering the store, the active-duty U.S. airman opened fire. One person was killed and another was injured before the shooter committed suicide at the scene.

June 17, 2015: Emanuel African Methodist Episcopal Church, Charleston, SC

Armed with a handgun, 21-year-old white supremacist Dylann Roof attended an evening Bible study at the Emanuel AME Church, a historically black congregation that is among the oldest in the South. When parishioners bowed their head in prayer, the shooter stood, retrieved his weapon, and opened fire. Over the next six minutes, the shooter had reloaded his weapon five times. Nine people were killed and one other was injured.

After the rampage, the shooter fled the church in his vehicle. He was captured the following morning during a routine traffic stop in Shelby, NC, approximately 245 miles from the church. He was charged with nine counts of first-degree murder and one count of possessing a firearm during the commission of a violent crime. The following month, he was charged on federal hate crime and civil rights violations, to which he pleaded not guilty.

The shooter initially chose to represent himself in the federal trial, though he later utilized a lawyer's services for the guilt phase, reserving self-representation for the penalty phase. He was convicted on all 33 charges and subsequently was sentenced to death. Four months later, he pleaded guilty to all state-related charges in an effort to avoid a second trial and was sentenced to nine consecutive terms of life in prison without the possibility of parole to be served in the state prison. He currently is incarcerated at the United States Penitentiary in Terra Haute, IN, pending mandatory appeals of his death sentence.

The End of an Era for a Symbol of the South

The Confederate flag, steeped in a long historical tradition, remained prominently displayed across South Carolina and other Southern states at the time of the shooting at the Charleston church. After images surfaced displaying the shooter holding the flag, there was pushback against the symbol of the Confederacy, which historically has been associated with slavery, racism, segregation, and white supremacy, themes that also all were present in his writings.

In an effort to abandon this historical cloud, steps were taken to discontinue its use. In the same month as the shooting, the National Park Service ceased flying Confederate flags over Fort Sumter. That same month, the governors of Virginia, Maryland, and North Carolina took steps to discontinue the issuance of specialty plates that bore the symbol. The next day, the governor of Alabama ordered the removal of the Confederate flag from the state capitol. Bills were introduced to revise the Mississippi state flag, which incorporated the symbol, but the attempts did not make it through the state's legislature.

In South Carolina, several civilians removed the Confederate flag from the capitol. On June 27, just 10 days after the shooting, Bree Newsome, a North Carolina activist, scaled the flagpole where the flag was flown and removed it, only to be arrested when she came back down. Her actions are one of the more iconic examples of civil disobedience in modern times. Within two weeks, the South Carolina Senate and House of Representatives both had voted to remove the flag by the required majorities. On July 10, 2015, the flag was permanently removed from the state capitol. In the years following, other symbols of the Confederacy, including the Jefferson Davis monument and the Robert E. Lee statue in New Orleans, Louisiana, also were removed from their long-standing posts.

July 16, 2015: Multiple Locations, Chattanooga, TN

Armed with a semiautomatic rifle, handgun, and shotgun, 24-year-old Muhammad Youssef Abdulazeez first drove by the Armed Forces Career Center, located in a local strip mall. From his vehicle, he fired between 30 and 45 rounds into the building, injuring a Marine. He sped off and drove approximately six miles to the Navy Support Operational Center. After ramming the security gate with his vehicle, the shooter opened fire, moving inside a building where Marines and sailors were working. Over nearly five minutes, five people were killed (one of whom died two days later at the hospital) and a second person was wounded. The gunman was shot and killed by responding law enforcement officers after they exchanged fire.

July 23, 2015: Grand 16 Theater, Lafayette, LA

Armed with a handgun, 59-year-old John Russel Houser purchased a ticket and took his seat in a theater. Approximately 20 minutes into the movie, the shooter rose and opened fire into the crowd. Two people were killed and another nine were injured in the attack. The shooter attempted to escape from the theater as patrons fled, but retreated back inside once he saw responding police officers. He reloaded his weapon and committed suicide in the theater.

October 1, 2015: Umpqua Community College, Roseburg, OR

Armed with five handguns and a semiautomatic rifle, 26-year-old student Christopher Harper-Mercer arrived at his writing class in Snyder Hall. Upon entering the room, he fired a warning shot to get everyone's attention before forcing everyone to the center of the room. One student was allowed to leave in order to deliver a package to police. The shooter then opened fire. He first shot and killed the professor before turning his weapons at his classmates. Eight students were killed and another nine were wounded. Police arrived on scene approximately six minutes after the shooting began and exchanged fire with the gunman, striking him once. After several minutes, the shooter retreated back into the classroom and committed suicide.

October 31, 2015: Residential Neighborhood, Colorado Springs, CO

After setting his house on fire, 33-year-old Noah Harpham walked through his neighborhood. Armed with two handguns and a rifle, he fired at people who were out on the street. Three people were killed by the time law enforcement responded; no other injuries were reported. The gunman then engaged in a shootout with police, in which he was killed.

November 22, 2015: Chaparral Night Club, Brownsville, Texas

Armed with a handgun, 30-year-old Marco Antonio Hernandez arrived at the nightclub. He opened fire in the parking lot, wounding four individuals before fleeing the scene. Identified by police several days later, the shooter then turned himself in to the authorities without further incidence. He was charged with four counts of aggravated assault with a deadly weapon and unlawful possession of a firearm by a felon. In May 2017, the shooter pleaded guilty to one count of aggravated assault with a deadly weapon; the remaining charges were dismissed. He was sentenced to 15 years in prison, which he currently is serving at the Garza West prison unit in Beeville, Texas.

November 27, 2015: Planned Parenthood Clinic, Colorado Springs, CO

Robert Lewis Dear entered the Planned Parenthood clinic armed with a rifle. The 59-year-old opened fire, killing three, including a police officer, and wounding nine others. After a five-hour standoff with police, the shooter surrendered. At trial, he expressed anti-abortion and anti–Planned Parenthood views. He was deemed incompetent to stand trial and confined to a Colorado state mental hospital for treatment. His competency standing has been reviewed several times, including in August 2017, but he remains unfit for trial at the time of this writing.

December 2, 2015: Inland Regional Center, San Bernardino, CA

Around 8:30 in the morning, nearly 80 coworkers gathered at the Inland Regional Center for a staff meeting that later would turn into a holiday party. Among the attendees that morning was 28-year-old Syed Rizwan Farook, a health inspector for the county. He exited the meeting about halfway through, leaving a backpack atop the table. He returned to the building a half hour later with his wife, 29-year-old Tashfeen Malik.

Armed with two semiautomatic rifles and two semiautomatic pistols, the couple first opened fire on two people who had been standing outside, killing both. They then made their way back to the room where the event was being held, continuing to fire their weapons. Many people had been able to flee when the shooting started but a number of individuals could not escape, instead seeking shelter under tables, in bathrooms, and even in cabinets if they could fit. Over the next three minutes, the shooters went table by table shooting at anyone they saw move. Several people were shot when they tried to tackle the shooters.

At the end of their rampage, the shooters retrieved the backpack that had been left earlier and set out the three pipe bombs, which were connected to one another, inside. The devices were hooked up to a remote detonator and were left to kill responding law enforcement; they never exploded. The shooters then fled the building as law enforcement arrived on scene. Fourteen people had been killed and 22 others were injured in the attack.

A victim at the scene had been able to identify the male shooter to police, who quickly determined that the pair had left in a rental SUV. Plainclothes officers were dispatched to the shooters' home in Redlands, and just after 3:00 p.m., the pair left the dwelling. They soon were pursued by law enforcement, entering, then exiting, a freeway. They stopped at a traffic light to put on their tactical vests and arm themselves with their rifles before speeding off; while the male shooter drove, the female shooter fired at the police chasing them through the back window.

The shooters came to a stop in a residential area, at which time both shooters fired at police from behind the doors of their vehicle, using them as a shield. One officer was struck as more units arrived to provide backup. The male shooter left his post and walked toward nearby homes. The officers concentrated their fire on him, striking him in the legs and torso. The gunman fell to the ground, continuing to shoot at the officers until his gun jammed; he then was shot and killed. Police then turned their full attention to the female shooter. Minutes later, she was struck in the head and body and killed, bringing the rampage to an end.

A Planned Attack

Nearly as soon as the gunfire subsided, questions arose as to how long this event had been planned. After killing the suspects in the shootout, police had found nearly 2,500 rounds of ammunition in their vehicle. A later search of their home uncovered an additional 4,500 rounds, as well as materials used to make pipe bombs. The evidence suggested that the pair had been planning their attack for more than a year.

The FBI announced that they were treating the case as an act of terrorism. Additional investigation determined that there was no definitive link between the shooters and ISIS, despite the fact that the shooters had communicated their jihadist ideologies to each other even before meeting face-to-face and getting married. The director of the FBI at the time, James Comey, testified that the shooters were self-radicalized based upon information they consumed on the Internet and that their radicalization process took place before ISIS even emerged.

February 20, 2016: Multiple Locations, Kalamazoo, MI

Armed with two semiautomatic handguns, 45-year-old Jason Brian Dalton first shot a random woman in an apartment parking lot. Four and a half hours later, the shooter arrived at a Kia dealership, where he continued shooting, striking several customers. He then continued to a Cracker Barrel restaurant, where he fired on additional people who were in their cars. In total, six people were killed and two were injured in the shootings. Police arrested him two hours after the final shooting. Further investigation revealed that the shooter also was an Uber driver who had been running routes in between shootings. He was charged with six counts of murder, two counts of assault with the intent to commit murder, and eight counts of using a firearm during the commission of a felony. He currently is incarcerated at the Kalamazoo County while his trial proceeds.

February 25, 2016: Multiple Locations, Newton and Heston, KS

Cedric Ford began his rampage in Newton by shooting at two vehicles from his car. Armed with a semiautomatic rifle and a semiautomatic handgun, the 38-year-old employee of Excel Industries, a lawn care equipment manufacturing company, then drove toward Heston, continuing to fire at oncoming vehicles. After crashing his vehicle into a ditch, the shooter exited the car and continued firing at people. He then made his way to the plant of his employer, shooting people outside before entering the building and firing at people working on the assembly lines. The police chief was the first on scene; the gunman fired at the officer, who shot back, killing him and ending the attack. In total, 3 people had been killed and 14 others were wounded in the shootings.

February 29, 2016: Madison Junior/Senior High School, Middletown, OH

Unhappy with his home life, 14-year-old James Austin Hancock went to school armed with a gun that he had taken from a family member. He opened fire in the cafeteria, wounding two students; two additional students were injured from shrapnel or when trying to flee. The shooter fled the scene, dropping his firearm along the way. He was taken into custody near the school after K-9 officers were able to track his scent. The shooter later pleaded guilty to four counts of attempted murder and one count of inducing a panic. He was sentenced to a juvenile detention facility until his 21st birthday.

April 23, 2016: Antigo High School, Antigo, WI

Armed with a rifle, 18-year-old Jakob Wagner arrived at the high school where the prom was taking place. The former student opened fire on students who were leaving the building, wounding two. Police officers, who also were in the parking lot to monitor the dance's activities, responded immediately. One of the officers returned fire, shooting the shooter. Though the shooter was transported to the hospital for medical care, he died the following day.

May 4, 2016: Knight Transportation, Harris County, TX

After being fired from the company two weeks earlier, 65-year-old Marion Guy Williams returned to his former workplace armed with a shotgun (the main weapon used in the attack) and a pistol. He went to the company breakroom, where he fired a warning round before starting to shoot. One person was killed in the attack and two others were injured. The shooter then committed suicide.

May 25, 2016: Beeline Highway, Phoenix, AZ

Armed with a rifle, 36-year-old James David Walker opened fire on passing vehicles on the Beeline Highway on the outskirts of Phoenix. He then carjacked a vehicle and fled the scene, after which time he hit a state trooper's patrol vehicle before crashing his car into a ditch. The shooter was spotted by a police air unit and taken into custody. Two people had been wounded in the shooting. The shooter was charged with multiple counts, including aggravated assault, attempted homicide, armed robbery, theft of means of transportation, and possession of dangerous drugs. He currently is incarcerated in the Fourth Avenue jail while awaiting trial.

May 29, 2016: Multiple Locations, Houston, TX

After breaking into the Memorial Auto and Tire shop and spending the night, 25-year-old Dionisio Garza opened fire with a semiautomatic rifle when a worker arrived in the morning. He killed the worker before fleeing on foot, shooting at passing cars as he walked. Police officers arrived on scene and set up a perimeter, exchanging gunfire with the shooter. The shooter then was killed in the attack. In addition to the man killed, six others were injured in the attack.

June 12, 2016: Pulse Nightclub, Orlando, FL

In the early morning hours, approximately 320 patrons were at the Pulse nightclub, enjoying the weekly Latin Night that was in session. At approximately 2:00 a.m., as the bar was serving last call drinks, 29-year-old Omar Mateen arrived at the venue armed with a semiautomatic rifle and semiautomatic pistol. As he tried to gain entry, the security guard (who also was an off-duty officer for the Orlando Police Department) engaged him, but the shooter was able to get inside the building.

Once inside, the shooter opened fire at the packed audience. He then made his way out onto the patio, where the security guard and additional responding police officers engaged him. The shooter then retreated into the club and began taking patrons as hostages. During the chaos, a Marine veteran was able to unlatch a door, allowing people to escape. A number of people took shelter in the bathroom, attempting to hide from the gunman. The shooter fired through the bathroom door and then over the stall doors, hitting additional people. After the rifle jammed, he switched to his handgun and continued shooting.

Twenty minutes after the shooting began, the gunman placed a call to 9-1-1 in which he pledged allegiance to ISIS's leader. Six officers shot out a window and entered the club, heading toward the bathroom where they determined the gunfire to be coming from. The shooter briefly stuck his head out and engaged the police before retreating back into the bathroom. The SWAT team that had arrived on scene ordered the officers to hold their positions. By that time, the shooter had stopped firing his weapon, transitioning the scene from active shooter to hostage.

At 2:45 a.m., the shooter called a local news station. A crisis negotiator arrived on scene and made contact with the shooter three times over the next 45 minutes. The shooter advised that he had explosive devices on his person; in a later call with police, he said he was going to strap similar bombs to his hostages and place them in the four corners of the room to blow the building up. Police then decided to end the standoff.

Just after 5:00 a.m., three hours after the ordeal began, SWAT officers breached the building's exterior wall. Once inside, they used flashbangs to draw the shooter out, engaging in a gunfight with him. By 5:17 a.m., the shooter had been killed by the police, ending the rampage and freeing the remaining hostages. A total of 49 people were killed, making the Pulse attack the deadliest mass shooting in U.S. history at the time. An additional 58 people were injured.

A Terrorist Attack, A Hate Crime, or Both?

People were quick to speculate about a potential motivation for the attack. The fact that the shooter was Muslim and also had told both 9-1-1 operators and news media that he had an allegiance to ISIS further fueled the speculation. Investigation into his past also revealed that in 2013, the shooter had been interviewed by the FBI after making statements to coworkers about being affiliated with al Qaeda. The investigation later was closed after the shooter was deemed not to be a threat. For many, the shooting at Pulse was a terror attack, making it the deadliest such incident on U.S. soil since 9/11.

Another set of rumors also fueled different speculations—that the shootings actually were retaliation against the LGBTQ community. Former acquaintances of the shooter claimed that he was a closeted homosexual who was exacting revenge after his advances toward other men were not reciprocated. This claim later was found to be without merit by the FBI during their investigation. Other people who knew him claimed that he was homophobic, suggesting that the shooting was instead a hate crime to eliminate people he did not view as worthy. Not only was Pulse a club for the LGBTQ community, but many of his victims were homosexual males.

Interestingly, the possibility of the attack being both often fails to be considered. It is possible, as former attorney general Loretta Lynch posed, that the shooter had multiple motivations.

Orlando United and the Future of Pulse

Residents of Orlando, also known as the City Beautiful, rallied around those affected by the shooting. People lined up in record numbers to donate blood, an effort that cast a light on an outdated policy preventing homosexual men from donating. A victims' assistance center opened up three days after the shooting and provided help to nearly 1,000 people over eight days. The hospitals that treated the patients from the shooting announced that they would not be billing anyone for medical services, and the City of Orlando offered free plots and funeral services for the deceased victims at a city-owned cemetery.

Monetary donations also poured in from across the globe. Equality Florida, the state's largest LGBT rights group, raised over $750,000 in the first nine hours of their campaign and nearly $8 million overall through a GoFundMe campaign. The City of Orlando also established a fundraising campaign, OneOrlando, which raised $23 million in the first month after the shooting. The phrase "Orlando United" rallied the community and helped raise money and awareness for the victims and their families.

The future of the Pulse nightclub became a subject of considerable debate in the wake of the attack. Some felt that it was a place of unimaginable tragedy that should be destroyed; others felt it provided a reminder of the lives lost in the attack. The City of Orlando announced plans to purchase the site for a memorial, but the club's owner declined to sell. Instead, she created the onePULSE Foundation and announced plans to turn the club into a memorial site and museum. The site is expected to open in 2020.

September 23, 2016: Cascade Mall, Burlington, WA

Arcan Cetin entered the Cascade Mall in the evening, first walking through Chuck E. Cheese and Macy's before leaving the building and moving his car closer to the department store. The 20-year-old removed a rifle from his trunk, which he had stolen from his stepfather, and made his way back into the store when he opened fire. He first shot a customer near some clothing racks and then made his way to the cosmetics counter, where he shot the other four victims. The shooter then set his weapon on the counter and left the building. Four of the victims died at the scene, and the last victim later died at the hospital. The shooter was found the next day, walking near his home, and was arrested. He was charged with five counts of first-degree murder and underwent several competency evaluations. On April 16, just a few weeks away from his next court date, he was found dead in his jail cell, having committed suicide.

September 25, 2016: Randall's Supermarket Strip Center, Houston, TX

Having struggled with his law practice in the months leading up to the event, 46-year-old Nathan DeSai parked his car at an intersection outside of Randall's Supermarket Strip Center. Armed with a pistol and a submachine gun, he opened fire at cars driving by and people who were in the area. Six people were shot and wounded; three additional people sustained injuries from broken glass. When police arrived on the scene, they and the shooter engaged in a chase, exchanging gunfire with one another. Amidst the struggle, the gunman was shot and killed.

September 28, 2016: Townville Elementary School, Townville, SC

After shooting and killing his father, 14-year-old Jesse Osborne drove into the fence of Townville Elementary School, exited the vehicle, and started firing into the air near the school's playground. The shooter then proceeded to jump the fence and continue firing at students. One teacher and two students were wounded; another student died several days after the shooting due to massive blood loss. The shooter was apprehended by a local firefighter, who wrestled him to the ground and held him until law enforcement arrived on scene. Further investigation revealed that prior to the rampage, the shooter had killed his father. He was charged in family court with two counts of murder and two counts of attempted murder. His trial is still pending at the time of this writing.

October 25, 2016: FreightCar America Plant, Roanoke, VA

After being fired from FreightCar America for not showing up to work, 53-year-old Getachew Fekede returned to the plant of his former employer. Armed with a pistol, he entered through the paint shop and began shooting at employees. He fired ten rounds from the gun, shooting and killing one worker and wounding three others. He then committed suicide as police arrived on scene, just two minutes after the first 9-1-1 call was received.

Mass Shootings Q&A:
The Experts Weigh In

Guns Affect Society Positively and the Data Proves It

Beverly Merrill Kelley

The right to bear arms should not be infringed in this country. On the whole, gun rights help more than hinder society.

This opinion seems to fly in the face of a scenario with which we have become familiar. It's become something of a crime story cliché. The wife nudges her snoozing husband and whispers that she hears a strange noise. The hubby opens the drawer of the nightstand, removes a revolver, snaps off the safety, and gingerly picks his way down the stairs. The intruder, whose identity is obscured by shadows, is stunned as he watches his father coldly aim and shoot. "I just wanted to surprise you" is the last thing he ever says.

ARGUMENTS BASED ON FLAWED EVIDENCE

Gun control advocates, who love heart-wrenching variations on the unintended victim theme, have claimed for decades that a homeowner's gun is 43 times more likely to kill a family member, friend, or acquaintance, than a prowler. The statistic, extrapolated from a study by Arthur Kellermann and Don Reay published in the *New England Journal of Medicine* 20 years ago, has wormed its way into medical journals, government publications, health newsletters, general interest magazines, op-ed pieces, and letters to the editor.

But Kellermann's and Reay's methodology was flawed. First, they calculated the number of intruders shot only in terms of those killed during the crime. They ignored the number of times that firearms stopped a crime without an assailant's death: those instances in which an intruder was wounded or scared off. In fact, they vastly underrepresented the effectiveness of guns in preventing crime.

Second, not only were over half of the deaths in the study suicides but the authors presupposed that without the presence of a gun, none of these desperate individuals would have died. Third, gun ownership as a risk for violent death in the home is meaningless unless violent deaths in the home not involving a firearm are considered as well. When the latter is factored in the calculations, it becomes clear that guns are not necessarily more dangerous to have around than knives, heavy objects, or a pair of strong hands.

EFFECTIVE PROTECTION

Reportedly, guns are used 2.5 million times a year for self-protection in this country—how effective are they?

A 1993 analysis, published in the *Journal of Quantitative Criminology* by Gary Kleck and Miriam Delone, found that robbery victims who used guns defensively are significantly less likely to either be injured or forced to surrender property than victims who employed another form of self-protection or did nothing. And every year, according to *Point Blank: Guns and Violence in America*, armed citizens kill at least twice as many criminals as police. Sadly, most of these shootings occur while the victim is either waiting for the police to arrive or for a 911 dispatcher to answer the phone.

James D. Wright and Peter Rossi, who surveyed 2,000 felons incarcerated in state prisons across the United States, report that 34 percent have been scared off, shot at, wounded, or captured by an armed victim; 34 percent stated that when thinking about committing a crime, they were often or regularly troubled that the victim might shoot them, and 57 percent agreed with the statement, "Most criminals are more worried about meeting an armed victim than they are about running into the police."

A similar study of Pennsylvania burglary inmates by George F. Rengert and John Wasilchick corroborates this finding. The convicts admitted that daytime break-ins are safer. At night, they feared "getting shot." Finally, according to international census figures, the rate of occupied dwelling burglaries in Britain and the Netherlands, where gun ownership is low, is approaching 45 percent. In the United States, where gun ownership is high, the figure is less than 13 percent.

Returning to our opening scene, we must ask: just how often does a gun owner, while defending the home, accidentally shoot a family member? According to *Targeting Guns: Firearms and Their Control*, fewer than 2 percent of fatal gun accidents, or about 20, occur during defensive gun use—certainly not the impression left by primetime television.

Nineteenth-century British prime minister Benjamin Disraeli once remarked, "There are lies, damned lies, and statistics." Not all Americans may feel comfortable with a gun in the house, yet facts, not figures skewed by a political agenda, should inform any decision that asks Americans to forfeit a right guaranteed by the Constitution.

Gun Ownership Should Be Protected; Gun Stockpiling Should Not

Gregg Lee Carter

Should the right to bear arms be restricted? Without doubt, the answer is yes—especially in an economically developed nation like the United States. This nation has a strong legal system, a long tradition of political stability, and extensive public safety organizations (from local, county, and state police to the FBI, Secret Service, Customs Service, and Drug Enforcement Administration). This degree of public protection greatly decreases the number and type of guns that the typical American could possibly need. So putting unlimited firepower in the hands of American citizens is both dangerous and needless.

PUBLIC OPINION ON GUN CONTROL

U.S. public opinion strongly favors strict gun control. In fact, Gallup, Pew Foundation, and other surveys indicate that most U.S. adults concur with the following gun control efforts. Importantly, gun owners and non–gun owners are generally in agreement with these efforts, though gun owners less strongly so:

1. a ban on high-capacity ammunition holders—with a 10-round magazine limit (60 percent of U.S. adults are in support)
2. a ban on military-style assault weapons (63 percent)
3. a ban on handguns for those less than 21 years old (66 percent)
4. creation of a federal database to track gun sales (tantamount to a national system of gun registration; 69 percent)
5. requiring guns in the home be locked up to prevent access by children and the mentally incompetent (69 percent)
6. mandatory licensing of gun buyers by local police (72 percent)

7. preventing the mentally ill from purchasing guns (77 percent)
8. requiring "universal" background checks on the purchasers of guns—whether the purchase is made from a licensed firearms dealers or a private individual; whether the purchase is made in person or online (84 percent).

THE NEED FOR SELF DEFENSE

But should the average world citizen have the right to bear arms? Without doubt, the answer is also yes. The unarmed Darfur villager in Sudan is almost helpless in trying to defend his or her family and person from the savage, armed attacks of Janjaweed militia. Similarly, in the early 1990s unarmed Bosnia Muslims fell easy prey to the viciousness of Serbian militiamen. And in contemporary Iraq and Syria, unarmed minority-religion citizens have been easily overwhelmed by the international terrorist organization variously labeled as ISIS, ISIL, or the Islamic State.

What is more, we have in American history an example of what can happen if guns are not available to people that need them. The so-called Black Codes in the post–Civil War South routinely barred African Americans from owning any kind of weapon. The codes also stripped many American blacks of legal protection. The law did not protect them, and they were unable to protect themselves. This left them defenseless in the face of a rising tide of violence from whites. Years of lynching and widespread terror were the result.

Our legal traditions recognize the need for self-defense. The right to protect oneself and one's family, with firearms if necessary, is fundamental and unquestioned within the tradition of Anglo-American law. The famous English jurist William Blackstone—whose language and thoughts were adopted by the writers of the U.S. Constitution—argued that the people have primary rights, an important one of which is "the free enjoyment of personal security, of personal liberty, and of private property." Blackstone further argued that this primary right implies an auxiliary right—"the right of having and using arms for self-preservation and defense."

THE NEED FOR LIMITS

However, this right does not imply that completely unregulated stockpiling of weapons is allowed. Some Americans are confused about the meaning of the Second Amendment to the U.S. Constitution. They believe that it guarantees an unfettered right for the average citizen to "keep and bear arms." But the amendment in its entirety reads: "A well regulated Militia, being necessary to the security of a free State, the right of the people to keep and bear Arms, shall not be infringed."

Until 2008, almost all federal court decisions involving the Second Amendment interpreted it as protecting the right of selected citizens to keep and bear arms—more specifically, those citizens who were able-bodied adults capable of serving in a state militia. However, in its landmark decisions in *District of Columbia v. Heller* (2008) and *McDonald v. Chicago* (2010), the U.S. Supreme Court ruled that the amendment protects the right of all ordinary adult citizens to possess a firearm unconnected with service in a militia and, further, to use that firearm for tradition-ally lawful purposes (including self-defense within the home). Importantly, in these same landmark decisions, the Court also affirmed that gun ownership is a limited right—both state and federal governments can "infringe" upon the posses-sion ("keeping") and carrying ("bearing") of arms throughout the entire popula-tion. Among other regulations, these governments can:

1. outlaw certain firearms (as done with machine guns)
2. deny certain individuals the right to possess firearms (as with felons and minors)
3. require that shooters be licensed and pass a firearms safety examination
4. require that the purchasers of certain classes of guns obtain special permits
5. mandate a background check to ensure a potential gun buyer or possessor meets all federal dictates (e.g., not being a felon; not having been involuntarily confined to a mental institution; not being under a domestic violence restrain-ing order)

In short, in the interests of responsibility and public safety, our legislative bod-ies have set limits on the right to bear arms—and our courts have upheld these limits. This is as it should be. How far these limits should be taken is at the heart of the highly contentious debate over gun control in the contemporary United States.

Those wanting to extend these limits believe that the increasing number of mass shootings in schools, malls, nightclubs, and other public venues can be curbed with more gun laws. For example, many of these—including the horrific mass shoot-ings in Aurora, Colorado (12 killed at the midnight opening of the Batman movie *Dark Knight Rises*; June 20, 2012), Newtown, Connecticut (26 killed, including 20 first-graders, at Sandy Hook Elementary School; December 14, 2012), and Orlando, Florida (49 killed at the Pulse nightclub; June 12, 2016)—have involved semiautomatic rifles equipped with high-capacity ammunition holders ("maga-zines" holding 30-plus rounds). Gun control proponents contend that at the very least the carnage in these kinds of mass shootings would be reduced if such weap-ons and ammunition holders were banned. Gun rights advocates, including the National Rifle Association, strongly disagree with this contention, and they also believe that such bans would be in violation of the Second Amendment. A small number of states have banned such weapons and magazines, and the federal court system has generally upheld the bans. However, no similar legislation has yet been passed at the national level, and most observers believe there will be no movement on such legislation until both houses of the U.S. Congress and the presidency are controlled by the Democrats.

Our Gun Laws Are Fine, the System That Implements Them Is Broken

William Vizzard

Americans have a right to laws that impose as little burden as possible upon them while serving the general public good. In the case of guns, the existence of 250 million guns in the United States makes any effort at prohibiting most people from possessing guns entirely impractical. Thus, any restriction on guns should focus on preventing their acquisition and use by those people who present the greatest threat to society.

Because more than 100 million Americans do own guns, the laws applying to them should be clear, consistent, and easy to understand and follow. This is a more difficult goal than it might seem. In addition to federal law, each state, city, and county can pass laws or ordinances applying to gun ownership, transportation, sales, or purchase. We should make every effort to follow the pattern of laws relating to automobiles, which provide uniform rules that are easy to follow.

THE NEED FOR UNIFORM LAWS

To effectively enforce gun laws, the laws must be simple, and they must allow those doing the enforcing to distinguish between law-abiding people and those intentionally violating the law. The law should also allow courts to distinguish between those who violate the law, but pose little risk to society, and those who pose serious risk. The problem for those making the law is to figure out how to accomplish these goals.

Too often, people try to reduce policy responses to simple formulas such as increased sentences. What matters more is the capacity to actually detect and prosecute the crimes. For example, cameras at red lights work better than increasing the fine for running the light. The solution may not lie with criminal justice, but with bureaucracy: a simple, universal system of gun licensing and registration. It would guarantee law-abiding people the right to acquire and possess guns and make people accountable for the guns they transfer to others. It would increase the chances for recovering stolen guns by keeping serial numbers.

A NATIONAL REGISTRY

Finally, a registry would create an environment in which "casual" gun sales that do not comply with the law would be recognized by the population in general as illegal. The law already prohibits dealers selling a gun to a convicted felon, but they usually get their guns from people they know.

These so-called "casual transactions" are very difficult to detect and control. Today, it is difficult to prosecute someone even when they sell to a convicted felon, because they claim ignorance of the person's felony status. Thus, the point is to create standard procedures that will separate the responsible and law-abiding from the irresponsible and the scofflaws.

This system would generate a pattern of regulated transfers, which would make excuses harder. It would become easier to preclude defenses based on ignorance ("it is my girlfriend's gun," "I didn't know it was a stolen gun," etc.), trace the history of the gun, and hold those who transfer to criminals accountable. Transferors who faced potential charges for an illegal transfer would become more cooperative witnesses. Registration would make the excuse that the gun was lost or stolen less viable, because theft and loss must be reported. It would increase the reporting of such thefts.

It would also be useful to increase sentences for serious repeat offenders with guns, though this has been done at the federal level and in several states.

No gun law will eliminate all crime with guns. But consistent, well-defined laws would provide a clear message to gun owners about what was legal and illegal with laws that both require responsible action by gun sellers and owners and provide them with uniform laws that they can easily comply with.

Guns Are Not the Problem

Harry L. Wilson

No single factor can explain school shootings, but we should be looking at the underlying causes of violent behavior rather than the instrument people use. The variety of possible causes of school shootings include socioeconomic conditions in the United States, culture, exposure to violence through entertainment, media coverage of such events, and history. The gun is the tool used to kill, but it is the human squeezing the trigger who is responsible for the killing.

Perhaps a better question, with no obvious answer, is "Why are Americans more violent, in general, than citizens of many developed countries?" Even with our comparatively ready access to firearms, the homicide rate in the United States not associated with guns is much higher than that of other nations. In simple terms, Americans are more likely to kill one another than are residents of most other developed nations.

RATES OF GUN OWNERSHIP WORLDWIDE

The idea of killing as many people as possible in a school is a more modern American phenomenon. Looking at the scores of school shootings throughout U.S. history, it is clear that mass school shootings did not begin until the 1966 University of Texas shooting, when a mentally ill man climbed a tower on that campus and killed 16 people and wounded 31 more before he was killed by police. The infamous Columbine High School shooting, in which two students killed 12 classmates and one teacher and wounded 31 others, was actually a failed attempt to bomb the school to kill hundreds in the cafeteria. More recently, 20 children were killed along with 6 teachers and administrators in the 2012 massacre at Sandy Hook Elementary School in Newtown, Connecticut.

Gun ownership rates do not appear, necessarily, to be tied to homicide rates. Private gun ownership rates in the United States are indeed much higher than rates in most other developed countries. School shootings are also more common in the United States than in those nations to which it is most often compared. However, political scientist Ryan McMaken argues that researchers should be comparing the United States to many other nations, not just a select few based primarily on economic considerations. For example, when he included nations such as Lithuania, Costa Rica, and Russia, all nations with relatively low gun ownership rates, McMaken discovered that their homicide rates were considerably higher than in the United States.

As noted by scholar Samarth Gupta, many nations have higher gun ownership than the United States but fewer or no school shootings. "Of the top ten countries with the most guns per capita, seven had no school shootings. Switzerland has 46 guns per 100 people, Finland 45, and Serbia 38, yet none of these countries had a school shooting in the period studied."

WHAT MOTIVATES SCHOOL SHOOTINGS?

We would like to find a simple, single cause for the monstrous act of killing school students because in finding the cause we could find a solution. It is simple and tempting to blame the gun. Assuming it is the gun that makes individuals violent, it would follow that getting rid of guns would make individuals less violent. But if one thinks about it based on the aforementioned information, many of the previously mentioned nations with many guns do not have school shootings. We also know that only a tiny percentage of gun owners and those who have access to firearms within the United States will ever engage in this criminality.

The honest answer to this question is that we don't know the answer. Some shooters are motivated by mental illness, although the vast majority of people with mental illness are not dangerous. Some are motivated by the desire to be famous. For example, both Seung-Hui Cho, the Virginia Tech shooter, and Adam Lanza, the Sandy Hook killer, were fascinated by Dylan Klebold and Eric Harris, the Columbine shooters. At the same time, both Cho and Lanza had histories of mental instability. Klebold and Harris were apparently angry and had bullied students prior to their rampage, which was a botched attempt to detonate bombs in the Columbine High School cafeteria in order to kill most of the student body, teachers, and administrators.

What we do know is that school shootings, as horrific as they may be, remain very rare events. We think they are common because they receive a great deal of attention from the news media. Yet, students are safer at school than they are away from school. That does not suggest that we should simply ignore these events or pretend they don't or can't happen. Rather, we should do what we can reasonably do to attend to student-centered problems, whether they be socioeconomic, emotional, or physical. With that said, we should not live in fear of events that are unlikely to occur.

Access to Guns Leads to Increased School Violence

Glenn H. Utter

Why are school shootings so prevalent in the United States, as compared to other countries? The answer is that many children and adolescents have unsupervised access to firearms. As a result, the rate of gun-related violence in U.S. schools, although not of epidemic proportions, is far higher than in other developed countries.

STUDIES ON GUN OWNERSHIP RATES AND SCHOOL VIOLENCE

Samarth Gupta, writing for the *Harvard Political Review*, presents data from research that Laura E. Agnich, assistant professor of criminal justice and criminology at Georgia State University, conducted on a cross-national comparison of school shootings resulting in at least one fatality. Gupta reports that from November 1991 to July 2013, there were 55 such incidents in the United States, but just three each in Canada and Germany; two each in Australia, France, and Finland; and one each in England, Denmark, and Austria.

Frank Ochberg, a clinical professor of psychiatry at Michigan State University, notes that the various causes for school shootings, such as revenge for bullying, interpersonal arguments, violent role models, serious mental illness, and a culture that often encourages extremism, apply to other nations as well, and therefore do not help to explain the higher rate of such incidents in the United States. The key distinction between the United States and other countries is the far greater number of firearms—estimated to be more than 300 million—in the general population and therefore the vast number of privately owned guns that can find their way into the hands of young people.

An ongoing study conducted by the Centers for Disease Control and Prevention concludes that "Firearms used in school-associated homicides and suicides came primarily from the perpetrator's home or from friends or relatives." The presence of firearms in the home, often easily accessible to minors, results in students taking firearms to school. A 2016 study from the National Center for Education Statistics reports that from 2009 to 2014, there were 7,824 incidents involving students bringing guns to a public school. David Hemenway, professor of health policy and director of the Harvard University Injury Control Research Center, notes that more than 6,000 students were expelled in the 1996–1997 school year because they brought guns to school.

GUN-FREE SCHOOLS AND CAP LAWS

Due to the troubling number of cases in which students have taken a firearm to school, a problem that other developed nations usually do not face, states and school districts ban firearms from school property. The Law Center to Prevent Gun Violence reports that 48 states prohibit anyone from possessing a firearm on K–12 school property, on school-authorized transportation, or at specified school-sponsored events. However, such measures ultimately fail to address the root problem, which is that children and adolescents often gain access to firearms at home, with devastating results.

Everytown for Gun Safety, an organization that monitors school shootings, has provided a list of more than 170 such incidents from January 2013 to February 2016 at all education levels. The list includes cases in which shooters killed or wounded themselves or others, as well as circumstances in which a gun was fired but no one was injured. Although the list contains examples in which shootings occurred after school hours and therefore may be overly broad, it provides a clear picture of the danger of guns in or near schools.

In addition to prohibiting guns in schools, several states have instituted child access prevention (CAP) laws that require gun owners to keep firearms unloaded and stored securely and that establish criminal liability for adults who allow minors to have unsupervised access to guns. However, such laws have not had a significant effect on the occurrence of school shootings. Just 27 states have enacted CAP laws, and Daniel W. Webster, director of the Johns Hopkins Center for Gun Policy and Research, and colleagues (2014) report that no additional states have enacted such laws since 1998. Even in states with CAP laws, effectiveness depends on the willingness of gun owners to take steps in their private homes to comply with the law. After a child or adolescent has accessed a firearm with tragic consequences, authorities face the difficult decision of whether to enforce the CAP law, often against grieving parents.

SOLUTIONS FOR CURBING SCHOOL SHOOTINGS

Keeping firearms away from young people requires more than gun-free school statutes, CAP laws, and the good judgment of gun-owning adults who have children in the home; even the most conscientious parent can suffer from "brain fade"—leaving a loaded firearm unattended and accessible to a minor. Many have promoted a promising technological solution: mandating the sale of personalized, so-called "smart" guns that can only be fired by authorized users. Although the gun industry and gun rights organizations have resisted the idea, smart-gun technology could provide a fail-safe mechanism to prevent children and adolescents from gaining unsupervised access to firearms. Several promising scientific applications have been developed—such as fingerprint recognition and radio frequency identification that involves a wristwatch programmed with a personal identification number—that make the firearm useless to an unauthorized person.

The extensive presence of guns in the United States has resulted in more school-related injuries and deaths than in other developed countries. Countering accidental and intentional shootings in schools requires preventing young people from obtaining unsupervised access to firearms. Many states have instituted CAP laws that hold parents, relatives, and other adults responsible for the secure storage of firearms, and government officials and school administrators often conclude that locked school doors and armed guards are necessary to prevent the sound of gunshots and the voices of children screaming. But these policies have not eliminated the occurrence of tragic incidents. Requiring the sale of technologically advanced firearms that allow only the legitimate owner to fire the weapon can help to resolve this stubborn problem.

Preventing Mass Shootings: Using Theory to Drive Evidence-Based Practice

Jaclyn Schildkraut and H. Jaymi Elsass

Despite their statistically rare occurrence, mass shootings have the ability to generate a considerable amount of concern, both in the general public and among the policymakers assigned to protect the people. In the days, weeks, and months after one of these events, a national discourse typically arises that focuses on the need to prevent future tragedies and the best ways in which to do so. A number of possible solutions are offered, including various proponents campaigning for either increased gun control or gun rights; better treatment for and reporting of mental illness; and restricting or outlawing violent media, including video games. While the risk of mass shootings can never be fully mitigated, that is, reduced to a zero percent chance, there are ways in which the occurrence of such events, and their subsequent lethality in the case of their occurrence, can be minimized. In order to be effective, however, such solutions must be grounded in academic research rather than based upon emotion or politics. More specifically, the use of criminological theory can help to base these strategies on research. Such theory offers testable propositions to determine if a particular proposed solution is, in fact, effective.

Lawrence Cohen and Marcus Felson's routine activities theory (1979) provides a way in which to base proposed preventive measures on academic research. The theory suggests that the opportunity for crime to occur increases when there is a convergence of a motivated offender and a suitable target in the absence of capable guardianship. Capable guardians are individuals or objects and devices that are designed to prevent the crime from taking place. Examples of capable guardians include, but are by no means limited to, police officers or security guards, alarm systems, dogs, and security cameras. A capable guardian performs two important functions—(1) to provide protection and oversight for the target and (2) to act as a control or deterrent for the offender—which can disrupt the opportunity for the crime to take place. It is important to note, however, that this theory does not consider the actual motivation of the offender. Rather, the theory assumes that all offenders are equally driven. As such, policies attempting to decrease the motivation of a particular individual are ill-suited to address possible preventive strategies for mass shootings. Instead, researchers and policymakers should focus on increasing capable guardianship while, at the same time, decreasing the suitability of targets in their proposed solutions to prevent future mass shootings.

INCREASED GUARDIANSHIP

Routine activities theory suggests that one strategy to reduce the likelihood of criminal victimization, including acts of mass shootings, is to increase capable guardianship. Routine activities theory outlines three necessary components for crime to occur: a suitable target, a motivated offender, and the lack of a capable guardian. It follows then, that crime does not occur in the presence of a capable guardian; therefore, by increasing capable guardianship, one can decrease the likelihood of victimization. Capable guardians have great utility in that they provide protection and oversight for potential targets and, when they engage a motivated offender, become possible captors. A number of strategies for increasing guardianship in public spaces have been introduced over the years, each with varying degrees of effectiveness.

Following mass shooting events, such as Columbine, Aurora, and Sandy Hook, those in favor of gun control often call for stricter regulations, such as the banning of assault weapons and large-capacity magazines. Gun rights advocates, on the other hand, often suggest that lesser restrictions should be imposed so that people are better able to protect themselves and others. Gun rights supporters really are advocating for increasing guardianship through reduced gun-carrying regulations—for example, pushing for more lenient restrictions on where firearms can be legally carried. The argument forwarded by proponents is that by allowing law-abiding citizens to carry firearms in a wider variety of environments, the likelihood of an armed citizen being present who can engage the shooter in a firefight and use deadly force to protect potential victims is raised. Frequently, in the wake of a mass shooting event, gun rights advocates assert that when a perpetrator is confronted by an individual with a firearm, the attacker is often killed by the guardian or takes his or her own life. Therefore, according to proponents, the occurrence of a mass shooting, or at least an event's lethality, can be reduced by increasing the likelihood that a law-abiding citizen carrying a firearm is present when an attack takes place.

The question becomes, however, whether the increased guardianship advocated for by gun rights proponents is indeed "capable." According to those favoring gun control, this is not the case. Those in favor of gun control often call for stricter firearms regulations, including the banning of assault weapons and large-capacity magazines, and further restricting locations where firearms can legally be carried. These restrictions are applicable from Columbine to Aurora to Sandy Hook. Gun control advocates argue that more guns does not necessarily equal the presence of more "capable" guardians, insinuating that lax regulations will increase the likelihood of a mass shooting occurring or increasing an event's lethality. While this is indeed a possibility, it is unknown at the current time which side of the debate is more realistic as, over time, events have occurred that seem to support the arguments of both sides. What is made clear, however, is the need for more scientific research to determine whether the proposed guardianship advocated by gun rights enthusiasts is, in fact, "capable." Only if it is proficient does it have the ability to disrupt the convergence of the three necessary components of routine activities theory, thereby reducing the likelihood of criminal victimization.

In an effort to find a compromise between the two sides of the firearms debate (those pushing for increased gun control and those advocating for increased gun rights), it periodically has been proposed that the number of armed peace officers in public places should be increased. Proponents assert that doing so will increase the likelihood of the presence of a capable guardian in the event of a mass shooting attempt. It has become clear, however, that unless armed officers receive specialized training on the proper procedures to take in the case of an active shooting event, they are not necessarily "capable" guardians. In a shooting that occurred outside of the Empire State Building in 2012, a gunman killed a former coworker. Two nearby NYPD officers opened fire on the gunman, killing him, but in the process of firing 16 rounds, they injured nine bystanders as well. This event brings to the forefront the difficulties in determining whether guardianship is indeed "capable." Recognizing the need for better training for law enforcement (and the general public) in the event of a mass shooting has resulted in the creation of active shooter training initiatives including the Advanced Law Enforcement Rapid Response Training (ALERRT) active shooter response program.

As mentioned, not all guardianship is necessarily capable, and it is proficient guardianship that is required to disrupt the convergence of necessary components to reduce criminal victimization. One attempt at increasing guardianship that has possibly been less effective in reducing the occurrence of mass shootings is the installation of security cameras throughout American society. Closed-circuit security systems allowing for the monitoring of both public and private spaces are commonplace today. The vast majority of businesses—from shopping malls, movie theaters, and a wide variety of workplaces to an increasing number of public and private schools—have been equipped with cameras in the hope of deterring crime, including mass shootings, by providing a watchful eye. It is unclear, however, to what extent such measures have reduced the occurrence of mass shooting events or the lethality of such incidents.

Indeed, a number of attacks have taken place in full view of security cameras that the perpetrators knew were in place. A civilian contractor at a facility where he had been employed opened fire at the Navy Yard in Washington, D.C., in 2013, killing 12 people and wounding 3 others. He likely knew that his attack would be caught on security cameras as they were in plain view. The two perpetrators of the 1999 Columbine High School shooting were fully aware that their school was equipped with two security cameras (one of which famously captured their movements in the cafeteria), and yet, they killed 13 people and wounded 20 others before committing suicide. Furthermore, a number of shooters have used video equipment to record messages to the general public before committing their attacks. For example, the perpetrators of the shootings at Columbine, Virginia Tech in 2007, and Santa Barbara in 2014 all used video equipment to communicate with the media and the general public, which suggests that they would not find the use of security cameras in their target locations as an adequate deterrent or capable guardianship. In order to be effective, guardianship must be capable, and for proficiency to be adequately assessed, continued scientific research focusing on the impact of different interventions must be conducted. Policy, both public and private, should be drafted in response to new research findings, rather than statutes and procedures being created out of fear and increased emotionality.

DECREASED SUITABILITY OF TARGETS

Another way to work toward the prevention of mass shootings is to decrease the suitability of potential targets which will make individuals less attractive to the offender. One way this can be accomplished is to decrease such suitability by ensuring that all doors are equipped with locks that can quickly be deployed in the event of a shooting. Research has shown that in incidents of mass shootings, no individual has ever been killed behind a locked door. In most instances, shooters are looking for easy targets that they can dispose of quickly; putting a barrier in place deters them, and they move on to others rather than spending time trying to breach a particular entrance. During the Columbine shooting, for example, the majority of individuals who sheltered in place within the school did so behind locked doors. Most of the individuals killed that day were in the library, which did not have locks that could be secured quickly. Similarly, at Sandy Hook Elementary School in Connecticut, the door locks that were in place had to be locked from outside the room, which left teachers with a choice: shelter students in the room without a locked door, or go into the hallway to secure the door and come face to face with the shooter.

It has been suggested that this issue could be addressed by installing lockdown mechanisms where, with the push of a button, all interior and exterior doors would be immediately secured. While this would improve the timing it takes to secure a building, these systems often require an override code that is typically only known by a handful of individuals at a given location, and technology malfunctions—particularly in consideration of fire safety—are of concern. One way to alleviate such apprehensions while providing a timely solution for securing rooms not fitted with quick-securing locks is a device called the Sleeve. Invented by an Iowa elementary school teacher, the Sleeve is a slide-on cover that fits over doors' arm joints, allowing rooms to be secured from the inside, within seconds, without a key or any prior installation of materials. The device is made of carbon steel and designed to withstand over 550 pounds per foot of force, making it particularly effective in attempted door breaches.

Another equally effective way to decrease the suitability of a target is through ongoing education and training, a strategy that has received a considerable amount of support from both the grassroots movement and the academic community. Individuals need to be educated about potential risks for mass shooting events, but also about ways in which to respond. Similar to evacuation routes in the event of a fire, all locations should have an active shooter response plan in place. Such plans should include information about the nearest exit (in the event an individual can flee during an attack), measures to take if they are required to shelter, a chain of command for notification in the event of an incident, and protocols for notifying others in the location of such an event. "Safe and Sound: A Sandy Hook Initiative," a grassroots organization formed in the wake of the 2012 shooting, provides a series of tool kits aimed at making schools safer, though their strategies can be applied more generally to other locations that have experienced or could be vulnerable to mass shootings, including malls, movie theaters, places of worship, and workplaces.

Education and training should be a collaborative effort between members of the community (both immediate, as in the case of schools or workplaces, or more broadly, such as the city or town), law enforcement, and other related service providers. By working together, these individuals can approach the potential issue from a proactive and multidisciplinary angle, allowing for a more robust solution to develop. Potential threats must be identified and emergency response plans designed accordingly to meet the individual needs of a particular location. Schools, for instance, provide different environmental design challenges than malls or workplaces. Once these plans are developed, individuals must be educated about the protocols through information sharing, training, and practice sessions. Drills for different types of emergencies, including (but not limited to) mass shootings, should be conducted routinely to ensure that all individuals, particularly those key players who are charged with overseeing the development and implementation of emergency planning, are up to date on the most current protocols. Still, even with plans in place, ongoing assessment of these strategies is crucial as it identifies weaknesses in the response implementation and ways in which preparedness can be improved.

It is important to note that not all suggested ways of minimizing target suitability are effective or practical. Following Sandy Hook, for example, a number of different prototypes of safety devices, including the aforementioned Sleeve, were introduced as ways of preventing the next mass shooting. Other such innovations included the Bodyguard Blanket, a bulletproof shield made from a material similar to Kevlar, and bulletproof whiteboards, both of which are designed to protect students from bullets and falling debris (in the event of a tornado or similar natural disaster). There are, however, obstacles that make both products less than effective solutions for mass shootings. Cost is a significant factor, as each Bodyguard Blanket is sold for $1,000, meaning that it would cost $50 billion to have one on hand for every student (excluding faculty and staff) in primary and secondary schools. The armored whiteboards, depending on their size, can range from $129 for a $10'' \times 13''$ clipboard to $999 for full-size boards designed to stop AR-15 bullets. By comparison, the Sleeve costs $65 per unit, and there are fewer doors than individuals in most locations.

The Bodyguard Blanket is worn like a backpack, which means that it takes time to put it on—time that individuals rarely have during an attack. Furthermore, the blanket is designed to be worn by people as they are curled up into a ball; while it shields their back from debris or bullets encroaching from the top, it leaves the individuals' sides fully exposed. The armored whiteboards also present concerns over exposure. Even more problematic, however, is that the Bodyguard Blanket and the whiteboards, to an extent, are meant to be used in a stationary position. Researchers, such as those from ALERRT, the national standard for active shooting training, suggest that staying in such a position or hiding should be the last possible response; instead, they advocate for a flight (evacuation to safety) or fight (engaging the shooter) strategy. Therefore, while there may be some benefits to these products, they should be used only as a last resort rather than as a first option.

CONCLUSION

It is impossible to completely prevent mass shootings because, due to the unpredictability of human nature, the risk never can be completely eliminated. Yet, it is possible to institute techniques that either reduce the opportunity for these events to occur or minimize their subsequent lethality if they do take place. Proposed tactics must be firmly grounded in academic research rather than based upon emotion or politics. Criminological theory, specifically routine activities theory, aids in such an undertaking as it offers testable propositions to determine if a particular proposed solution is, in fact, effective.

Routine activities theory, holding offender motivation constant, contends that criminal victimization will occur when a suitable target and a motivated offender converge in the absence of a capable guardian. This theory lends itself to real-world application as it implies that the likelihood of criminal victimization can be reduced if the suitability of targets is lessened or capable guardianship is increased. This allows for the design and implementation of specific techniques to reach these ends. Moreover, through the use of scientific research, tactics can be systematically evaluated, therefore increasing knowledge and, as a result, reducing victimization.

With respect to increasing guardianship, it must be recognized that not all watchful eyes are necessarily "capable," and it is the proficiency of the guardian, rather than their existence, that impacts the likelihood of victimization. Therefore, strategies to increase guardianship, such as the installation of security systems, increasing gun rights for law-abiding citizens, increasing the presence of peace officers (including unarmed school resource officers), and educating individuals (especially law enforcement) on how to properly respond in an active shooter situation, must be systematically studied and assessed for their proficiency. Findings from this research must be used to influence future policy. In regard to reducing the suitability of targets, scientific research, along with education and evaluation, are equally essential. It is only with continued, intense study that the lethality of mass shooting events or even their occurrence may be more generally reduced.

REFERENCE

Cohen, L. E., & Felson, M. (1979). Social change and crime rate trends: A routine activity approach. *American Sociological Review, 44*(4), 588–608.

A Problem Entailing Many Policy Ideas—But Few Likely to Have Complete Success

James A. Beckman

School shootings are a transcendent problem in society that unfortunately spans decades—and indeed centuries—in the United States. School shootings transcend time, place, motivation, and policy measures intended to prevent such events. While many policy ideas have been put forth in recent years, few are likely to have complete success. Clearly, each time a school shooting occurs in the United States, numerous understandable emotions flow through the populace, emotions ranging from anger and sadness to outrage and demand for an immediate governmental and social response. With each new horrific incident, demands for government action are often splashed across the nation's newspapers (Jennings, 2012). The morally indignant lament the shooting incident to be yet another example of behavior wrought by a morally defunct society. Many simply throw up their hands and lament through a bewildered voice or pen, words to the effect of "why? why?" (Candiotti & Aarthun, 2012).

Children are one of the country's most precious resources, and the most innocent of those among us. As such, the death of even one child is horrific and heart wrenching. Further, the schoolyard and classroom has in many ways become one the last bastions of "freedom" and "safety" in the United States, where one can, or should, be able to pursue knowledge without concern for threats to one's personal safety. Phrased another way, schools and classrooms at any level should be the last places to be encumbered with high-security apparatus, chain-linked fences, armed guards and guns, and a "police state"–like presence. Thus, school shootings target the most innocent and vulnerable in society and strike at a place where these individuals should be entitled to feel the most secure.

However, and as difficult as this is to admit and write, no simple legislative measure can or ever will eliminate these horrific situations from arising in the future. Beyond simple measures that have long been employed and implemented with common sense—and as delineated later in this essay—no single "silver bullet" catch-all solutions will eradicate this particular plague. While a plethora of policy measures have been proposed in the last several decades, few if any of these ideas are likely to completely succeed. As one author has posited, "school systems' reaction to schoolyard shootings was visceral, emotional, and often poorly conceived" (Hawley, 2012, p. 735). That is, government cannot prophylactically legislate to guard against the actions of every lunatic, psychopathic, and deranged person in society. Perhaps author Dave Cullen (2009) summarized it best in his book entitled *Columbine,* wherein he said that one of the high school shooters was not some misunderstood victim of bullying from a socioeconomically backward childhood environment, but rather, and unfortunately quite simply, a criminal sociopath. Likewise, the other shooter was just a lackey and follower. The issue of how to stop school shootings is as problematic and timeless as how one stops crime and criminals generally.

TRANSCENDS TIME

School shootings are not a new phenomenon. School shootings have transcended decades, generations, and even centuries in the United States. Indeed, school shootings in the United States can be traced back to at least July 26, 1764, the date of the so-called Enoch Brown School Massacre, wherein the teacher, Enoch Brown, and at least nine children were shot, killed, and scalped by Native American warriors as part of the Pontiac War between settlers and the Native American Delaware (Lenape) tribe (Dixon, 2005; Middleton, 2007). This would only be the first of hundreds of school shootings that would occur in the United States between 1764 and 2013. Another early example can be found in radical abolitionist John Brown's famous raid of the federal arsenal at Harpers Ferry, Virginia—now West Virginia—in October 1859 in an effort to free slaves and usher in slave insurrection throughout the South—one of the sparks of the American Civil War. While no known schoolchildren were actually killed or hurt during the raid, one of the raiders seized a schoolhouse there, containing approximately 30 children ranging in age from 8 to 16, temporarily holding the children and teacher hostage. The students were eventually released and the schoolhouse used for a potential rendezvous point and depot for the storage of guns and ammunition during Brown's famous raid (Lubet, 2012). Scholars have estimated that these various school shootings over the centuries have resulted in over 400 students killed and over 500 injured (Lubet, 2012).

TRANSCENDS MOTIVATION

The motivations of school shooters transcend every rationale imaginable, ranging from personal disputes and arguments between students, to being upset with a grade or disciplinary action taken by the school, to disgruntled former students, to rejected romantic suitors, to those committing crime, such as burglary, or acting under general mental illness. Four brief examples—from literally hundreds of cases—illustrate this point.

One of the more infamous school shootings in the latter half of the 20th century occurred on August 1, 1966, when an ex–United States Marine and 25-year-old University of Texas student climbed the University of Texas Tower in the middle of the University of Texas at Austin campus and committed a murderous rampage by killing 17 students and bystanders, and wounding at least 32 other individuals. At least 3 people were killed inside of the Tower as the shooter climbed to the 28th-floor observation deck, and 11 others were killed by what only can be described as "sniper fire" as the victims innocently walked the grounds of the campus below.

Immediately prior to the mass murder rampage, the shooter had executed his wife and mother as well. A myriad of possible motivations were put forth for the shooter's motivations after the killing spree, including the possibility of a tumor in his brain, which may have adversely impacted his decision-making process and other inexplicable prior episodes of anger; prescription drug abuse of amphetamines, Dexedrine, and Valium; and anger and hostility over his discharge from the U.S. Marine Corps—and a recent court-martial (Douglas, Burgess, Burgess, & Ressler, 2013; "Jury Blames Tumor," 1966; Lavergne, 1997). The exact cause, and therefore possible information about how to prevent similar events based on this one, will never be fully known.

In 1996, in what is known as the Frontier Middle School shooting, in Moses Lake, Washington, a 14-year-old student killed his algebra teacher, 2 students, and held 16 students hostage in the algebra class until subdued by a gym teacher. In explaining his motivation for the shooting at one point, the 14-year-old student alleged being bullied by students and being inspired by Stephen King's first novel, *Rage*, published under the pen name Richard Bachman. During the trial of the real school shooter, he alleged that he "tried to model his life after the novel *Rage*'s protagonist Charlie Decker, who kills two teachers and takes his algebra class hostage" (Carroll, 2013). King's book was also cited as a motivating or influencing factor in at least three other school shootings, wherein the shooters shot or held hostage fellow students, and copies of King's book were found among the shooters' possessions, and in one incident, allegedly read and re-read multiple times by the shooter.

These other incidents occurred in San Gabriel, California in 1988, McKee, Kentucky in 1989, and West Paducah, Kentucky in 1997. The West Paducah incident involved a 14-year-old student shooter who had fantasies about killing his classmates. He entered his high school and shot at a group of students in a prayer circle, killing three and injuring five. After the shooting, it was believed that the shooter lashed out because he felt bullied by other students and was paranoid. Additionally, a search of the shooter's locker revealed a copy of King's book *Rage*. This last incident prompted Stephen King to withdraw the book from future publication, reportedly as the "right thing to do." King (1999) commented that "the incident was enough for me. I asked my publisher to take the damned thing out of print. They concurred."

A further illustrative example of the lack of a concrete identifiable motive—or perhaps the confluence of a multitude of differing motives—is seen in the case of the Columbine High School massacre on April 20, 1999, in Colorado. The two shooters—both high school seniors at the school, one aged 18 and one 17—went on a shooting rampage, killing and executing at close range a total of 12 of their fellow students and 1 teacher—along with injuring approximately 20 more students. After the shootings, a variety of motivations were put forth to explain the horrific event, most of which have since been proven to be untrue. Those various motivations included a panoply of maladies: being the alleged prior victims of bullying; being social outcasts and not part of certain popular cliques; being the victims of adverse effects of antidepressants on teenagers; being part of Gothic subculture; obsessive Internet usage; and even prolonged exposure to violent videos. These early theories were mostly unsubstantiated. In reality, the shooters were not bullied or abused as children or suffer from undiagnosed medical ailments; rather they were "cold blooded, predatory psychopaths" (Gumbel, 2009; Toppo, 2009). As authors David Kopel and Carol Oyster (2012) have written, both of the shooters were "narcissists and sadists" and "during their high school career together, they were bullies, vandals, arsonists, and thieves" (p. 183). Phrased another way, the shooters were motivated not by any of the above often commonly attributed maladies of a "school shooter," but were simple criminal miscreants, bent on the destruction and imposition of pain on others as a means of gratifying themselves and their grandiose view of themselves in the process.

TRANSCENDS PLACE

As shooter motivations have been elusive, so too is the location of these events over time. The argument that some parts of the country are more subject to school shootings than other areas is a fallacy. Indeed, school shootings have transcended geographical lines, making little distinction between "red states" and "blue states." In preparation for this article, this author conducted newspaper database searches of each of the 50 states using queries like "school shootings" for each of the 50 states. These searches were conducted in various research/newspaper databases—as well as general Internet searches. The result of this research was that the author could identify in a very short period of time school shooting incidents that have occurred in at least 48 of the 50 states. The only two states that did not appear to have a school shooting occurring on school grounds were Maine and Utah, though Utah has had two very close calls since 2012, including an 11-year-old sixth-grader brandishing a gun at his classmates and a separate chilling but thwarted incident involving a "Columbine-like" attack planned by two Utah high school students who intended to set off a bomb during a school assembly. Thus, this author's review of school shootings throughout the United States reveals that virtually every state in the country has had an episode occur within the state.

TRANSCENDS (OR IS RESISTANT TO) MODERN LEGISLATIVE AND GOVERNMENTAL EFFORTS

School shootings have transcended and thwarted efforts to curtail such eruptions of violence. Such efforts have included increased security and sign-in procedures at schools, more robust mental health screening and assistance, reduction of bullying in school, armed guards, armed teachers, metal detectors, banning assault weapons generally in society, and so on.

INCREASED MEDICAL SCREENING AND SERVICES WILL NOT PREVENT SHOOTINGS

After the horrific Sandy Hook Elementary School shooting on December 14, 2012, in which 20 children and 6 adults were killed in a murderous rampage by a 20-year-old autistic former student, some argued that more robust mental health screening and care could have avoided the situation. This position was taken in spite of strong medical evidence that suggests that autism and Asperger's syndrome do not cause individuals to engage in such violent behavior. That is, some argued that better treatment and screening for autism and Asperger's syndrome would better defuse the possible violence of future shooters, while not recognizing that the very violence at issue in the Sandy Hook shooting was not a manifestation of these particular mental/medical disorders. Further, in addition to not being an effective tool to screen would-be mass murderers, focusing on a policy of mental screening foregoes all of the other types of motivations attached to school shootings. While effective health screening has many positive ramifications to society and is a laudable society goal generally, it unfortunately would not entirely eliminate the scourge of school shootings and violence. It would not have prevented killings like those that took place in Newtown in 2012 or Columbine in 1999. Further, even screening for specific psychopathic behavior would not prevent all future school shootings. For instance, even a case where the shooter was identified, targeted, and treated for mental illness and abnormal psychopathic behavior before going on a rampage—like the shooter in the April 16, 2007, Virginia Tech massacre—such screening and counseling did not deter that person from killing 32 people and wounding another 17 (Wilson, 2012).

While shooters generally can be said to be more depressed, suicidal, and interested in violent themes, this classification does not narrow down the pool of potential shooters to a manageable number, as such classifications are already somewhat prevalent among hormonal pubescent teenagers. Further, it has been noted that these individuals are likely to strike out at a bevy of potential targets, from teachers, to athletes, to girls who rejected romantic overtures (Hawley, 2012). According to one recent article, which reported on research efforts by the U.S. Secret Service and U.S. Department of Education in identifying potential shooters, the agencies concluded in 2002 that school shooters "followed no set profile, but most were depressed and felt persecuted" (Gumbel, 2009; Toppo, 2009).

BULLY AWARENESS WILL NOT PREVENT SCHOOL SHOOTINGS

In the wake of recent shootings, many schools have instituted antibullying campaigns and increased resources in this area. While these are generally laudable and worthy policies aimed at protecting the more vulnerable children from abuse, scholars have found "there is no evidence that [these] effort[s] have been effective [in thwarting school shootings]. In fact, in schools where SROs [school resource officers] were employed prior to the shootings, they played no major role in ending the incidents" (Hawley, 2012, 733–734). Indeed, the perpetrators of the Columbine school shooting often bullied other students themselves (e.g., freshman, effeminate male students, etc.), and were not those subject to the bullying themselves.

INCREASED SECURITY MEASURES CAN BE EASILY THWARTED AND ARE NOT COST EFFECTIVE

The 2012 Newtown tragedy also illustrates the ineffectiveness of screening and visitor reception areas. The 20-year-old shooter was able to gain access to the building despite a recently upgraded security protocol, which required doors to be locked at 9:30 a.m. after all children arrived for school in the morning, and required that all visitors had to be signed in at a front desk after showing identification; also, the main entrance was subject to video monitoring (Barron, 2012). The shooter easily gained access about five minutes after the front door had already been "locked down" for the morning.

Likewise, the "armed guard at every school entrance" proposed by the National Rifle Association (NRA) is not an effective solution. First, such procedures are incredibly costly and lead to a false sense of security. That is, all a shooter needs to do is unexpectedly shoot the guard upon entrance, while the rest of the school remains vulnerable to an impending attack because of a false sense of security that they are protected by the friendly armed guard at the front door. Likewise, arming teachers is not a viable option, as law enforcement figures will attest that being a trained armed responder takes many hours of practice, and without such practice, armed teachers create as many risks as benefits (e.g., shooting inappropriately or at innocent bystanders by mistake, increased injury by misfires, and the obvious problem of a ready supply of firearms for a student to steal when the teacher is distracted or disabled).

BAN WEAPONS IN SOCIETY, BAN HIGH-CAPACITY AMMUNITION MAGAZINES AND SO-CALLED "ASSAULT WEAPONS"

Many of the shootings were done by individuals who obtained their weapons lawfully under existing laws, or by taking them from their parents—who also had the weapons lawfully. Beyond the Second Amendment problems of restricting lawful gun ownership in an overbroad approach to curtail a specific problem involving a statistically miniscule level of abuse by lawful gun owners or their children, this solution also fails to take into account the many other methods that have been explored and utilized to create death and destruction of students and teachers, ranging from explosives to knives, and in one case, using rat poison in the attempt to poison teachers and students by putting the rat poison in coffee, water coolers, and so on. Additionally, the proposed solution of limiting "high-capacity" magazines imposed by President Obama is faulty in that shooters can bring multiple clips or weapons, and can just switch weapons or substitute clips—it can take only seconds to exchange clips, according to weapon experts.

DECREASE ACCESS TO VIOLENT VIDEO GAMES AND BOOKS

Censor books and video games? While there is conflicting evidence about whether violent video games and books are correlated with subsequent violence, there are major First Amendment free speech and free press impediments to this suggestion. While King's response in removing *Rage* from publication is laudable, even he admits that he was not obligated to do so under the First Amendment and that each of the shooters had other problems that arguably led to the shootings, despite King's book (Carroll, 2013).

CONCLUSION: ARE SOLUTIONS POSSIBLE?

This essay is not encouraging the reader to abdicate responsibility, and in fact, is advocating quite the opposite. This essay attempts to explain that the knee-jerk, visceral reaction to try to prophylactically legislate following each incident, while understandable, is not effective in the long run, and few of these policy initiatives are likely to have complete success in substantially curtailing such horrible events. There is no single "silver bullet" in preventing future shootings. The single best solution is for the continued exercise of common sense by school officials, teachers, parents, and other impacted individuals. Through the exercise of common sense, the public can remain vigilant on a variety of fronts ranging from identifying students of concern, paying attention to warning signs—which the U.S. Secret Service identified as a particularly viable approach, as many shooters leave clues in paintings, diaries, journals, social media sites, and comments to classmates leading up to the shootings—offering mental health screening and benefits, and having reasonable security measures in place to restrict unapproved visitors to schools—simple and long practiced measures—which will not completely eliminate shootings, but might discourage a few. The use of lockable, bulletproof doors and whiteboards is something many schools are now investing resources in, and are worth the cost of implementation as another reasonable, commonsense action. While these are not complete solutions and do not have the likelihood of completely eradicating the plague of school shootings, such an approach is better than simply abdicating individual responsibility and waiting for the government to pass its next across-the-board prophylactic measure—measures envisioned to immediately make our schools 100 percent safe from violence, but which will only give the public a false sense of security and will not ultimately obtain the full results intended.

Finally, a voluntary effort should be made by the media and society not to sensationalize, publicize, and give attention to these shooters. The reader will note that this author has intentionally chosen not to use shooter names in this essay. Potential shooters should know and be aware that their actions will not result in infamous immortality in news accounts, but rather obscurity and ultimately, darkness in their inevitable death from perpetrating such despicable acts of violence against our country's most vulnerable.

REFERENCES

Barron, J. (2012, December 14). Nation reels after gunman massacres 20 children at school in Connecticut. *New York Times.* Retrieved from https://mobile.nytimes.com/2012/12/15 /nyregion/shooting-reported-at-connecticut-elementary-school.html?mcubz=1

Candiotti, S., & Aarthun, S. (2012, December 15). Police: 20 children among 26 victims of Connecticut school shooting. *CNN.* Retrieved from http://www.edition.cnn.com /2012/12/14/us/connecticut-school-shooting/index.html

Carroll, R. (2013, January 25). Stephen King risks wrath of NRA by releasing pro–gun control essay. *The Guardian.* Retrieved from https://www.theguardian.com/books /2013/jan/25/stephen-king-gun-control-essay-amazon-nra

Cullen, D. (2009). *Columbine.* New York: Hatchette Books.

Dixon, D. (2005). *Never come to peace again: Pontiac's uprising and the fate of the British empire in North America.* Norman: University of Oklahoma Press.

Douglas, J., Burgess, A. W., Burgess, A. G., & Ressler, R. K. (2013). *Crime classification manual: A standard system for investigating and classifying violent crime* (3rd ed.). New York: John Wiley & Sons.

Gumbel, A. (2009, April 16). The truth about Columbine. *The Guardian.* Retrieved from http://www.theguardian.com/world/2009/apr/17/columbine-massacre-gun-crime -us

Hawley, R. F. (2012). Schoolyard shootings. In G. L. Carter (Ed.), *Guns in American society: An encyclopedia of history, politics, culture, and the law* (732–735). Santa Barbara, CA: ABC-CLIO.

Jennings, N. (2012, December 14). Mark Kelly: Action on guns "can no longer wait." *Washington Post.* Retrieved from http://www.washingtonpost.com/blogs/post-politics /wp/2012/12/14/mark-kelly-action-on-guns-can-no-longer-wait

Jury blames tumor for killings. (1966, August 5). *The News and Courier* (9A). Retrieved from http://nl.newsbank.com/nl-search/we/Archives/?p_product=HA -PC&p_theme=histpaper&p_nbid=&p_action=doc&p_docid=159C1B037502C 33B&s_lastnonissuequeryname=2&d_viewref=search&p_queryname=2&p _docnum=1&p_docref=v2:13CCA871AD118D5A@HA-PC-159C1ED33858 765A@2439343-159C1B037502C33B@8-159C1B037502C33B@

King, S. (1999). *Stephen King's keynote address.* Presented at Vermont Library Conference, VEMA Annual Meeting. Retrieved from http://www.horrorking.com/inter view7.html

Kopel, D. B., & Oyster, C. (2012). Columbine High School tragedy (1999). In G. L. Carter (Ed.), *Guns in American society: An encyclopedia of history, politics, culture, and the law* (181–189). Santa Barbara, CA: ABC-CLIO.

Lavergne, G. (1997). *A sniper in the tower.* Denton, TX: University of North Texas Press.

Lubet, S. (2012). *John Brown's spy: The adventurous life and tragic confession of John E. Cook.* New Haven, CT: Yale University Press.

Middleton, R. (2007). *Pontiac's war: Its causes, courses, and consequences.* New York: Routledge.

Toppo, G. (2009, April 13). 10 years later, the real story behind Columbine. *USA Today.* Retrieved from http://usatoday30.usatoday.com/news/nation/2009-04-13-columbine-myths_n.htm

Wilson, H. L. (2012). Virginia Tech massacre. In G. L. Carter (Ed.), *Guns in American society: An encyclopedia of history, politics, culture, and the law* (907–912). Santa Barbara, CA: ABC-CLIO.

Government Options to Stop School Shootings

Lawrence Southwick Jr.

Why are school shootings a problem? We need to look at the numbers of these events, how many people are harmed, who the shooters are, how school environments might contribute to the problem, the extent to which the numbers or attributes of guns affect the issue, and the proposals made to remedy the problem. In light of these, some evaluation of proposed solutions is needed as well.

WHAT ARE SCHOOL SHOOTINGS?

School shootings are generally thought of as a subset of the category "mass murder." However, they are actually more inclusive in that they include individual killings or injuries. Of course, school shootings do not include shootings that are not associated with schools.

The FBI defines "mass murder" as: "Generally, mass murder was described as a number of murders (four or more) occurring during the same incident, with no distinctive time period between the murders." These events typically involved a single location, where the killer murdered a number of victims in an ongoing incident (e.g., the 1984 San Ysidro McDonald's incident in San Diego, California; the 1991 Luby's Restaurant massacre in Killeen, Texas; and the 2007 Virginia Tech murders in Blacksburg, Virginia) (Morton & Hilts, 2008).

School killing events have been collected for a number of cases since 1764. Not all of these are shootings, but many have been, simply because it may well be the most readily available way to commit such killings. However, a would-be mass murderer who uses explosives is more likely to have a large number of victims. The largest number of victims killed in a single school event was committed by a person who dynamited a school in 1927, killing 50 (Associated Press, 1927). (Another major bombing was that of the Murrah Building in Oklahoma City in 1995, killing 168 and injuring 680, including 19 children in a day care center. However, this is not generally considered a school killing. See History.com, n.d.)

WHO ARE THE SHOOTERS?

Wikipedia provides a list of 271 school murder/injury events in the United States over the past 2.5 centuries. Academics generally do not like to use Wikipedia (n.d.) as a reference, but the school shootings list it provides is currently the best available. This list provides information about the attackers and about the victims as well as the circumstances reported in the press for each. Over that period, there were 186 events that resulted in the deaths of one or more victims. There were 484 victims killed and 522 injured. This does not include individual suicides (19) and attempted suicides when these did not include attacks on others as murders; in attacks on others followed by a suicide, I have included the attacker's death (49 cases). Accidents are also included. In many cases, I have needed to look up various other news reports about the events.

It would seem that the major issue to be considered in order to reduce these events is to have some better way of treating mental health issues. Some 56.1 percent of deaths and 53.3 percent of injuries occur when the killers are apparently mentally ill. The next highest category is rejected suitors/domestic disputes at 10.3 percent of deaths and 1.3 percent of injuries.

It is also worthwhile to ask how this number of deaths relates to murders in other than school settings. In 2010, there were a total of 14,722 murders, according to the FBI (U.S. Department of Justice, 2012). That is down by more than 37 percent from 1990 (U.S. Department of Justice, 2012). Over the entire history of school killings, they total less than 3.3 percent of just one recent year's murders. While that is not to say they are unimportant, they are not as important as many other murders or other causes of deaths.

ARE SCHOOL ENVIRONMENTS CHANGING FOR THE WORSE?

Are there trends in such school-related events over time? Of course, there are more people in schools over time as population increases. There has also been a major increase in college/university populations as more and more people, as a percentage of college-age people, choose to attend college. In the primary and secondary schools, there have been mergers that resulted in larger-sized schools.

There were about 139,000 schools in the United States in 2009–2010 (U.S. Department of Education, 2016). Given the total number of shooting events during 2012 of 11, that implies a probability of any school having one of these of less than one hundredth of 1 percent.

Keep in mind that events in earlier years are less likely to have been reported accurately or reported at all (U.S. Census Bureau, 2008, 2010). Further, while the number of events in the first four years of the current decade appears very high, so too was the number in the decade 1900–1909. In fact, there is no significant trend found when a regression is run with the year as the independent variable and the number of events as the dependent variable.

A more telling statistic is reported by the Bureau of Justice Statistics (Robers, Kemp, Truman, & Snyder, 2013). That is, "The percentage of youth homicides occurring at school remained at less than 2% of the total number of youth homicides over all available survey years" (Robers et al., 2013, p. 6). There is a vastly greater problem of homicide outside of school than there is in school. These data are currently available for school years 1992–1993 through 2010–2011.

Using these same BJS data to run regressions with School Homicides, Youth Homicides in School, and Youth Suicides as dependent variables and, in each case, Year as the independent variable (running from 1 in 1992–1993 to 19 in 2010–2011), the result is that in all three regressions there is no trend coefficient significant at the 95 percent level, the usual level required for social science significance, although there is a negative coefficient for Youth Homicides, which is barely significant at the 90 percent level. It may be that Youth Homicides are decreasing, although there is little confidence that is so. The usual standard for significance for social statistics is at the 95 percent level using a two-tailed test. (All three slope coefficients are negative, although not significant, possibly showing a declining trend.)

While it may seem, based on news coverage, that most school killings are of grade school children, that is not the case, based on a rough analysis. Grade school students through middle school accounted for about 118 of the victims, high school students accounted for 96, college students accounted for 46, and adults accounted for 169. About 55 could not be placed as to grade. Many of the incidents saw adult teachers or administrators killed in the school.

The perpetrators were of varying ages as well. There were about 83 adults, 73 high school students (or of high school age), 22 of grade school age including middle school, and 18 apparently in college or graduate school. At least 52 could not be categorized by age. It seems unlikely that much can be made of this.

WHAT ABOUT GUNS?

Some would suggest that it is the wide availability of guns that results in school killings. As noted above, the total U.S. numbers of murders dropped from 23,438 in 1990, a rate of 9.4 per 100,000 people, to 14,722 in 2010, a rate of 4.8 per 100,000 people (U.S. Department of Justice, 2012). That is a drop in the number of murders of over 37 percent and a drop in the murder rate of over 48 percent.

What about the guns? Using ATF data (U.S. Department of Justice, 2011), I have started with the post–World War II time and data, added annual production, subtracted annual exports, and added annual imports of guns. Starting in 1990, there were 68.8 million handguns, 74.0 million rifles, and 63.4 million shotguns in the hands of the public for a total of 206.2 million guns. By 2010, there were 118.2 million handguns, 113.0 million rifles, and 86.6 million shotguns for a total of 318.8 million guns in the hands of the public. That was an increase of over 54 percent in the number of guns. The population increased over the same period by almost 24 percent with the result that the number of guns per capita went from 0.83 to 1.03, or a more than 24 percent increase. In the United States, we now have more than one gun per person. (Of course, many people have no gun and others have more than one. Some would argue that fewer people actually own guns while the increase is due to those who already own guns buying more. However, this is generally supported only by relatively poor survey data. Self-reporting of gun ownership to an interviewer is likely to be skewed by current social perceptions of what the answer may be expected to be.)

The number of guns per capita went up and the number of murders relative to population went down. Perhaps the argument that guns really do have a self-defense use is valid. If potential murderers are deterred by the possibility that they may end up shot by the intended victim, that should be considered a benefit of gun ownership (Wright & Rossi, 1986). Any proposed change to more restrictive gun rules should take into account both the benefit in reduced murders due to reduced guns in the hands of would-be murderers and the cost in increased murders of the reduced numbers of guns in the hands of potential defenders against murders. The author is aware of only one school case in which a person retrieved his gun after hearing shots fired and stopped the shooter. This was in 1997 in Pearl, Mississippi. However, the potential threat to potential shooters is difficult to quantify, especially inasmuch as possession of guns is typically forbidden to potential responders to shooters.

WHAT PROPOSALS ARE OFFERED AND HOW WELL WOULD THEY WORK?

There have been several proposals offered to help deal with the school shooting problem. Let us set aside for now the fact that the problem is not as bad as it has been portrayed by the media (which generally reports on infrequent events as newsworthy) and look at some of these proposals.

Reduce Bullying

This suggests several methods of reducing the bullying problem (Hellwig, 2011). Because these require interventions by parents and teachers, this is more appropriate to local schools than to government. However, a number of school killings were done in retaliation for bullying.

Metal Detectors

These are already used in some schools. However, there are both positives and negatives about their use. For a good listing of both, see National School Safety and Security Services (n.d.). The cost is substantial, involving both equipment and personnel, and failures of either may occur. Further, the perceived security may make other efforts become more relaxed. How do you handle buses and their security, for example, since students may go directly from their bus to class?

Cut Down on Violence in the Media

In order for this to make a difference, it needs to be shown that violence in media has a causal relationship with violence in the real world. Several articles in the

Journal of Experimental Social Psychology co-authored by Brad Bushman argue that it does (see, for example, Carnagey, Anderson, & Bushman, 2007). Gene Beresin, MD, director of Child and Adolescent Psychiatry Residency Training at Massachusetts General Hospital and director of the MGH Center for Mental Health and Media, and Steve Schlozman, MD, examine research that shows no causal relationship between violent games and violent behavior (Beresin & Schlozman, 2012). Whether it is true or not, the next question is whether those affected were already disturbed individuals. Naturally, there is a reluctance to interfere with free speech, which is enshrined in the Constitution. Keep in mind that a single country will only keep particular materials from young people with great difficulty. While it is a commodity rather than speech, notice the lack of success in the "War on Drugs." Smuggling speech is almost certainly easier than smuggling commodities.

Improve Children's Social Skills

One potentially helpful improvement in particular is anger management (Beresin & Schlozman, 2012). Because these are lesson plans, they are more appropriate for implementation by teachers and individual schools than they are for governments. An interesting article in the *Wall Street Journal* pointed out that professionals can't agree whether angry outbursts are a symptom of mental illness or simply a behavior problem (Beck, 2010). Further, these anger management courses do not necessarily reduce violence; the Columbine shooters attended anger management classes. This article noted that "Psychiatrists generally recommend a psychiatric exam for people with severe anger problems, because anger can often accompany depression, anxiety, bipolar disorder or obsessive-compulsive disorder" (Beck, 2010). These are vastly differing mental issues and may have differing effects.

Focus on Parenting: Too Much "Self-Esteem"

It appears that being low on self-esteem can reduce initiative, but having too much self-esteem can lead to narcissism and people who do "seriously objectionable things" (Macaro & Baggini, 2013).

NRA Training Courses for First Graders, with Updates Annually, in How to Respond to a Shooter/Intruder

Proposed by Missouri State Senator Dan Brown

An important flaw in this plan is that it is by no means clear just how children should respond to a shooter/intruder. At present, they appear to be taught to mainly hide under their desks, but that leaves the shooter free to continue shooting. Any child who actually engages an adult is very unlikely to prevail and, unless many respond, will simply be an earlier target. Even a dozen six year olds will not necessarily be able to overcome a single adult. It will take more than a short course to actually teach something useful to children. Further, that may well represent a substantial waste of time away from educational pursuits. Keep in mind that we are considering very rare events. See also a pamphlet prepared by the U.S. Department of Homeland Security (2008; see also Goode, 2013). This basically says: (1) evacuate; if this is not possible, (2) hide; and if this is not possible, (3) take direct action against the shooter. (Obviously, children will not be armed.)

Ban "Military-Style Assault Weapons"

Proposed by President Obama

This proposal is unlikely to be helpful. Assault weapons necessarily include fully automatic firing capability (Fox, 2012). Their purpose is to get enemies to keep their heads down while an army is assaulting their positions, not specifically to kill people. Very few people have licenses to purchase full auto guns, certainly not most licensed gun owners in the United States. In fact, the actual proposal is based on looks rather than on function and was basically a renewal of the 1994 law. In the 1994 law restricting some of these guns, a factor included was whether it had the capability of holding a bayonet. A bayonet actually reduces the functionality of a rifle in many uses. The 1994 law was generally found to have no effect on crime.

Ban High-Capacity Ammunition Magazines

Proposed by President Obama

As pointed out to me by a retired colonel of Special Forces, one of the major problems with such high-capacity magazines is an increased tendency to malfunction. Two major malfunctions are the failure of a cartridge to fire and the misfeeding of a cartridge; either can jam a gun. The state of New York recently passed a law that magazines could hold no more than 7 rounds. (One wonders where this figure came from.) When it was pointed out that most such detachable clips hold 10 rounds, the legislation was revised to allow 10-round clips but restricted the owner from loading it with more than 7 rounds. I assume a would-be shooter will certainly obey that restriction! (See, for example, Daily Mail Reporter, 2013.) The time necessary to change a magazine is as little as two seconds. Another argument is that "you don't need a high-capacity magazine for deer hunting." This is a non-sequitur. You might need it for self-defense. In a recent event, a woman and her nine-year-old twins retreated from a home invader to their attic where she ended up emptying the handgun's magazine into him, hitting him five times out of six, but still not really stopping him; she continued by bluffing (Daily Mail Reporter, 2013). Suppose there had been multiple home invaders; what then? However, for a school attacker, the unavailability of large magazines will simply be replaced by the use of multiple magazines.

Lockable, Bulletproof Doors for Classrooms and School Entrances

This was proposed by Selwyn Duke (Daily Mail Reporter, 2013). This would probably slow down such a shooter, although, by the time someone thinks to lock a door because they have received advance warning, the shooter would probably already be in the first classroom. This might possibly help in the second room. It needs to be kept in mind that children and various staff members come in and out of classrooms rather frequently so that doors cannot or will not always be locked. As to the entrances, there may be a better argument for this if people remember to use the locks. People often prop doors open and that clearly defeats the purpose. Hotels that have their back doors unattended often have automatic locking mechanisms, but many people prop them open while making multiple trips to their car to get their suitcases. The cost for 139,000 schools each of which has multiple doors and multiple classrooms is likely to be quite high for the hardened doors, locks, and the requisite maintenance of that hardware.

Permit Licensed Gun Owners Who Are Teachers/Administrators to Carry Guns into Schools

If this is done and made known, it will certainly increase the risk to any potential shooter. However, given the low percentage of teachers and administrators who have carry licenses, the potential risk to a shooter will still be very low. On October 1, 1997, a 16-year-old killed his mother at home, killed an ex-girlfriend and another girl at school, and wounded seven others. He was confronted by the vice principal who had retrieved his own gun from his car and stopped the shooter. We don't know, of course, how long he would have continued shooting had he not been stopped that way. We also don't know how many fewer he might have shot if the vice principal had been carrying his gun. Some will argue that armed personnel will increase accidents as well as improper use of these guns; generally licensed civilians have not had such results, but training and practice is well advised before this is authorized. Further, if it is known generally that some teachers and administrators may be armed, this may make teachers and administrators primary targets for the shooter.

Armed Guards at Schools

This was proposed by the NRA. This has much the same problem as the prior proposal. Shall we have guards at all entrances at all times? This is a substantial cost for very low-frequency events. Further, the attacker has only to shoot the unsuspecting guard first to obtain unimpeded access to the rest of the school population.

Pay Attention to Warning Signs

This is effectively a summary of the Secret Service/Department of Education Report (Vossekuil, Fein, Reddy, Borum, & Modzeleski, 2002). This report comes to the conclusion that attackers who target people in schools tend to give warning signs as well as telling others about their plans. We don't know how many give such signs but never carry them out, however. Thus, it will be difficult to act on the warning signs without acting on others who really may not have such intentions.

Suppose a student appears to have mental health issues and some action is taken. Will that be a violation of that student's rights? How many false positives and consequent actions will be taken at what cost? We are currently suspending students who eat a cookie into the shape of a gun or point a finger at another student. What level of reaction is appropriate? Statistically, there are two types of errors; in this case the errors are (a) missing a person who becomes a shooter and (b) doing something adverse to a person who would not have become a shooter.

CONCLUSIONS

There appear to be no easy answers. Knives, hammers, guns, and explosives are available. They are not going away. Mental illness is always a problem. There is no magic cure or even an always correct diagnosis. Whatever is done implies steering a course between violating people's rights and allowing bad things to happen. We are discussing rather rare events at a probable cost of ignoring other problems that may have higher costs.

REFERENCES

Associated Press. (1927, May 19). Survivors tell of explosion. *New York Times.* Retrieved from https://timesmachine.nytimes.com/timesmachine/1927/05/19/97232747.html?pageNumber=2

Beck, M. (2010, March 9). When anger is an illness, "intermittent explosive disorder," or just a temper tantrum? *Wall Street Journal.* Retrieved from https://search.proquest.com/

Beresin, E., & Schlozman, S. (2012, December 22). Violent video games and movies causing violent behavior. *Psychology Today.* Retrieved from https://www.psychologytoday.com/blog/inside-out-outside-in/201212/violent-video-games-and-movies-causing-violent-behavior

Carnagey, N. L., Anderson, C. A., & Bushman, B. J. (2007). The effect of video game violence on physiological desensitization to real-life violence. *Journal of Experimental Social Psychology, 43*(3), 489–496.

Daily Mail Reporter. (2013, January 6). Mother shoots home intruder five times in face and neck after he cornered her in attic with her twins, 9. *Daily Mail.* Retrieved from http://www.dailymail.co.uk/news/article-2257966/Paul-Ali-Slater-Intruder-shot-times-face-neck-cornering-mother-kids-attic.html

Fox, J. A. (2012, December 19). Top 10 myths about mass shootings. *Boston.com.* Retrieved from http://boston.com/community/blogs/crime_punishment/2012/12/top_10_myths_about_mass_shooti.html

Goode, E. (2013, January 16). Even defining "assault rifles" is complicated. *New York Times.* Retrieved from http://www.nytimes.com/2013/01/17/us/even-defining-assault-weapons-is-complicated.html?_r=0

Hellwig, E. (2011). 10 ways to help reduce bullying in schools. *Crisis Prevention Institute (CPI).* Retrieved from https://www.crisisprevention.com/Blog/November-2011/10-Ways-to-Help-Reduce-Bullying-in-Schools

History.com. (n.d.). *Oklahoma City bombing.* Retrieved from http://www.history.com/topics/oklahoma-city-bombing

Macaro, A., & Baggini, J. (2013, January 25). Can we have too much self-esteem? *Financial Times Magazine*. Retrieved from http://www.ft.com/cms/s/2/a44911ae-486c-11e2-a1c0-00144feab49a.html#axzz2ZAAgsD62

Morton, R. J., & Hilts, M. A. (Eds.). (2008). *Serial murder: Multi-disciplinary perspectives for investigators*. Washington, D.C.: U.S. Department of Justice, Federal Bureau of Investigation. Retrieved from http://www.fbi.gov/stats-services/publications/serial-murder/serial-murder-july-2008-pdf

National School Safety and Security Services. (n.d.). *School metal detectors*. Retrieved from http://www.schoolsecurity.org/trends/school_metal_detectors.html

Robers, S., Kemp, J., Truman, J., & Snyder, T.D. (2013). *Indicators of school crime and safety: 2012*. Washington, D.C.: National Center for Education Statistics and Bureau of Justice Statistics. Retrieved from https://nces.ed.gov/pubs2013/2013036.pdf

U.S. Census Bureau. (2008). *2008 national population projection tables*. Washington, D.C.: U.S. Census Bureau. Retrieved from https://www.census.gov/data/tables/2008/demo/popproj/2008-summary-tables.html

U.S. Census Bureau. (2010). *2010 national population projection tables*. Washington, D.C.: U.S. Census Bureau. Retrieved from http://www.census.gov/history/www/through_the_decades/fast_facts/2010_fast_facts.html

U.S. Department of Education, National Center for Education Statistics. (2016). *Digest of Education Statistics, 2015 (NCES 2016-014), Table 105.50*. Washington, D.C.: U.S. Department of Education, National Center for Education Statistics. Retrieved from https://nces.ed.gov/fastfacts/display.asp?id=84

U.S. Department of Homeland Security. (2008). *Active shooter: How to respond.* Washington, D.C.: U.S. Department of Homeland Security. Retrieved from http://www.dhs.gov/xlibrary/assets/active_shooter_booklet.pdf

U.S. Department of Justice. Bureau of Alcohol, Tobacco, Firearms, and Explosives. (2011). *Firearms commerce in the United States, 2011*. Washington, D.C.: U.S. Department of Justice, Bureau of Alcohol, Tobacco, Firearms, and Explosives. Retrieved from https://www.atf.gov/firearms/docs/report/firearms-commerce-united-states-2011/download

U.S. Department of Justice. Federal Bureau of Investigation. (2012). *Crime in the United States, 2011: Annual Uniform Crime Report; Crime in the United States by volume and rate per 100,000 inhabitants, 1992–2011*. Washington, D.C.: U.S. Department of Justice, Federal Bureau of Investigation. Retrieved from https://ucr.fbi.gov/crime-in-the-u.s/2011/crime-in-the-u.s.-2011/tables/table-1

Vossekuil, B., Fein, R. A., Reddy, M., Borum, R., & Modzeleski, W. (2002). *The final report and findings of the Safe School Initiative: Implications for the prevention of school attacks in the United States*. Washington, D.C.: United States Secret Service and United States Department of Education. Retrieved from https://www2.ed.gov/admins/lead/safety/preventingattacksreport.pdf

Wikipedia. (n.d.). *List of school shootings in the United States*. Retrieved from https://en.wikipedia.org/wiki/List_of_school_shootings_in_the_United_States

Wright, J. D., & Rossi, P. H. (1986). *Armed and considered dangerous: A survey of felons and their firearms*. New York: Aldine de Gruyter.

Let the Locals Decide How to Stop School Shootings

Harry L. Wilson

On December 14, 2012, 20-year-old Adam Lanza walked into the Sandy Hook Elementary School in Newtown, Connecticut, where he shot and killed 20 schoolchildren and 6 teachers and administrators. Earlier, he had killed his mother and taken several of her semiautomatic firearms, which he used in the school shootings. His actions changed the landscape of the gun control debate in the United States.

Everyone agrees that we should act to reduce the possibility of mass shootings. School shootings, though thankfully rare, stir emotions and provoke calls to action. Like most major social problems, gun violence has neither a simple explanation nor a simple solution.

School-related deaths are very rare. According to the Centers for Disease Control, 17 school-age youths, ages 5 to 18 were killed at school during the 2009–2010 school year. Of all youth homicides, less than 2 percent occur at school. Contrary to common perception, that percentage has been steady for a decade (Centers for Disease Control, n.d.). In short, there is no epidemic of school shootings. Still, for many of us, the tragedy of Newtown calls for some type of action.

Some people think that the country needs a single nationwide response—one that would have to result from congressional action with presidential approval. This essay argues that such a solution is not workable, either politically or practically. Therefore, we should allow individual states, and even individual school districts to adopt their own policies which they believe will reduce the possibility of a school shooting in their town or city.

Politically, we have seen clearly that the nation is not able to agree on gun-related polices. Elected officials disagree, and, if public opinion polls are to be believed, then that disagreement is a reflection of the differing views of Americans, not just "politics" (Pew Research Center for the People and the Press, 2013). In practical terms, we do not know which policies will work and which will not (or if one policy would work in all environments), so it makes sense for us to allow different policies in different places.

The United States is governed by a federal system in which both the national government and state governments have responsibilities. Some powers fall fully under the purview of the national government; others are reserved for the states. Many powers are shared. There are numerous examples of current contentious policies where both levels of government exert power, including abortion, same-sex marriage, and marijuana regulation. As is true of gun control, the country has found it difficult to reach a national consensus on those issues, and individual states have enacted laws to reflect their own views. States, of course, may not adopt laws that violate the Constitution, but within those often broad parameters, they are free to adopt policies they believe best fit their state. Those who hope for a national "solution" to problems are often unhappy with this approach, but it has merits, insofar as it allows us to move forward state by state until a consensus is found. That may take decades, or even longer, but may be less contentious because citizens can feel that their state government reflects their opinion when the national government may not.

Prior to the Newtown tragedy, violent crime had been declining nationally for more than a decade, and polls showed a gradual, but clear, shift in favor of gun rights. The National Rifle Association (NRA) had successfully helped to move laws, both nationally and in many states, away from stricter regulations on firearms. The Assault Weapons Ban of 1994 expired a decade later with little impetus in Congress to renew the legislation. The Supreme Court of the United States had issued two landmark rulings in 2008 and 2010, both in close votes, clearly stating that the Second Amendment to the Constitution protected an individual right to bear arms for self-defense.

Even President Barack Obama, who had been a strong supporter of gun control in the state of Illinois and as a U.S. senator, stated that he supported an individual right in the Second Amendment. In his first term as president, he took no action to restrict gun rights, and gun control was largely absent from the presidential campaign in 2012.

Obama was reluctant to press for gun control in his first term, understanding that he was not likely to be successful in getting legislation passed. While the Democrats controlled Capitol Hill from 2009 to 2011, there was insufficient time and little congressional support, even among Democrats, for gun control. After the Republican victories in the midterm elections of 2010, when they regained control of the House of Representatives, the opportunity for gun control legislation had passed. All of that changed dramatically with the Newtown shooting.

To be sure, this was not the only mass shooting in recent history. Several other shootings had also received significant media attention, including, in recent years, an Aurora, Colorado, movie theater (July 20, 2012; 70 killed and injured); a Safeway grocery store in Tucson, Arizona (Jan. 8, 2012; 19 injured and killed, including Rep. Gabrielle Giffords); Fort Hood, Texas, army base (Nov. 5, 2009; 43 killed and injured); Northern Illinois University (Feb. 14, 2008; 26 killed and injured); and the Virginia Tech shootings, the largest in U.S. history up to that point in time (April 16, 2007; 55 killed and injured). (Editor's Note: The victim count for the Northern Illinois University and Virginia Tech shootings has been updated from the author's original work to not include the perpetrators in the victim count.) One of the first school shootings to receive significant news media coverage occurred at Columbine High School in Colorado on April 20, 1999 (13 killed; 21 wounded). (Editor's Note: This figure has been updated from the author's original work to not include the perpetrators in the victim count.)

After each of these tragedies there were calls for stricter gun laws, but little action was taken. In each case there was significant coverage by the news media; often intense for a short period—but that coverage usually waned shortly after the funerals for the victims were held. In most cases, the guns were legally purchased, and the shooters were clearly mentally unstable. Thus, the threat to most people was not viewed as proximate.

But Sandy Hook was different. First, the victims were primarily small children and their teachers. This was a new experience for America. Even though the shooter had stolen the firearms from his mother, who had them registered in a state with very strict gun laws, making it difficult to envision a law that would have prevented it, this was different. Even though [the shooter] was mentally unstable, at least at the time of the shooting, like many other mass shooters, this was different. Even if the number of victims was large, we had seen more victims in previous shootings, but this was different because the victims were mostly young children between five and ten years old and the teachers who tried in vain to protect them.

It is painful to imagine a group of college students at Virginia Tech huddled in a classroom, trying to plot a way out, which only a few successfully utilized. It gives us all pause to consider people in a movie theater with no place to run and no clear path of escape. We have difficulty comprehending a shooter in a parking lot, targeting an elected official and many others at a political rally. But none of this comes close to the horror of little children huddled in a corner of a classroom, with only a teacher to protect them, too young to understand what may have been happening and too small and almost certainly too frightened to fight back. The emotional impact was something we had not witnessed before. The victims at Columbine were teens; those at Virginia Tech and NIU were young adults. Those at Newtown were young children. The country's response was visceral, and emotion has typically been on the side of gun control.

For those who support stricter gun control laws, including President Obama, this was their opportunity. The policy window had opened. It is difficult to imagine a political climate more sympathetic to gun laws than that which followed the Newtown tragedy. In the weeks and months following the shootings, gun control remained in the news. Obama expressed the feelings of many of us:

> "No single law, no set of laws can eliminate evil from the world or prevent every senseless act of violence in our society," he said. "But that can't be an excuse for inaction." He added that "in the coming weeks I'll use whatever power this office holds" in an effort "aimed at preventing more tragedies like this.
>
> "Because what choice do we have?" he added. "We can't accept events like this as routine. Are we really prepared to say that we're powerless in the face of such carnage? That the politics are too hard? Are we prepared to say that such violence visited on our children year after year after year is somehow the price of our freedom?" (Landler & Baker, 2012)

On December 18, the president announced that he was putting Vice President Joe Biden, one of the authors of the original Assault Weapons Ban, in charge of a task force that would investigate gun violence, issue a report, and make specific recommendations for action prior to the State of the Union address in February. On January 16, President Obama announced four legislative proposals and 23 executive actions. Flanked by four young schoolchildren who had written letters to the president regarding gun violence, he called for passage of a strengthened assault weapons ban, a ban on magazines that can hold more than 10 rounds of ammunition, universal background checks to include all private firearms transactions, and legislation banning "armor-piercing" bullets and stronger penalties for straw-purchasers, those who legally purchase firearms but then sell or give them to persons prohibited from buying firearms themselves.

The NRA was silent for nearly a week after the shootings. At a press conference on December 18, 2012, Wayne LaPierre suggested that violent media, "gun-free" zones, lax law enforcement, and a lack of school security put children at risk. Vowing to use the resources of the NRA to create programs to help train and deploy armed security for those schools that wanted it, he argued that the media and some elected officials perpetuate the problems by misstating the causes of violence and misrepresenting firearms ("NRA: Full Statement," 2012).

> The only thing that stops a bad guy with a gun is a good guy with a gun. You know, five years ago, after the Virginia Tech tragedy, when I said we should put armed security in every school, the media called me crazy. But what if, when Adam Lanza started shooting his way into Sandy Hook Elementary School last Friday, he had been confronted by qualified, armed security? Will you at least admit it's possible that 26 innocent lives might have been spared? Is that so abhorrent to you that you would rather continue to risk the alternative?

The *Washington Post* described the response as "simplistic" and "crude." The *New York Times* stated, "[W]e were stunned by Mr. LaPierre's mendacious, delusional, almost deranged rant" ("The NRA Crawls," 2012). *USA Today* quoted several Newtown residents, suggesting that LaPierre's remarks were "off the mark," "rude," "completely ludicrous," and "just an awful slap to the face" and suggested that the timing was too soon after the shootings (Jervis, 2012). Other news outlets were equally effusive in their condemnation. In his speech, LaPierre stated, "Now, I can imagine the shocking headlines you'll print tomorrow morning: More guns, you'll claim, 'are the NRA's answer to everything!'" His prediction was not inaccurate.

On April 17, 2013, the Senate voted down an amendment that would have expanded background checks to include all firearms transactions at gun shows and Internet sales (which was defined as any firearm that had been advertised in any medium that had an Internet presence). The amendment had been crafted by moderate Democrat Joe Manchin (WV) and conservative Republican Pat Toomey (PA) working with Chuck Schumer (D-NY) and Mark Kirk (R-IL) and was thought to have the best chance of passage of any gun control measure. It received 54 votes, falling 5 short of what was necessary to stall another filibuster. Only four Republicans voted for the amendment, including the two co-sponsors, and five

Democrats, including Harry Reid, voted against it. In comparison, an amendment to ban assault weapons got 40 votes, while one that would have allowed persons with a concealed-gun carry permit to carry across state lines—even in states that do not allow concealed carry—received 57 votes. The nature of the Senate smaller states, which tend to be more rural, more Republican, and more pro-gun, have disproportionate power because each state has two votes. In essence, the two votes from low-population Alaska canceled out the two from high-population California. At the same time, the red-state, blue-state divide was clearly evident in the vote (Todd, Murray, Montenaro, & Brower, 2013).

Despite the legislative failures at the national level, several states passed very strict laws in the wake of the Newtown shootings. Most prominent among them were Connecticut, New York, Maryland, and Colorado. At the same time, more than a dozen states loosened gun restrictions, mostly dealing with concealed carry laws, although Kansas declared that no federal gun laws could be enforced in the state, a law that realistically could not be enforced or pass constitutional muster (Drash & Lyles, 2013).

Policy responses at the local level have varied even more widely. For example, schools have suspended young students for allegedly chewing a pastry into the shape of a gun, pointing a finger and saying "Pow" to another student, or a young girl for "threatening" to shoot another with a plastic toy that "shoots" bubbles. In other incidents, a school refused to serve birthday cupcakes to a third-grade class because they had World War II toy soldiers on them and another threatened suspension if an eighth-grade student did not remove his T-shirt, which featured the insignia of the U.S. Marine Corps, which includes interlocking guns. In June 2013, an elementary school in Hayward, CA, sponsored a toy gun buyback event in which children received a book and a chance to win a bike in return for their toy guns. The school principal said that such toys desensitized children and made it easier for them to use real guns (Chasmar, 2013).

Some schools adopted policies were more in line with NRA recommendations. An Arkansas school district had planned to arm 20 teachers who had spent more than 50 hours training over the summer, but the state's attorney general said the program was not covered by state law, and it was abandoned (Stanglin, 2013). Even within the state of Connecticut, school responses to enhanced security needs varied tremendously. Some schools opted for armed guards, while others installed cameras, adopted buzz-in systems, card-swipe entry, and other structural changes designed to enhance safety. Others improved mental health systems.

The states have been described as "laboratories of democracy" by Supreme Court Justice Louis Brandeis in *New State Ice Co. v. Liebmann* (1932). The concept was also referenced by the liberal dissenters in *McDonald v. Chicago* (2010), which struck down Chicago's handgun ban. In dissent, Justice Stevens argued that permitting state laws to differ regarding firearms restrictions would allow us to essentially test various policies' impacts.

While neither side in the debate will be satisfied with the state-by-state approach to gun control, it allows both sides to press their case and tout the results of policies implemented in various states. With no national consensus in sight, this is not only a practical approach, but it also reflects the founding ideals of the nation. So long as the president and Congress cannot agree on a gun control policy, those policies will largely continue to be made in the states.

While the motives for the Newtown shootings remain unclear, we know that [the gunman] shot and killed his mother before taking several of her legally registered firearms to the elementary school where he killed the others and shot himself when police arrived on the scene. Ms. Lanza had legally obtained her firearms in a state with some of the most restrictive laws in the country. She underwent a background check. It is difficult to see how a gun control law, short of confiscation of some guns, would have prevented the shootings. Allowing different states and even school districts to adopt different polices regarding firearms seems to be a reasonable response to a problem which does not have a clear solution and which arouses strong and differing responses from different people.

REFERENCES

Centers for Disease Control. (n.d.). *Understanding school violence: Fact sheet 2012*. Retrieved from http://www.cdc.gov/violenceprevention/pdf/schoolviolence_factsheet-a.pdf

Chasmar, J. (2013, June 10). Calif. elementary school offers toy gun buyback. *Washington Times*. Retrieved from http://www.washingtontimes.com/news/2013/jun/10/calif-elementary-school-offers-toy-gun-buyback/

Drash, W., & Lyles, T. (2013, June 8). States tighten, loosen gun laws after Newtown. *CNN*. Retrieved from http://www.cnn.com/2013/06/08/us/gun-laws-states/index.html?hpt=hp_t1

Jervis, R. (2012, December 21). Newtown on NRA speech: "Completely off the mark." *USA Today*. Retrieved from http://www.usatoday.com/story/news/nation/2012/12/21/nra-guns-newtown-reaction/1784957/

Landler, M., & Baker, P. (2012, December 16). These tragedies must end, Obama says. *New York Times*. Retrieved from http://www.nytimes.com/2012/12/17/us/politics/bloomberg-urges-obama-to-take-action-on-gun-control.html?pagewanted=all

The NRA crawls from its hidey hole. (2012, December 21). *New York Times*. Retrieved from http://www.nytimes.com/2012/12/22/opinion/the-nra-crawls-from-its-hidey-hole.html

NRA: Full statement by Wayne LaPierre in response to Newtown shootings. (2012, December 21). *The Guardian*. Retrieved from http://www.theguardian.com/world/2012/dec/21/nra-full-statement-lapierre-newtown

Pew Research Center for the People and the Press. (2013, January 14). *In gun control debate, several options draw majority support*. Retrieved from http://www.people-press.org/2013/01/14/in-gun-control-debate-several-options-draw-majority-support/

Stanglin, D. (2013, August 2). Ark. school district's plan to arm teachers nixed by AG. *USA Today*. Retrieved from http://www.usatoday.com/story/news/nation/2013/08/02/arkansas-school-district-armed-staff-teachers-attorney-general/2611897/

Todd, C., Murray, M., Montenaro, D., & Brower, B. (2013, April 18). First thoughts: Why the gun measure went down to defeat. *NBC News*. Retrieved from http://firstread.nbcnews.com/_news/2013/04/18/17809775-first-thoughts-why-the-gun-measure-went-down-to-defeat

Pivotal Documents in Mass
Shootings Research

Gun Control Act of 1968

Following the assassinations of President John F. Kennedy (1963), Dr. Martin Luther King Jr. (1968), and Senator Robert F. Kennedy (1968), Congress passed the Gun Control Act of 1968, also known as the State Firearms Control Assistance Act. The primary focus of the legislation, which President Lyndon B. Johnson signed into law on October 22, 1968, was to regulate interstate firearms commerce, including the prohibition of interstate transfers by anyone other than licensed manufacturers, dealers, or importers. The act also prohibited certain groups of people, including convicted felons and mentally ill individuals (with certain provisions), from owning a firearm.

"§ 922. Unlawful acts

"(a) It shall be unlawful—

"(1) for any person, except a licensed importer, licensed manufacturer, or licensed dealer, to engage in the business of importing, manufacturing, or dealing in firearms, or in the course of such business to ship, transport, or receive any firearm in interstate or foreign commerce;

"(2) for any importer, manufacturer, dealer, or collector licensed under the provisions of this chapter to ship or transport in interstate or foreign commerce any firearm to any person other than a licensed importer, licensed manufacturer, licensed dealer, or licensed collector, except that—

"(A) this paragraph and subsection (b)(3) shall not be held to preclude a licensed importer, licensed manufacturer, licensed dealer, or licensed collector from returning a firearm or replacement firearm of the same kind and type to a person from whom it was received; and this paragraph shall not be held to preclude an individual from mailing a firearm owned in compliance with Federal, State, and local law to a licensed importer, licensed manufacturer, licensed dealer, or licensed collector;

"(B) this paragraph shall not be held to preclude a licensed importer, licensed manufacturer, or licensed dealer from depositing a firearm for conveyance in the mails to any officer, employee, agent, or watchman who, pursuant to the provisions of section 1715 of this title, is eligible to receive through the mails pistols, revolvers, and other firearms capable of being concealed on the person, for use in connection with his official duty; and

"(C) nothing in this paragraph shall be construed as applying in any manner in the District of Columbia, the Commonwealth of Puerto Rico, or any possession of the United States differently than it would apply if the District of Columbia, the Commonwealth of Puerto Rico, or the possession were in fact a State of the United States;

"(3) for any person, other than a licensed importer, licensed manufacturer, licensed dealer, or licensed collector to transport into or receive in the State where he resides (or if the person is a corporation or other business entity, the State where it maintains a place of business) any firearm purchased or otherwise obtained by such person outside that State, except that this paragraph (A) shall not preclude any person who lawfully acquires a firearm by bequest or intestate succession in a State other than his State of residence from transporting the firearm into or receiving it in that State, if it is lawful for such person to purchase or possess such firearm in that State, (B) shall not apply to the transportation or receipt of a firearm obtained in conformity with subsection (b)(3) of this section, and (C) shall not apply to the transportation of any firearm acquired in any State prior to the effective date of this chapter;

"(4) for any person, other than a licensed importer, licensed manufacturer, licensed dealer, or licensed collector, to transport in interstate or foreign commerce any destructive device, machinegun (as defined in section 5845 of the Internal Revenue Code of 1986), short-barreled shotgun, or short-barreled rifle, except as specifically authorized by the Attorney General consistent with public safety and necessity;

"(5) for any person (other than a licensed importer, licensed manufacturer, licensed dealer, or licensed collector) to transfer, sell, trade, give, transport, or deliver any firearm to any person (other than a licensed importer, licensed manufacturer, licensed dealer, or licensed collector) who the transferor knows or has reasonable cause to believe does not reside in (or if the person is a corporation or other business entity, does not maintain a place of business in) the State in which the transferor resides; except that this paragraph shall not apply to (A) the transfer, transportation, or delivery of a firearm made to carry out a bequest of a firearm to, or an acquisition by intestate succession of a firearm by, a person who is permitted to acquire or possess a firearm under the laws of the State of his residence, and (B) the loan or rental of a firearm to any person for temporary use for lawful sporting purposes;

"(6) for any person in connection with the acquisition or attempted acquisition of any firearm or ammunition from a licensed importer, licensed manufacturer, licensed dealer, or licensed collector, knowingly to make any false or fictitious oral or written statement or to furnish or exhibit any false, fictitious, or misrepresented identification, intended or likely to deceive such importer, manufacturer, dealer, or collector with respect to any fact material to the lawfulness of the sale or other disposition of such firearm or ammunition under the provisions of this chapter.

"(b) It shall be unlawful for any licensed importer, licensed manufacturer, licensed dealer, or licensed collector to sell or deliver—

"(1) any firearm or ammunition to any individual who the licensee knows or has reasonable cause to believe is less than eighteen years of age, and, if the firearm, or ammunition is other than a shotgun or rifle, or ammunition for a shotgun or rifle, to any individual who the licensee knows or has reasonable cause to believe is less than twenty-one years of age;

"(2) any firearm to any person in any State where the purchase or possession by such person of such firearm would be in violation of any State law or any published ordinance applicable at the place of sale, delivery or other disposition, unless the licensee knows or has reasonable cause to believe that the purchase or possession would not be in violation of such State law or such published ordinance;

"(3) any firearm to any person who the licensee knows or has reasonable cause to believe does not reside in (or if the person is a corporation or other business entity, does not maintain a place of business in) the State in which the licensee's place of business is located, except that this paragraph (A) shall not apply to the sale or delivery of any rifle or shotgun to a resident of a State other than a State in which the licensee's place of business is located if the transferee meets in person with the transferor to accomplish the transfer, and the sale, delivery, and receipt fully comply with the legal conditions of sale in both such States (and any licensed manufacturer, importer or dealer shall be presumed, for purposes of this subparagraph, in the absence of evidence to the contrary, to have had actual knowledge of the State laws and published ordinances of both States), and (B) shall not apply to the loan or rental of a firearm to any person for temporary use for lawful sporting purposes;

"(4) to any person any destructive device, machinegun (as defined in section 5845 of the Internal Revenue Code of 1986), short-barreled shotgun, or short-barreled rifle, except as specifically authorized by the Attorney General consistent with public safety and necessity; and

"(5) any firearm or armor-piercing ammunition to any person unless the licensee notes in his records, required to be kept pursuant to section 923 of this chapter, the name, age, and place of residence of such person if the person is an individual, or the identity and principal and local places of business of such person if the person is a corporation or other business entity.

Paragraphs (1), (2), (3), and (4) of this subsection shall not apply to transactions between licensed importers, licensed manufacturers, licensed dealers, and licensed collectors. Paragraph (4) of this subsection shall not apply to a sale or delivery to any research organization designated by the Attorney General.

"(c) In any case not otherwise prohibited by this chapter, a licensed importer, licensed manufacturer, or licensed dealer may sell a firearm to a person who does not appear in person at the licensee's business premises (other than another licensed importer, manufacturer, or dealer) only if—

"(1) the transferee submits to the transferor a sworn statement in the following form:

"'Subject to penalties provided by law, I swear that, in the case of any firearm other than a shotgun or a rifle, I am twenty-one years or more of age, or that, in the case of a shotgun or a rifle, I am eighteen years or more of age; that I am not prohibited by the provisions of chapter 44 of title 18, United States Code, from receiving a firearm in interstate or foreign commerce; and that my receipt of this firearm will not be in violation of any statute of the State and published ordinance applicable to the locality in which I reside. Further, the true title, name, and address of the principal law enforcement officer of the locality to which the firearm will be delivered are _____

Signature _____ Date _____.'

and containing blank spaces for the attachment of a true copy of any permit or other information required pursuant to such statute or published ordinance;

"(2) the transferor has, prior to the shipment or delivery of the firearm, forwarded by registered or certified mail (return receipt requested) a copy of the sworn statement, together with a description of the firearm, in a form prescribed by the Attorney General, to the chief law enforcement officer of the transferee's place of residence, and has received a return receipt evidencing delivery of the statement or has had the statement returned due to the refusal of the named addressee to accept such letter in accordance with United States Post Office Department regulations; and

"(3) the transferor has delayed shipment or delivery for a period of at least seven days following receipt of the notification of the acceptance or refusal of delivery of the statement.

A copy of the sworn statement and a copy of the notification to the local law enforcement officer, together with evidence of receipt or rejection of that notification shall be retained by the licensee as a part of the records required to be kept under section 923(g).

"(d)It shall be unlawful for any person to sell or otherwise dispose of any firearm or ammunition to any person knowing or having reasonable cause to believe that such person—

"(1) is under indictment for, or has been convicted in any court of, a crime punishable by imprisonment for a term exceeding one year;

"(2) is a fugitive from justice;

"(3) is an unlawful user of or addicted marihuana or any depressant or stimulant drug (as defined in section 201 (v) of the Federal Food, Drug, and Cosmetic Act) or narcotic drug (as defined in section 4731(a) of the Internal Revenue Code of 1954); or

"(4) has been adjudicated as a mental defective or has been committed to any mental institution.

This subsection shall not apply with respect to the sale or disposition of a firearm or ammunition to a licensed importer, licensed manufacturer, licensed dealer, or licensed collector who pursuant to subsection (b) of section 925 of this chapter is not precluded from dealing in firearms or ammunition, or to a person who has been granted relief from disabilities pursuant to subsection (c) of section 925 of this chapter.

Source: An Act to amend title 18, United States Code, to provide for better control of the interstate traffic in firearms, H.R. 17735, 90th Cong., 2nd Sess (1968). Retrieved from https://www.gpo.gov/fdsys/pkg/STATUTE-82/pdf/STATUTE -82-Pg1213-2.pdf

The Brady Handgun Violence Prevention Act (Enacted November 30, 1993 by President Bill Clinton)

Named after President Ronald Reagan's press secretary, James Brady, who was wounded in an assassination attempt against the commander-in-chief, the act amended some of the provisions outlined in the Gun Control Act of 1968. Specifically, it required that firearm purchasers submit to a federal background check prior to purchase, and that all purchases be subjected to a five-day mandatory waiting period before transfer, the latter of which remained in place until the national instant background check system (NICS) was implemented in 1998. The law originally was introduced in 1991, but was never brought to a vote. It was reintroduced in 1993, when it passed through both houses of Congress. Between November 30, 1998, the five-year anniversary of the law's enactment and the date the system was implemented, and May 31, 2017, more than 263 million background checks were performed, with the number of checks steadily increasing each year. As of the end of the 2016 calendar year, 1,393,729 applications for purchase had been rejected, representing less than 0.6 percent in denials.

SEC. 102. FEDERAL FIREARMS LICENSEE REQUIRED TO CONDUCT CRIMINAL BACKGROUND CHECK BEFORE TRANSFER OF FIRE-ARM TO NON-LICENSEE.

(a) INTERIM PROVISION.—

(1) IN GENERAL.—Section 922 of title 18, United States Code, is amended by adding at the end the following:

"(s)(1) Beginning on the date that is 90 days after the date of enactment of this subsection and ending on the day before the date that is 60 months after such date of enactment, it shall be unlawful for any licensed importer, licensed manufacturer, or licensed dealer to sell, deliver, or transfer a handgun to an individual who is not licensed under section 923, unless—

"(A) after the most recent proposal of such transfer by the transferee—

"(i) the transferor has—

"(I) received from the transferee a statement of the transferee containing the information described in paragraph (3);

"(II) verified the identity of the transferee by examining the identification document presented;

"(III) within 1 day after the transferee furnishes the statement, provided notice of the contents of the statement to the chief law enforcement officer of the place of residence of the transferee; and

"(IV) within 1 day after the transferee furnishes the statement, transmitted a copy of the statement to the chief law enforcement officer of the place of residence of the transferee; and

"(ii)(I) 5 business days (meaning days on which State offices are open) have elapsed from the date the transferor furnished notice of the contents of the statement to the chief law enforcement officer, during which period the transferor has not received information from the chief law enforcement officer that receipt or possession of the handgun by the transferee would be in violation of Federal, State, or local law; or

"(II) the transferor has received notice from the chief law enforcement officer that the officer has no information indicating that receipt or possession of the handgun by the transferee would violate Federal, State, or local law;

"(B) the transferee has presented to the transferor a written statement, issued by the chief law enforcement officer of the place of residence of the transferee during the 10-day period ending on the date of the most recent proposal of such transfer by the transferee, stating that the transferee requires access to a handgun because of a threat to the life of the transferee or of any member of the household of the transferee;

"(C)(i) the transferee has presented to the transferor a permit that—

"(I) allows the transferee to possess or acquire a handgun; and

"(II) was issued not more than 5 years earlier by the State in which the transfer is to take place; and

"(ii) the law of the State provides that such a permit is to be issued only after an authorized government official has verified that the information available to such official does not indicate that possession of a handgun by the transferee would be in violation of the law;

"(D) the law of the State requires that, before any licensed importer, licensed manufacturer, or licensed dealer completes the transfer of a handgun to an individual who is not licensed under section 923, an authorized government official verify that the information available to such official does not indicate that possession of a handgun by the transferee would be in violation of law;

"(E) the Secretary has approved the transfer under section 5812 of the Internal Revenue Code of 1986; or

"(F) on application of the transferor, the Secretary has certified that compliance with subparagraph (A)(i)(III) is impracticable because—

"(i) the ratio of the number of law enforcement officers of the State in which the transfer is to occur to the number of square miles of land area of the State does not exceed 0.0025;

"(ii) the business premises of the transferor at which the transfer is to occur are extremely remote in relation to the chief law enforcement officer; and

"(iii) there is an absence of telecommunications facilities in the geographical area in which the business premises are located.

"(2) A chief law enforcement officer to whom a transferor has provided notice pursuant to paragraph (1)(A)(i)(III) shall make a reasonable effort to ascertain within 5 business days whether receipt or possession would be in violation of the law, including research in whatever State and local recordkeeping systems are available and in a national system designated by the Attorney General.

"(3) The statement referred to in paragraph (1)(A)(i)(I) shall contain only—

"(A) the name, address, and date of birth appearing on a valid identification document (as defined in section 1028(d)(1)) of the transferee containing a photograph of the transferee and a description of the identification used;

"(B) a statement that the transferee—

"(i) is not under indictment for, and has not been convicted in any court of, a crime punishable by imprisonment for a term exceeding 1 year;

"(ii) is not a fugitive from justice;

"(iii) is not an unlawful user of or addicted to any controlled substance (as defined in section 102 of the Controlled Substances Act);

"(iv) has not been adjudicated as a mental defective or been committed to a mental institution;

"(v) is not an alien who is illegally or unlawfully in the United States;

"(vi) has not been discharged from the Armed Forces under dishonorable conditions; and

"(vii) is not a person who, having been a citizen of the United States, has renounced such citizenship;

"(C) the date the statement is made; and

"(D) notice that the transferee intends to obtain a handgun from the transferor.

"(4) Any transferor of a handgun who, after such transfer, receives a report from a chief law enforcement officer containing information that receipt or possession of the handgun by the transferee violates Federal, State, or local law shall, within 1 business day after receipt of such request, communicate any information related to the transfer that the transferor has about the transfer and the transferee to—

"(A) the chief law enforcement officer of the place of business of the transferor; and

"(B) the chief law enforcement officer of the place of residence of the transferee.

"(5) Any transferor who receives information, not otherwise available to the public, in a report under this subsection shall not disclose such information except to the transferee, to law enforcement authorities, or pursuant to the direction of a court of law.

"(6)(A) Any transferor who sells, delivers, or otherwise transfers a handgun to a transferee shall retain the copy of the statement of the transferee with respect to the handgun transaction, and shall retain evidence that the transferor has complied with subclauses (III) and (IV) of paragraph (1)(A)(i) with respect to the statement.

"(B) Unless the chief law enforcement officer to whom a statement is transmitted under paragraph (1)(A)(i)(IV) determines that a transaction would violate Federal, State, or local law—

"(i) the officer shall, within 20 business days after the date the transferee made the statement based on which the notice was provided, destroy the statement, any record containing information derived from the statement, and any record created because of the notice required by paragraph (1)(A)(i)(III);

"(ii) the information contained in the statement shall not be conveyed to any person except a person who has a need to know to carry out this subsection; and

"(iii) the information contained in the statement shall not be used for any purpose other than to carry out this subsection.

"(C) If a chief law enforcement officer determines that an individual is ineligible to receive a handgun and the individual requests the officer to provide the reason for such determination, the officer shall provide such reasons to the individual in writing within 20 business days after receipt of the request.

"(7) A chief law enforcement officer or other person responsible for providing criminal history background information pursuant to this subsection shall not be liable in an action at law for damages—

"(A) for failure to prevent the sale or transfer of a handgun to a person whose receipt or possession of the handgun is unlawful under this section; or

"(B) for preventing such a sale or transfer to a person who may lawfully receive or possess a handgun.

"(8) For purposes of this subsection, the term 'chief law enforcement officer' means the chief of police, the sheriff, or an equivalent officer or the designee of any such individual.

"(9) The Secretary shall take necessary actions to ensure that the provisions of this subsection are published and disseminated to licensed dealers, law enforcement officials, and the public.".

(2) HANDGUN DEFINED.—Section 921(a) of title 18, United States Code, is amended by adding at the end the following: "(29) The term 'handgun' means—

"(A) a firearm which has a short stock and is designed to be held and fired using a single hand; and

"(B) any combination of parts from which a firearm described in subparagraph (A) can be assembled.".

(b) PERMANENT PROVISION.—Section 922 of title 18, United States Code, as amended by subsection (a)(1), is amended by adding at the end the following:

"(t)(1) Beginning on the date that is 30 days after the Attorney General notifies licensees under section 103(d) of the Brady Handgun Violence Prevention Act that the national instant criminal background check system is established, a licensed importer, licensed manufacturer, or licensed dealer shall not transfer a firearm to any other person who is not licensed under this chapter, unless—

"(A) before the completion of the transfer, the licensee contacts the national instant criminal background check system established under section 103 of that Act;

"(B)(i) the system provides the licensee with a unique identification number; or

"(ii) 3 business days (meaning a day on which State offices are open) have elapsed since the licensee contacted the system, and the system has not notified the licensee that the receipt of a firearm by such other person would violate subsection (g) or (n) of this section; and

"(C) the transferor has verified the identity of the transferee by examining a valid identification document (as defined in section 1028(d)(1) of this title) of the transferee containing a photograph of the transferee.

"(2) If receipt of a firearm would not violate section 922 (g) or (n) or State law, the system shall—

"(A) assign a unique identification number to the transfer;

"(B) provide the licensee with the number; and

"(C) destroy all records of the system with respect to the call (other than the identifying number and the date the number was assigned) and all records of the system relating to the person or the transfer.

"(3) Paragraph (1) shall not apply to a firearm transfer between a licensee and another person if—

"(A)(i) such another person has presented to the licensee a permit that—

"(I) allows such other person to possess or acquire a firearm; and

"(II) was issued not more than 5 years earlier by the State in which the transfer is to take place; and

"(ii) the law of the State provides that such a permit is to be issued only after an authorized government official has verified that the information available to such official does not indicate that possession of a firearm by such other person would be in violation of law;

"(B) the Secretary has approved the transfer under section 5812 of the Internal Revenue Code of 1986; or

"(C) on application of the transferor, the Secretary has certified that compliance with paragraph (1)(A) is impracticable because—

"(i) the ratio of the number of law enforcement officers of the State in which the transfer is to occur to the number of square miles of land area of the State does not exceed 0.0025;

"(ii) the business premises of the licensee at which the transfer is to occur are extremely remote in relation to the chief law enforcement officer (as defined in sub-section (s)(8)); and

"(iii) there is an absence of telecommunications facilities in the geographical area in which the business premises are located.

"(4) If the national instant criminal background check system notifies the licensee that the information available to the system does not demonstrate that the receipt of a firearm by such other person would violate subsection (g) or (n) or State law, and the licensee transfers a firearm to such other person, the licensee shall include in the record of the transfer the unique identification number provided by the system with respect to the transfer.

"(5) If the licensee knowingly transfers a firearm to such other person and knowingly fails to comply with paragraph (1) of this subsection with respect to the transfer and, at the time such other person most recently proposed the transfer, the national instant criminal background check system was operating and information was available to the system demonstrating that receipt of a firearm by such other person would violate subsection (g) or (n) of this section or State law, the Secretary may, after notice and opportunity for a hearing, suspend for not more than 6 months or revoke any license issued to the licensee under section 923, and may impose on the licensee a civil fine of not more than $5,000.

"(6) Neither a local government nor an employee of the Federal Government or of any State or local government, responsible for providing information to the national instant criminal background check system shall be liable in an action at law for damages—

"(A) for failure to prevent the sale or transfer of a firearm to a person whose receipt or possession of the firearm is unlawful under this section; or

"(B) for preventing such a sale or transfer to a person who may lawfully receive or possess a firearm.".

(c) PENALTY.—Section 924(a) of title 18, United States Code, is amended—

(1) in paragraph (1), by striking "paragraph (2) or (3) of"; and

(2) by adding at the end, the following:

"(5) Whoever knowingly violates subsection (s) or (t) of section 922 shall be fined not more than $1,000, imprisoned for not more than 1 year, or both.".

Source: The Brady Handgun Violence Prevention Act, H.R. 1025, 103d Cong., 1st Sess. (1993). Retrieved from https://www.congress.gov/103/bills/hr1025/BILLS-103hr1025enr.pdf

The Public Safety and Recreational Firearms Use Protection Act

During the second session of the 103rd Congress, lawmakers passed the Violent Crime Control and Law Enforcement Act of 1994. The act was signed into law by President Bill Clinton on September 13, 1994. The law was designed to prevent incidents of violent crime within the nation. Provisions included an expansion in the number of police officers, assessment of the nation's prisons, grant programs to fund crime control and violence against women initiatives, and enhanced penalties for drug-related offenses. Also included in the package was a section dedicated to addressing assault weapons; this legislation—the Public Safety and Recreational Firearms Use Protection Act—is more commonly referred to as the Federal Assault Weapons Ban. In addition to defining what constitutes a semiautomatic assault weapon (and identifying several hundred different guns that fit the description in an added appendix [not included in this excerpt]), the law effectively limited the number of rounds a magazine could hold and outlawed the ownership and manufacturing of such firearms. Among those weapons listed was the IntraTec TEC-DC9, later used by one of the Columbine shooters. The bill also included a sunset provision, meaning that it expired 10 years after its enactment if it was not renewed, which it was not. An updated version of the legislation was presented to Congress in 2013 (H.R. 437 and S. 150) but died nearly instantly after introduction.

TITLE XI—FIREARMS
Subtitle A—Assault Weapons

SEC. 110101. SHORT TITLE.

This subtitle may be cited as the "Public Safety and Recreational Firearms Use Protection Act".

SEC. 110102. RESTRICTION ON MANUFACTURE, TRANSFER, AND POSSESSION OF CERTAIN SEMIAUTOMATIC ASSAULT WEAPONS.

(a) RESTRICTION.—Section 922 of title 18, United States Code, is amended by adding at the end the following new subsection:

"(v)(1) It shall be unlawful for a person to manufacture, transfer, or possess a semiautomatic assault weapon.

"(2) Paragraph (1) shall not apply to the possession or transfer of any semiautomatic assault weapon otherwise lawfully possessed under Federal law on the date of the enactment of this subsection.

"(3) Paragraph (1) shall not apply to—

"(A) any of the firearms, or replicas or duplicates of the firearms, specified in Appendix A to this section, as such firearms were manufactured on October 1, 1993;

"(B) any firearm that—

"(i) is manually operated by bolt, pump, lever, or slide action;

"(ii) has been rendered permanently inoperable; or "(iii) is an antique firearm;

"(C) any semiautomatic rifle that cannot accept a detachable magazine that holds more than 5 rounds of ammunition; or

"(D) any semiautomatic shotgun that cannot hold more than 5 rounds of ammunition in a fixed or detachable magazine.

The fact that a firearm is not listed in Appendix A shall not be construed to mean that paragraph (1) applies to such firearm. No firearm exempted by this subsection may be deleted from Appendix A so long as this subsection is in effect.

"(4) Paragraph (1) shall not apply to—

"(A) the manufacture for, transfer to, or possession by the United States or a department or agency of the United States or a State or a department, agency, or political subdivision of a State, or a transfer to or possession by a law enforcement officer employed by such an entity for purposes of law enforcement (whether on or off duty);

"(B) the transfer to a licensee under title I of the Atomic Energy Act of 1954 for purposes of establishing and maintaining an on-site physical protection system and security organization required by Federal law, or possession by an employee or contractor of such licensee on-site for such purposes or off-site for purposes of licensee-authorized training or transportation of nuclear materials;

"(C) the possession, by an individual who is retired from service with a law enforcement agency and is not otherwise prohibited from receiving a firearm, of a semiautomatic assault weapon transferred to the individual by the agency upon such retirement; or

"(D) the manufacture, transfer, or possession of a semiautomatic assault weapon by a licensed manufacturer or licensed importer for the purposes of testing or experimentation authorized by the Secretary.".

(b) DEFINITION OF SEMIAUTOMATIC ASSAULT WEAPON.—Section 921(a) of title 18, United States Code, is amended by adding at the end the following new paragraph:

"(30) The term 'semiautomatic assault weapon' means—

"(A) any of the firearms, or copies or duplicates of the firearms in any caliber, known as—

"(i) Norinco, Mitchell, and Poly Technologies Avtomat Kalashnikovs (all models);

"(ii) Action Arms Israeli Military Industries UZI and Galil;

"(iii) Beretta Ar70 (SC–70);

"(iv) Colt AR–15;

"(v) Fabrique National FN/FAL, FN/LAR, and FNC;

"(vi) SWD M–10, M–11, M–11/9, and M–12;

"(vii) Steyr AUG;

"(viii) INTRATEC TEC–9, TEC–DC9 and TEC–22; and

"(ix) revolving cylinder shotguns, such as (or similar to) the Street Sweeper and Striker 12;

"(B) a semiautomatic rifle that has an ability to accept a detachable magazine and has at least 2 of—

"(i) a folding or telescoping stock;

"(ii) a pistol grip that protrudes conspicuously beneath the action of the weapon;

"(iii) a bayonet mount;

"(iv) a flash suppressor or threaded barrel designed to accommodate a flash suppressor; and

"(v) a grenade launcher;

"(C) a semiautomatic pistol that has an ability to accept a detachable magazine and has at least 2 of—

"(i) an ammunition magazine that attaches to the pistol outside of the pistol grip;

"(ii) a threaded barrel capable of accepting a barrel extender, flash suppressor, forward handgrip, or silencer;

"(iii) a shroud that is attached to, or partially or completely encircles, the barrel and that permits the shooter to hold the firearm with the nontrigger hand without being burned;

"(iv) a manufactured weight of 50 ounces or more when the pistol is unloaded; and

"(v) a semiautomatic version of an automatic firearm; and

"(D) a semiautomatic shotgun that has at least 2 of—

"(i) a folding or telescoping stock;

"(ii) a pistol grip that protrudes conspicuously beneath the action of the weapon;

"(iii) a fixed magazine capacity in excess of 5 rounds; and

"(iv) an ability to accept a detachable magazine.".

(c) PENALTIES.—

(1) VIOLATION OF SECTION 922(v).—Section 924(a)(1)(B) of such title is amended by striking "or (q) of section 922" and inserting "(r), or (v) of section 922".

(2) USE OR POSSESSION DURING CRIME OF VIOLENCE OR DRUG TRAFFICKING CRIME.—Section 924(c)(1) of such title is amended in the first sentence by inserting ", or semiautomatic assault weapon," after "short-barreled shotgun,".

(d) IDENTIFICATION MARKINGS FOR SEMIAUTOMATIC ASSAULT WEAPONS.—Section 923(i) of such title is amended by adding at the end the following: "The serial number of any semiautomatic assault weapon manufactured after the date of the enactment of this sentence shall clearly show the date on which the weapon was manufactured.".

SEC. 110103. BAN OF LARGE CAPACITY AMMUNITION FEEDING DEVICES.

(a) PROHIBITION.—Section 922 of title 18, United States Code, as amended by section 110102(a), is amended by adding at the end the following new subsection:

"(w)(1) Except as provided in paragraph (2), it shall be unlawful for a person to transfer or possess a large capacity ammunition feeding device.

"(2) Paragraph (1) shall not apply to the possession or transfer of any large capacity ammunition feeding device otherwise lawfully possessed on or before the date of the enactment of this subsection.

"(3) This subsection shall not apply to—

"(A) the manufacture for, transfer to, or possession by the United States or a department or agency of the United States or a State or a department, agency, or political subdivision of a State, or a transfer to or possession by a law enforcement officer employed by such an entity for purposes of law enforcement (whether on or off duty);

"(B) the transfer to a licensee under title I of the Atomic Energy Act of 1954 for purposes of establishing and maintaining an on-site physical protection system and security organization required by Federal law, or possession by an employee or contractor of such licensee on-site for such purposes or off-site for purposes of licensee-authorized training or transportation of nuclear materials;

"(C) the possession, by an individual who is retired from service with a law enforcement agency and is not otherwise prohibited from receiving ammunition, of a large capacity ammunition feeding device transferred to the individual by the agency upon such retirement; or

"(D) the manufacture, transfer, or possession of any large capacity ammunition feeding device by a licensed manufacturer or licensed importer for the purposes of testing or experimentation authorized by the Secretary.".

"(4) If a person charged with violating paragraph (1) asserts that paragraph (1) does not apply to such person because of paragraph (2) or (3), the Government shall have the burden of proof to show that such paragraph (1) applies to such person. The lack of a serial number as described in section 923(i) of title 18, United States Code, shall be a presumption that the large capacity ammunition feeding device is not subject to the prohibition of possession in paragraph (1).".

(b) DEFINITION OF LARGE CAPACITY AMMUNITION FEEDING DEVICE.—

Section 921(a) of title 18, United States Code, as amended by section 110102(b), is amended by adding at the end the following new paragraph:

"(31) The term 'large capacity ammunition feeding device'—

"(A) means a magazine, belt, drum, feed strip, or similar device manufactured after the date of enactment of the Violent Crime Control and Law Enforcement Act of 1994 that has a capacity of, or that can be readily restored or converted to accept, more than 10 rounds of ammunition; but

"(B) does not include an attached tubular device designed to accept, and capable of operating only with, .22 caliber rimfire ammunition.".

(c) PENALTY.—Section 924(a)(1)(B) of title 18, United States Code, as amended by section 110102(c)(1), is amended by striking "or (v)" and inserting "(v), or (w)".

(d) IDENTIFICATION MARKINGS FOR LARGE CAPACITY AMMUNITION FEEDING DEVICES.—Section 923(i) of title 18, United States Code, as amended by section 110102(d) of this Act, is amended by adding at the end the following: "A large capacity ammunition feeding device manufactured after the date of the enactment of this sentence shall be identified by a serial number that clearly shows that the device was manufactured or imported after the effective date of this subsection, and such other identification as the Secretary may by regulation prescribe.".

SEC. 110104. STUDY BY ATTORNEY GENERAL.

(a) STUDY.—The Attorney General shall investigate and study the effect of this subtitle and the amendments made by this subtitle, and in particular shall determine their impact, if any, on violent and drug trafficking crime. The study shall be conducted over a period of 18 months, commencing 12 months after the date of enactment of this Act.

(b) REPORT.—Not later than 30 months after the date of enactment of this Act, the Attorney General shall prepare and submit to the Congress a report setting forth in detail the findings and determinations made in the study under subsection (a).

SEC. 110105. EFFECTIVE DATE.
This subtitle and the amendments made by this subtitle—

(1) shall take effect on the date of the enactment of this Act; and
(2) are repealed effective as of the date that is 10 years after that date.

> **Source:** Violent Crime Control and Law Enforcement Act of 1994, H.R. 3355, 103d Cong., 2nd Sess. (1994). Retrieved from https://www.congress.gov/103/bills /hr3355/BILLS-103hr3355enr.pdf

President Clinton's Remarks on School Violence Following Columbine (1999)

On April 30, 1999, just 10 days after the shooting at Columbine High School, President Clinton addressed the nation from the Rose Garden at the White House in Washington, D.C. During his speech, he discussed his plans to address school violence, including regulating violent media and access to firearms, and encouraging parental involvement in children's lives.

Ladies and gentlemen, in the last several days, like most Americans, I have spent an enormous amount of time following the events in Colorado, talking to family and friends and others. And I have some thoughts on that that I want to share with you today.

Let me begin by saying we got some more good news today on the economic front, with the word that our economy expanded by 4.5 percent in the first quarter of this year. This news provides both more evidence that we should stick with our economic strategy and also is a worthwhile reminder that for all the challenges we face at home and abroad, we are indeed a fortunate people. We are strong enough to meet those challenges.

Over the past 10 days our whole Nation has been united in grief with the people of Littleton, Colorado. We have also been profoundly moved by the courage, the common sense, and the fundamental goodness of Littleton students, teachers, parents, and public servants as they have spoken to us of the tragic events there. I have listened carefully to what they have said and to other young people and parents who have been on the townhall meetings and those whom I have met personally.

We should recognize the simple truth that there is no simple, single answer. We should not be fighting about who takes the blame. Instead, we should all be looking for ways to take responsibility, and we should be doing that together.

As we have united in grief, now we should unite in action. If we ask the right question, "What can we do to give your children safe, whole childhoods?" then there will be answers for parents and children, for teachers, communities, and for those who influence the lives and the environment in which our children live, including those of us in government, religious leaders, the entertainment and Internet communities, those who produce explosives and weapons, and those who use them lawfully.

I am inviting representatives of all these groups to come to the White House on May 10th for a strategy session on children, violence, and responsibility. The First Lady, the Vice President, and Mrs. Gore, all of whom have worked for years to give our children the childhoods they deserve, will join me. I ask everyone to come to this meeting with ideas about how we can move forward together.

As Hillary said yesterday, we need nothing less than a grassroots effort to protect our children and turn them away from violence. If citizens, parents and children alike, working together in their communities, can reduce teen pregnancy, reduce drunk driving, make seatbelt use nearly universal, then working together, we can protect our children.

I want to briefly set out a framework for how this challenge can best be addressed. The push and pull of modern life adds incalculable new burdens to the work of parents. We must strive to find ways to bring parents and children together more, to get parents more involved with their children's lives, to get negative influences and guns out of the lives of our children, and to give families the tools to meet these challenges.

First, we must help parents to pass on their values to their children in the face of a blizzard of popular communications that too often undermine those values. For young people who are particularly vulnerable and isolated, the violent video games they play can seem more real than conversations at home or lessons at school. We've been working to give parents stronger tools to protect their children, and we must do more.

The V-chip will be included in half the new televisions sold this year. And together with the voluntary rating system adopted by broadcasters, it will give parents a new ability to screen the images their children see. Meanwhile, we've launched the most ambitious media plan ever to educate our children about the dangers of drugs.

The Vice President and Internet service providers have given parents the ability to block access to violent or otherwise inappropriate websites. The Vice President will continue to work with industry to find ways to help parents guide their children through cyberspace, and we'll have more to say on that in the days ahead.

We have worked to give our parents the tools to protect children from violence and to take guns out of the hands of children. The policy of zero tolerance for guns in schools led to 6,000 expulsions or suspensions in the last year alone.

This week I proposed new measures to keep guns away from criminals and children; requiring background checks for buying guns at gun shows, as they are required at gun stores now, and background checks for the purchase of explosives; banning handgun ownership for people under 21; and restoring the Brady bill's cooling off period; and closing the loopholes in the assault weapons law.

Even on these contentious issues, I believe we can reach across party lines and find common ground. I hope that sportsmen, gun manufacturers, and lawmakers of all parties will see these steps for what they are, commonsense measures to promote the common good. We all love our children. I respect the rights of hunters and sportsmen. Let's bury the hatchet and build a future for our children together.

We must help parents fulfill their most important responsibilities. We all say we want parents to talk to their children more, but we all know that too many families have too little time even to have dinner together.

Because parents too often have too little time, we've passed the Family and Medical Leave Act, and we're working to expand it. Because too many children leave school at 3, with nowhere to go and no adult to talk to, we're giving a quarter-million kids access to after-school and summer school programs, and we're working to triple that number. Because many parents need help in recognizing the signs of illness in their children, we're working to expand access to mental health care for children of all ages. Next month, Mrs. Gore will host the first White House Conference on Mental Health. We are also working to expand counseling, mentoring, and mental health services in our schools.

Most important of all, and perhaps most difficult, parents must be more active participants in their children's lives. It is not for us to pass judgment on how those two young men in Colorado descended into darkness. We may never know what can be or even what could have been done. But this should be a wake-up call for all parents. We can never take our children for granted. We must never let the lines of communication, no matter how frayed, be broken altogether. Our children need us, even if they don't know it sometimes.

This terrible tragedy must not be an occasion for silence. This weekend I ask all parents, if they have not already done so, to sit down and talk to their children about what happened at Littleton and what is happening in their schools and their lives.

If we are not careful, when our children move through their teen years and begin to create their own separate lives, the bustle and burden of our daily lives can cause families to drift too far apart, to ignore the still-strong needs of children for genuine concern and guidance and honest conversation. This is sometimes the hardest thing of all, but it is vital, and lives depend on it.

Finally, I ask students to do more to help each other. Next week, if you have not already done so, I ask every student in America to look for someone at school who is not in your group. You know, there have always been different crowds in schools, and there always will be. This, too, is an inevitable part of growing up and finding your own path through life. But it should not be an occasion for disrespect or hostility in our schools. After all, our children are all on the same journey, even if they're trying to chart different paths. And this can be profoundly important in building a safer future.

The spirit of America can triumph in this troubling moment, and I am convinced it will. But we must build the energy and will and passion of our country and the fundamental goodness of our people into a grassroots movement to turn away from violence and to give all our children the safe and wholesome childhoods they richly deserve.

Thank you very much.

> **Source:** Public Papers of the Presidents of the United States. William J. Clinton, 1999, Book 1. Washington, D.C.: Government Printing Office, 2000, 661–662.

Federal Bureau of Investigation's Report on Threat Assessment of School Shooters (2000)

Several months after the 1999 shooting at Columbine High School, the National Center for the Analysis of Violent Crime (NCAVC) held a symposium in Leesburg, Virginia, aimed at gaining insight on school shootings and associated threat assessment. Supported by U.S. attorney general Janet Reno and FBI director Louis Freeh, schoolteachers and administrators, members of the law enforcement community, and staff from the NCAVC joined together to discuss adolescent violence. The report, authored by Mary Ellen O'Toole, a supervisory special agent and senior criminal profiler for the FBI, provides a systematic procedure for identifying potential threats and responding to them.

This excerpt is from Chapter II: Assessing Threats.

What Is a Threat?

A threat is an expression of intent to do harm or act out violently against someone or something. A threat can be spoken, written, or symbolic—for example, motioning with one's hands as though shooting at another person.

Threat assessment rests on two critical principles: first, that all threats and all threateners are not equal; second, that most threateners are unlikely to carry out their threat. However, all threats must be taken seriously and evaluated.

In National Center for the Analysis of Violent Crime's (NCAVC) experience, most threats are made anonymously or under a false name. Because threat assessment relies heavily on evaluating the threatener's background, personality, lifestyle, and resources, identifying the threatener is necessary for an informed assessment to be made—and also so criminal charges can be brought if the threat is serious enough to warrant prosecution. If the threatener's identity cannot be determined, the response will have to be based on an assessment of the threat alone. That assessment may change if the threatener is eventually identified: a threat that was considered low risk may be rated as more serious if new information suggests the threatener is dangerous, or conversely, an assessment of high risk may be scaled down if the threatener is identified and found not to have the intent, ability, means, or motive to carry out the threat.

Motivation

Threats are made for a variety of reasons. A threat may be a warning signal, a reaction to fear of punishment or some other anxiety, or a demand for attention. It may be intended to taunt; to intimidate; to assert power or control; to punish; to manipulate or coerce; to frighten; to terrorize; to compel someone to do something; to strike back for an injury, injustice or slight; to disrupt someone's or some institution's life; to test authority, or to protect oneself. The emotions that underlie a threat can be love; hate; fear; rage; or desire for attention, revenge, excitement, or recognition.

Motivation can never be known with complete certainty, but to the extent possible, understanding motive is a key element in evaluating a threat. A threat will reflect the threatener's mental and emotional state at the time the threat was made, but it is important to remember that a state of mind can be temporarily but strongly influenced by alcohol or drugs, or a precipitating incident such as a romantic breakup, failing grades, or conflict with a parent. After a person has absorbed an emotional setback and calmed down, or when the effects of alcohol or drugs have worn off, his motivation to act on a violent threat may also have diminished.

Signposts

In general, people do not switch instantly from nonviolence to violence. Nonviolent people do not "snap" or decide on the spur of the moment to meet a problem by using violence. Instead, the path toward violence is an evolutionary one, with signposts along the way. A threat is one observable behavior; others may be brooding about frustration or disappointment, fantasies of destruction or revenge, in conversations, writings, drawings, and other actions.

Types of Threats

Threats can be classed in four categories: *direct, indirect, veiled*, or *conditional*.

A direct threat identifies a specific act against a specific target and is delivered in a straightforward, clear, and explicit manner: "I am going to place a bomb in the school's gym."

An indirect threat tends to be vague, unclear, and ambiguous. The plan, the intended victim, the motivation, and other aspects of the threat are masked or equivocal: "If I wanted to, I could kill everyone at this school!" While violence is implied, the threat is phrased tentatively—"If I wanted to"—and suggests that a violent act COULD occur, not that it WILL occur.

A veiled threat is one that strongly implies but does not explicitly threaten violence. "We would be better off without you around anymore" clearly hints at a possible violent act, but leaves it to the potential victim to interpret the message and give a definite meaning to the threat.

A conditional threat is the type of threat often seen in extortion cases. It warns that a violent act will happen unless certain demands or terms are met: "If you don't pay me one million dollars, I will place a bomb in the school."

Factors in Threat Assessment

Specific, plausible details are a critical factor in evaluating a threat. Details can include the identity of the victim or victims; the reason for making the threat; the means, weapon, and method by which it is to be carried out; the date, time, and place where the threatened act will occur; and concrete information about plans or preparations that have already been made.

Specific details can indicate that substantial thought, planning, and preparatory steps have already been taken, suggesting a higher risk that the threatener will follow through on his threat. Similarly, a lack of detail suggests the threatener may not have thought through all of the contingencies, has not actually taken steps to carry out the threat, and may not seriously intend violence but is "blowing off steam" over some frustration or seeking to frighten or intimidate a particular victim or disrupt a school's events or routine.

Details that are specific but not logical or plausible may indicate a less serious threat. For example, a high school student writes that he intends to detonate hundreds of pounds of plutonium in the school's auditorium the following day at lunch time. The threat is detailed, stating a specific time, place, and weapon. But the details are unpersuasive. Plutonium is almost impossible to obtain, legally or on the black market. It is expensive, hard to transport, and very dangerous to handle, and a complex high explosive detonation is required to set off a nuclear reaction. No high school student is likely to have any plutonium at all, much less hundreds of pounds, nor would he have the knowledge or complex equipment to detonate it. A threat this unrealistic is obviously unlikely to be carried out.

The emotional content of a threat can be an important clue to the threatener's mental state. Emotions are conveyed by melodramatic words and unusual punctuation—"I hate you!!!!!" "You have ruined my life!!!!" "May God have mercy on your soul!!!!"—or in excited, incoherent passages that may refer to God or other religious beings or deliver an ultimatum.

Though emotionally charged threats can tell the assessor something about the temperament of the threatener, they are not a measure of danger. They may sound frightening, but no correlation has been established between the emotional intensity in a threat and the risk that it will be carried out.

Precipitating stressors are incidents, circumstances, reactions, or situations which can trigger a threat. The precipitating event may seem insignificant and have no direct relevance to the threat, but nonetheless becomes a catalyst. For example, a student has a fight with his mother before going to school. The argument may have been a minor one over an issue that had nothing to do with school, but it sets off an emotional chain reaction leading the student to threaten another student at school that day—possibly something he has thought about in the past.

The impact of a precipitating event will obviously depend on *"predisposing factors"*: underlying personality traits, characteristics, and temperament that predispose an adolescent to fantasize about violence or act violently. Accordingly, information about a temporary "trigger" must be considered together with broader information about these underlying factors, such as a student's vulnerability to loss and depression.

Levels of Risk

Low Level of Threat: A threat which poses a minimal risk to the victim and public safety.

- Threat is vague and indirect.
- Information contained within the threat is inconsistent, implausible or lacks detail.
- Threat lacks realism.
- Content of the threat suggests person is unlikely to carry it out.

Medium Level of Threat: A threat which could be carried out, although it may not appear entirely realistic.

- Threat is more direct and more concrete than a low level threat.
- Wording in the threat suggests that the threatener has given some thought to how the act will be carried out.
- There may be a general indication of a possible place and time (though these signs still fall well short of a detailed plan).
- There is no strong indication that the threatener has taken preparatory steps, although there may be some veiled reference or ambiguous or inconclusive evidence pointing to that possibility—an allusion to a book or movie that shows the planning of a violent act, or a vague, general statement about the availability of weapons.
- There may be a specific statement seeking to convey that the threat is not empty: "I'm serious!" or "I really mean this!"

High Level of Threat: A threat that appears to pose an imminent and serious danger to the safety of others.

- Threat is direct, specific and plausible.
- Threat suggests concrete steps have been taken toward carrying it out, for example, statements indicating that the threatener has acquired or practiced with a weapon or has had the victim under surveillance.

Example: ***"At eight o'clock tomorrow morning, I intend to shoot the principal. That's when he is in the office by himself. I have a 9mm. Believe me, I know what I am doing. I am sick and tired of the way he runs this school."*** This threat is direct, specific as to the victim, motivation, weapon, place, and time, and indicates that the threatener knows his target's schedule and has made preparations to act on the threat.

NCAVC's experience in analyzing a wide range of threatening communications suggests that in general, the more direct and detailed a threat is, the more serious the risk of its being acted on. A threat that is assessed as high level will almost always require immediate law enforcement intervention.

In some cases, the distinction between the levels of threat may not be as obvious, and there will be overlap between the categories. Generally, obtaining additional information about either the threat or the threatener will help in clarifying any confusion. What is important is that schools be able to recognize and act on the most serious threats, and then address all other threats appropriately and in a standardized and timely fashion.

Source: O'Toole, M. E. (2000). *The school shooter: A threat assessment perspective.* Washington, D.C.: Federal Bureau of Investigation, 6–9. Retrieved from https://www.fbi.gov/file-repository/stats-services-publications-school-shooter -school-shooter

The Report of Governor Bill Owens' Columbine Review Commission (2001)

In January 2000, then-Colorado governor Bill Owens signed an executive order creating the Columbine Review Commission to conduct an independent review of the April 20, 1999, shooting carried out by two students at Columbine High School, resulting in the deaths of 12 other students and a teacher. The Commission spent more than a year on their investigation before compiling their findings into this report. The report itself not only examines the events on the day of the shooting, but it also offers a series of recommendations related to responding to these tragedies (e.g., crisis response actions, improved communications and advanced planning for critical emergencies, interaction with media representatives, medical treatment for victims, reunification of students with their families, victim identification), tasks for school resource officers, threat assessment of potential offenders prior to action, and dealing with community needs in the aftermath (e.g., suicide prevention).

The following is an excerpt from Part VII: Lessons from Columbine: Preventing School Violence.

A. Introduction

The Governor directed the Commission to identify key factors that might have contributed to the Columbine High School tragedy, in particular with the prevention of similar future incidents in view. In this Part, the Commission focuses on issues associated with violence prevention in schools.

B. Knowledge About the Perpetrators Before the Columbine Attack

A most disturbing aspect of the tragedy at Columbine High School was the fact that many people had pieces of information about perpetrators Harris and Klebold well before they launched their attack, but that information was never acted upon, in part because at the time no protocols or procedures were in place that would have allowed all of the pieces of information to be assembled in one place and evaluated.

C. Knowledge Possessed by the Parents of the Perpetrators and Other Students

The parents of the two Columbine perpetrators must have had inklings that disturbing things were going on, including such suspicious circumstances as the construction and storage of some 90 bombs in the homes of Harris and Klebold, the purchase of weapons by the two, and other evident preparations for an attack.

Students at Columbine High School are not reported to have heard either directly or indirectly from either Harris or Klebold that they were planning an attack at the school. But granted the fact that Harris' website bragged about the bombs the pair had assembled and tested, as well as the fact that the website contents virtually screamed the gunmen's murderous intentions, it would be quite surprising if the two had not given some indication to fellow students, though veiled and indirect, that they were planning a violent incident at the school.

D. The Importance of "Leakage" About Impending Acts of Violence

In the wake of the events at Columbine High School and other instances of school violence, many experts, as well as federal agencies including the Secret Service and the FBI, have studied the phenomenon in an effort to understand it. Expert witnesses before the Commission emphasized that instances of school violence do not occur because students "suddenly snapped," due to a particular incident on a particular day. Instead, school shooters usually give very clear advance indications of their violent intentions, so that school officials and law enforcement agencies are in fact able to prevent violence whenever (1) they have information about such threats; (2) they are able to draw together information about dangerous students from a variety of sources; and (3) the authorities understand how to evaluate the threats. Experts who study school violence refer to this spectrum of direct and indirect communications by perpetrators in advance of an event as "leakage."

E. The Reasons Students Failed to Come Forward Even Though Worried About Violence
(1) *The Code of Silence*
Granted the probability there had been leakage about the attack at Columbine High School before April 20, 1999, one clear issue concerns appropriate responses on the part of education and law enforcement authorities who have acquired troubling evidence, albeit merely indirect evidence, that violence is threatened in or near a school. Before those authorities can address the issue effectively, however, they must devise means to encourage students, who are most likely to know about impending violence, to come forward to disclose their information to school authorities.

Why have students failed to come forward with their information in advance of many instances of school violence before and after Columbine? Often, that reluctance may stem from a student culture that fosters and enforces a code of silence, under which students cannot be seen to "rat" on their fellow students. Students may well not understand that even jokes about violence or indirect threats of violence may be significant. Schools have begun to work to change this code of silence by talking to students about the limits of loyalty to friends.

Another basis for student failures or refusals to report threats of violence is a fear of repercussions should their worries about violence prove groundless. One way to encourage students to report their concerns about potential violence, without their having to worry about repercussions, is to put in place a mechanism through which students may report their concerns or worries anonymously. The Colorado Attorney General has been working to develop a hotline number students can use to report their concerns or worries about student violence to school authorities.

(2) *Youthfulness of Perpetrators of School Violence*
A notable feature about school shooters is their extreme youth—many are only 13, 14 or 15 years old. The Commission stresses the youth of school shooters for several reasons. First, their youth may play a role in the failures of their contemporaries, their parents, or school faculty and staff to identify them before their violent acts. Most adults do not tend to associate aggravated violence, often directed at

multiple targets, with younger adolescents. The perpetrators often appear to be what they are—children—on whose youthful countenances it is difficult to perceive evil. Perhaps such inherited societal perceptions are changing, however, as we become accustomed to seeing on evening television young persons in jail clothing much too large for their slight bodies, handcuffed to police officers who bulk over them in size. The youthfulness of so many perpetrators may help explain the reluctance of people who knew them to take their threats of violence seriously. Students, teachers, staff and parents need to be reminded that school shooters are often quite young.

A second important aspect of the youth of perpetrators is their extreme immaturity. This is not a criticism, but fact. Adults often forget the perpetrators' extreme youth when they endeavor to understand the motivations for school violence. Student-perpetrated violence appears to adults vastly disproportionate to any possible cause or gain. But young perpetrators, almost by definition, lack perspective on both themselves and their acts. Their crimes make no sense to adults because they make no sense to anyone who is not 13, 14, or 15 years old.

A third aspect of the significance of the youth of so many perpetrators of school violence is the difficulty it poses in developing treatment and sanctions designed to deter violence among members of an age group that is emotionally immature. Most mature persons who commit serious crimes try to commit them so as not to be apprehended and sanctioned. Young school shooters, in contrast, do not adopt the same calculus as mature offenders, perhaps because they act on the basis of rage or other extreme emotion, and thus never calculate the consequences of their activity. Even if they do project those consequences, they sometimes intend to kill themselves or to be killed.

Despite the great difficulty adults have in understanding school violence committed by young perpetrators, the Commission nevertheless recommends that school officials continue to work to change the "code of silence" dimension of the prevailing student culture, by emphasizing to students that loyalty to fellow students has its limits, one of which is that statements or conduct carrying with them a possible threat of violence, even an indirect threat, must be reported to school authorities. Students, teachers, administrators and parents also must be reminded that many perpetrators of school violence are quite young. Therefore, threats of violence must not be discounted because a student issuing a threat is young.

The Commission recommends that each school district establish a mechanism like an anonymous telephone line, through which students and others may anonymously report statements or conduct that worries or concerns them. The Commission endorses the efforts of the Colorado Attorney General to develop a hotline number that students and others can use to report threats and other forms of behavior that concern them. Whatever the mechanism for anonymous reporting eventually established in a school district, it is important that students learn of it and be advised of its importance to their safety and the security of school premises.

F. The Relationship Between Bullying and School Violence

The Commission heard conflicting testimony about the significance of bullying and related disciplinary concerns at Columbine High School. The Commission's interest in the matter of bullying rests on the fact that victimization by bullies has been increasingly recognized as an important precursor of school violence. It cannot be said that bullying causes school violence, or even that youthful perpetrators of school violence have all been bullied by other students. Nevertheless, bullying is a risk factor in assessing the potential for school violence, in that many of those who have carried out lethal acts of violence had in fact been taunted and bullied at their schools.

Because bullying is such a pervasive problem in America's schools, and because it has long been a documented dimension of school life, there has been a tendency to minimize its importance or to deny any link between bullying and school violence. Admittedly, most students seem to be able to tolerate a moderate amount of bullying and taunting. But experts on school violence believe that a significant number of students are less able to tolerate bullying and peer rejection than their fellow students, particularly when that bullying becomes intimidation. These students can become seriously depressed as a consequence of harassing treatment by fellow students, which in turn can lead to an internal building-up of smoldering anger and resentment. Lethal results can ensue when that anger and resentment are set within the matrix of societal factors, for example, an entertainment industry that glorifies violence, news coverage that concentrates on sensational violence, the ready availability of weapons, and even the dissemination of Internet diagrams for the construction of explosives and incendiary devices.

It is against this broader background that we are forced to view "school rage." The problem is certainly not confined to the state's and nation's schools, but schools seem unable to obtain needed assistance from state or national sources to help them cope with these broader issues.

In the wake of the Columbine High School tragedy, Congress enacted legislation attempting to control Internet sites that can be accessed for information about construction of explosive and incendiary devices. First Amendment issues aside, such legislation reportedly has been almost completely ineffective, and bomb "recipes flourish on the Internet." As a consequence, information relating to the construction and use of explosive and incendiary devices and firearms is available without restriction to school-age youth as well as adults; school administrators are left to their own resources in addressing the resulting problem, as they are with so many problems generated by contemporary American society.

The task of coping with school rage is rendered even more difficult by the fact that our schools have become larger and larger in both number of students and building capacity. Large schools are generally preferred by state and local governments because of their fiscal advantages in terms of land and construction costs; one large school facility is less expensive to a community than two or three smaller facilities. Nevertheless, recent studies document the fact that a community pays a price for larger schools: Students at large schools tend to feel marginalized and less a part of a school community in comparison to their counterparts in smaller facilities. Still, there are ways to make students feel part of a smaller school community even if they are educated in a larger school facility.

It is clear to the Commission that Colorado's schools operate under substantial pressures in the wake of Columbine to safeguard staff and students against all dangers of violence, and are being treated as responsible for problems that in fact are generated by modern American society and not the schools themselves. Regrettable as that may be, officials responsible to maintain safety and security within the state's and nation's schools have no alternative but to create as effectively as they can a supportive environment in which students are listened to, and encouraged to come forward to articulate their worries and concerns. That is a very difficult task under the best of circumstances, and we do not now function under the best of circumstances.

Accordingly, the Commission endorses the efforts of the Colorado Attorney General to combat school bullying, and recommends that all schools in the state adopt one or more of the bullying-prevention programs that have already been tested and proven effective. It also believes that every school administration should adopt a code of behavior that sets forth clearly the rights and responsibilities of both students and adults within the school community, and should ensure that its code is enforced equably against all violators: students will not voluntarily report bullying or other problems at a school if they feel the school's administrators do not enforce its rules fairly. Finally, the Commission concludes that it is difficult for administrators in large schools to create a supportive atmosphere for students. Therefore, if fiscal and other concerns do not allow for the continuation of smaller schools, communities should explore the use of alternative approaches in larger facilities like schools-within-a-school.

> **Source:** Columbine Review Commission. (2001). *The report of Governor Bill Owens' Columbine Review Commission.* Part VII: Lessons from Columbine: Preventing School Violence. Denver, CO: State of Colorado, 91–102.
> Retrieved from http://trac.state.co.us/Documents/Reports%20and%20Publications /Columbine_2001_Governor_Review_Commission.pdf

President Bush's Weekly Radio Address Following Virginia Tech (2007)

On April 20, 2007, just four days after the shooting at Virginia Tech and on the eighth anniversary of the attack at Columbine High School, President Bush addressed the nation from the Cabinet Room at the White House in Washington, D.C. During his speech, recorded for broadcast nationwide the following day, the president spoke not only about the event and honoring the victims, but also about the directives he had initiated to help address warning signs that had been missed and make institutions of higher education safer for students.

Good morning. This week, the thoughts and prayers of millions of Americans are with the victims of the Virginia Tech attacks. We mourn promising lives cut short, we pray for the wounded, and we send our love to those who are hurting.

The day after the attack, Laura and I attended a memorial service on the campus in Blacksburg. We met with faculty members who lost students and colleagues and shared hugs with grieving moms and dads, including parents who had lost their only child. We offered what words of comfort we could, and we were moved by the solidarity and strength of spirit we found. We wanted everyone at the university to know that this tragedy saddened our entire Nation and that the American people stand with them in an hour of darkness.

We can never fully understand what would cause a student to take the lives of 32 innocent people. What we do know is that this was a deeply troubled young man, and there were many warning signs. Our society continues to wrestle with the question of how to handle individuals whose mental health problems can make them a danger to themselves and to others.

Colleges and State and local officials are now confronting these issues, and the Federal Government will help. I've asked top officials at the Departments of Education, Justice, and Health and Human Services to provide the Virginia Tech community with whatever assistance we can and to participate in a review of the broader questions raised by this tragedy.

I have directed these officials to travel to communities across our Nation to meet with educators, mental health experts, and State and local officials. I have asked the Secretary of Health and Human Services, Mike Leavitt, to summarize what they learn and report back to me with recommendations about how we can help to avoid such tragedies.

This week at Virginia Tech, we saw a glimpse of humanity at its worst, and we also saw humanity at its best. We learned of students who risked their own safety to tend to wounded classmates. We heard of a teacher who used his body to barricade a classroom door and gave his life so his students could escape through windows. And we saw the good people of Blacksburg embrace victims of this tragedy and help their neighbors endure and heal and hope.

That hope was expressed in a letter written by a Virginia Tech graduate shortly after the attack. He wrote: "Today there is pain everywhere in our community and our hearts are troubled. Yet I am certain our university will persevere." He continued, "Evil can never succeed, not while there are men and women like the people of Virginia Tech, who reach every day for success and endeavor for the improvement of the human condition across the planet."

This week, we reflect on what has been lost and comfort those enduring a profound grief. And somehow we know that a brighter morning will come. We know this because together Americans have overcome many evils and found strength through many storms. And we know there will be a day, as promised in Scripture, when evil will meet its reckoning and when every tear shall be wiped away.

May God bless those who mourn, and may God bless our wonderful country. Thank you for listening.

> **Source:** Public Papers of the Presidents of the United States: George W. Bush (2007, Book I). Washington, D.C. Government Printing Office, 2011, 463–464.

Virginia Tech Review Panel Report (2007)

Three days after the April 16, 2007, shooting at Virginia Tech, then-governor Tim Kaine convened a panel of experts to independently review the events of that day and those leading up to the attack. Furthermore, the panel was tasked with assessing the handling of the shootings by the university and its representatives, public safety officials, and emergency service providers, as well as evaluating the services that were provided to survivors, families of the victims, and the community as a whole. Over a five-month period, the panel interviewed over 200 individuals and reviewed thousands of pages of documents relevant to the case. Their final report, delivered to Governor Kaine in August 2007, includes key findings of their inquiry, as well as recommendations for improvements in different areas of response moving forward. Following are several excerpts from the report.

From Chapter II. University Setting and Security.

KEY FINDINGS

The Emergency Response Plan of Virginia Tech was deficient in several respects. It did not include provisions for a shooting scenario and did not place police high enough in the emergency decision-making hierarchy. It also did not include a threat assessment team. And the plan was out of date on April 16; for example, it had the wrong name for the police chief and some other officials.

The protocol for sending an emergency message in use on April 16 was cumbersome, untimely, and problematic when a decision was needed as soon as possible. The police did not have the capability to send an emergency alert message on their own. The police had to await the deliberations of the Policy Group, of which they are not a member, even when minutes count. The Policy Group had to be convened to decide whether to send a message to the university community and to structure its content.

The training of staff and students for emergencies situations at Virginia Tech did not include shooting incidents. A messaging system works more effectively if resident advisors in dormitories, all faculty, and all other staff from janitors to the president have instruction and training for coping with emergencies of all types.

It would have been extremely difficult to "lock down" Virginia Tech. The size of the police force and absence of a guard force, the lack of electronic controls on doors of most buildings other than residence halls, and the many unguarded roadways pose special problems for a large rural or suburban university. The police and security officials consulted in this review did not think the concept of a lockdown, as envisioned for elementary or high schools, was feasible for an institution such as Virginia Tech.

It is critical to alert the entire campus population when there is an imminent danger. There are information technologies available to rapidly send messages to a variety of personal communication devices. Many colleges and universities, including Virginia Tech, are installing such campus-wide alerting systems. Any purchased system must be thoroughly tested to ensure it operates as specified in the purchase contract. Some universities already have had problems with systems purchased since April 16.

An adjunct to a sophisticated communications alert system is a siren or other audible warning device. It can give a quick warning that something is afoot. One can hear such alarms regardless of whether electronics are carried, whether the electronics are turned off, or whether electric power (other than for the siren, which can be self-powered) is available. Upon sounding, every individual is to immediately turn on some communication device or call to receive further instructions. Virginia Tech has installed a system of six audible alerting devices of which four were in place on April 16. Many other colleges and universities have done something similar.

No security cameras were in the dorms or anywhere else on campus on April 16. The outcome might have been different had the perpetrator of the initial homicides been rapidly identified. Cameras may be placed just at entrances to buildings or also in hallways. However, the more cameras, the more intrusion on university life.

Virginia Tech did not have classroom door locks operable from the inside of the room. Whether to add such locks is controversial. They can block entry of an intruder and compartmentalize an attack. Locks can be simple manually operated devices or part of more sophisticated systems that use electromechanical locks operated from a central security point in a building or even university-wide. The locks must be easily opened from the inside to allow escape from a fire or other emergency when that is the safer course of action. While adding locks to classrooms may seem an obvious safety feature, some voiced concern that locks could facilitate rapes or assaults in classrooms and increase university liability. (An attacker could drag someone inside a room at night and lock the door, blocking assistance.) On the other hand, a locked room can be a place of refuge when one is pursued. On balance, the panel generally thought having locks on classroom doors was a good idea.

Shootings at universities are rare events, an average of about 16 a year across 4,000 institutions. Bombings are rarer but still possible. Arson is more common and drunk driving incidents more frequent yet. There are both simple and sophisticated improvements to consider for improving security (besides upgrading the alerting system). A risk analysis needs to be performed and decisions made as to what risks to protect against.

There have been several excellent reviews of campus security by states and individual campuses (for example, the states of Florida and Louisiana, the University of California, and the University of Maryland). The Commonwealth of Virginia held a conference on campus security on August 13, 2007.

The Virginia Tech Police Department (VTPD) and Blacksburg Police Department (BPD) were well-trained and had conducted practical exercises together. They had undergone active shooter training to prepare for the possibility of a multiple victim shooter. The entire police patrol force must be trained in the active shooter protocol, because any officer may be called upon to respond.

It was the strong opinion of groups of Virginia college and university presidents with whom the panel met that the state should not impose required levels of security on all institutions, but rather let the institutions choose what they think is appropriate. Parents and students can and do consider security a factor in making a choice of where to go to school.

Finally, the panel found that the VTPD statement of purpose in the Emergency Response Plan does not reflect that law enforcement is the primary purpose of the police department.

RECOMMENDATIONS

EMERGENCY PLANNING

II-1   *Universities should do a risk analysis (threat assessment) and then choose a level of security appropriate for their campus.*
How far to go in safeguarding campuses, and from which threats, needs to be considered by each institution. Security requirements vary across universities, and each must do its own threat assessment to determine what security measures are appropriate.

II-2   *Virginia Tech should update and enhance its Emergency Response Plan and bring it into compliance with federal and state guidelines.*

II-3   *Virginia Tech and other institutions of higher learning should have a threat assessment team that includes representatives from law enforcement, human resources, student and academic affairs, legal counsel, and mental health functions.* The team should be empowered to take actions such as additional investigation, gathering background information, identification of additional dangerous warning signs, establishing a threat potential risk level (1 to 10) for a case, preparing a case for hearings (for instance, commitment hearings), and disseminating warning information.

II-4   *Students, faculty, and staff should be trained annually about responding to various emergencies and about the notification systems that will be used.* An annual reminder provided as part of registration should be considered.

II-5   *Universities and colleges must comply with the Clery Act, which requires timely public warnings of imminent danger.* "Timely" should be defined clearly in the federal law.

CAMPUS ALERTING

II-6   *Campus emergency communications systems must have multiple means of sharing information.*

II-7   *In an emergency, immediate messages must be sent to the campus community that provide clear information on the nature of the emergency and actions to be taken.* The initial messages should be followed by update messages as more information becomes known.

II-8   *Campus police as well as administration officials should have the authority and capability to send an emergency message.*
Schools without a police department or senior security official must designate someone able to make a quick decision without convening a committee.

POLICE ROLE AND TRAINING

II-9   *The head of campus police should be a member of a threat assessment team as well as the emergency response team for the university.* In some cases where there is a security department but not a police department, the security head may be appropriate.

II-10 *Campus police must report directly to the senior operations officer responsible for emergency decision making.* They should be part of the policy team deciding on emergency planning.

II-11 *Campus police must train for active shooters (as did the Virginia Tech Police Department).* Experience has shown that waiting for a SWAT team often takes too long. The best chance to save lives is often an immediate assault by first responders.

II-12 *The mission statement of campus police should give primacy to their law enforcement and crime prevention role.* They also must to be designated as having a function in education so as to be able to review records of students brought to the attention of the university as potential threats. The lack of emphasis on safety as the first responsibility of the police department may create the wrong mindset, with the police yielding to academic considerations when it comes time to make decisions on, say, whether to send out an alert to the students that may disrupt classes. On the other hand, it is useful to identify the police as being involved in the education role in order for them to gain access to records under educational privacy act provisions. . . .

***

Excerpt from Chapter VII. Double Murder at West Ambler Johnston.

KEY FINDINGS

Generally the VTPD and BPD officers responded to and carried out their investigative duties in a professional manner in accordance with accepted police practices. However, the police conveyed the wrong impression to the university Policy Group about the lead they had and the likelihood that the suspect was no longer on campus.

The police did not have the capability to use the university alerting system to send a warning to the students, staff, and faculty. That is, they were not given the keyword to operate the alerting system themselves, but rather they had to request a message be sent from the Policy Group or at least the associate vice president for University Relations, who did have the keyword. The police did have the authority to request that a message be sent, but did not request that be done. They gave the university administration the information on the incident, and left it to the Policy Group to handle the messaging.

The university administration failed to notify students and staff of a dangerous situation in a timely manner. The first message sent by the university to students could have been sent at least an hour earlier and been more specific.

The university could have notified the Virginia Tech community that two homicides of students had occurred and that the shooter was unknown and still at large. The administration could have advised students and staff to safeguard themselves by staying in residences or other safe places until further notice. They could have advised those not en route to school to stay home, though after 8 a.m. most employees would have been en route to their campus jobs and might not have received the messages in time.

Despite the above findings, there does not seem to be a plausible scenario of university response to the double homicide that could have prevented a tragedy of considerable magnitude on April 16. Cho had started on a mission of fulfilling a fantasy of revenge. He had mailed a package to NBC identifying himself and his rationale and so was committed to act that same day. He could not wait beyond the end of the day or the first classes in the morning. There were many areas to which he could have gone to cause harm.

RECOMMENDATIONS

VII-1   *In the preliminary stages of an investigation, the police should resist focusing on a single theory and communicating that to decision makers.*

VII-2   *All key facts should be included in an alerting message, and it should be disseminated as quickly as possible, with explicit information.*

VII-3   *Recipients of emergency messages should be urged to inform others.*

VII-4   *Universities should have multiple communication systems, including some not dependent on high technology.* Do not assume that 21st century communications may survive an attack or natural disaster or power failure.

VII-5   *Plans for canceling classes or closing the campus should be included in the university's emergency operations plan.* It is not certain that canceling classes and stopping work would have decreased the number of casualties at Virginia Tech on April 16, but those actions may have done so. Lockdowns or cancellation of classes should be considered on campuses where it is feasible to do so rapidly.

***

Excerpt from Chapter VIII. Mass Murder at Norris Hall.

KEY FINDINGS

Overall, the police from Virginia Tech and Blacksburg did an outstanding job in responding quickly and using appropriate active-shooter procedures to advance to the shooter's location and to clear Norris Hall.

The close relationship of the Virginia Tech Police Department and Blacksburg Police Department and their frequent joint training saved critical minutes. They had trained together for an active shooter incident in university buildings. There is little question their actions saved lives. Other campus police and security departments should make sure they have a mutual aid arrangement as good as that of the Virginia Tech Police Department.

Police cannot wait for SWAT teams to arrive and assemble, but must attack an active shooter at once using the first officers arriving on the scene, which was done. The officers entering the building proceeded to the second floor just as the shooting stopped. The sound of the shotgun blast and their arrival on the second floor probably caused Cho to realize that attack by the police was imminent and to take his own life.

Police did a highly commendable job in starting to assist the wounded, and worked closely with the first EMTs on the scene to save lives.

Several faculty members died heroically while trying to protect their students. Many brave students died or were wounded trying to keep the shooter from entering their classrooms. Some barricading doors kept their bodies low or to the side and out of the direct line of fire, which reduced casualties.

Several quick-acting students jumped from the second floor windows to safety, and at least one by dropping himself from the ledge, which reduced the distance to fall. Other students survived by feigning death as the killer searched for victims.

People were evacuated safely from Norris Hall, but the evacuation was not well organized and was frightening to some survivors. However, being frightened is preferable to being injured by a second shooter. The police had their priorities correct, but they might have handled the evacuation with more care.

RECOMMENDATIONS

VIII-1 Campus police everywhere should train with local police departments on response to active shooters and other emergencies.

VIII-2 Dispatchers should be cautious when giving advice or instructions by phone to people in a shooting or facing other threats without knowing the situation. This is a broad recommendation that stems from reviewing other U.S. shooting incidents as well, such as the Columbine High School shootings. For instance, telling someone to stay still when they should flee or flee when they should stay still can result in unnecessary deaths. When in doubt, dispatchers should just be reassuring. They should be careful when asking people to talk into the phone when they may be overheard by a gunman. Also, local law enforcement dispatchers should become familiar with the major campus buildings of colleges and universities in their area.

VIII-3 Police should escort survivors out of buildings, where circumstances and manpower permit.

VIII-4 Schools should check the hardware on exterior doors to ensure that they are not subject to being chained shut.

VIII-5 Take bomb threats seriously. Students and staff should report them immediately, even if most do turn out to be false alarms.

Source: Virginia Tech Review Panel. (2007). *Mass shootings at Virginia Tech April 16, 2007: Report of the review panel.* Arlington, VA: Governor's Office of the Commonwealth of Virginia, 17–20, 86–87, 98–99. Retrieved from http://www .governor.virginia.gov/TempContent/techpanelreport.cfm. Used by permission of the Governor's Office of the Commonwealth of Virginia.

The NICS Improvement Amendments Act of 2007

Following the 2007 shooting at Virginia Tech, which identified gaping loopholes in the national background check system for firearms purchases, then-President Bush signed the NICS Improvement Amendments Act of 2007 into law on January 8, 2008. After identifying that a large number of records similar to that of the Virginia Tech shooter were missing from the NICS, which would have disqualified him and others from purchasing firearms, the act designated nearly $1.3 billion total in federal funding for states to overhaul their existing systems or implement new systems in order to ensure that the NICS had the most up-to-date records about mental health adjudications and commitments. Between the passage of the act and the *shooting at Sandy Hook Elementary School, only about $50 million of these funds were appropriated; another $50 million in awards was granted to states between 2012 and 2016. The Brady Campaign, however, notes that there still are millions of records missing from the system, and in 2015, FBI director James Comey suggested missing information from the system allowed the Charleston church shooter to legally purchase his weapons, though others suggest that there would not have been any disqualifying information on him in the records. On February 2, 2017, the Senate passed a resolution to repeal a rule enacted by the Obama administration that required the Social Security Administration to report mentally impaired individuals to the NICS if they were no longer capable of managing their financial affairs, thereby disqualifying them from being able to legally purchase a firearm.*

SEC. 2. FINDINGS.

Congress finds the following:

(1) Approximately 916,000 individuals were prohibited from purchasing a firearm for failing a background check between November 30, 1998, (the date the National Instant Criminal Background Check System (NICS) began operating) and December 31, 2004.

(2) From November 30, 1998, through December 31, 2004, nearly 49,000,000 Brady background checks were processed through NICS.

(3) Although most Brady background checks are processed through NICS in seconds, many background checks are delayed if the Federal Bureau of Investigation (FBI) does not have automated access to complete information from the States concerning persons prohibited from possessing or receiving a firearm under Federal or State law.

(4) Nearly 21,000,000 criminal records are not accessible by NICS and millions of criminal records are missing critical data, such as arrest dispositions, due to data backlogs.

(5) The primary cause of delay in NICS background checks is the lack of—

(A) updates and available State criminal disposition records; and

(B) automated access to information concerning persons prohibited from possessing or receiving a firearm because of mental illness, restraining orders, or misdemeanor convictions for domestic violence.

(6) Automated access to this information can be improved by—

(A) computerizing information relating to criminal history, criminal dispositions, mental illness, restraining orders, and misdemeanor convictions for domestic violence; or

(B) making such information available to NICS in a usable format.

(7) Helping States to automate these records will reduce delays for law-abiding gun purchasers.

(8) On March 12, 2002, the senseless shooting, which took the lives of a priest and a parishioner at the Our Lady of Peace Church in Lynbrook, New York, brought attention to the need to improve information-sharing that would enable Federal and State law enforcement agencies to conduct a complete background check on a potential firearm purchaser. The man who committed this double murder had a

prior disqualifying mental health commitment and a restraining order against him, but passed a Brady background check because NICS did not have the necessary information to determine that he was ineligible to purchase a firearm under Federal or State law.

(9) On April 16, 2007, a student with a history of mental illness at the Virginia Polytechnic Institute and State University shot to death 32 students and faculty members, wounded 17 more, and then took his own life. The shooting, the deadliest campus shooting in United States history, renewed the need to improve information-sharing that would enable Federal and State law enforcement agencies to conduct complete background checks on potential firearms purchasers. Despite a proven history of mental illness, the shooter could purchase the two firearms used in the shooting. Improved coordination between State and Federal authorities could have ensured that the shooter's disqualifying mental health information was available to NICS.

***

TITLE I—TRANSMITTAL OF RECORDS

SEC. 101. ENHANCEMENT OF REQUIREMENT THAT FEDERAL DEPARTMENTS AND AGENCIES PROVIDE RELEVANT INFORMATION TO THE NATIONAL INSTANT CRIMINAL BACKGROUND CHECK SYSTEM

(a) IN GENERAL.—Section 103(e)(1) of the Brady Handgun Violence Prevention Act (18 U.S.C. 922 note) is amended—

(1) by striking "Notwithstanding" and inserting the following:

(A) IN GENERAL.—Notwithstanding";

(2) by striking "On request" and inserting the following:

"(B) REQUEST OF ATTORNEY GENERAL.—On request";

(3) by striking "furnish such information" and inserting "furnish electronic versions of the information described under subparagraph (A)"; and

(4) by adding at the end the following:

"(C) QUARTERLY SUBMISSION TO ATTORNEY GENERAL.—If a Federal department or agency under subparagraph (A) has any record of any person demonstrating that the person falls within one of the categories described in subsection (g) or (n) of section 922 of title 18, United States Code, the head of such department or agency shall, not less frequently than quarterly, provide the pertinent information contained in such record to the Attorney General.

"(D) INFORMATION UPDATES.—The Federal department or agency, on being made aware that the basis under which a record was made available under subparagraph (A) does not apply, or no longer applies, shall—

"(i) update, correct, modify, or remove the record from any database that the agency maintains and makes available to the Attorney General, in accordance with the rules pertaining to that database; and

"(ii) notify the Attorney General that such basis no longer applies so that the National Instant Criminal Background Check System is kept up to date.

The Attorney General upon receiving notice pursuant to clause (ii) shall ensure that the record in the National Instant Criminal Background Check System is updated, corrected, modified, or removed within 30 days of receipt.

"(E) ANNUAL REPORT.—The Attorney General shall submit an annual report to Congress that describes the compliance of each department or agency with the provisions of this paragraph.".

(b) PROVISION AND MAINTENANCE OF NICS RECORDS.—

(1) DEPARTMENT OF HOMELAND SECURITY.—The Secretary of Homeland Security shall make available to the Attorney General—

(A) records, updated not less than quarterly, which are relevant to a determination of whether a person is disqualified from possessing or receiving a firearm under subsection (g) or (n) of section 922 of title 18, United States Code, for use in background checks performed by the National Instant Criminal Background Check System; and

(B) information regarding all the persons described in subparagraph (A) of this paragraph who have changed their status to a category not identified under section 922(g)(5) of title 18, United States Code, for removal, when applicable, from the National Instant Criminal Background Check System.

(2) DEPARTMENT OF JUSTICE.—The Attorney General shall—

(A) ensure that any information submitted to, or maintained by, the Attorney General under this section is kept accurate and confidential, as required by the laws, regulations, policies, or procedures governing the applicable record system;

(B) provide for the timely removal and destruction of obsolete and erroneous names and information from the National Instant Criminal Background Check System; and

(C) work with States to encourage the development of computer systems, which would permit electronic notification to the Attorney General when—

(i) a court order has been issued, lifted, or otherwise removed by order of the court; or

(ii) a person has been adjudicated as a mental defective or committed to a mental institution.

***

TITLE III—GRANTS TO STATE COURT SYSTEMS FOR THE IMPROVEMENT IN AUTOMATION AND TRANSMITTAL OF DISPOSITION RECORDS

SEC. 301. DISPOSITION RECORDS AUTOMATION AND TRANSMITTAL IMPROVEMENT GRANTS.

(a) GRANTS AUTHORIZED.—From amounts made available to carry out this section, the Attorney General shall make grants to each State, consistent with State plans for the integration, automation, and accessibility of criminal history records, for use by the State court system to improve the automation and transmittal of criminal history dispositions, records relevant to determining whether a person has been convicted of a misdemeanor crime of domestic violence, court orders, and mental health adjudications or commitments, to Federal and State record repositories in accordance with sections 102 and 103 and the National Criminal History Improvement Program.

(b) GRANTS TO INDIAN TRIBES.—Up to 5 percent of the grant funding available under this section may be reserved for Indian tribal governments for use by Indian tribal judicial systems.

(c) USE OF FUNDS.—Amounts granted under this section shall be used by the State court system only—

(1) to carry out, as necessary, assessments of the capabilities of the courts of the State for the automation and transmission of arrest and conviction records, court orders, and mental health adjudications or commitments to Federal and State record repositories; and

(2) to implement policies, systems, and procedures for the automation and transmission of arrest and conviction records, court orders, and mental health adjudications or commitments to Federal and State record repositories.

(d) ELIGIBILITY.—To be eligible to receive a grant under this section, a State shall certify, to the satisfaction of the Attorney General, that the State has implemented a relief from disabilities program in accordance with section 105.

(e) AUTHORIZATION OF APPROPRIATIONS.—There are authorized to be appropriated to the Attorney General to carry out this section $62,500,000 for fiscal year 2009, $125,000,000 for fiscal year 2010, $125,000,000 for fiscal year 2011, $62,500,000 for fiscal year 2012, and $62,500,000 for fiscal year 2013.

Source: NICS Improvement Amendments Act of 2007, H.R. 2640, 110th Cong., 1st Sess. (2007). Retrieved from https://www.uscis.gov/ilink/docView/PUBLAW/ HTML/PUBLAW/0-0-0-38245.html

New York City Police Departments Report *Active Shooter: Recommendations and Analysis for Risk Mitigation* (2012)

After examining active shooter incidents occurring between 1966 and 2010, the New York City Police Department's (NYPD) Counterterrorism Bureau compiled a report offering recommendations to help mitigate the risk of active shooter events. Though the report is geared toward security personnel, the recommendations offered by the NYPD can easily be adapted to any type of establishment that seeks to strengthen its proactive practices against potential active and/or mass shooters. The report also includes the study's methodology and analysis that led to the recommendations, as well as an appendix of attacks that form the basis of the research.

Excerpt from Part II: Recommendations.

The NYPD compiled a list of recommendations to mitigate the risks from active shooter attacks. The NYPD developed these recommendations based on analysis of past active shooter incidents and careful review of previous studies. Unlike other works on active shooter attacks, this guide provides recommendations tailored to building security personnel. The NYPD organized its recommendations into three categories: procedures, systems, and training.

Procedures:

- Conduct a realistic security assessment to determine the facility's vulnerability to an active shooter attack.
- Identify multiple evacuation routes and practice evacuations under varying conditions; post evacuation routes in conspicuous locations throughout the facility; ensure that evacuation routes account for individuals with special needs and disabilities.
- Designate shelter locations with thick walls, solid doors with locks, minimal interior windows, first-aid emergency kits, communication devices, and duress alarms.
- Designate a point-of-contact with knowledge of the facility's security procedures and floor plan to liaise with police and other emergency agencies in the event of an attack.
- Incorporate an active shooter drill into the organization's emergency preparedness procedures.
- Vary security guards' patrols and patterns of operation.
- Limit access to blueprints, floor plans, and other documents containing sensitive security information, but make sure these documents are available to law enforcement responding to an incident.
- Establish a central command station for building security.

Systems:

- Put in place credential-based access control systems that provide accurate attendance reporting, limit unauthorized entry, and do not impede emergency egress.
- Put in place closed-circuit television systems that provide domain awareness of the entire facility and its perimeter; ensure that video feeds are viewable from a central command station.
- Put in place communications infrastructure that allows for facility-wide, real-time messaging.
- Put in place elevator systems that may be controlled or locked down from a central command station.

Training:

- Train building occupants on response options outlined by the Department of Homeland Security in "Active Shooter: How to Respond" when an active shooter is in the vicinity:
  - **Evacuate**: Building occupants should evacuate the facility if safe to do so; evacuees should leave behind their belongings, visualize their entire escape route before beginning to move, and avoid using elevators or escalators.
  - **Hide**: If evacuating the facility is not possible, building occupants should hide in a secure area (preferably a designated shelter location), lock the door, blockade the door with heavy furniture, cover all windows, turn off all lights, silence any electronic devices, lie on the floor, and remain silent.

    o   **Take Action**: If neither evacuating the facility nor seeking shelter is possible, building occupants should attempt to disrupt and/or incapacitate the active shooter by throwing objects, using aggressive force, and yelling.

- Train building occupants to call 911 as soon as it is safe to do so.
- Train building occupants on how to respond when law enforcement arrives on scene: follow all official instructions, remain calm, keep hands empty and visible at all times, and avoid making sudden or alarming movements.

Note: A new version of the Active Shooter report should be published soon, per the New York City Police Department Deputy Commissioner of Public Information Office. In the new edition, "Evacuate, Hide, Take Action" will be replaced with "Avoid, Barricade, Confront":

- **Avoid**
  - Evacuate the building immediately if can be done in a safe manner
  - Do NOT carry any personal belongings with you and avoid elevators if possible
  - When evacuating in a stairwell stay pressed to the wall to allow responding officers room to ascend quickly and safely

- **Barricade**
  - If possible to do safely, move to a central and secure area of the building. Block the door with large heavy objects to make entry as difficult as possible, desk, tables, file cabinets, furniture etc.

- **Confront**
  - If hiding or flight is impossible remain quiet to avoid detection
  - As a last resort attempt to quickly overpower the individual with the most force possible, if you are with others you should work as a group to overcome the shooter

  Source: New York City Police Department. (2012). *Active shooter: Recommendation and analysis for risk mitigation.* New York: New York City Police Department, 2–3. Retrieved from http://www.nypdshield.org/public/SiteFiles /documents/Activeshooter.pdf

President Obama's Remarks on Gun Violence Following Sandy Hook (2013)

On January 16, 2013, just over a month after the 2012 Sandy Hook Elementary School shooting, President Barack Obama addressed the nation from the South Court Auditorium at the White House in Washington, D.C. As a part of his ongoing efforts to address gun violence in the United States, including and beyond mass shootings, the president's remarks accompanied his signing of memorandums to (1) increase research by federal agencies into the causes and prevention of gun violence, (2) improve the availability of records to the National Instant Criminal Background Check System, and (3) strengthen firearms tracing efforts by federal law enforcement agencies.

Thank you. Thank you so much. Thank you, everybody. Please have a seat. Good afternoon, everybody.

Let me begin by thanking our Vice President, Joe Biden, for your dedication, Joe, to this issue, for bringing so many different voices to the table. Because while reducing gun violence is a complicated challenge, protecting our children from harm shouldn't be a divisive one.

Over the month since the tragedy in Newtown, we've heard from so many, and obviously, none have affected us more than the families of those gorgeous children and their teachers and guardians who were lost. And so we're grateful to all of you for taking the time to be here and recognizing that we honor their memories in part by doing everything we can to prevent this from happening again.

But we also heard from some unexpected people. In particular, I started getting a lot of letters from kids. Four of them are here today: Grant Fritz, Julia Stokes, Hinna Zeejah, and Taejah Goode. They're pretty representative of some of the messages that I got. These are some pretty smart letters from some pretty smart young people.

Hinna, a third-grader—you can go ahead and wave, Hinna. Yes, you. [*Laughter*] Hinna wrote: "I feel terrible for the parents who lost their children. . . . I love my country, and I want everybody to be happy and safe."

And then, Grant—go ahead and wave, Grant. [*Laughter*] Grant said: "I think there should be some changes. We should learn from what happened at Sandy Hook. I feel really bad." And then, Julia said—Julia, where are you? There you go. "I'm not scared for my safety, I'm scared for others. I have four brothers and sisters, and I know I would not be able to bear the thought of losing any of them."

These are our kids. This is what they're thinking about. And so what we should be thinking about is our responsibility to care for them and shield them from harm and give them the tools they need to grow up and do everything that they're capable of doing, not just to pursue their own dreams, but to help build this country. This is our first task as a society: keeping our children safe. This is how we will be judged. And their voices should compel us to change.

And that's why, last month, I asked Joe to lead an effort, along with members of my Cabinet, to come up with some concrete steps we can take right now to keep our children safe, to help prevent mass shootings, to reduce the broader epidemic of gun violence in this country.

And we can't put this off any longer. Just last Thursday, as TV networks were covering one of Joe's meetings on this topic, news broke of another school shooting, this one in California. In the month since 20 precious children and 6 brave adults were violently taken from us at Sandy Hook Elementary, more than 900 of our fellow Americans have reportedly died at the end of a gun—900 in the past month. And every day we wait, that number will keep growing.

So I'm putting forward a specific set of proposals based on the work of Joe's task force. And in the days ahead, I intend to use whatever weight this office holds to make them a reality. Because while there is no law or set of laws that can prevent every senseless act of violence completely, no piece of legislation that will prevent every tragedy, every act of evil, if there is even one thing we can do to reduce this violence, if there is even one life that can be saved, then we've got an obligation to try.

And I'm going to do my part. As soon as I'm finished speaking here, I will sit at that desk, and I will sign a directive giving law enforcement, schools, mental health professionals, and the public health community some of the tools they need to help reduce gun violence.

We will make it easier to keep guns out of the hands of criminals by strengthening the background check system. We will help schools hire more resource officers, if they want them, and develop emergency preparedness plans. We will make sure mental health professionals know their options for reporting threats of violence, even as we acknowledge that someone with a mental illness is far more likely to be a victim of violent crime than the perpetrator.

And while year after year, those who oppose even modest gun safety measures have threatened to defund scientific or medical research into the causes of gun violence, I will direct the Centers for Disease Control to go ahead and study the best ways to reduce it. And Congress should fund research into the effects that violent video games have on young minds. We don't benefit from ignorance. We don't benefit from not knowing the science of this epidemic of violence.

Now, these are a few of the 23 executive actions that I'm announcing today. But as important as these steps are, they are in no way a substitute for action from Members of Congress. To make a real and lasting difference, Congress, too, must act, and Congress must act soon. And I'm calling on Congress to pass some very specific proposals right away.

First, it's time for Congress to require a universal background check for anyone trying to buy a gun. The law already requires licensed gun dealers to run background checks, and over the last 14 years, that's kept 1.5 million of the wrong people from getting their hands on a gun. But it's hard to enforce that law when as many as 40 percent of all gun purchases are conducted without a background check. That's not safe. That's not smart. It's not fair to responsible gun buyers or sellers.

If you want to buy a gun—whether it's from a licensed dealer or a private seller—you should at least have to show you are not a felon or somebody legally prohibited from buying one. This is common sense. And an overwhelming majority of Americans agree with us on the need for universal background checks, including more than 70 percent of the National Rifle Association's members, according to one survey. So there's no reason we can't do this.

Second, Congress should restore a ban on military-style assault weapons and a 10-round limit for magazines. The type of assault rifle used in Aurora, for example, when paired with high-capacity magazines, has one purpose: to pump out as many bullets as possible, as quickly as possible; to do as much damage, using bullets often designed to inflict maximum damage.

And that's what allowed the gunman in Aurora to shoot 70 people—70 people—killing 12 in a matter of minutes. Weapons designed for the theater of war have no place in a movie theater. A majority of Americans agree with us on this.

And by the way, so did Ronald Reagan, one of the staunchest defenders of the Second Amendment, who wrote to Congress in 1994, urging them—this is Ronald Reagan speaking—urging them to listen to the American public and to the law enforcement community and support a ban on the further manufacture of military-style assault weapons.

And finally, Congress needs to help, rather than hinder, law enforcement as it does its job. We should get tougher on people who buy guns with the express purpose of turning around and selling them to criminals. And we should severely punish anybody who helps them do this. Since Congress hasn't confirmed a Director of the Bureau of Alcohol, Tobacco and Firearms in 6 years, they should confirm Todd Jones, who will be—who has been Acting, and I will be nominating for the post.

And at a time when budget cuts are forcing many communities to reduce their police force, we should put more cops back on the job and back on our streets.

Now, let me be absolutely clear. Like most Americans, I believe the Second Amendment guarantees an individual right to bear arms. I respect our strong tradition of gun ownership and the rights of hunters and sportsmen. There are millions of responsible, law-abiding gun owners in America who cherish their right to bear arms for hunting or sport or protection or collection.

I also believe most gun owners agree that we can respect the Second Amendment while keeping an irresponsible, law-breaking few from inflicting harm on a massive scale. I believe most of them agree that if America worked harder to keep guns out of the hands of dangerous people, there would be fewer atrocities like the one that occurred in Newtown. That's what these reforms are designed to do. They're commonsense measures. They have the support of the majority of the American people.

And yet that doesn't mean any of this is going to be easy to enact or implement. If it were, we'd already have universal background checks. The ban on assault weapons and high-capacity magazines never would have been allowed to expire. More of our fellow Americans might still be alive, celebrating birthdays and anniversaries and graduations.

This will be difficult. There will be pundits and politicians and special interest lobbyists publicly warning of a tyrannical, all-out assault on liberty, not because that's true, but because they want to gin up fear or higher ratings or revenue for themselves. And behind the scenes, they'll do everything they can to block any commonsense reform and make sure nothing changes whatsoever.

The only way we will be able to change is if their audience, their constituents, their membership says this time must be different, that this time, we must do something to protect our communities and our kids.

I will put everything I've got into this, and so will Joe. But I tell you, the only way we can change is if the American people demand it. And by the way, that doesn't just mean from certain parts of the country. We're going to need voices in those areas, in those congressional districts, where the tradition of gun ownership is strong to speak up and to say this is important. It can't just be the usual suspects. We have to examine ourselves and our hearts and ask ourselves what is important.

This will not happen unless the American people demand it. If parents and teachers, police officers and pastors, if hunters and sportsmen, if responsible gun owners, if Americans of every background stand up and say: "Enough. We've suffered too much pain and care too much about our children to allow this to continue." Then change will come. That's what it's going to take.

In the letter that Julia wrote me, she said, "I know that laws have to be passed by Congress, but I beg you to try very hard." [*Laughter*] Julia, I will try very hard. But she's right: The most important changes we can make depend on congressional action. They need to bring these proposals up for a vote, and the American people need to make sure that they do.

Get them on record. Ask your Member of Congress if they support universal background checks to keep guns out of the wrong hands. Ask them if they support renewing a ban on military-style assault weapons and high-capacity magazines. And if they say no, ask them why not. Ask them what's more important: doing whatever it takes to get a A grade from the gun lobby that funds their campaigns or giving parents some peace of mind when they drop their child off for first grade?

This is the land of the free, and it always will be. As Americans, we are endowed by our Creator with certain inalienable rights that no man or government can take away from us. But we've also long recognized, as our Founders recognized, that with rights come responsibilities. Along with our freedom to live our lives as we will comes an obligation to allow others to do the same. We don't live in isolation. We live in a society, a government of and by and for the people. We are responsible for each other.

The right to worship freely and safely, that right was denied to Sikhs in Oak Creek, Wisconsin. The right to assemble peacefully, that right was denied shoppers in Clackamas, Oregon, and moviegoers in Aurora, Colorado. That most fundamental set of rights to life and liberty and the pursuit of happiness, fundamental rights that were denied to college students at Virginia Tech and high school students at Columbine and elementary school students in Newtown and kids on street corners in Chicago on too frequent a basis to tolerate and all the families who've never imagined that they'd lose a loved one to a bullet, those rights are at stake. We're responsible.

When I visited Newtown last month, I spent some private time with many of the families who lost their children that day. And one was the family of Grace McDonnell. Grace's parents are here. Grace was 7 years old when she was struck down, just a gorgeous, caring, joyful little girl. I'm told she loved pink. She loved the beach. She dreamed of becoming a painter.

And so just before I left, Chris, her father, gave me one of her paintings, and I hung it in my private study just off the Oval Office. And every time I look at that painting, I think about Grace. And I think about the life that she lived and the life that lay ahead of her, and most of all, I think about how, when it comes to protecting the most vulnerable among us, we must act now. For Grace. For the 25 other innocent children and devoted educators who had so much left to give. For the men and women in big cities and small towns who fall victim to senseless violence each and every day. For all the Americans who are counting on us to keep them safe from harm. Let's do the right thing. Let's do the right thing for them and for this country that we love so much.

Thank you. Let's sign these orders . . . [Orders Signed] . . . All right, there we go.

Source: Obama, B. (2013). Remarks on Gun Violence, January 16, 2013. Daily Compilation of Presidential Documents, DCPD-201300018.

U.S. Senate Judiciary Committee Hearing on Gun Violence (2013)

On January 30, 2013, approximately a month and a half after the Sandy Hook Elementary School shootings, the United States Senate Committee on the Judiciary held a hearing asking what America should do about gun violence. Statements from committee members Patrick Leahy (D-UT), Orrin Hatch (R-UT), and Ted Cruz (R-TX) were offered. Five expert witnesses also offered remarks, including Mark Kelly, a retired Navy captain and husband of Congresswoman Gabrielle Giffords, who was shot by a gunman during a mass shooting in 2011 in Tucson, Arizona, and James Johnson, the chief of police for the Baltimore County Police Department. In addition to these testimonies (provided here), comments also were offered by NRA president Wayne LaPierre (provided here), Denver University law professor David Kopel, and Gayle Trotter, an attorney and senior fellow with the Independent Women's Forum in Washington, D.C.

Testimony of Captain Mark Kelly, United States Navy (Ret.) and Americans for Responsible Solutions

As you know, our family has been immeasurably affected by gun violence. Gabby's gift for speech is a distant memory. She struggles to walk, and she is partially blind. Her right arm is completely paralyzed. And a year ago she left a job she loved serving the people of Arizona.

But in the past two years, we have watched Gabby's determination, spirit, and intellect conquer her disabilities.

We aren't here as victims. We're speaking to you today as Americans.

We're a lot like many of our fellow citizens following this debate about gun violence:

- We're moderates. Gabby was a Republican long before she was a Democrat.
- We're both gun owners, and we take that right and the responsibilities that come with it very seriously.
- And we watch with horror when the news breaks to yet another tragic shooting. After 20 kids and six of their teachers were gunned down in their classrooms at Sandy Hook, we said, this time must be different. Something needs to be done.

We are simply two reasonable Americans who realize we have a problem with gun violence, and we need Congress to act.

At 10:10 am on January 8, 2011, a young man walked up to Gabby at her constituent event at a Safeway in Tucson, leveled his gun, and shot her through the head. He then turned down the line and continued firing. In 15 seconds, he emptied his magazine. It contained 33 bullets; there were 33 wounds.

As the shooter attempted to reload, he fumbled. A woman grabbed the next magazine, and others tackled and restrained him.

Gabby was the first victim. Christina-Taylor Green, nine years old, born on 9/11 2001, was shot with the thirteenth bullet or after. And others followed.

The killer in the Tucson shooting suffered from severe mental illness. He is a paranoid schizophrenic who had been deemed unqualified for service in the United States Army and exhibited increasingly bizarre behavior as he spiraled toward murder. At Pima Community College, his disruptions led to run-ins with the campus police and his expulsion, but he was never reported to mental health authorities.

On November 30, 2010, he walked into a sporting goods store, passed a federal NICS background check, and walked out with a Glock 19 semiautomatic handgun. He had never been legally adjudicated as mentally ill, and, even if he had, Arizona at the time had over 121,000 records of disqualifying mental illness it had not submitted to the background check system.

Looking back, we can't say with certainty, "Only if we had done this, it wouldn't have happened." There isn't a single action or law that could have elegantly prevented the Tucson shooting from being written into the history books.

Gabby is one of roughly 100,000 victims of gun violence in America every year. Behind every victim lays a matrix of failure and inadequacy—in our families, communities, and values; in our society's approach to poverty, violence, and mental illness; and, yes, in our politics and in our gun laws.

One of our messages is simple: The breadth and complexity of the problem of gun violence is great, but it is not an excuse for inaction.

As you know, there's another side to our story.

Gabby is a gun owner. I am a gun owner.

We have our firearms for the same reasons millions of Americans just like us have guns—to defend ourselves, our family, and our property, and to go hunting or target shooting.

We believe wholly and completely in the Second Amendment of our Constitution—and that it confers upon all Americans the right to own a firearm for protection, collection, and recreation.

We take that right very seriously, and we would never, ever give it up—just like Gabby would never relinquish her gun, and I would never relinquish mine.

But rights demand responsibility. And this right does not extend to terrorists. It does not extend to criminals. It does not extend to the mentally ill.

When dangerous people get guns, we are all vulnerable—at the local movie theater, worshipping at church, conducting our everyday business, exercising our civic responsibilities as Americans, and—time after time after time—at school, on our campuses, in our children's classrooms.

When dangerous people get dangerous guns, we are all the more vulnerable. Dangerous people with weapons specifically designed to inflict maximum lethality upon others have turned every corner of our society into places of carnage and gross human loss.

Our rights are paramount. But our responsibilities are serious. And as a nation we are not taking responsibility for the gun rights our founders conferred upon us.

Gabby and I are pro–gun ownership. We are anti–gun violence.

And we believe that in this debate Congress should look not toward special interests and ideology, which push us apart, but toward compromise, which brings us together. We believe whether you call yourself pro-gun or anti–gun violence, or both—that you can work together to pass laws that save lives.

We have some ideas for you.

Fix background checks. Currently up to 40 percent of all gun transfers are made through private sales and without background checks. Not surprisingly, 80 percent of criminals reported obtaining their weapons through private sales with no background check. This makes a mockery of our background check system. Congress should close the private sales loophole and strengthen the background check system by requiring states and the federal government to supply the necessary records.

Remove the limitations on the CDC and other public health organizations on collecting data and conducting scientific research on gun violence. As a fighter pilot and astronaut, I saw the value of using data to achieve our military and scientific objectives. We wouldn't have gotten to the Moon or built the International Space Station without robust use of data to make informed decisions. It is simply crazy that we limit gun violence data collection and analysis when we could use that knowledge to save lives.

Enact a federal gun trafficking statute with real penalties for people in the business of helping criminals get guns. Let's get law enforcement the tools they need to stop violent criminals from killing people with illegal guns.

And, finally, let's have a careful and civil conversation about the lethality of the firearms we permit to be legally bought and sold. You can't just walk into a store and buy a machine gun, but you can easily buy a semiautomatic high velocity assault rifle and/or high capacity ammunition magazines. We should come together and decide where to draw that line in such a way that it protects our rights and communities alike.

This country and this Congress can find a commonsense consensus on preventing gun violence and protecting our inviolable Second Amendment rights. We went to the Moon and back within a decade of deciding we were going to do it. We have prevailed over adversaries big and small. Surely when the safety of our communities, our schools, and our children is at stake, our politics can provide a path toward compromise, and not an obstacle that can't be overcome.

Thank you.

***

Testimony of Wayne LaPierre, executive vice president of the National Rifle Association (NRA)

Mr. Chairman and Members of the Committee:

It's an honor to be here today on behalf of more than 4.5 million moms and dads and sons and daughters, in every state across our nation, who make up the National Rifle Association of America. Those 4.5 million active members are joined by tens of millions of NRA supporters.

And it's on behalf of those millions of decent, hardworking, law-abiding citizens . . . to give voice to their concerns . . . that I'm here today. The title of today's hearing is "What should America do about gun violence?"

We believe the answer to that question is to be honest about what works—and what doesn't work.

Teaching safe and responsible gun ownership works—and the NRA has a long and proud history of teaching it.

Our "Eddie Eagle" children's safety program has taught over 25 million young children that if they see a gun, they should do four things: "Stop. Don't touch. Leave the area. Tell an adult." As a result of this and other private sector programs, fatal firearm accidents are at the lowest levels in more than 100 years.[1]

The NRA has over 80,000 certified instructors who teach our military personnel, law enforcement officers and hundreds of thousands of other American men and women how to safely use firearms. We do more—and spend more—than anyone else on teaching safe and responsible gun ownership.

We joined the nation in sorrow over the tragedy that occurred in Newtown, Connecticut. There is nothing more precious than our children. We have no more sacred duty than to protect our children and keep them safe. That's why we asked former Congressman and Undersecretary of Homeland Security, Asa Hutchison, to bring in every expert available to develop a model School Shield Program—one that can be individually tailored to make our schools as safe as possible.

It's time to throw an immediate blanket of security around our children. About a third of our schools have armed security already—because it works.[2] And that number is growing. Right now, state officials, local authorities and school districts in all 50 states are considering their own plans to protect children in their schools.

In addition, we need to enforce the thousands of gun laws that are currently on the books. Prosecuting criminals who misuse firearms works. Unfortunately, we've seen a dramatic collapse in federal gun prosecutions in recent years. Overall in 2011, federal weapons prosecutions per capita were down 35 percent from their peak in the previous administration.[3] That means violent felons, gang members and the mentally ill who possess firearms are not being prosecuted. And that's unacceptable.

And out of more than 76,000 firearms purchases denied by the federal instant check system, only 62 were referred for prosecution and only 44 were actually prosecuted.[4] Proposing more gun control laws—while failing to enforce the thousands we already have—is not a serious solution to reducing crime.

---

[1] Pre-1981 data from National Safety Council, Accident Facts (annual); 1981 forward from Centers for Disease Control and Prevention, available at http://www.cdc.gov/injury/wisqars/fatal_injury_reports .html.

[2] Gary Fields et al., "NRA Calls for Arms in School," *Wall Street Journal*, Dec. 22, 2012, available at http://online.wsj.com/article/SB10001424127887324461604578193364201364432.html

[3] Calculated from U.S. Department of Justice data available through Transactional Records Access Clearinghouse, http://tracfed.syr.edu

[4] Ronald J. Frandsen, "Enforcement of the Brady Act, 2010: Federal and State Investigations and Prosecutions of Firearm Applicants Denied by a NICS Check in 2010," available at https://www .ncjrs.gov/pdffiles1/bjs/grants/239272.pdf

I think we can also agree that our mental health system is broken. We need to look at the full range of mental health issues, from early detection and treatment, to civil commitment laws, to privacy laws that needlessly prevent mental health records from being included in the National Instant Criminal Background Check System.

While we're ready to participate in a meaningful effort to solve these pressing problems, we must respectfully—but honestly and firmly—disagree with some members of this committee, many in the media, and all of the gun control groups on what will keep our kids and our streets safe.

Law-abiding gun owners will not accept blame for the acts of violent or deranged criminals. Nor do we believe the government should dictate what we can lawfully own and use to protect our families.

As I said earlier, we need to be honest about what works and what does not work. Proposals that would only serve to burden the law-abiding have failed in the past and will fail in the future.

Semiautomatic firearms have been around for over 100 years. They are among the most popular guns made for hunting, target shooting and self-defense. Despite this fact, Congress banned the manufacture and sale of hundreds of semiautomatic firearms and magazines from 1994 to 2004. Independent studies, including a study from the Clinton Justice Department, proved that ban had no impact on lowering crime.[5]

And when it comes to the issue of background checks, let's be honest—background checks will never be "universal"—because criminals will never submit to them.

But there are things that can be done and we ask you to join with us. The NRA is made up of millions of Americans who support what works . . . the immediate protection for all—not just some—of our schoolchildren; swift, certain prosecution of criminals with guns; and fixing our broken mental health system.

We love our families and our country. We believe in our freedom. We're the millions of Americans from all walks of life who take responsibility for our own safety and protection as a God-given, fundamental right.

Mr. Chairman and members of the Committee, I thank you for your time and consideration.

***

Testimony of James Johnson, Baltimore County Police Department chief and chair of the National Law Enforcement Partnership to Prevent Gun Violence

Mr. Chairman, Ranking Member, and Members of the Committee, I want to thank you for the opportunity to testify today. I am here on behalf of the National Law Enforcement Partnership to Prevent Gun Violence, an alliance of the nation's

---

[5] Jeffrey A. Roth & Christopher S. Koper, "Impact Evaluation of the Public Safety and Recreational Firearms Use Protection Act of 1994" (1997), available at http://www.sas.upenn.edu/jerrylee/research/aw_ban.htm

law enforcement leadership organizations concerned about the unacceptable level of gun violence in the United States.

The Partnership, founded in 2010, includes: the Commission on Accreditation of Law Enforcement Agencies; Hispanic American Police Command Officers Association; International Association of Campus Law Enforcement Administrators; International Association of Chiefs of Police; Major Cities Chiefs Association; National Association of Women Law Enforcement Executives; National Organization of Black Law Enforcement Executives; Police Executive Research Forum; and the Police Foundation.

We mourn those lost to gun violence, including the 20 children in Newtown, along with the six brave adults whose lives were cut short by a deranged individual armed with firepower originally designed for combat, not for gunning down innocent members of our communities.

More than 30 homicides occur in America each day. Two thousand children, ages 18 and under, die of firearm-related deaths in the U.S. every year. In 2011, for the first time in 14 years, firearms were the leading cause of death for police officers killed in the line of duty. In just the two-week period after the Newtown massacre, six police officers were killed and 10 injured in 12 separate shootings.

In a one-week period in 2011, the Police Executive Research Forum (PERF) found that gun crime in six cities cost more than $38 million, and in the year 2010 cost the entire country more than $57 billion.

We urgently need Congress to address the rising epidemic of gun violence. Law enforcement leaders support the President's comprehensive approach, which includes enhancing safety at educational institutions and addressing mental health issues. But on behalf of my colleagues across the nation, I am here today to tell you that we are long overdue in strengthening our nation's gun laws. Doing so must be a priority for Congress.

The organizations in the National Law Enforcement Partnership to Prevent Gun Violence are united in urgently calling on Congress to:

- Require background checks for all firearm purchasers;
- Ensure that prohibited purchaser records in the National Instant Criminal Background Check System (NICS) are up-to-date and accurate; and
- Limit high capacity ammunition feeding devices to ten rounds.

Seven of our nine groups, including the largest organizations among us, also support a ban on 2 assault weapons and Senator Feinstein's legislation.

Federal law prohibits dangerous individuals, such as convicted felons and those with mental health disqualifiers, from possessing firearms. While background checks are required for purchases through federally licensed gun dealers, no check is required for private sales, such as those through Internet postings, print ads or gun shows.

From November 2011 to November 2012, an estimated 6.6 million firearm transactions occurred without a background check. Up to 40 percent of firearm transactions occur through private individuals rather than licensed gun dealers.

Allowing 40 percent of those acquiring guns to bypass background checks is like allowing 40 percent of airline passengers to board a plane without going through airport security.

Last October, in Brookfield, Wisconsin, seven women were shot by a prohibited purchaser who was under a domestic violence restraining order. The shooter answered an online ad and was able to buy a gun without a background check. Had the sale required a check, this tragedy could have been prevented.

Background checks work. They stopped nearly 2 million prohibited purchases between 1994 and 2009. We already have a national background check system in place. Therefore, extending background checks to all firearm purchasers can easily be implemented—and should be, without delay.

States can't do it alone. Interstate firearms trafficking is a serious problem that must be addressed federally. The problem is rampant: According to the ATF, in 2009, 30 percent of guns recovered at crime scenes had crossed state lines.

Submissions to NICS must be improved, especially mental health and drug abuse records. The 2007 massacre at Virginia Tech is a tragic example of a prohibited purchaser slipping between the cracks due to incomplete NICS records.

The ban on assault weapons and high-capacity ammunition magazines must be reinstated. Like assault weapons, high-capacity magazines are not used for hunting, do not belong in our homes and wreak havoc in our communities. Banning these magazines will reduce the number of bullets a shooter can use before having to reload. Reloading can provide a window of time in which to take down a shooter, as we saw in Tucson.

In 1998, four years after the assault weapons and high-capacity ammunition magazine ban was enacted, the percentage of firearms with large-capacity magazines recovered by Virginia police decreased and continued to drop until it hit a low of 9 percent in 2004, the year the ban expired. It hit a high of 20 percent in 2010, according to a *Washington Post* analysis.

After the 1994 law expired, 37 percent of police agencies saw increases in criminals' use of assault weapons, according to a 2010 PERF survey.

I have been in law enforcement for nearly 35 years, and have seen an explosion in firepower since the assault weapons ban expired. It is common to find many shell casings at crime scenes these days, as victims are being riddled with multiple gunshots.

The common-sense measures we are calling for will not infringe on Second Amendment rights, but will ensure that we keep guns out of dangerous hands and excessive firepower out of our communities.

Generations of Americans, including our youngest ones, are depending on you to ensure they will grow up and fulfill their roles in the great human experience. None of us can fail them. I urge you to follow the will of the American public and stand with law enforcement to enact these common-sense public safety measures.

Thank you.

Source: United States Senate Committee on the Judiciary. (2013). *What should America do about gun violence?* Retrieved from https://www.judiciary.senate.gov /meetings/what-should-america-do-about-gun-violence

Federal Bureau of Investigation's Study of Active Shooter Incidents (2014)

Following the passage of the Investigative Assistance for Violent Crimes Act of 2012 (H.R. 2076) on January 14, 2013—one month after the shooting at Sandy Hook Elementary School—the FBI conducted a study of 160 active shooter incidents occurring between 2000 and 2013. The term "active shooter" refers to an incident where a shooting is in progress. This differs from other types of events, including a mass shooting, that typically relate to categorizing attacks after the fact. The information collected in the FBI report can be used to inform law enforcement practices in respect to how they respond to such events, as well as how they can prevent such incidents, plan for potential attacks, and address recovery in the aftermath should one take place.

The FBI initiated this study to add to the resources available to law enforcement and others who must consider their best course of action to prepare for, respond to, and recover from active shooter incidents. Using the same criteria over a 14-year span, the FBI sought to determine whether the number of active shooter incidents had changed, concluding the trend over the study period showed a steady rise. In the first half of the years studied, the average annual number of incidents was 6.4, but that average rose in the second half of the study to 16.4, an average of more than one incident per month.

Of the 160 incidents studied, 64 (40.0%) would have met the criteria to fall under the federal statute passed in 2012 which defines mass killing as three or more killed in a single incident. Of the 64, 39 of these mass killings occurred within the final 7 years studied.

Study results also indicate that, of the 11 defined location categories, the majority of incidents—45.6% of the 160—occurred in an environment related to commerce. The second most common incident locations were in educational environments (24.4%), and the study results established that some of these incidents involved some of the highest casualty numbers.

Study results provided added clarity on instances where law enforcement appeared to be most at risk when responding to the scene. For example, though law enforcement responded to a large number of school incidents, no law enforcement officers were killed or wounded when responding to a school incident. However, in 45 of the 160 incidents where law enforcement did engage a shooter, law enforcement suffered casualties in 21 (46.7%) of the incidents, resulting in 9 officers killed and 28 wounded.

Significantly, 10 of the officers were wounded in gunfights categorized as occurring in open spaces where the shooters were moving through streets and between buildings. In addition, 3 of the officers were wounded on military property, and another 3 were killed and 9 wounded in gunfights on other government properties. Based on these study results, therefore, the FBI will no longer use the term "confined" as part of the "active shooter" definition.

Though this study did not focus on the motivation of the shooters, the study did identify some shooter characteristics. In all but 2 of the incidents, the shooter chose to act alone. Only 6 female shooters were identified. Shooter ages as a whole showed no pattern. However, some patterns were seen in incident sub-groups. For example, 12 of 14 shooters in high school shootings were students at the schools, and 5 of the 6 shooters at middle schools were students at the schools.

In addition, research results identified some location categories where victim targets were more readily identifiable, in part because of the shooters' connections to the locations. For example, in businesses generally closed to pedestrian traffic, 22 of the 23 shooters were employees or former employees of the involved company. In other instances, the location category appeared less significant than the victims targeted. For example, in 15 (9.3%) of the 160 incidents, the shooter targeted family members. And in 15 (9.3%) of the 160 incidents, the shooter targeted his current, estranged, or former spouse or his current or former girlfriend.

This study helps clarify the environment with regard to both the level of risk citizens face and the speed with which active shooter incidents occur. A majority of the 160 incidents (90 [56.3%]) ended on the shooter's initiative before the police arrived—sometimes when the shooter committed suicide or stopped shooting, and other times when the shooter fled the scene. In 63 incidents where the duration of the incident could be ascertained, 44 (69.8%) of 63 incidents ended in 5 minutes or less, with 23 ending in 2 minutes or less.

The study identified 21 (13.1%) of 160 incidents where unarmed citizens made the selfless and deeply personal choices to face the danger of an active shooter. In those instances, the citizens safely and successfully disrupted the shootings. In 11 of those 21 incidents, unarmed principals, teachers, other school staff and students confronted the shooters to end the threat. In 10 incidents, citizens, working or shopping when the shootings began, successfully restrained shooters until police could arrive. And in 6 other incidents, armed off-duty police officers, citizens, and security guards risked their lives to successfully end the threat. These actions likely saved the lives of students and others present.

Recognizing the increased active shooter threat and the swiftness with which active shooter incidents unfold, these study results support the importance of training and exercises—not only for law enforcement but also for citizens. It is important, too, that training and exercises include not only an understanding of the threats faced but also the risks and options available in active shooter incidents.

Finally, the FBI recognizes that seeking to avoid these tragedies is clearly the best result. The FBI remains dedicated to supporting prevention efforts within all communities affected by these tragedies. As the FBI continues to study the active shooter phenomenon, the Bureau remains committed to assist state, local, tribal, and campus law enforcement in developing better prevention, response, and recovery practices involving active shooter incidents.

> **Source:** Blair, J. P., & Schweit, K. W. (2014). *A study of active shooter incidents, 2000–2013*. Washington, D.C.: Federal Bureau of Investigation. https://www.fbi .gov/file-repository/active-shooter-study-2000-2013-1.pdf/view

Final Report of the Sandy Hook Advisory Commission (2015)

The Sandy Hook Advisory Commission was convened by Connecticut governor Dannel P. Malloy shortly after the 2012 shooting at Sandy Hook Elementary

School. The commission—which was comprised of 16 experts in various fields, including education, law enforcement, mental health, and public policy—spent two years examining laws, policies, and practices that were in place on the day of the shooting. Their mission was not necessarily to explain why the shooter had committed the attack, but rather to understand shortfalls in security and other systems that had allowed the event to happen in order to remedy such issues so as to prevent future similar tragedies. Three key areas were the focus of the inquiry— safe school design and operation; law enforcement, public safety, and emergency response; and mental health/mental wellness. Based on the information collected, the commission made a number of recommendations within these key areas that not only are applicable to the Newtown community or even the state of Connecticut, but to communities across the nation.

Excerpt from Part I: Findings and Recommendations of the Safe School Design and Operations Writing Group, as Adopted and Approved by the Full Commission.

III. RECOMMENDATIONS

The Commission's Interim Report included twenty-two (22) recommendations addressing safe school design and human resource emergency preparedness. As previously noted, virtually all those recommendations were acknowledged and adopted in P.A. 13-3, the Report of the School Safety Infrastructure Council and/ or the School Security and Safety Plan Standards.

The Commission's work did not end, however, with the issuance of the Interim Report. The Commission continued to hear testimony on all issues within the scope of its mission, including SSDO. Considering that testimony, and having considered P.A. 13-3 and the work of the commissions and task forces that it established, the Commission makes the following additional recommendations:

RECOMMENDATION NO. 1: The SSIC Report includes a standard requiring classroom and other safe-haven areas to have doors that can be locked from the inside. The Commission cannot emphasize enough the importance of this recommendation. *The testimony and other evidence presented to the Commission reveals that there has never been an event in which an active shooter breached a locked classroom door.* Accordingly, the Commission reiterates its recommendation that all classrooms in K–12 schools should be equipped with locked doors that can be locked from the inside by the classroom teacher or *substitute*.

RECOMMENDATION NO. 2: The Commission also reiterates its recommendation that all exterior doors in K–12 schools be equipped with hardware capable of implementing a full perimeter lockdown.

RECOMMENDATION NO. 3: A feasibility study should be conducted to develop additional safety standards concerning the issuance of classroom keys to substitute teachers.

The Commission makes this recommendation due to the absence of standardized school district policies regarding the issuance of classroom keys to substitute teachers. Testimony provided to the Commission confirms that the lack of such policies remains a national problem even after the Sandy Hook tragedy. The Commission recommends the development of realistic, manageable and secure approach to key access and control to ensure that all teachers charged with the well-being of students can lock their assigned classroom doors, but also to address the overall need for maintaining strict building security requirements. The management of classroom access control should be determined not only through the lens of new locking hardware, but also by examining the control and issuance of keys within all K–12 schools. The logistics behind the monitor, control, and record keeping of classroom keys will be instrumental for improving school security plans moving forward.

RECOMMENDATION NO. 4: School custodians should be included as members of school security and safety committees. Custodians have a wealth of knowledge and experience to share about the physical school building and grounds. Accordingly, the Commission requests that the Governor submit the following recommendation for consideration by the General Assembly during the 2015 legislative session:

Section 10-222m of the general statutes is repealed and the following is substituted in lieu thereof (*Effective from passage*):

(a) For the school year commencing July 1, 2014, and each school year thereafter, each local and regional board of education shall develop and implement a school security and safety plan for each school under the jurisdiction of such board. Such plans shall be based on the school security and safety plan standards developed by the Department of Emergency Services and Public Protection, pursuant to section 86 of this act. Each local and regional board of education shall annually review and update, if necessary, such plans.

(b) For the school year commencing July 1, 2014, and each school year thereafter, each local and regional board of education shall establish a school security and safety committee at each school under the jurisdiction of such board. The school security and safety committee shall be responsible for assisting in the development of the school security and safety plan for the school and administering such plan. Such school security and safety committee shall consist of: **(1)** a local police officer;, **(2)** a local first responder;, **(3)** a teacher **employed at the school, selected with the consent and approval of other school or district employees of that classification**; and **(4)** an administrator **employed at the school, selected with the consent and approval of other school or district employees of that classification**; **(5) a custodian** employed at the school, **selected with the consent and approval of other school or district employees of that classification; (6) the school facilities managers; (7)** a mental health professional, as defined in section 10-76t of the general statutes; **(8)** a parent or guardian of a student enrolled in the school; and any other person the board of education deems necessary. Any parent or guardian serving as a member of a school security and safety committee shall not have access to any information reported to such committee, pursuant to subparagraph (c) of subdivision (2) of subsection (c) of section 10-222k of the general statutes, as amended by this act.

(c) Each local and regional board of education shall annually submit the school security and safety plan for each school under the jurisdiction of such board, developed pursuant to subsection of this section, to the Department of Emergency Services and Public Protection.

(d) In furtherance of this recommendation, the Commission also recommends that the School Security and Safety Plan Standards and Template should be changed so that school districts realize the importance of placing custodians on these vital committees.

RECOMMENDATION NO. 5: Teachers, administrators and custodians should be appointed to school security and safety committees with the consent and approval of other employees of their same classification. The Commission believes that committee members so appointed may be more empowered to voice their concerns. Accordingly, the Commission recommends the following:

Section 10-222m of the general statutes is repealed and the following is substituted in lieu thereof (*Effective from passage*):

(a) For the school year commencing July 1, 2014, and each school year thereafter, each local and regional board of education shall develop and implement a school security and safety plan for each school under the jurisdiction of such board. Such plans shall be based on the school security and safety plan standards developed by the Department of Emergency Services and Public Protection, pursuant to section 86 of this act. Each local and regional board of education shall annually review and update, if necessary, such plans.

(b) For the school year commencing July 1, 2014, and each school year thereafter, each local and regional board of education shall establish a school security and safety committee at each school under the jurisdiction of such board. The school security and safety committee shall be responsible for assisting in the development of the school security and safety plan for the school and administering such plan. Such school security and safety committee shall consist of: **(1)** a local police officer; **(2)** a local first responder; **(3)** a teacher **employed at the school, selected with the consent and approval of other school or district employees of that classification**; and **(4)** an administrator **employed at the school, selected with the consent and approval of other school or district employees of that classification**; **(5) a custodian** employed at the school**, selected with the consent and approval of other school or district employees of that classification; (6) the school facilities managers; (7)** a mental health professional, as defined in section 10-76t of the general statutes; **(8)** a parent or guardian of a student enrolled in the school; and any other person the board of education deems necessary. Any parent or guardian serving as a member of a school security and safety committee shall not have access to any information reported to such committee, pursuant to subparagraph (c) of subdivision (2) of subsection (c) of section 10-222k of the general statutes, as amended by this act.

(c) Each local and regional board of education shall annually submit the school security and safety plan for each school under the jurisdiction of such board, developed pursuant to subsection (a) of this section, to the Department of Emergency Services and Public Protection.

RECOMMENDATION NO. 6: Consistent with the guiding principle that the successful implementation of SSDO standards and strategies requires—local champions, ‖ as described previously at p. 31**,** the Commission recommends that the State require each school district to create a permanent committee or commission, the purpose of which shall be to ensure SSDO standards and strategies are implemented in the district. The Commission suggests that the committee consist of the following persons: 1) one person selected by the Superintendent of Schools; 2) one person selected by the local chief of police; 3) one person selected by the local fire chief; 4) one person selected by local EMS; 5) one person selected to represent local public health and safety; and 6) one mental/behavioral health professional.

Additionally, the State should designate an individual at the state Commissioner-level, such as the Commissioner of Education or Commission of the Department of Emergency Services and Public Protection, to whom the local committee shall be required to submit a written status report on or before December 31 of each year.

RECOMMENDATION NO. 7: The State should amend section 80 (a) of P.A. 13-3 to include an architect licensed in the State of Connecticut among the members of the School Safety Infrastructure Council. Therefore, the Commission requests that the Governor submit this recommendation for consideration by the General Assembly during the 2015 legislative session.

RECOMMENDATION NO. 8: The State should amend section 80(b) of P.A. 13-3 as follows:

> The School Safety Infrastructure Council shall develop school safety infrastructure standards for school building projects under chapter 173 of the general statutes and projects receiving reimbursement as part of the school security infrastructure competitive grant program, pursuant to section 84 of this act. Such school safety infrastructure standards shall conform to Connecticut and national industry best practice standards for school building safety infrastructure and shall include, but not be limited to, standards regarding ~~(1) entryways to school buildings and classrooms, such as, reinforcement of entryways, ballistic glass, solid core doors, double door access, computer-controlled electronic locks, remote locks on all entrance and exits and buzzer systems~~ (1) entryways to school buildings, classrooms and other space that can become areas of safe haven, such as, reinforcement of entryways, forced entry and/or ballistic rated glazing, solid core (FE and/or BR) doors, double door access, computer-controlled electronic locks, remotely controlled locks on all entrance and exits and buzzer systems, (2) the use of cameras throughout the school building and at all entrances and exits, including the use of closed-circuit television monitoring, (3) penetration resistant vestibules, and (4) other security infrastructure improvements and devices as they become industry standards. The council shall meet at least

annually to review and update, if necessary, the school safety infrastructure standards and make such standards available to local and regional boards of education.

Therefore, the Commission requests that the Governor submit this recommendation for consideration by the General Assembly during the 2015 legislative session.

RECOMMENDATION NO. 9: Each school shall maintain an accurate list of faculty, staff and students, complete with emergency contact information, which shall include, but not be limited to, parents and guardians of students. This information shall be kept at two locations within each school known by appropriate school staff and the emergency response teams for that school.

RECOMMENDATION NO. 10: Each school shall provide safety and security training for faculty, staff and students on how to respond to hazards and/or events to provide competent compliance with the All Hazards School Security and Safety Plan Standards. This training shall include live exercises to test the efficacy of the training program and to provide a means to develop that program as informed by these exercises. These training programs and exercises shall also include the identification and use of rendezvous points, escape routes, location of safe havens, the means of emergency communication and the role of faculty, staff, emergency responders, etc. These training and exercise programs may benefit from the participation of parents as part of post-event response and recovery operations as determined by each school and school district in accordance with their incident response plans.

RECOMMENDATION NO. 11: The Commission recommends that each school identify specific individuals to serve as safety and security wardens, who shall be responsible for executing and managing the safety and security strategies set forth in Recommendation No. 10.

RECOMMENDATION NO. 12: In the design of schools, the Commission recommends that classrooms and other spaces of denser population occupancy be located away from the points of building entry and that spaces of lesser occupancy be adjacent to school entry points, without giving up human visual surveillance and situational awareness of the entry points.

> **Source:** Sandy Hook Advisory Commission. (2015). *Final report of the Sandy Hook Advisory Committee*. Hartford, CT: Sandy Hook Advisory Committee, 32–38. Retrieved from http://www.shac.ct.gov/SHAC_Final_Report_3-6-2015.pdf

Recommended Readings

The following resource list is a compilation of key works in the research areas of school and mass shootings. Though not an exhaustive inventory of the existing literature, the works listed here will provide students with a strong foundation from which to understand specific events and the broader phenomenon as a whole.

BOOKS

Blair, J. P., Nichols, T., Burns, D., & Curnett, J. (2013). *Active shooter events and response*. Boca Raton, FL: CRC Press.

Brown, B., & Merritt, R. (2002). *No easy answers: The truth behind death at Columbine*. New York: Lantern Books.

Cullen, D. (2009). *Columbine*. New York: Twelve.

Fast, J. (2008). *Ceremonial violence: A psychological explanation of school shootings*. New York: Overlook Press.

Fox, J. A., Levin, J., & Fridel, E. E. (2018). *Extreme killing: Understanding serial and mass murder* (4th ed.). Thousand Oaks, CA: Sage Publications.

Gimpel, D. M. (2012). *Columbine shootings*. Minneapolis, MN: ABDO Publishing.

Kellner, D. (2008). *Guys and guns amok: Domestic terrorism and school shootings from the Oklahoma City bombing to the Virginia Tech massacre*. Boulder, CO: Paradigm Publishers.

Klarevas, L. (2016). *Rampage nation: Securing America from mass shootings*. Amherst, NY: Prometheus Books.

Klein, J. (2013). *The bully society: School shootings and the crisis of bullying in America's schools*. New York: New York University Press.

Langman, P. (2010). *Why kids kill: Inside the minds of school shooters*. New York: St. Martin's Press.

Langman, P. (2015). *School shooters: Understanding high school, college, and adult perpetrators*. Lanham, MD: Rowman & Littlefield.

Larkin, R. W. (2007). *Comprehending Columbine*. Philadelphia, PA: Temple University Press.

Lavergne, G. M. (1997). *A sniper in town: The Charles Whitman mass murders*. Denton: University of North Texas Press.

Lebrun, M. (2009). *Books, blackboards, and bullets: School shootings and violence in America*. Lanham, MD: Rowman & Littlefield.

Lysiak, M. (2014). *Newtown: An American tragedy*. New York: Gallery Books.

Madfis, E. (2014). *The risk of school rampage: Assessing and preventing threats of school violence.* New York: Palgrave Pivot.

McCluskey, M. (2017). *News framing of school shootings: Journalism and American social problems.* Lanham, MD: Lexington Books.

Newman, K. S., Fox, C., Harding, D. J., Mehta, J., & Roth, W. (2004). *Rampage: The social roots of school shootings.* New York: Basic Books.

Ownings, L. (2014). *The Newtown school shooting.* Minneapolis, MN: ABDO.

Roy, L. (2009). *No right to remain silent: What we've learned from the tragedy at Virginia Tech.* New York: Three Rivers Press.

Schildkraut, J., & Elsass, H. J. (2016). *Mass shootings: Media, myths, and realities.* Santa Barbara, CA: Praeger.

Vann, D. (2013). *Last day on Earth: Portrait of the NIU school shooter.* Athens: University of Georgia Press.

EDITED BOOKS[*]

Agger, B., & Luke, T. W. (eds.). (2008). *There is a gunman on campus: Tragedy and terror at Virginia Tech.* Lanham, MD: Rowman & Littlefield.

Böckler, N., Seeger, T., Sitzer, P., & Heitmeyer, W. (eds.). (2013). *School shootings: International research, case studies, and concepts for prevention.* New York: Springer.

Hunnicutt, S. C. (ed.). (2006). *School shootings.* Farmington Hills, MI: Greenhaven Press.

Muschert, G. W., Henry, S., Bracy, N. L., & Peguero, A. A. (eds.). (2014). *Responding to school violence: Confronting the Columbine effect.* Boulder, CO: Lynne Rienner.

Muschert, G. W., & Sumiala, J. (eds.). *School shootings: Mediatized violence in a global age.* Bingley, UK: Emerald Publishing Group.

Wilson, L. (ed.). (2017). *The Wiley handbook of the psychology of mass shootings.* Malden, MA: John Wiley & Sons.

JOURNAL ARTICLES

Addington L. (2003). Students' fear after Columbine: Findings from a randomized experiment. *Journal of Quantitative Criminology, 19*(4), 367–387.

Addington, L. A. (2009). Cops and cameras: Public security as a policy response to Columbine. *American Behavioral Scientist, 52*(10), 1426–1446.

Agnich, L. E. (2015). A comparative analysis of attempted and completed school-based mass murder attacks. *American Journal of Criminal Justice, 40*(1), 1–22.

Altheide, D. L. (2009). The Columbine shooting and the discourse of fear. *American Behavioral Scientist, 52*(10), 1354–1370.

Barry, C. L., McGinty, E. E., Vernick, J. S., & Webster, D. W. (2013). After Newtown—public opinion on gun policy and mental illness. *New England Journal of Medicine, 368*(12), 1077–1081.

Birkland, T. A., & Lawrence, R. G. (2009). Media framing and policy change after Columbine. *American Behavioral Scientist, 52*(10), 1405–1425.

Bonnie, R. J., Reinhard, J. S., Hamilton, P., & McGarvey, E. L. (2009). Mental health system transformation after the Virginia Tech tragedy. *Health Affairs, 28*(3), 793–804.

---

[*] Featuring works by multiple expert researchers compiled into a single volume.

Borum, R., Cornell, D., Modzeleski, W., & Jimerson, S. (2010). What can be done about school shootings? A review of the evidence. *Educational Researcher, 39*(1), 27–37.

Brener N. D., Simon T. R., Anderson M., Barrios L., & Small M. L. (2002). Effect of the incident at Columbine on students' violence- and suicide-related behaviors. *American Journal of Preventive Medicine, 22*(3), 146–150.

Burns, R., & Crawford, C. (1999). School shootings, the media, and public fear: Ingredients for a moral panic. *Crime, Law & Social Change, 32*(2), 147–168.

Bushman, B. (Forthcoming). Narcissism, fame-seeking, and mass shootings. *American Behavioral Scientist*, special issue on the "Media Coverage of Mass Shooters" (2018).

Carvalho, E. J. (2010). The poetics of a school shooter: Decoding political significance in Cho Seung-Hui's multimedia manifesto. *Review of Education, Pedagogy, and Cultural Studies, 32*(4–5), 403–430.

Chyi, H. I., & McCombs, M. E. (2004). Media salience and the process of framing: Coverage of the Columbine school shootings. *Journalism and Mass Communication Quarterly, 81*(1), 22–35.

Crepeau-Hobson, M. F., Filaccio, M., & Gottfired, L. (2005). Violence prevention after Columbine. *Children & Schools, 27*(3), 157–165.

Dahmen, N. (Forthcoming). Visually reporting mass shootings: U.S. newspaper photographic coverage of three mass school shootings. *American Behavioral Scientist*, special issue on the "Media Coverage of Mass Shooters" (2018).

De Apodaca, R. F., Brighton, L. M., Perkins, A. N., Jackson, K. N., & Steege, J. R. (2012). Characteristics of schools in which fatal shootings occur. *Psychological Reports, 110*(2), 363–377.

De Venanzi, A. (2012). School shootings in the USA: Popular culture as risk, teen marginality, and violence against peers. *Crime Media Culture, 8*(3), 261–278.

Dutton, D. G., White, K. R., & Fogarty, D. (2013). Paranoid thinking in mass shooters. *Aggression and Violent Behavior, 18*(5), 548–553.

Duwe, G. (2000). Body-count journalism: The presentation of mass murder in the news media. *Homicide Studies, 4*(4), 364–399.

Duwe, G. (2004). The patterns and prevalence of mass murder in twentieth-century America. *Justice Quarterly, 21*(4), 729–761.

Duwe, G. (2005). A circle of distortion: The social construction of mass murder in the United States. *Western Criminology Review, 6*(1), 59–78.

Elsass, H. J., Schildkraut, J., & Stafford, M. C. (2014). Breaking news of social problems: Examining media effects and panic over school shootings. *Criminology, Criminal Justice, Law & Society, 15*(2), 31–42.

Elsass, H. J., Schildkraut, J., & Stafford, M. C. (2016). Studying school shootings: Challenges and considerations for the research. *American Journal of Criminal Justice, 41*(3), 444–464.

Fallahi, C. R., Austad, C. S., Fallon, M., & Leishman, L. (2009). A survey of the perceptions of the Virginia Tech tragedy. *Journal of School Violence, 8*(2), 120–135.

Ferguson, C. J. (2008). The school shooting/violent video game link: Causal relationship or moral panic? *Journal of Investigative Psychology and Offender Profiling, 5*(1), 25–37.

Ferguson, C. J. (2014). Violent video games, mass shootings, and the Supreme Court: Lessons for the legal community in the wake of recent free speech cases and mass shootings. *New Criminal Law Review, 17*(4), 553–586.

Fisher, B. W., Nation, M., Nixon, C. T., & McIlroy, S. (2016). Students' perceptions of safety at school after Sandy Hook. *Journal of School Violence.* https://doi.org/10.1080/15388220.2015.1133310

Fox, C., & Harding, D. (2005). School shootings as organizational deviance. *Sociology of Education, 78*(1), 69–97.

Fox, J. A., & DeLateur, M. J. (2014). Mass shootings in America: Moving beyond Newtown. *Homicide Studies, 18*(1), 125–145.

Fox, J. A., & Levin, J. (1994). Firing back: The growing threat of workplace homicide. *Annals of the American Academy of Political & Social Sciences, 536*, 126–130.

Fox, J. A., & Savage, J. (2009). Mass murder goes to college: An examination of changes on college campuses following Virginia Tech. *American Behavioral Scientist, 52*(10), 1465–1485.

Frymer, B. (2009). The media spectacle of Columbine: Alienated youth as an object of fear. *American Behavioral Scientist, 52*(10), 1387–1404.

Gerard, F. J., Whitfield, K. C., Porter, L. E., & Browne, K. D. (2016). Offender and offence characteristics of school shooting incidents. *Investigative Psychology and Offender Profiling, 13*(1), 22–38.

Harding, D. J., Fox, C., & Mehta, J. D. (2002). Studying rare events through qualitative case studies: Lessons from a study of rampage school shootings. *Sociological Methods & Research, 31*(2), 174–217.

Harris, J. M., & Harris, R. B. (2012). Rampage violence requires a new type of research. *American Journal of Public Health, 102*(6), 1054–1057.

Heilbrun, K., Dvoskin, J., & Heilbrun, A. (2009). Toward preventing future tragedies: Mass killings on college campuses, public health, and threat/risk assessment. *Psychological Injury and Law, 2*(2), 93–99.

Henry, S. (2009). School violence beyond Columbine: A complex problem in need of an interdisciplinary analysis. *American Behavioral Scientist, 52*(9), 1246–1265.

Hoffner, C. A., Fujioka, Y., Cohen, E. L., & Atwell Seate, A. (2017). Perceived media influence, mental illness, and responses to news coverage of a mass shooting. *Psychology of Popular Media Culture, 6*(2), 159–173.

Holody, K. J., & Daniel, E. S. (2017). Attributes and frames of the Aurora shootings. *Journalism Practice, 11*(1), 80–100.

Hong, J. S., Cho, H., Allen-Meares, P., & Espelage, D. L. (2011). The social ecology of the Columbine High School shootings. *Children and Youth Services Review, 33*(6), 861–868.

Hong, J. S., Cho, H., & Lee, A. S. (2010). Revisiting the Virginia Tech shootings: An ecological systems analysis. *Journal of Loss and Trauma, 15*(6), 561–575.

Kalish, R., & Kimmel, M. (2010). Suicide by mass murder: Masculinity, aggrieved entitlement, and rampage school shootings. *Health Sociology Review, 19*(4), 451–464.

Kaminski, R. J., Koons-Witt, B. A., Thompson, N. S., & Weiss, D. (2010). The impacts of Virginia Tech and Northern Illinois University shootings on the fear of crime on campus. *Journal of Criminal Justice, 38*(1), 88–98.

Killingbeck, D. (2001). The role of television news in the construction of school violence as a "moral panic." *Journal of Criminal Justice and Popular Culture, 8*(3), 186–202.

Kimmel, M. S., & Mahler, M. (2003). Adolescent masculinity, homophobia, and violence: Random school shootings, 1982–2001. *American Behavioral Scientist, 46*(10), 1439–1458.

Kleck, G. (2009). Mass shootings in schools: The worst possible case for gun control. *American Behavioral Scientist, 52*(10), 1447–1464.

Kuby, R. L., & Kunstler, W. M. (1995). So crazy he thinks he is sane: The Colin Ferguson trial and the competency standard. *Cornell Journal of Law & Public Policy, 5*(1), 19–26.

Kupchik, A., & Bracy, N. L. (2009). The news media on school crime and violence. *Youth Violence and Juvenile Justice, 7*(2), 136–155.

Langman, P. (2009). Rampage school shooters: A typology. *Aggression and Violent Behavior, 14*(1), 79–86.

Langman, P. (Forthcoming). Different types of role-model influence and fame-seeking among mass killers and copycat offenders. *American Behavioral Scientist*, special issue on the "Media Coverage of Mass Shooters" (2018).

Lankford, A. (2015). Mass shooters in the USA, 1966–2010: Differences between attackers who live and die. *Justice Quarterly, 32*(2), 360–379.

Lankford, A. (2016). Are America's public mass shooters unique? A comparative analysis of offenders in the United States and other countries. *International Journal of Comparative and Applied Criminal Justice, 40*(2), 71–183.

Lankford, A., & Madfis, E. (2017). Don't name them, don't show them, but report everything else: A pragmatic proposal for denying mass killers the attention they seek and deterring future offenders. *American Behavioral Scientist.* https://doi.org/10.1177/0002764217730854

Larkin, R. W. (2009). The Columbine legacy: Rampage shootings as political acts. *American Behavioral Scientist, 52*(9), 1309–1326.

Lawrence, R., & Mueller, D. (2003). School shootings and the man-bites-dog criterion of newsworthiness. *Youth Violence and Juvenile Justice, 1*(4), 330–345.

Lawrence, R. G., & Birkland, T. A. (2004). Guns, Hollywood, and school safety: Defining the school-shooting problem across public arenas. *Social Science Quarterly, 85*(5), 1193–1207.

Leary, M. R., Kowalski, R. M., Smith, L., & Phillips, S. (2003). Teasing, rejection, and violence: Case studies of the school shootings. *Aggressive Behavior, 29*(3), 202–214.

Leavy, P., & Maloney, K. P. (2009). American reporting of school violence and "people like us": A comparison of newspaper coverage of the Columbine and Red Lake school shootings. *Critical Sociology, 35*(2), 273–292.

Levin, J., & Madfis, E. (2009). Mass murder at school and cumulative strain: A sequential model. *American Behavioral Scientist, 52*(9), 1227–1245.

Levin, J., & Wiest, J. B. (Forthcoming). Explaining public interest in mass murder: Effect of fear and news focus. *American Behavioral Scientist*, special issue on the "Media Coverage of Mass Shooters" (2018).

Lindberg, N., Oksanen, A., Sailas, E., & Kaltiala-Heino, R. (2012). Adolescents expressing school massacre threats online: Something to be extremely worried about? *Child and Adolescent Psychiatry and Mental Health, 6*(1), 39–46.

Lindgren, S. (2011). YouTube gunmen? Mapping participatory media discourse on school shooting videos. *Media, Culture & Society, 33*(1), 123–136.

Lipschultz, J. H., & Hilt, M. L. (2011). Local television coverage of a mall shooting: Separating facts from fiction in breaking news. *Electronic News, 5*(4), 197–214.

Madfis, E. (2017). In search of meaning: Are school rampage shootings random and senseless violence? *Journal of Psychology: Interdisciplinary and Applied, 151*(1), 21–35.

Maguire, B., Weatherby, G. A., & Mathers, R. A. (2002). Network news coverage of school shootings. *Social Science Journal, 39*(3), 465–470.

Martaindale, M. H., Sandel, W. L., & Blair, J. P. (In press). Active shooter events in the workplace: Findings and policy implications. *Journal of Business Continuity and Emergency Planning*.

Martin, M. L. (2008). Lessons learned from the Virginia Tech tragedy. *Journal of Collective Bargaining in the Academy, 3*, 1–8.

Meindl, J. N., & Ivy, J. W. (Forthcoming). Reducing media induced mass killings: Lessons from suicide prevention. *American Behavioral Scientist*, special issue on the "Media Coverage of Mass Shooters" (2018).

Metzl, J. M., & MacLeish, K. T. (2015). Mental illness, mass shootings, and the politics of American firearms. *American Journal of Public Health, 105*(2), 240–249.

Murray, J. L. (2017). Mass media reporting and enabling of mass shootings. *Cultural Studies (Critical Methodologies, 17*(2), 114–124.

Muschert, G. W. (2007a). Research in school shootings. *Sociology Compass, 1*(1), 60–80.

Muschert, G. W. (2007b). The Columbine victims and the myth of the juvenile superpredator. *Youth Violence and Juvenile Justice, 5*(4), 351–366.

Muschert, G. W. (2009). Frame-changing in the media coverage of a school shooting: The rise of Columbine as a national concern. *Social Science Journal, 46*(1), 164–170.

Muschert, G. W., & Carr, D. (2006). Media salience and frame changing across events: Coverage of nine school shootings, 1997–2001. *Journalism and Mass Communication Quarterly, 83*(4), 747–766.

Newman, K. S., & Fox, C. (2009). Repeat tragedy: Rampage shootings in American high school and college settings, 2002–2008. *American Behavioral Scientist, 52*(9), 1286–1308.

Ogle, J. P., Eckman, M., & Leslie, C. A. (2003). Appearance cues and the shootings at Columbine High: Construction of a social problem in the print media. *Sociological Inquiry, 73*(1), 1–27.

Raitanen, J., & Oksanen, A. (Forthcoming). Global online subculture surrounding school shootings. *American Behavioral Scientist*, special issue on the "Media Coverage of Mass Shooters" (2018).

Rocque, M. (2012). Exploring school rampage shootings: Research, theory, and policy. *Social Science Journal, 49*(3), 304–313.

Schildkraut, J. (2012). Media and massacre: A comparative analysis of the reporting of the 2007 Virginia Tech shootings. *Fast Capitalism, 9*(1). Retrieved from http://www.uta.edu/huma/agger/fastcapitalism/9_1/schildkraut9_1.html

Schildkraut, J., Elsass, H. J., & Meredith, K. (2015). Mass shootings and the media: Why all events are not created equal. *Journal of Crime and Justice.* https://doi.org/10.1080/0735648X.2017.1284689

Schildkraut, J., Elsass, H. J., & Stafford, M. C. (2015). Could it happen here? Moral panics, school shootings, and fear of crime among college students. *Crime, Law and Social Change, 63*(1–2), 91–110.

Schildkraut, J., & Hernandez, T. C. (2014). Laws that bit the bullet: A review of legislative responses to school shootings. *American Journal of Criminal Justice, 39*(2), 358–374.

Schildkraut, J., & Muschert, G. W. (2013). Violent media, guns, and mental illness: The three ring circus of causal factors for school massacres, as related in media discourse. *Fast Capitalism, 10*(1). Retrieved from http://www.uta.edu/huma/agger/fastcapitalism/10_1/schildkraut10_1.html

Schildkraut, J., & Muschert, G. W. (2014). Media salience and the framing of mass murder in schools: A comparison of the Columbine and Sandy Hook school massacres. *Homicide Studies, 18*(1), 23–43.

Schultz, J. M., Muschert, G. W., Dingwall, A., & Cohen, A. M. (2013). The Sandy Hook Elementary School shooting as tipping point: "This time is different." *Disaster Health, 1*(2), 65–73.

Serazio, M. (2010). Shooting for fame: Spectacular youth, Web 2.0 dystopia, and the celebrity anarchy of generation mash-up. *Communication, Culture & Critique, 3*(3), 416–434.

Soraghan, M. (2000). Colorado after Columbine: The gun debate. *State Legislatures, 26*(6), 14–21.

Springhall, J. (1999). Violent media, guns, and moral panics: The Columbine High School massacre, 20 April 1999. *Paedagogica Historica, 35*(3), 621–641.

Sumiala, J., & Tikka, M. (2010). "Web first" to death: The media logic of the school shootings in the era of uncertainty. *Nordicom review: Nordic research on media & communication, 31*(2), 17–29.

Sumiala, J., & Tikka, M. (2011a). Imagining globalized fears: School shooting videos and circulation of violence on YouTube. *Social Anthropology/Anthropologie Sociale, 19*(3), 254–267.

Sumiala, J., & Tikka, M. (2011b). Reality on circulation: School shootings, ritualised communication, and the dark side of the sacred. *ESSACHESS: Journal for Communication Studies, 4*(8), 145–159.

Tonso, K. L. (2009). Violent masculinities as tropes for school shooters: The Montréal massacre, the Columbine attack, and rethinking schools. *American Behavioral Scientist, 52*(9), 1266–1285.

Towers, S., Gomez-Lievano, A., Khan, M., Mubayi, A., & Castillo-Chávez, C. (2015). Contagion in mass killings and school shootings. *PLoS one, 10*. Retrieved from https://doi.org/10.1371/journal.pone.0117259

Turchan, B., Zeoli, A. M., & Kwiatkowski, C. (2017). Reacting to the improbable: Handgun carrying permit application rates in the wake of high-profile mass shootings. *Homicide Studies*. https://doi.org/10.1177/1088767917699657

U.S. Secret Service, National Threat Assessment Center. (2002). Preventing school shootings: A summary of a U.S. Secret Service Safe School Initiative report. *NIJ Journal, 248*, 10–15. Retrieved from https://www.illinois.gov/ready/plan/Documents/PreventingSchoolShootingsSecretService.pdf

Verlinden, S., Hersen, M., & Thomas, J. (2000). Risk factors in school shootings. *Clinical Psychology Review, 20*(1), 3–56.

Wallace, L. (2015). Responding to violence with guns: Mass shootings and gun acquisition. *Social Science Journal, 52*(2), 156–167.

Warnick, B. R., Johnson, B. A., & Rocha, S. (2010). Tragedy and the meaning of school shootings. *Educational Theory, 60*(3), 371–390.

Wigley, S., & Fontenot, M. (2009). Where media turn during crises: A look at information subsidies and the Virginia Tech Shootings. *Electronic News, 3*(2), 94–108.

Wike, T. L., & Fraser, M. W. (2009). School shootings: Making sense of the senseless. *Aggression and Violent Behavior, 14*(3), 162–169.

Wozniak, K. H. (2015). Public opinion about gun control post–Sandy Hook. *Criminal Justice Policy Review, 28*(3), 255–278.

GOVERNMENT REPORTS (BOTH STATE AND NATIONAL)

Bjelopera, J. P., Bagalman, E., Caldwell, S. W., Finklea, K. M., & McCallion, G. (2013). *Public mass shootings in the United States: Selected implications for federal public health and safety policy*. Washington, D.C.: Congressional Research Service. Retrieved from http://fas.org/sgp/crs/misc/R43004.pdf

Blair, J. P., & Schweit, K. W. (2014). *A study of active shooter incidents, 2000–2013.* Washington, D.C.: U.S. Department of Justice, Federal Bureau of Investigation. Retrieved from http://www.fbi.gov/news/stories/2014/september/fbi-releases -study-on-active-shooter-incidents/pdfs/a-study-of-active-shooter-incidents-in-the -u.s.-between-2000-and-2013

Columbine Review Commission. (2001). *The report of Governor Bill Owens' Columbine Review Commission.* Denver: State of Colorado. Retrieved from http://trac.state .co.us/Documents/Reports%20and%20Publications/Columbine_2001_Governor _Review_Commission.pdf

Donohue, E., Schiraldi, V., & Ziedenberg, J. (1998, July). *School house hype: School shootings and the real risks kids face in America.* Washington, D.C.: Justice Policy Institute. Retrieved from http://www.justicepolicy.org/uploads/justicepolicy /documents/98-07_rep_schoolhousehype_jj.pdf

Northern Illinois University. (2008). *Report of the February 14, 2008 shootings at Northern Illinois University.* DeKalb: Northern Illinois University. Retrieved from http:// www.niu.edu/feb14report/Feb14report.pdf

Office of the Child Advocate. (2014). *Shooting at Sandy Hook Elementary School: Report of the Office of the Child Advocate.* Hartford, CT: Office of the Child Advocate. Retrieved from www.ct.gov/oca/lib/oca/sandyhook11212014.pdf

O'Toole, M. E. (2000). *The school shooter: A threat assessment perspective.* Quantico, VA: Critical Incident Response Group, FBI Academy, National Center for the Analysis of Violent Crime. Retrieved from https://www.fbi.gov/file-repository/stats -services-publications-school-shooter-school-shooter

Sandy Hook Advisory Commission. (2015). *Final report of the Sandy Hook Advisory Committee.* Hartford, CT: Sandy Hook Advisory Committee. Retrieved from http:// www.shac.ct.gov/SHAC_Final_Report_3-6-2015.pdf

Santa Barbara County Sheriff's Office. (2015). *Isla Vista mass murder, May 23, 2014: Investigative summary.* Santa Barbara, CA: Santa Barbara County Sheriff's Office. Retrieved from http://www.sbsheriff.us/documents/ISLAVISTAINVESTIGATI VESUMMARY.pdf

Sedensky, S. J. (2013). *Report of the State's Attorney for the judicial district of Danbury on the shootings at Sandy Hook Elementary School and 36 Yogananda Street, Newtown, Connecticut on December 14, 2012.* Danbury, CT: Office of the State's Attorney, Judicial District of Danbury.

U.S. Department of Defense. (2013). *Internal review of the Washington Navy Yard shooting: A report to the Secretary of Defense.* Washington, D.C.: Secretary of Defense for Intelligence. Retrieved from http://www.defense.gov/pubs/DoD-Internal -Review-of-the-WNY-Shooting-20-Nov-2013.pdf

U.S. Department of Education. (2007). *Issue brief: Public school practices for violence prevention and reduction: 2003–04.* Washington, D.C.: National Center for Education Statistics. Retrieved from http://nces.ed.gov/pubs2007/2007010.pdf

U.S. Department of Education, et al. (2013). *Guide for developing high-quality school emergency operations plans.* Washington, D.C.: U.S. Department of Education. Retrieved from http://www2.ed.gov/about/offices/list/oese/oshs/rems-k-12-guide.pdf

U.S. Department of Homeland Security. (2008). *Active shooter: How to respond.* Washington, D.C.: Department of Homeland Security. Retrieved from http://www.dhs.gov /xlibrary/assets/active_shooter_booklet.pdf

U.S. Department of Justice. (2002). *Reporting school violence.* Washington, D.C.: Office of Justice Programs. Retrieved from https://www.ncjrs.gov/ovc_archives/bulletins /legalseries/bulletin2/ncj189191.pdf

Vossekuil, B., Fein, R. A., Reddy, M., Borum, R., & Modzeleski, W. (2002). *The final report and findings of the Safe School Initiative: Implications for the prevention of school attacks in the United States*. Washington, D.C.: United States Secret Service and United States Department of Education. Retrieved from https://www2.ed.gov /admins/lead/safety/preventingattacksreport.pdf

About the Editor and Contributors

EDITOR

JACLYN SCHILDKRAUT, PhD, is an assistant professor of public justice at the State University of New York (SUNY) at Oswego. Her research interests include mass/school shootings, homicide trends, mediatization effects, moral panics, and crime theories. She is the co-author of *Mass Shootings: Media, Myths, and Realities* and has published in academic journals including *Homicide Studies, American Journal of Criminal Justice, Journal of Qualitative Criminal Justice & Criminology, Fast Capitalism, Journal of Crime and Justice, Criminal Justice Studies, Security Journal, Journal of Homeland Security & Emergency Management, Crime, Law and Social Change*, and *Criminology, Criminal Justice, Law & Society*, as well as several edited volumes. Her research also has been featured throughout various national news sources, including the *Wall Street Journal* and the *Washington Post*, following mass shooting events. She currently serves as a research analyst for *Safe and Sound: A Sandy Hook Initiative*.

FOREWORD

FRANK DEANGELIS, retired principal of Columbine High School, served as an educator for the Jeffco School District in Littleton, Colorado, since 1979. A national-level speaker, Frank has addressed numerous professional and school audiences on the topic of recovery after a school-based tragedy. He has visited, consulted, and assisted school communities across the country following incidents of violence and tragedy, including Platte Canyon, Chardon, Virginia Tech, and Sandy Hook. He recently received the Jefferson Country Lifetime Achievement Award and the Gandhi, King, Ikeda Community Builders Award. He retired in June 2014 after 35 years at Columbine and presently serves as a consultant for safety and emergency management for the Jeffco School District, as well as speaking and consulting both nationally and internationally.

THEMATIC OPENING ESSAY CONTRIBUTORS

LYNN A. ADDINGTON, JD, PhD, is a professor in the Department of Justice, Law and Criminology at American University in Washington, D.C. She earned her PhD in criminal justice from the University at Albany (SUNY) and her JD from the University of Pennsylvania Law School. Her research focuses on criminal victimization with an emphasis on school violence as well as policy responses to preventing violence and serving victims. In 2016, she received AU's top faculty research award. She also has served as a Visiting Fellow with the Bureau of Justice Statistics (U.S. Department of Justice). Her recent publications have appeared in a range of outlets including the *Journal of Quantitative Criminology, Justice Quarterly*, and *Trauma, Violence and Abuse*. She is the co-editor (with James P. Lynch) of a volume of original research entitled *Understanding Crime Statistics: Revisiting the Divergence of the NCVS and UCR* (2007).

KRISTINA ANDERSON is an international advocate in the fields of bystander intervention, active shooter response, and violence prevention within schools, workplaces, and public spaces. Kristina is founder of the Koshka Foundation for Safe Schools, a nonprofit that provides training on the prevention of school and workplace violence, education on active shooter preparedness, and consultation on postcrisis recovery. Ms. Anderson travels extensively within the United States and Canada to spread the importance of preparedness and joint training between citizens, educators, law enforcement, emergency managers, and first responders. She started the nonprofit after becoming one of the most critically injured survivors of the 2007 Virginia Tech school tragedy, where she was shot three times. Ms. Anderson is also co-founder of LiveSafe, a mobile technology communication platform for sharing safety-related information that is used by over 100 college campuses, as well as corporations and hospitals. Ms. Anderson has delivered training to numerous law enforcement and government agencies, as well as schools and workplaces, including school resource officers, university administrators, fire and emergency managers, FEMA, the FBI, and private corporations. She is a member of the Association of Threat Assessment Professionals and graduated from Virginia Tech with a BS in International Studies.

AMANDA L. FARRELL, PhD, is an assistant professor of criminal justice at Marymount University in Arlington, Virginia. She received her PhD from Old Dominion University. During her MSc and PhD programs, she interned with a police department, primarily in field forensics. She worked many crime scenes with forensic personnel, informally consulted on homicide investigations, and assisted with instruction at both the police academy and in-service training. As an ORISE research fellow for the FBI, she worked on multiple projects, including ones related to the prevention and investigation of mass shootings. Her research and teaching interests include homicide, criminal investigations, field forensics, and policing in general, with her dissertation and other recent work seeking to holistically explore officer mental health and resilience, particularly in the context of police use of deadly force incidents. She has published in *International Criminal*

Justice Review, *Homicide Studies*, and *Journal of Investigative Psychology and Offender Profiling*.

CHRISTOPHER J. FERGUSON, PhD, is a professor of psychology at Stetson University. He has his PhD in clinical psychology from the University of Central Florida and is licensed as a psychologist. He is a fellow of the American Psychological Association. He has published dozens of articles on media effects, including video game violence, and also studied criminal violence including mass shootings. He has published a book, *Moral Combat: Why the War on Violent Video Games Is Wrong,* along with a mystery novel set in Renaissance Florence, *Suicide Kings.* He lives in Orlando with his wife and son.

MICHELE GAY is a mother, former teacher, and now one of the founders of *Safe and Sound: A Sandy Hook Initiative*. After losing her daughter, Josephine Grace, on December 14, 2012, she chose to take action as an advocate for improved school security and safety in our nation's schools. Michele's background as a teacher and involved parent, along with her personal loss and posttragedy perspective, have left her uniquely positioned to help school communities prevent tragedy and better prepare and respond in the event of an emergency in their own schools. Michele holds a bachelor of science in Elementary Education from Towson University and a master's degree in Curriculum and Instruction from McDaniel College. She taught at the elementary level in Maryland and Virginia public schools before staying home to raise her three daughters and advocate for the special needs of her youngest daughter, Josephine. Michele is dedicated to honoring Josephine in her work to make schools in our country more safe and secure.

JEFF GRUENEWALD, PhD, is an assistant professor in the School of Public and Environmental Affairs at Indiana University–Purdue University, Indianapolis. His research interests broadly include lethal violence, terrorism and homeland security policy, and media coverage of crime and justice issues. Dr. Gruenewald is also an investigator for the National Consortium for the Studies of Terrorism and Responses to Terrorism (START), a Department of Homeland Security Center of Excellence. In addition to receiving support from START, he is a co-investigator for two multiyear projects examining patterns of terrorism in the United States, which are currently funded by the National Institute of Justice. Some of his recent published work has appeared in journals such as *Justice Quarterly*, *Journal of Quantitative Criminology*, *Criminology and Public Policy*, *Terrorism & Political Violence*, and *Crime & Delinquency*.

JENNIFER JOHNSTON, PhD, is a media psychologist and assistant professor of psychology at Western New Mexico University. She was also a licensed mental health clinician for many years before joining the faculty. She conducts research in the area of media effects and psychological disorder, and provides quantitative consultation and content analysis expertise for research teams. Dr. Johnston has written about the effects of early viewing of pornography and sexual satisfaction, American pornography diet across generations and genders, psychological sexual disorders and media diet, and sexual trauma and later psychological disorder. Current research on mass shootings, the role of media contagion, and mental health has been featured in international and national newspapers, television, and radio.

JACK LEVIN, PhD, is professor emeritus of sociology and criminology and co-director of the Brudnick Center on Violence and Conflict at Northeastern University. He has published a number of books about multiple homicide including *Extreme Killing: Understanding Serial and Mass Murder, The Will to Kill: Making Sense of Senseless Murder, Serial Killers and Sadistic Murderers: Up Close and Personal, Killer on Campus,* and *Mass Murder: America's Growing Menace.* Levin was honored by the Massachusetts Council for Advancement and Support of Education as its "Professor of the Year" and by the American Sociological Association for his contributions to the public understanding of sociology. He also has received awards from the Eastern Sociological Society, Association of Clinical and Applied Sociology, New England Sociological Association, and Society for the Study of Social Problems.

ERIC MADFIS, PhD, is an associate professor of criminal justice at the University of Washington–Tacoma, where his research focuses on theoretical criminology, the criminalization of American public schools, and the causes and prevention of school violence, hate crime, and mass murder. His work has been published in *American Behavioral Scientist, Critical Criminology, Homicide Studies, Journal of Hate Studies, Journal of Psychology, Men and Masculinities, Social Justice, Social Science Journal, Youth Violence and Juvenile Justice,* and in numerous edited volumes. His book, *The Risk of School Rampage* (2014), explores how threats of multiple-victim rampage school shootings are assessed and prevented.

GLENN W. MUSCHERT, PhD, is professor of sociology and social justice studies, and faculty affiliate in comparative media studies at Miami University in Oxford, Ohio. He earned a BS in international area studies from Drexel University (1992) and a PhD in sociology from the University of Colorado, Boulder (2002). He has been in his current position at Miami University since 2003. His research interests lie in the intersection of crime and deviance, social control, and mass media phenomena. He has edited numerous academic volumes and special issues, and written numerous journal articles and chapters in edited volumes in the fields of sociology, criminology, and media studies.

MARC SETTEMBRINO, PhD, is assistant professor of sociology at Southeastern Louisiana University, where he teaches graduate- and undergraduate-level courses on race and ethnic relations, globalization, and social problems. Dr. Settembrino's research examines how socially marginalized populations prepare for, respond to, and recover from disasters. He has published peer-reviewed articles in *Justice Policy Journal, Natural Hazards Observer, Journal of Emergency Management,* and *Natural Hazards Review.* A former resident of Orlando, Dr. Settembrino also is a member of the LGBTQ community and a prior patron of Pulse Nightclub.

SVEN SMITH, PhD, is a professor of psychology at Stetson University. He earned his PhD in Law and Society from the University of Florida and is also a practicing attorney. His research areas and publications involve the intersection of crime, media, and courts. He lives in Deland, Florida, with his daughter.

MELISSA J. TETZLAFF-BEMILLER, PhD, is an assistant professor in the Department of Sociology, Criminal Justice, and Social Work at Augusta University. Her research interests include homicide, particularly the murdering of children, sex crimes, and criminological theories. She is a member of the American Society of Criminology and the Homicide Research Working Group, where she currently serves as the Treasurer. Her research has been published in *Homicide Studies*, *Criminal Justice Review*, and *International Journal of Cyber Criminology*.

PERSPECTIVE ESSAY CONTRIBUTORS

JAMES A. BECKMAN (JD, Ohio State, LLM, Georgetown University) is an associate professor of legal studies at the University of Central Florida, where he also serves as the inaugural chair of the Department of Legal Studies. He is the author of *Comparative Legal Approaches to Homeland Security and Anti-terrorism* (2007) and *Affirmative Action Now: A Guide for Students, Families, and Counselors* (2006); he is also the general editor of *Affirmative Action: An Encyclopedia* (2004). Before his entrance into academia in 2000, he served as an attorney-advisor for the Bureau of Alcohol, Tobacco and Firearms (ATF) at its headquarters in Washington, D.C. Among other awards, he was the recipient of the United States Department of Defense Meritorious Service Medal for his legal work as an active duty judge advocate from 1994 to 1998, and the Department of Justice Meritorious Service Award (1999) for legal work on behalf of the Department of Justice and ATF.

GREGG LEE CARTER (PhD, Columbia University) is professor of sociology at Bryant University in Smithfield, Rhode Island, where he is the chair of the Department of History and Social Sciences. He has authored or edited 22 books, including the first and revised editions of *Guns in American Society: An Encyclopedia of History, Politics, Culture, and the Law* (ABC-CLIO, 2002, 2012) and *Gun Control in the United States: A Reference Handbook* (ABC-CLIO, 2006). His writings on contemporary social issues have also appeared in more than a dozen academic journals. He is a former president of the New England Sociological Association and a former associate editor of the journal *Teaching Sociology*. He is the recipient of the New England Sociological Association's "Sociologist of the Year Award" and the American Sociological Association's sectional "Outstanding Contributions to Instruction Award."

H. JAYMI ELSASS, PhD, is a lecturer in the School of Criminal Justice at Texas State University. Her primary research interests include episodic violent crime, moral panics, fear of crime, and juvenile delinquency. She is the co-author of *Mass Shootings: Media, Myths, and Realities*, as well as published in several edited volumes and a variety of academic journals including *Journal of Crime & Justice*, *American Journal of Criminal Justice*, *Journal of Homeland Security & Emergency Management*, and *Crime, Law & Social Change*.

BEVERLY MERRILL KELLEY earned her PhD from UCLA in 1977. She founded the Communication Department at California Lutheran University in 1981 and was elected Professor of the Year in 1987. She has taught every communication course in the curriculum during the past 30 years and helped start the KCLU FM radio station and the Educational Television for the Conejo TV channel. She is the author of the three-volume *Reelpolitik* series on film and political ideologies, and she has been a *Ventura County Star* opinion columnist since 1997. She also contributed monthly "Ventura County Perspective" op/ed pieces to the *Los Angeles Times* from 1997 to 2000, and she is the author of numerous scholarly articles and convention papers. She managed a California State Assembly campaign in 1999 and is frequently invited to speak at public events, to moderate election debates, and to provide analysis on politics, pop culture, and the media for radio, television, and newspapers.

LAWRENCE SOUTHWICK JR. has a PhD in Economics from Carnegie Mellon University and taught in the School of Management at the University at Buffalo for almost four decades.

GLENN H. UTTER is a distinguished professor emeritus of political science at Lamar University in Beaumont, Texas. He received his BA in political science from the State University of New York at Binghamton; his MA and PhD in political science from the State University of New York at Buffalo; and his MA in philosophy from Bedford College, University of London. He served as professor and chair of the political science department at Lamar University. He is the editor of *Guns and Contemporary Society: The Past, Present, and Future of Firearms and Firearm Policy* (Praeger, 2016), coauthor of *Encyclopedia of Gun Control and Gun Rights* (2011), and author of *Youth and Political Participation* (ABC-CLIO, 2012).

DR. WILLIAM VIZZARD is the chair of the Criminal Justice Division at California State University–Sacramento. Before he began teaching he spent 30 years in law enforcement as a deputy with the Fresno County (California) Sheriff's Department and the Bureau of Alcohol, Tobacco, Firearms and Explosives. He is the author of *Shots in the Dark: The Policy, Politics and Symbolism of Gun Control* and *In the Crossfire: A Political History of ATF*, as well as numerous journal articles on gun control, policing, and investigation.

HARRY L. WILSON received his PhD from Rutgers University and is a professor of political science and director of the Institute for Policy and Opinion Research at Roanoke College in Salem, Virginia. Dr. Wilson is the author of *The Triumph of the Gun-Rights Argument* (2015), *Guns, Gun Control, and Elections* (2007), and editor of *Gun Politics in America* (2015). He has written numerous articles in academic journals and book chapters and spent a year in Pskov, Russia, as a Fulbright scholar.

Index

DATE DUE

PRINTED IN U.S.A.